Batza Téna
Trail to Obsidian
Archaeology at an Alaskan
Obsidian Source

Donald W. Clark and
A. McFadyen Clark

Archaeological Survey of Canada
Mercury Series Paper 147

Canadian Museum of Civilization

© Canadian Museum of Civilization 1993

CANADIAN CATALOGUING IN PUBLICATION DATA

Clark, Donald W.

Batza Téna : trail to obsidian : archaeology at an Alaskan obsidian source

(Mercury series, ISSN 0316-1854)
(Paper / Archaeological Survey of Canada, ISSN 0317-2244; no. 147)
Includes an abstract in French.
Includes bibliographical references.
ISBN 0-660-14016-0

1. Koyukon Indians – Antiquities. 2. Koyukuk River (Alaska) – Antiquities. 3. Excavation (Archaeology) – Alaska – Koyukuk River. 4. Athapaskan Indians – Antiquities. I. McFadyen Clark, A. (Annette). II. Canadian Museum of Civilization. III. Archaeological Survey of Canada. IV. Title. V. Title: Archaeology at an Alaskan obsidian source. VI. Series. VII. Series: Paper (Archaeological Survey of Canada); no. 147.

E99.K79C52 1993   979.8′6   C93-099659-3

PRINTED IN CANADA

Published by
Canadian Museum of Civilization
100 Laurier Street
P.O. Box 3100, Station B
Hull, Quebec
J8X 4H2

COVER PHOTO: Sunset from the 1971 field camp at the base of the hill Batza Tiga. A camp of people who evidently came from the west to visit Batza Téna, and the Batza Téna Tuktu site, are located on the shore of the small lake.

HEAD OF PRODUCTION: Deborah Brownrigg

PRODUCTION OFFICER: Lise Rochefort

COVER DESIGN: Purich Design Studio

PRODUCTION EDITOR: Richard E. Morlan

OBJECT OF THE MERCURY SERIES

The Mercury Series is designed to permit the rapid dissemination of information pertaining to the disciplines in which the Canadian Museum of Civilization is active. Considered an important reference by the scientific community, the Mercury Series comprises over three hundred specialized publications on Canada's history and prehistory.

Because of its specialized audience, the series consists largely of monographs published in the language of the author.

In the interest of making information available quickly, normal production procedures have been abbreviated. As a result, grammatical and typographical errors may occur. Your indulgence is requested.

Titles in the Mercury Series can be obtained by writing to:

> Mail Order Services
> Publishing Division
> Canadian Museum of Civilization
> 100 Laurier Street
> P.O. Box 3100, Station B
> Hull, Quebec
> J8X 4H2

BUT DE LA COLLECTION MERCURE

La collection Mercure vise à diffuser rapidement le résultat de travaux dans les disciplines qui relèvent des sphères d'activités du Musée canadien des civilisations. Considérée comme un apport important dans la communauté scientifique, la collection Mercure présente plus de trois cents publications spécialisées portant sur l'héritage canadien préhistorique et historique.

Comme la collection s'adresse à un public spécialisé celle-ci est constituée essentiellement de monographies publiées dans la langue des auteurs.

Pour assurer la prompte distribution des exemplaires imprimés, les étapes de l'édition ont été abrégées. En conséquence, certaines coquilles ou fautes de grammaire peuvent subsister : c'est pourquoi nous réclamons votre indulgence.

Vous pouvez vous procurer la liste des titres parus dans la collection Mercure en écrivant au :

> Service des commandes postales
> Division de l'édition
> Musée canadien des civilisations
> 100, rue Laurier
> C.P. 3100, succursale B
> Hull (Québec)
> J8X 4H2

Canada

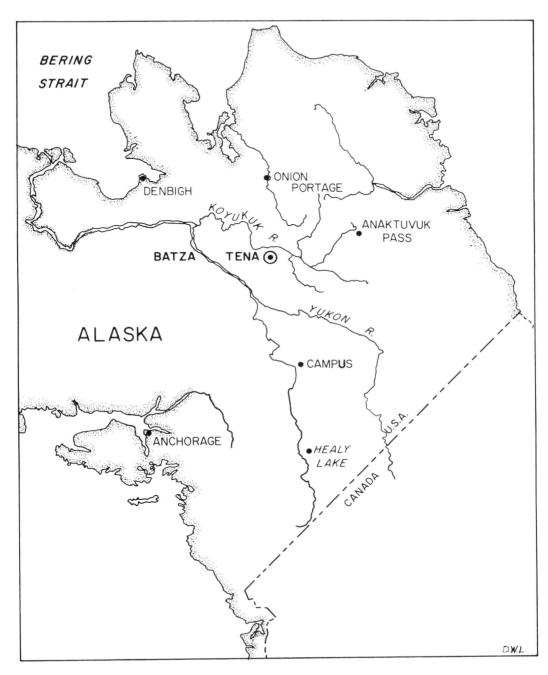

Frontispiece. Batza Téna and the State of Alaska.

Abstract

Thirty years ago the sources of obsidian used prehistorically in northwestern Alaska and adjacent regions were an archaeological and geological mystery. In 1967 the principal geologic source for this region was located by the United States Geological Survey on the Koyukuk River. During the next four seasons it was investigated by Canadian Museum of Civilization archaeologists. This volume reports on these surveys, excavations and archaeological collections.

The geologic source is located between the Indian and Little Indian rivers in the area known to the local Koyukon Athapaskans as "Batza Téna." The high-grade obsidian occurs as nodules in perlitic ash at the outcrop and is widely distributed westward nearly to the banks of the Koyukuk River in the gravels and colluvium of the Indian and Little Indian drainages. Surrounding and within the source area, though usually more than one kilometre distant from the primary outcrop, are numerous flaking stations where obsidian was reduced to biface roughouts and made into other artifacts. Within this array of sites are several that have yielded assemblages, which by their nature represent a broader range of activities than lithic reduction and may be regarded as campsites. From these it has been possible to construct a tentative sequence of occupation at Batza Téna, based primarily on typological comparisons with assemblages reported elsewhere in Alaska.

Résumé

En 1967, le United States Geological Survey annonçait la découverte de la source principale d'obsidienne des peuples préhistoriques du nord-ouest de l'Alaska et des régions limitrophes, mettant ainsi fin à une énigme géologique et archéologique. Dans la foulée de cette découverte, les archéologues du Musée canadien des civilisations ont consacré les quatre saisons suivantes à l'analyse de la source; le présent ouvrage décrit les levés et les fouilles qui ont été effectués et les collections archéologiques qu'ils ont réunies. La source géologique est située sur la rivière Koyukuk, entre les rivières Indian et Little Indian, dans la région baptisée Batza Téna par les Athapascans.

Se présentant sous forme de nodules dans de la cendre perlitique, cette obsidienne de très grande qualité se retrouve en grande quantité à l'ouest, près des rives de la rivière Koyukuk, dans le gravier et la colluvion des dépôts des rivières Indian et Little Indian. Dans la zone immédiate, mais normalement à plus d'un kilomètre du point d'affleurement, on a découvert de nombreuses stations d'écaillage où l'on taillait l'obsidienne en bifaces grossiers pour la fabrication d'outillages lithiques. Sur plusieurs sites, qui présentent toutes les caractéristiques d'un campement, on a pu réunir des collections d'articles qui témoignent que les habitants s'adonnaient aussi à bien d'autres activités. On a pu hypothétiquement établir une chronologie de l'occupation de la région de Batza Téna, à partir essentiellement de comparaisons typologiques avec d'autres vestiges signalés ailleurs en Alaska.

Preface

This volume reports archaeological surveys and excavations done in the vicinity of the obsidian source located in the Koyukuk River drainage south of Hughes, Alaska. The area has been designated <u>Batza Téna</u> (obsidian trail, Baats'a Tina in Koyukon orthography) following local Koyukon Athapaskan usage. Collections were made at nearly 100 localities or points, and this has resulted in a mass of data that often is difficult to synthesise. Sites and artifacts are grouped by chapter in a tentative chronological sequence determined primarily on the basis of index artifacts, especially fluted points, microblades and sidenotched points. Minor collection localities are placed in a separate chapter. Description is to a certain degree summary, but the depth of treatment varies according to the author's perception of the relevance of the material. The complexion of most Batza Téna sites reflects their association with the natural source of raw material; that is, most sites are flaking stations where relatively nondiagnostic flake cores, flaking detritus and broken biface roughouts are abundant. The emphasis in this report, however, will be primarily historiographic rather than on the mode of resource exploitation.

Archaeological field research was undertaken in the Koyukuk drainage in 1961 by A. McFadyen (Clark) and 1968 through 1972 by the Canadian Museum of Civilization as part of a programme to document Koyukuk Indian (branch of Koyukon) ethnography, Indian-Eskimo relationships in the Koyukuk drainage, and the native history and prehistory of the Koyukuk region. In addition to the research at Batza Téna reported here, and ethnographic research, the project has undertaken the following archaeologic work which is reported elsewhere: inventory of historic sites and survey of selected localities for prehistoric sites (A. Clark 1991, see also Andrews 1977) brief investigation of Norutak Lake in the Kobuk Eskimo-Koyukuk Indian border region (Clark 1974a), excavation of contact period semisubterranean houses located near Allakaket (Clark and Clark 1974, A. Clark 1991), and excavation of settlements of an Ipiutak-related people located near Huslia (Clark 1977).

Acknowledgements

For more than two decades research on Batza Téna has generated a number of journal and symposium articles which together with the response of our colleagues, have contributed to the final product presented here. The acknowledgements to be made, then, go far beyond what is to be seen in these pages.

Two infrastructures have made this work possible. One is the staff of the Canadian Museum of Civilization (formerly National Museum of Man), particularly the Archaeological Survey of Canada and Canadian Ethnology Service divisions. The other is at the opposite end of the long traverse between Ottawa and Alaska and the field. There include the University of Alaska, the Institute of Arctic Biology and Dr. John Cook; the local Koyukuk River flying service, Bettles

Aviation, and residents of the region, particularly the people of Allakaket-Alatna as well as many persons from Hughes and Huslia. It was the local people who told us about Batza Téna and provided collateral information and assistance.

Others provided technical information and assistance, as will be described in later chapters. Among them are V.C. Armstrong, Atomic Energy of Canada Commercial Products, Ltd.; William Patton, Jr., U.S. Geological Survey; Leslie B. Davis, Montana State University; D.G. Fong, Canadian Geological Survey; David Laverie, draftsman, and David Morrison, who reviewed the draft manuscript, Archaeological Survey of Canada; Steve Darby, photographer, Canadian Museum of Civilization; J.W. Michels, MOHLAB; the late Sterling Presley, lab technician, Archaeological Survey of Canada; and M. E. Wheeler, Canadian Conservation Institute. D. Clark participated in the project as staff of the Museum; and the three 1971 field assistants--Knut Fladmark, Jonathan Nobleman and William Peacock--were hired by the Museum for the summer under a Canadian government student employment programme. The frequent use of "we"in this report is not simply an editorial convention but reflects co-research and consultation between the authors.

CONTENTS

xi

FIGURES

TABLES

CHAPTER 1: BATZA TENA

Geographical Setting

South of Anaktuvuk Pass, several streams rise in the Arctic heartland of the Brooks Range to coalesce in the Kanuti Basin, between Bettles and Allakaket, forming the Koyukuk River. The Koyukuk then flows southwestward breaching the Hodzana highlands. A few kilometres below the settlement of Hughes the river leaves the highlands to enter the Koyukuk Lowlands, a 250-km-long enclave extending south to the Yukon River, between the Nulato Hills and Hogatza Highland on one side, and the Kokrines-Hodzana Highlands. Batza Téna is found a short distance below Hughes at the head of the Koyukuk Lowlands and the edge of the Kokrines-Hodzana Highlands (Fig. 1.1). The obsidian deposits are only a few kilometres from the river. From them one can look westward across the Koyukuk valley which is still relatively narrow at

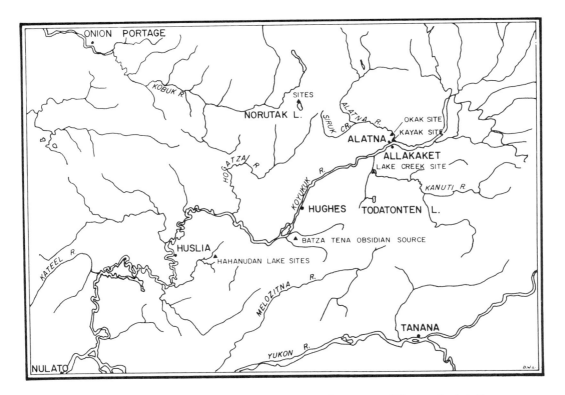

Figure 1.1. Map of the middle Koyukuk region including Batza Téna and vicinity.

this point. Beyond are the Hogatza Highlands traversed by "roads" to the Kobuk River taken by prehistoric and historic Native traders and travellers. In the opposite direction, through the hills to the southeast are routes taken in historic times to the trading rendezvous at the confluence of the Tanana and Yukon River. Down the Koyukuk River itself, and beyond, lay the relatively large Koyukon villages of the lower Koyukuk and Yukon River.

Climatic conditions at Batza Téna are more severe than those at Fairbanks in the heart of Alaska, but are less severe than those at Wiseman, in the Koyukuk headwaters region (Fig 1.2). The latter may be known to the reader as Marshall's (1933) "Arctic Village." The Utopia recording station is located at the edge of Batza Téna, but at higher elevation than most of the Batza Téna sites. Although the central interior climatic zone is characterized by relatively low rainfall, thunder showers and extended periods of wet weather are common during the spring and summer. Local residents reported that thunder showers were very rare in the region until after 1962. One six-day period of rain hindered our second field trip in 1970, and in 1971 at one camp we experienced more days with rain than without. Similar conditions would have been especially detrimental to people who had to depend on the preparation and storage of dried food. Extremely low winter temperatures in the order of 70-80 degrees below zero F. are experienced in the basins north of Batza Téna. Summer temperatures are variable and range from unpleasantly chilly to eneveratingly hot.

Topography at the obsidian source and environs is divided between hilly ridges and lowlands flanked by low mountains 600 m and greater in height (Fig. 1.3). The subdued hilly ridges, which rise 100-150 m above the Koyukuk Flats, are forested with groves of birch trees or mixed aspen (*Populus tremuloides*), spruce (*Picea mariana*) and birch (*Betula papifera*) with an undercover of shrubs, especially *Alnus*, *Salix spp.*, *Betula spp.* and Ledum, moss and lichens. Locally, forest groves are composed of small or scrub trees, largely because of permafrost and topography. Interspersed with the forested ridges, particularly in upland draws, are grassy tussock meadows and muskeg tundra dotted with stunted spruce trees. The composition and distribution of forests and size of the trees also has been affected by forest fires, several of which have swept the region in historic times. Recent Bureau of Land Management investigations suggest that these fires occurred every 50-100 years (Kunz 1991 citing unpublished 1991 study by D.H. Mann). One fire cleared the undercover at Batza Téna in 1968, partially exposing many surficial sites. The sparse soil of the forested hills contains a considerable amount of stone rubble derived from local bedrock. An alpine environment is found in the higher hills and mountains that flank the obsidian source south of Little Indian River and, especially, north of Indian River.

The lowlands, elevation c 80 m above sea level, are dominated by smaller rivers and streams and by features of the Koyukuk River. They are underlain by stream and river gravels, and probably also by colluvium from the adjacent hills. Ponds and small lakes of irregular form and large open reaches of tundra are found on the lowlands. At the very margins of the streams, including Indian and Little Indian River, there are ribbons of cottonwood forest (*Populus balsamifera*) and thickets of large willows. The portion of the lowlands under the influence of the

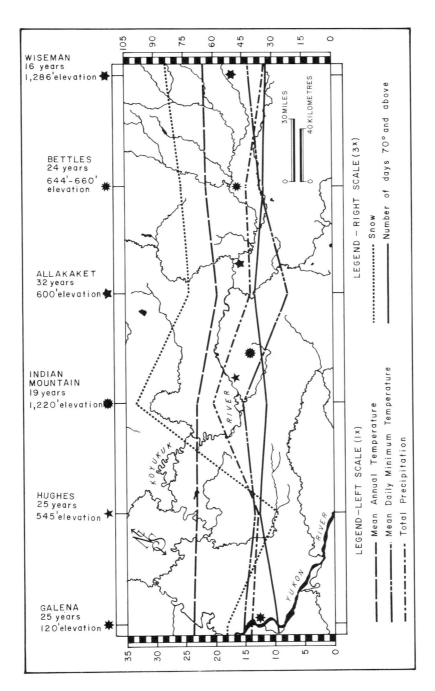

Figure 1.2. Graph of the climate of the Koyukuk River Valley.

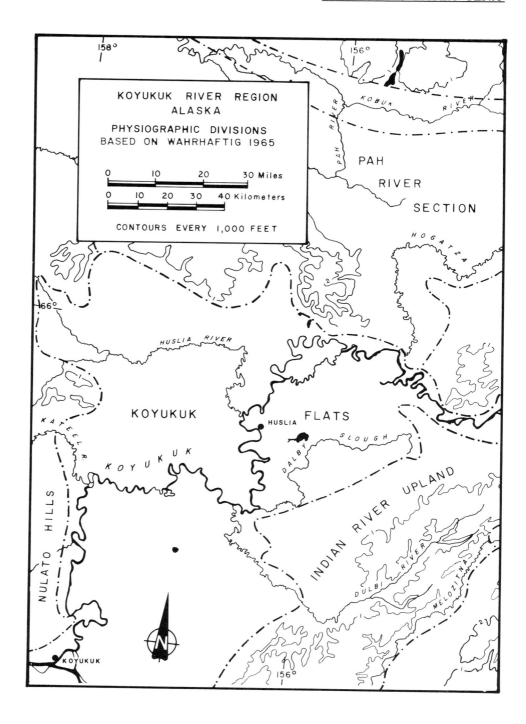

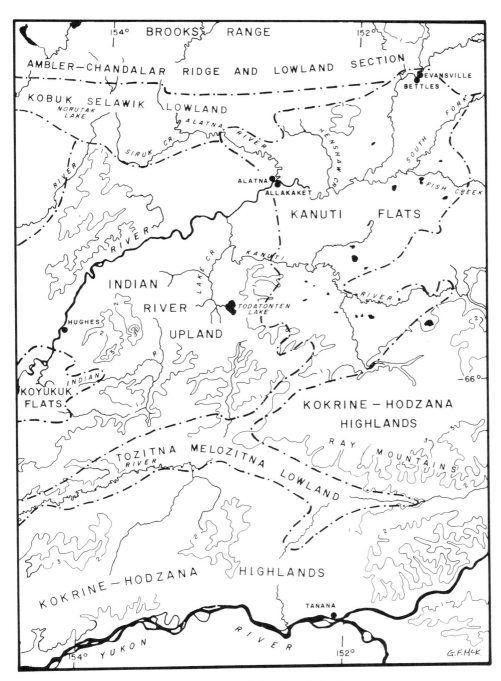

Figure 1.3. Map of the physiography of the Koyukuk Region.

Koyukuk River is typically a terrain of sloughs, horseshoe lakes, swales and silted-in channels. Plant communities include dense brush, cottonwood forest and spruce forest, and grassy swales. Archaeological sites were found on the hills to the edge of the lowlands. Historic sites are reported for the banks of the Koyukuk River, and presumably there was earlier occupation along the river.

Numerous moose were seen in the hills and on the lowlands. In the 1960s this reach of the Koyukuk valley was acknowledged as a good moose area. Additional game observed includes six encounters with black bears, single wolves and a wolf pack, otter, beaver and muskrat sightings, red squirrels, a white owl, one porcupine and a single caribou that had failed to migrate northward. Grouse (spruce hen and ptarmigan) were uncommon and no hare were sighted although their spoor was seen. Many other species are known to exist in the region. Chum salmon (*O. keta*) were observed spawning in the Indian River.

The obsidian source is located within the Pleistocene glacial refugium of interior Alaska, which forms part of the region designated by palaeoecologists as Beringia (Hopkins et al 1982). Accordingly, there is a potential for very considerable time depth of human occupation at Batza Téna. Maps showing the extent of Quaternary glaciation in Alaska (Péwé 1975, U.S. Geological Survey 1965) indicate that the immediate area under consideration was distant from the nearest Wisconsinan stage glaciers (cf. Hamilton 1969) excepting small glaciers in the highland hills between Indian River and the Yukon River. Anderson, Reanier and Brubaker (1990) found at Sithylemenkat Lake, east of the obsidian source, a 14,000 year pollen sequence similar to that being revealed elsewhere in northern Alaska. According to their report *Betula* (birch) shrub tundra was present 13,500 to 9000 years ago, with increased *Populus* about 10,000 to 9000 years ago. *Picia glauca* (white spruce) appeared about 9000 B.P. However, spruce then declined between 7800 and 500 years ago, followed by a rise, again, of white spruce along with black spruce (*P. mariana*).

The lower hills at Batza Téna are not mantled by eolian loess deposits. This situation may relate to the fact that the Koyukuk passes through confining hills north of Batza Téna in a course not conducive to the production of potential wind-carried sediments (explanation suggested to the writer by S. Schweger). This situation reduces the potential for finding stratified sites there. Dune and fine sediment deposits are found farther southwest in the Koyukuk valley (Péwé et al. 1965:Fig. 1 and 361-62).

Frost riving, stirring, sorting, and soil creep or solifluction are evident at Batza Téna. The flats display polygonal ground, easily observed from the air. Sites on the hilly ridges have been affected by frost heaving and sorting. Soil creep may account for rounding of the lower hills and the absence of developed soil profiles. Together with frost sorting this may have resulted in rearranged sites. These processes acting upon a jointed and fractured bedrock have produced the large amount of stone found in the thin soil mantle.

In addition to the surficial deposits, three geologic units are represented at Batza Téna (Fig. 1.4). These are volcanic rocks (TKv), volcanic greywacke and mudstone (Kgm) and andesitic volcanic rocks (Kv) (Patton, Miller, Chapman and Yeend 1977). The primary source of the Indian River obsidian is found in Tkv volcanic rocks which occupy a substantial part of the upland saddle between Indian and Little Indian River. This formation is tentatively assigned a mid-Tertiary age and is described as composed mainly of light-grey to pink rhyolite tuff, possible welded tuff, and breccia. Volcanic greywacke forms most of the hills and low ridges at Batza téna and underlies the majority of archaeological sites. This unit of probable Early Cretaceous age consists of "chiefly dark-greenish grey, fine-grained to gritty, poorly sorted greywacke composed largely of first- and second-cycle volcanic debris..."(Patton et al 1979. The third group, andesitic volcanic rocks, forms the hill known as Batzatiga and another, smaller hill southwest of that locality, and are present elsewhere in the middle Koyukuk region. Where visited by the archaeological party, this Lower Cretaceous rock presented the appearance of weathered disintegrating lava. The unit is described as "pillow basalt and andesite flows; andesitic tuff, volcanic conglomerate and breccia" (Patton et al 1977).

The terrain probably has changed during the history of human occupation at Batza Téna. As far as we are aware, though, the several Pleistocene or early Holocene events there are poorly dated. Reger (Reger and Reger 1972:26) reports that a proglacial lake that formerly occupied the Kanuti basin drained into the upper Indian River east of Utopia. This apparently was early in Wisconsinan time, possibly long before humans had set foot in North America. Another event is the capture of the upper Little Indian River drainage by the Indian River. We have not found any published discussion of this feature. If stream capture occurred after the first occupation, it could have significantly affected Little Indian river as a route for canoe travel (presently nil because of its small size), as a fishery, and as a gravel-bar source of obsidian. Except in small catchment basins and for the Koyukuk flats joined by a small area of Indian River flats, there are almost no fine sediment deposits at Batza Téna. On the low hills broken up bedrock outcrops in many places. There is an area of fine sediments at the southwest end of Batzatiga, a hill south of Little Indian River approximately opposite the southwest end of Huggins Island. Seen from the surface, this area appears to be one of undifferentiated alluvial flats that with imperceptible slope joins and forms part of the Koyukuk flats. But the more abrupt slope at the front of site RkIh-35 provides a different perspective, which is that of a terrace remnant composed of finegrained sediments. It would be useful to know more about the age and genesis of these deposits in order to determine if they have any potential to contain ancient archaeological remains.

The age and genesis of the numerous small lakes that abut the flats and elevated terrain, respectively, also may be pertinent to the human history of the region. These lakes are not remnants of old river meanders. Nor are they typical thaw lakes though most are shallow enough to be inhabited by moose.

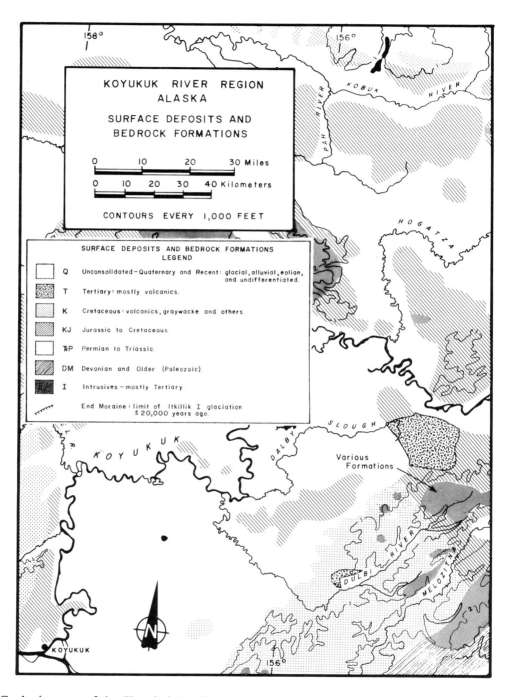

Figure 1.4. Geologic map of the Koyukuk Region.

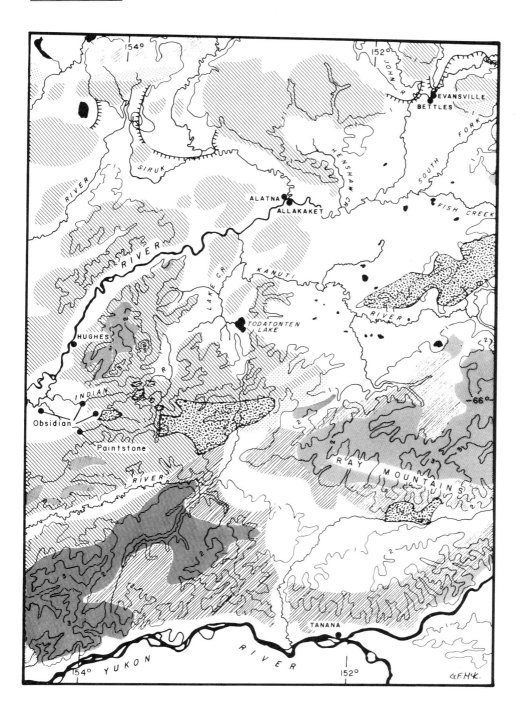

Trail to Obsidian

History of Regional Research

The first archaeological work on the Koyukuk River was done by Frederica de Laguna in 1935 when she examined the lower river as far as Kateel, located below Huslia. Three structures excavated at Kateel were of early historic age (de Laguna 1947:46-51).

Frank Hibben surveyed the area around the mouth of the Koyukuk in 1941 for traces of Palaeo-Indian occupation but apparently found none (Hibben 1943:255). Nearly thirty years later his foresight, that there would be early remains in the drainage, was validated by finds at Batza Téna. James L. Giddings traversed the Alatna drainage by foot overland to Norutak Lake and the Kobuk River in 1940 but he states that the "determined search for sites really began at Shungnak [on Kobuk River]" (Giddings 1952:2). After the Second World War, one of Gidding's associates, J.S. Newcomb and one companion, ascended the Koyukuk and Alatna River by canoe, and portaged from the head of the Alatna to the Kobuk which they descended (anon. nd). The objectives of this trip appear to have been both recreation and an archaeological site survey. No sites were reported in the Koyukuk and Alatna drainage.

In 1961 A. McFadyen, encouraged to do fieldwork in the region by J.L. Giddings, Diamond Jenness, John Campbell, and Cornelieus Osgood, surveyed part of the Koyukuk and Alatna drainage shores in the vicinity of Allakaket. No lithic material was recovered and the housepit sites examined by and reported to her appear to be protohistoric and historic in age. Also in 1961 William Irving and Thomas Hamilton traversed the Alatna River from its headwaters to Allakaket in a folding kayak. No sites were discovered except at the headwaters. However, as Irving points out (1962:82), little time could be expended looking for sites inasmuch as the party, which had been making surveys in the Brooks Range, was racing against freeze up to reach Allakaket. One of the small housepit sites reported by McFadyen for the Alatna River at the mouth of Siruk Creek was excavated in 1963 by John M. Campbell assisted by Richard E. Morlan (Morlan 1967). Since 1956 Campbell had been doing archaeological research in the central Brooks Range including the headwaters of the John River, a northern tributary of the Koyukuk utilized by Inupiat and, on its lower reaches, by Koyukon (Campbell 1962).

A. McFadyen (Clark) returned to Allakaket in 1968 with Donald W. Clark to continue ethnological and archaeological work under sponsorship of the Canadian Museum of Civilization. Houses were excavated at contact period sites, but no lithic sites were found although at one site on Todatonten Lake a single obsidian flake was found associated with a small group of potsherds. Later in the year, after freeze up, we heard from local inhabitants of an obsidian source located southeast of the village of Hughes. In 1969 and 1970 A. and D. Clark returned to the Koyukuk to make brief surveys at the obsidian source, and in 1971 D. Clark went to Batza Téna and to

Hahanudan Lake with a crew of four persons for more extensive investigations. Also in 1969, while studying altoplanation terraces in the vicinity of Indian Mountain Reger collected flakes and artifacts from approximately twelve sites at the northeastern edge of Batza Téna (Reger and Reger 1972).

By this time salvage, rescue and, later, resource inventory archaeology had started in the upper Koyukuk region and its headwaters in the Brooks Range as well as along the pipeline route east of Batza Téna in the headwaters of the Kanuti River. Initially this work was done for the Trans-Alaska Pipeline System (TAPS) (Cook ed. 1970, 1971; Holmes 1973) which with realization of construction became ALYESKA (Cook ed. 1977, Fetter and Shinkwin 1978). Later, agency archaeologists also began to survey the headwaters areas, particularly in the Gates of the Arctic National Monument (Kunz 1984), and this work has continued essentially to the present. Their area of research is geographically removed from Batza Téna but we will have occasion to refer to the upper drainage archaeology in comparing and interpreting the results from the middle Koyukuk drainage.

Discovery of the Obsidian Source

Obsidian lancets used by the Indians of interior Alaska were reported more than one hundred years ago. But the occasional presence of obsidian in archaeological sites apparently drew little interest until it was found to be a major material in the microblade industry at Cape Denbigh. Further interest was aroused by the abundance of obsidian in certain layers at Onion Portage on the Kobuk River (Giddings 1962:13, 18-19; 1964:262-263). At this time, and particularly during the 1950s obsidian artifacts also were being recovered as a minor component of archaeological assemblages found in the central Brooks Range (Campbell 1962; also discovered by Irving but not discussed in his 1963 publication).

In 1961 Giddings received reports of obsidian on the Koyukuk but he was unable to obtain specific data about source localities (Giddings 1962:19). His information actually was based on Patton's recovery of float obsidian in 1958. W.W. Patton had found obsidian near the village of Huslia but had not yet located a natural source or outcrop (Patton, personal communication to D. Clark, 1971). During the 1960s geologists also were finding devitrified obsidian deposits in the interior of Alaska, none of the quality used for stone implements. Archaeological and geological activity and garnering of clues thus served to create an awareness and interest in obsidian. Finally, in 1967 Patton located and examined the bedrock source below Hughes on the Koyukuk, south of Indian Mountain. We can note in retrospect, though, that the U.S. Geological Survey earlier had obtained the translated Indian name "Obsidian Hill" for Indian Mountain (Orth 1967:454). As well, Schrader had reported that "the river gravels of the middle part of the Koyukuk Valley...carry cobbles of obsidian or true volcanic glass" (1900:481), but this report appears to have attracted little notice. Patton and Miller (1970) published a brief description of the Indian River natural source including an analysis indicating that this locality is the probable source for obsidian utilized elsewhere in northwestern Alaska, including analyzed Kobuk River specimens published the preceding year (Griffin, Wright and Gordus 1969).

Meanwhile, at Allakaket, in 1968 the Clarks, unaware of Patton's work, showed to local Koyukuk residents the obsidian artifacts obtained that season at Norutak Lake. Although no one knew any of its English names, the obsidian was readily recognized as batza. It had been used until recently to cut blisters or swollen blood vessels of the eye lids caused by snow blindness. A terminological or language barrier coupled with the lack of specimens to demonstrate may be the reason why A. McFadyen earlier, in 1961, alerted by Giddings to the possibility of there being obsidian on the Koyukuk, had obtained negative responses to inquires regarding the presence of this material in the region. Initially, no person indicated precisely where the batza was found. Later, in the autumn one of the Koyukuk men, who had been away returned to Allakaket and informed us that it was found in the region southeast of Hughes inclusive of Takbatzahullanten -- "Obsidian-is-found-in-the-water Lake." The occurrence of batza was confirmed by another person, but by this time freeze-up had set in and it was impractical for us to visit the source.

We were still beset by uncertainty inasmuch as we had not seen any actual specimens from the Koyukuk source, and reports from elsewhere in Alaska of batz had led only to discoveries of archaeological sites or chert outcrops (J. P. Cook personal communication 1968). However, subsequent correspondence with Patton reassured us by confirming that Koyukuk batza was not flint. He further provided us with precise information on the location of the bedrock source. A brief period only was allocated for a reconnaissance of the source in 1969 inasmuch as we did not know if there would be any significant distribution of archaeological sites around the geologic source. The positive results of the initial surveys in 1969 and 1970 indicated that more comprehensive work would be worthwhile in 1971.

We also learned that residents of Hughes and Huslia were more familiar with the obsidian occurrences than people at Allakaket. A trader and lodge keeper at Hughes, Les James, had even considered the possible commercial value of the obsidian nodules as semiprecious gem material. Two of the Hughes Koyukon travelled to the outcrop, later reported by the geologists, and obtain a box of the nodules for James. It hardly is proper to state that the obsidian source was "discovered." It always had been known to local people. The history of its recognition illustrates that lacunae sometimes exist in our knowledge through not asking the right questions of the right persons in the right manner.

Fieldwork at Batza Téna

Neutron activation analysis done for Patton by the University of Michigan confirmed the probability that Batza Téna or Indian River was the source for previously tested obsidian utilized prehistorically in northwestern Alaska (Patton and Miller 1970). As no sources had heretofore been located for the obsidian found in archaeological sites in Alaska, the Aleutian Islands

Figure 1.5.   Surface collecting on "Basecamp Ridge" in 1970. "Basecamp Lake" is in the background.

Figure 1.6.   Surface collecting on the north side of "Basecamp Ridge" in 1970, showing the stark devegetated terrain after a wildfire in 1968.

excepted, it was considered highly desirable to examine the natural source area on the Koyukuk and to determine the nature of archaeological remains there.

Our knowledge of the local occurrence of obsidian come too late in the 1968 season to allow us to undertake a reconnaissance then. A. and D. Clark returned to the Koyukuk in early June 1969. Eight full days were spent in the source area. During this period we examined, from our camp on a small unnamed lake east of the Koyukuk River ("Basecamp Lake") two aspects of the natural source deposit (primary outcrop, Little Indian River gravels), and collected from approximately 30 sites or flaking locations (Fig. 1.5, 1.7). The time allocated for this initial reconnaissance was not sufficient to fully examine the area, but when the field trip was initiated the extent of the archaeological remains was unknown and we had made commitments for other work during the summer. The principal reconnaissance routes taken during this and two subsequent seasons are indicated in Figure 1.7.

In 1970 we again returned to the Koyukuk and during the latter part of May and in June we made two field trips from Allakaket to the vicinity of the obsidian source. On the first trip we went down the Koyukuk River by boat and, each day, walked inland four kilometres to a hill called Batzatiga (local name, translates Obsidian Hill) (Fig. 1.10, 1.11). Several sites were found on the west side of Batzatiga. This trip was of eight days duration, half of which was taken up by the river travel and examination of historic camps along the route.

For the second trip of eleven days duration we returned to "Basecamp Lake" by float plane. This camp placed us in a satisfactory position to undertake foot reconnaissances in and around the area briefly surveyed in 1969. Several additional sites or localities with chipping detritus were discovered (Fig. 1.6). Brief stops were made by float plane at two lakes within the Batza Téna area and at Sithylemenkat Lake located about 120 km to the east. Survey in 1970 was stimulated by the search for and discovery of sites with fluted points following the recognition of two fluted point fragments of presumed Palaeo-Indian affiliation among specimens collected the preceding year. Several additional fluted point fragments and one complete point were picked up from the surface. A preliminary report on these finds has been published (Clark 1972).

Figure 1.7 Key: NATIVE TOPONYMS AT BATZATENA

1. Kitsel hhakhten [lake] "we kill something", also reported as Kikgat'tik
2. Nagatla-tio todlioden [lake]
3. Kaish'ta-litno [stream], published at Kitalitna but misplaced
4. Klugatog'goshnoden [lake]
5. Hotitihichlen [lake]
6. Tabescot [lake]
7. Batzaténa [lake, cabin site, spring camp site, reported site of 1884 village]
8. Hogataak'tiga [a large lake] same as or near Keekh lake
9. Tonitzkanatlili [small lake]

10. Twenty Five Mile Cabin [traditional fishing camp site]
11. Lavine Williams' spring camp
12. Batzati-munket [lake] also reported as Toban noka'ish todlioden
13. Hellodilithta [lake]
14. Kik'ghatila [lake]
15. Kikhleet [lake] "all around birch", reported as one of two lakes called Batzati-munket
16. The Lake on the South Side of the Hill
17. Batzatiga [hill]
18. Kohodo Batzitna, Little Batzitna [stream, also is pronounced Batza-ta-tena]
19. Batza-zeehee, [range of hills off the map to the south]
20. Baaknahokodawi [mountain, off map to southeast, one source applied this name to benchmark "cone", "animal (bear) takes old hair off"]
21. Takajian-tokten [lake]
22. Takagian-dioghten [?, across from and slightly below mouth of Indian River.
23. Chitena [lake with islet]
24. Tak'batzahullanten, Taah Baats'a Hoolaanh Dinh*, [lake]
25. Lake said to bear same name as No. 24.
26. Tikyeet [lake], may be in error, same name may apply to a lake in or just off the SW corner of the map.
27. Sikdondidlikno [stream, Pocahontas Creek]
28. Twelve mile Fishing Camp [formerly Sarah Simon's] across from mouth of the stream Allen misnamed "Batza River," the name that should have been applied to Indian River. Batza River is Siskatonten ("Looks Good for Bear Upstream") or "Bear Creek."
29. Batzitgla [Indian Mountain, off map to northeast].the one in Allen's report. One local source stated that Baats'akkaakk'at* was the mouth of a slough (evidently Mathews Slough) near Little Indian River.

The results of the first two surveys showed that Batza Téna merited more intensive investigation. This was accomplished to a certain extent when D. Clark assisted by Knut Fladmark, William Peacock and Jonathan Nobleman spent two months excavating and surveying in the Koyukuk drainage in 1971, though more work still is needed. Goals in 1971 were to extend the survey over a greater part of Batza Téna, to undertake test excavations, and to investigate peripheral areas. The objectives of this investigation were to outline the prehistory of the middle Koyukuk region and to determine what bearing it has in the broader context of New World prehistory. The obsidian source was interpreted as a probable magnet that attracted people to exploit the desired raw material there, and this, it was anticipated would result in a concentration of sites and spectrum of prehistoric phases difficult to duplicate elsewhere in the region. The discovery of fluted points of apparent Palaeo-Indian affiliation further showed that the local prehistory could be significant to the prehistory of North America.

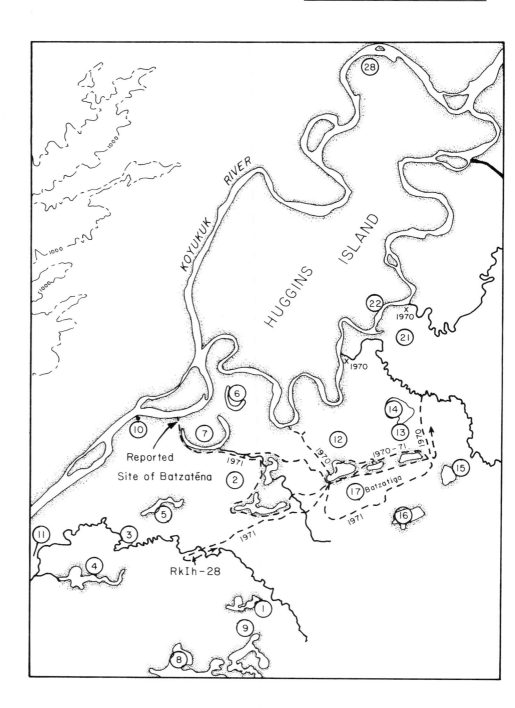

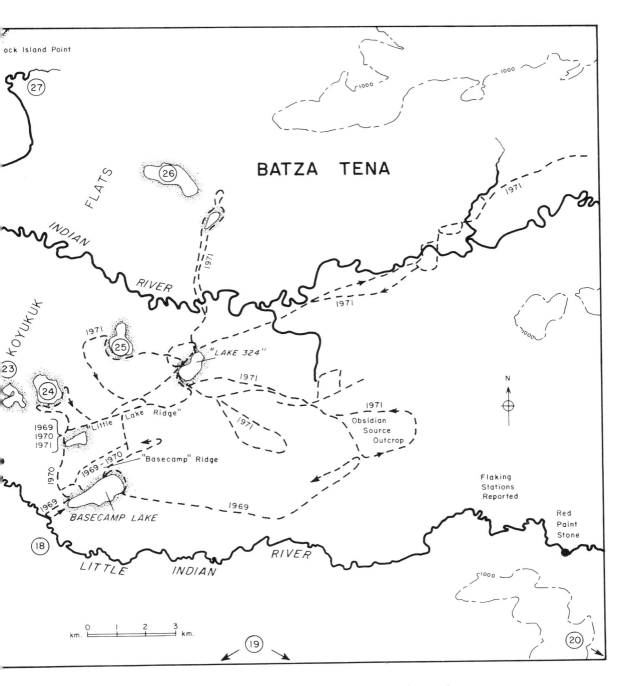

Figure 1.7. Map showing the archaeological surveys at Batza Téna and toponyms.

Figure 1.8. The northeast end of Batzatiga as it is approached by foot across the tundra from the Little Indian River.

To be situated closer to the obsidian source and a site cluster that had yielded several fluted points, we established the first 1971 camp on a small lake located a short distance up the Indian River drainage (Fig. 1.10). This lake is not named on topographic maps and has been designated here, according to its elevation, as Lake El. 324. We arrived there by float plane chartered from Bettles Aviation on June 27, 1971, after an early season on Kodiak (Afognak) Island. From this camp we surveyed up the Indian River, visited the primary source, and made test excavations at several fluted point sites. Six or seven additional fluted points were recovered.

Figure 1.9.   The northeast end of Batzatiga, from the air looking westward. Figure 1.10 was taken from the tundra that shows as a large light area in the right middle ground.

On July 21 we moved by float plane to a small lake at the base of Batzatiga in order to work on sites discovered there in 1970 and to further survey the promising Batzatiga locality. Work there was hampered by an inordinate number of rainy days. It did result in the excavation of Batza Téna Tuktu components described in Chapter 5.

During the preceding season we had observed that soil conditions close to the obsidian source were poor for the development of stratified archaeological contexts. With the hope of finding stratified sites, we undertook survey and excavation in an area of undulating terrain and lakes located approximately 75 km west-southwest of the obsidian source. Our camp there was at Hahanudan Lake where we arrived on August 11. The primary objective again was to find stratified early man sites, but after a couple days of reconnaissance we became convinced that our prospects of finding such sites by foot survey were poor. The remaining time at Hahanudan Lake was profitably spent excavating prehistoric house depressions from a Norton/Ipiutak-related occupation. This work is reported elsewhere (Clark 1977).

Figure 1.10. Two views of site RIIg-33 and the 1971 field camp at Lake 324, taken from onshore and from the air.

Chronology

The primary basis for organizing this volume is a chronology which entails both chronometric dating and hypotheses concerning artifact typology. One technique common for relative dating, that of superposition, has been of no use because of the lack of stratified sites. Dating is discussed here to provide a summary and overview though further details will be given in each chapter. In brief, the sequence described in succeeding chapters, is as follows (Fig. 1.11):

1. Palaeo-Indian occupation identified as such by fluted points.
2. A phase of tenuous integrity and uncertain age characterized by leafshaped and oblanceolate points.
3. Microblade and blade components, poorly dated to the middle time range of microblade industries in Alaska.
4. A late-dating approximation of the Tuktu complex of the Northern Archaic tradition defined principally on the basis of side-notched points.
5. A late microblade component possibly dating to the same period as Batza-Téna Tuktu.
6. Norton/Ipiutak-related assemblages from houses at Hahanudan Lake, dating to the middle of the first millennium A.D.
7. The Lake 324 complex is possible Athapaskan, although presently its type of industry emphasising tools made on bladelike flakes has not been traced to the Koyukon Athapaskans. A radiocarbon date of uncertain reliability dates this complex to the beginning of the present millennium.
8. The late-prehistoric Koyukuk Koyukon are represented by occasional isolated artifacts, especially a Kavik stemmed point, potsherds, a grooved adze, a grinding slab, and cache pits.
9. Finally, there are protohistoric and early historic houses. Their excavation has yielded limited collections of persisting precontact type implements as well as a wide range of European items plus important details on the construction and size of structures.

Radiocarbon Dating

The excavations at Batza Téna produced little material suitable for radiocarbon dating. This may be laid to the fact that hearths were not located within clusters of lithic detritus, have been disturbed or destroyed by soil processes, and also have been rendered unrecognizable by forest fires. Most of the dates that have been obtained come from features and are for Hahanudan Lake (Clark 1977, Table 1.1). In addition to the dates reported in Table 1.1, there are geological dates pertinent to the Pleistocene history of the upper Koyukuk region (see Hamilton refs.) and the Hogatza River. There are several dates for upper drainage archaeological sites investigated by the Alyeska or Trans-Alaska Pipeline project (Cook, ed. 1977:37, 83-84) but in some cases the associations remain to be published.

Figure 1.11. Representative artifacts illustrating the archaeological sequence of the middle
Koyukuk region: a) fluted point base, b) broad oblanceolate point from RkIg-28,
c) wedgeshaped microblade core RkIn-1:1, d) side-notched point, e-g) points and
sideblade from Hahanudan Lake, h-i) points from the Lake 324 complex, j) late
-style stemmed point from RlIg-33; k) 44 cartridge case slipped over wooden shaft
(only a stub remains) to form a blunt point, from an early historic house floor.

The two dates for Batza Téna sites proper are not of good quality because of the material (calcined bone) and the possibility that the association of dated material and artifacts is coincidental. Nevertheless, the dates are compatible with current models of regional prehistory and, in the case of the one applied to the Batza Téna Tuktu component, with obsidian hydration measurements.

Obsidian Hydration Dating

Obsidian hydration dating at Batza Téna was initiated by Leslie B. Davis, at the request of D. Clark, as a means for dating the fluted point occupation, but soon was expanded to cover other components of occupation. It has not been used to the fullest extent possible there, however, because methodological problems, especially poorly controlled variables that have blunted the results. Elsewhere I have discuss the results of the hydration dating programme at Batza Téna and the problems of applying this dating method (Clark 1984). Use of obsidian hydration dating in the upper Koyukuk region has continued (Cook, Kunz and Reanier personal communications to D. Clark; Davis in Cook, ed., 1977; Holmes 1983; Kunz 1984, 1992) as well as elsewhere in Alaska (cf Schoenberg 1985). At present (1989-92) collaborative research by Kunz, Reanier and Cook is leading to better control of the environmental variables that affect the hydration rate in the Koyukuk region, including some of the sites reported here (Kunz 1991). This research should enhance the accuracy of hydration dating and its usefulness at Batza Téna.

The problems encountered in applying hydration dating to the Arctic and Subarctic regions may not be unique to that area but may be better recognized there. Stated in another way, hydration data for temperate zone sites may not be as good, and the applications made of it not as valid as some investigators have assumed. One possible misuse of hydration measurements is to sort out mixed components. A related problem concerns the variance within a single data set. For instance, some samples consist of specimens from a single, sealed dwelling floor all of which likely originated within the span of a few years. Yet, hydration readings are not tightly clustered. The method we have used to cope with such variance is to take an average and not to date on the basis of single specimens.

Another problem concerns establishment of a hydration rate for a particular area, site and microenvironment. Hydration rates can be determined experimentally (Michels 1984) for a particular hydration environment, e.g., "induced," or, with more confidence in my estimation, calculated through utilizing obsidian samples from dated archaeological deposits. Our experience is that the application of induced Batza Téna rates sometimes produces incongruous results, and Kunz (citing C.M. Stevenson) questions that method (Kunz 1991). One limitation to accuracy is the error range in the true age of the radiocarbon dates used for correlation. Hydration rates have been calculated for a number of sites (Clark 1984; Davis 1977; Holmes 1973, 1983; Kunz 1984, 1992) but many of the results are widely variant. A number of microenvironmental factors may be at play, including local microclimate, site orientation, depth of burial, and history of the site or changes in microclimate. These factors are partially controllable, and present research involving the burial of sensors in sites of the Brooks Range and Koyukuk region is intended to provide more accurate, site specific, effective hydration temperatures (R.E. Reanier, M. Kunz and J. P. Cook, personal communications to D. Clark 1989--1991; Kunz 1992).

It became evident early in the history of northern hydration dating that some "wipeout" factor was operative. Within a series there were specimens that lacked hydration, and sections of the same specimen might yield both moderate measurements and nil hydration. One probable wipeout factor--perhaps the major one--is forest fires. This can cause dehydration of obsidian or, so-to-speak, turn the clock back. Not all fires are sufficiently intense to do this, but fires are of sufficient frequency in the north that a site of several millennia age is likely to have been burned over many times. After being dehydrated, the obsidian again starts to hydrate, though in some cases it may be so badly "burned" or altered on the surface that it is unsuitable for hydration observations. As far as we are aware, though, there are no case examples demonstrating that forest fires actually are the cause of nil hydration on Alaskan specimens. However, several Batza Téna thinsections showed evidence of burning, in some cases with, and in other cases without measurable hydration. Studies by Trembour (1990), summarized by Kunz (1992) indicate that for complete elimination of the hydration rind (which follows a stage in which it becomes diffuse or indistinct), the obsidian in his experiments had to be heated to 430 °C, and that at 540 °C the surface became thermally crazed. We found that obsidian exposed on the surface to the 1968 Utopia wildfire still had a fresh glassy appearance, especially after the dirt was washed off. In many places litter and organic rich soil had been burned down to mineral soil, exposing clusters of obsidian. At only two sites, and these were subsurface deposits, had obsidian been heated to the point that the surface had become frosted, crazed or melted. Judging from Trembor's experiments, obsidian can be heated to a level that destroys hydration and still have a fresh appearance. Kunz (1992) cites Mann's work indicating that in order not to kill the root systems of aspen trees the temperature within the shallow ground would not have exceeded 130 °C during fires. We noted that within two years after the 1968 wildfire there was a dense regrowth of aspen saplings on some sites. It appears, then, that the numerous fires at Batza Téna were too cool to destroy the hydration rinds on buried obsidian, but in some places where roots, fallen timber or thick litter and organic soil layers burned temperatures may have been high enough to destroy hydration. This possibility needs to be verified by field observations, which might be made in the face of advancing forest fires or through experimental firing of selected plots of ground.

Both thick and thin hydration sometimes occurs on the same specimen. A common explanation for this is reuse or refashioning of an old implement. We believe, though, that physicists investigating hydration should look for other causes.

TABLE 1.1. RADIOCARBON DATES FROM BATZA TENA AND HAHANUDAN LAKE

Number	Age	Date*	Material	Dates	Applies to
S-975	285~95	AD 1665	Charcoal from cache cover supports	RkIk-5 Cache Pit A	Late prehist. Koyukon
S-921	765~455	AD 1185	Calcined bone	RkIk-4 open area	Uncertain**
S-920	885~80	AD 1065	Calcined bone	Part of RlIg-52	Lake 324 Com.
S-976	1325~260	AD 625	Calcined bone	Dispersed hearth centre RkIh-36	Batza Téna Tuktu
S-656	1285~75	AD 665	Charcoal from floor	RkIk-5 House 2	Inland Norton-Ipiutak
S-655	1360~90	AD 590	Charcoal from hearth	RkIk-5 House 1	" "
S-658	1465~75	AD 485	Structural charcoal	RkIk-3 House B	" "
S-657	1500~90	AD 450	Charcoal from floor	RkIk-3 House C	" "

* Clark 1977 Table IV gives the date range taking into account MASCA calibration. The reader may wish to make appropriate corrections and calibration.
**The problem of applying this date to a probable multiple component site is discussed in Clark 1977.

Typological Crossdating

In the absence of any direct chronometric dating, sites or artifacts may be compared or crossdated with similar material of known age found elsewhere. The fluted points at Batza Téna are correlated with those of the mid-continent region, though there are persons who suggest that the northern fluted points are an independent development (Clark 1984a). In this monograph we begin the sequence with the fluted points, but it remains possible that there are older sites at Batza Téna that have not yielded diagnostic chronological indicators. As well, the temporal separation of fluted points and the earliest microblade industries in the Koyukuk region is undetermined. Some investigators suggest that microblades and fluted points validly co-occur (Holmes 1973, Gal 1976).

Similarities between the Tuktu complex of Anaktuvuk Pass (Campbell 1961), and to a lesser extent the Palisades complex of Onion Portage (Anderson 1968, 1988) establish Batza Téna Tuktu as a Northern Archaic complex, though it is proposed that the Koyukuk River assemblage is considerably younger than the one from the Kobuk drainage.

Among the most difficult artifacts for comparative chronology are the microblade cores. Initially thought to be very ancient in northwestern North America, microblade technology presently is seen to have both early and young aspects (cf Cook 1975; West 1967a, 1975, 1981). Opinions have differed, though, on just how recent microblade technology can be, and some archaeologists have rejected first millennium A.D. dates as being too young. A number of core forms were utilized, and it has been proposed by various investigators that certain core attributes occurred during different periods than others.

Obsidian Sources

Local Toponyms

Obsidian sources reported to us at Allakaket and Hughes are the Little Indian River, one person also named Indian River, the upland between the two Indian rivers, a lake called Takbatzahullanten , and certain other lakes and river sloughs within the Indian River area (spellings here are approximations as heard by D. or A. Clark; translations were provided by the native speakers). Little Indian River is known to local Koyukon people as Batzitna which translates "Obsidian River" but the immediate proximity frequently is referred to as Batza Téna which means "Obsidian Trail." We have used this term for the source area and associated sites. Batza Téna refers specifically to a formerly occupied locality not far below the mouth of Little Indian River. One explanation offered locally is that from Batza Téna it is easy to see the way to the source. The Koyukuk people use the same basic words for Indian River and Little Indian River but distinguish the former with a prefix for upper or big . Local information supports Orth's (1967) statement implying that the Batza River identified on modern maps on the west side of the Koyukuk River represents a cartographer's mislocation of Batzitna or Batzakaket (Batza mouth). The stream indicated as Batza River on topographic maps was reported to A. Clark as Siskatonten ("Looks-Good-for-Bear-Upstream" or simply "Bear Creek"). Several additional toponyms for the area contain the term batza (Fig. 1.7). Takbatzahullanten means "There is batza in the lake water." It was explained that obsidian pebbles could be found on gravel bars in the lake or be seen on the bottom if one was coasting along the shore in a canoe. There was a 19th century settlement, Batzaténa , located in the vicinity of a lake of the same name. Batzatimunket ("Obsidian Hill Lake") is located at Batzatiga or "Obsidian Hill" where we made surveys and excavations. Batzazeehe * is a range of hills flanking Little Indian River on the south. Batzitgla ("Obsidian Mountain") is a prominent landmark behind Hughes known today as Indian Mountain. One resident of Hughes pointed out that neither of the last two locations had any obsidian but that they received these names because of their proximity to the source area. This array of names and landmarks must have advertised widely were batza could be obtained

Among some Athapaskan-speaking groups the term batza and its cognates has a generalized meaning used in reference to hard cutting materials and implements (M. Krauss oral communication 1968). We queried several native speakers at Allakaket, Hughes and Huslia about this term, and especially whether it could refer to other hard lithic materials used for tools. Invariably, we were informed that it referred only to the glassy rock (obsidian), not to any other rock, not to a tool, and not to tools made of batza . One person however misidentified a dark chert scraper as being made of batza . But another person when shown two colours of chert and one of obsidian identified the last as batza and said he did not know the term for the others. Today people recall that until relatively recently flakes of batza were used to cut the blisters

Figure 1.12. View of the upland source outcrop area in 1971, looking northward (W. Peacock, K. Fladmark, J. Nobleman left to right).

under eyelids resulting from snow blindness. There is information from a single source that it was used for "fire sparks" (as a fire flint) and that it was traded to Kobuk people for seal oil and oogruk rope. Although some aspects of indigenous technology continued in the Koyukuk region into the second half of the 19th century, tools and weapon tips knapped from obsidian and other stones may have been replaced by bone, ground slate and early traded Eurasian metal sufficiently prior to contact that little information has survived on the earlier use of batza as a lithic material.

Natural Sources

Natural sources at Batza Téna include the Indian River bedrock source in the 250-300 metre-high upland between Little Indian and Indian River, colluvium in the Indian River valley opposite the bedrock source, gravel bars of the Indian and Little Indian River, shore gravels at Ta'batzahullanten (Lake), and colluvial deposits at the southwest corner of Batzatiga including the shore of a small lake there.

Patton and Miller describe the primary source as...

> ...a nearly horizontal tabular body of rhyolite flows and tuffs of probable mid-Tertiary age, which rests with angular discordance upon deformed sedimentary strata of Cretaceous age. Bedrock exposures of the obsidian have been completely reduced to rubble, and the obsidian is found as subround pelletal and globular fragments up to 10 cm in length strewn across a sandy surface of finely divided vitric and pumiceous debris. The size and shape of the obsidian fragments suggest that they formed as residual inclusions (sometimes called "marekanites" or "Apache tears") in a hydrated perlitic glass (1970:761; see also Patton, Miller, Chapman and Yeend 1977).

Further study of the geologic source is being undertaken by the Bureau of Land Management which has located an additional outcrop littered with small fragments of obsidian about 2 km northeast of the one described above (Mann unpublished 1991 report cited by Kunz 1992; J.P. Cook personal communication to D. Clark 1993).

We made two trips to the upland source area in 1969 and 1971 and found the sandy pumiceous surface but saw only small obsidian pebbles. Larger pieces were found in adjacent cobble fields (Fig. 1.12, 1.13). Flaking stations are uncommon in the immediate area. Local people informed us that large obsidian cobbles and flakes could be found farther east towards a conical peak (VABM 2139 CONE). This small but distinctive peak could have served as a landmark identifying the source to persons lacking previous familiarity with the area.

Gravel bars were examined on Little Indian River immediately west of "Basecamp" lake. Upon close scrutiny we were able to find several small pebbles of obsidian, and eventually a few larger pebbles barely within the size range of the utilized pieces seen at flaking stations. Fewer but larger obsidian cobbles were found on gravel bars of the Indian River immediately north of

Figure 1.13. Upland country east of the obsidian source, seen from the north side of the uplands. The peak benchmark "cone" is on the horizon.

lake elevation 324. A single obsidian cobble was found in shore gravels of the lake we believe the one called Tak'batzahullanten, reported locally to have been a source. Gravels at this locality may be derived from the alluvium of the Indian River.

The source at the southwest end of Batzatiga is primarily colluvial but the obsidian there may be derived from unobserved local bedrock deposits (Fig. 1.14). This location is 17-19 km from the verified upland source. Evidence for it consists of lakeshore, slope and frost boil occurrences and the presence of abundant obsidian pebbles in colluvial material mantling volcanic rock. Inasmuch as this source has not been previously reported, details are provided below.

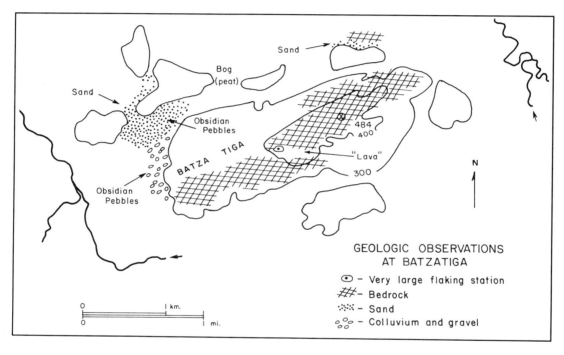

Figure 1.14. Map with geological observations at Batzatiga.

Numerous pebbles were found, in 1969 during low water, along the shore of a lake at the southwest end of Batzatiga. One Koyukuk person identified the lake as <u>Toban Naka'ish Tod-li-oden</u>. Several archaeological sites, especially of the Batza Téna Tuktu phase, are located around this lake and the pebbles co-occur with flaked material. The possibility that the pebbles are unused material derived from the archaeological sites was considered but was rejected because some pebbles are so small that they are not likely have been collected for raw material. As well, the amount of obsidian not utilized is peculiarly high if it had been brought in from a distant source.

Inland from these sites about 100 meters, towards the hill, obsidian pebbles were found in frost boils. The surface there, as well as at the lake, is underlain by fine-grained sand or silt sediment. Farther up the slope of Batzatiga small obsidian pebbles are abundant near the surface of the gravelly soil and in frost stripes, but occasional flakes of human derivation occur in the same context. A cluster of obsidian pebbles also was found on the slope exposed by one tree throw.

Obsidian pebbles occur on a low subridge of the southwest end of Batzatiga in yellow-green gravelly soil. At one location, designated RkIh-31, 30-cm-deep test pit with about 2.3 cubic feet volume yielded at least 86 unmodified obsidian pebbles. Flakes of apparent human production occurred abundantly at all depths together with the obsidian. The matrix there was unsorted yellowish clayey colluvium. Stones were up to 15 cm in maximum dimension (the obsidian pebbles were considerably smaller) and include obviously water rounded cobbles, among them quartz cobbles as well as volcanic rock. This site presents two problems: one is to explain the development of this natural occurrence of obsidian cobbles, including the presence of alluvial cobbles in an apparent colluvial deposit; the second to account for apparent archaeological material in what may be a very old natural context.

Reconnaissance showed that obsidian occurs naturally only on the southwestern third of Batzatiga where it was limited there to the northwest-facing side of the hill. Elsewhere on Batzatiga decomposed lava-like rock is exposed, but without associated obsidian pebbles. Bedrock lithology at Batzatiga belongs to a different volcanic rock unit than that at the primary geologic source (Patton et al 1977). Possibly, if not a natural bedrock source itself Batzatiga retains old colluvial deposits from a once more continuous distribution in the region extending eastward to the upland bedrock source. However, the high frequency of obsidian pebbles found in the test noted above is hardly compatible with the explanation of dispersal from a source several km distant, though chemical data indicate that a single source is involved. The one unique obsidian or fourth chemical source type in the Canadian Conservation Institute analysis comes from Batzatiga, but other Batzatiga specimens conform to the Group 2 and 3 types (Appendix III). Therefore a Batzatiga source wholly separate from that in the uplands between Indian and Little Indian River is unlikely. It remains significant, however, that in prehistoric times it was not necessary go to the upland source area to obtain obsidian. This material could be obtained very close to the Koyukuk River and the historic Batza Téna settlement.

Archaeological Sites

Table 1.2 lists all collection locations designated as sites, while selected sites and collections are described in succeeding chapters. Site location is plotted on the map figures. For the majority of sites, which are principally single cluster flaking stations, aggregates of flaking station clusters, and flake scatters a single generalized description will be provided. Many sites are located on two short ridges that form the transition between the Koyukuk River flats and the upland source area between Indian and Little Indian River (Fig. 1.15-1.17). Both of these small streams are tributaries of the Koyukuk River. A few additional sites occur in the upland source area between these two streams. More sites are located on both sides of Indian River near and downriver from Utopia as determined from a single reconnaissance by D. Clark and discoveries by R. Reger (Reger and Reger 1972). Many additional sites were found at Batzatiga or Obsidian Hill which rises from the flats three km east of the Koyukuk River (Fig. 1.9). Finally, a microblade site was found at the end of a small hill located south of Batzatiga. This exploration does not completely delimit the Batza Téna site focus. Undoubtedly many more sites or site clusters are present in areas we did not examine, particularly east of the source. A few exposed sites have been seen in the vicinity by geologists. For recording, the two short ridges noted above were designated "Basecamp Ridge" (site of 1969 and 1970 camps) and "Little Lake Ridge." Sites are distributed from the very edge of ridges, were they meet the flats, to their crests. The concentration of sites on these ridges and Batzatiga is noteworthy, although there are additional sites elsewhere. Logically, to a certain degree, the distribution of discovered sites correlates with the routes of reconnaissance and areas given especial attention, as is indicated in Figure 1.7. However, surveys focused on and extended to topographic features or terrain considered to be optimal for site location and visibility, and therefore discovery is based on more than chance proximity to a path of reconnaissance.

With a few exceptions, primarily Batzatiga, some indication of each site was visible on the surface inasmuch as the ground cover had been burned off, and most of the trees killed, by a forest fire in 1968, the Utopia burn. As well, some sites are exposed on partially denuded stony ground. Effects of the Utopia burn vary from place to place. Locally it missed a grove of trees; elsewhere it only burned off the leaf litter and scorched the shrubs; but in other places the fire was so intense that nearly all the organic matter on the ground, including organic components of the soil, was consumed leaving a relatively barren surface of ash, mineral soil and stones. Many groves of fire-killed trees were still standing when we surveyed, but we also encountered impenetrable jungles of deadfalls. To a certain degree, reconnaissance was oriented towards examining ground exposed by the Utopia burn, as well as toward places where there was sparse vegetation or natural exposure. This has resulted in certain locations receiving more attention than others. In a few cases where exposures were lacking, as on Batzatiga, shovel probes and metal rod probes were used. An obsidian flake emits a very distinctive screech when stuck by an iron probe. By 1971, three years after the burn, regeneration of the vegetation was well advanced, especially the aspen which was propagating from surviving roots.

The unsystematic nature of the site survey and observations must be emphasised. Not all sites were exposed, or some were only partially exposed, and information on them is limited to judgemental test probes, as noted above. At times sites were discovered at the end of arduous traverses, during poor weather or in the failing light at the end of the day, while various circumstances operated to prevent our returning to them to make more thorough investigations.

Many sites have the same characteristics which can be described summarily. Usually a site

Figure 1.15. "Basecamp Lake" and "Basecamp Ridge" with "Little Lake Ridge" in the background and the Indian Mountains on the horizon, from the air looking slightly east of north.

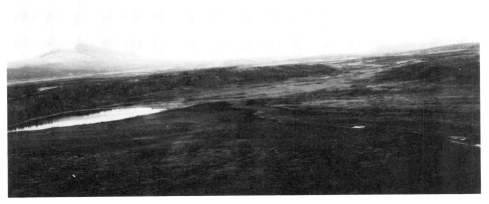

Figure 1.16. "Little Lake" and "Little Lake Ridge", from the same flight line as Figure 1.14.

consists of one to several obsidian flake clusters and a thinner, wider, sometimes discontinuous scatter of flakes. A concentration might be as small as 60 cm in diameter or as large as 5 metres, and in maximum dimension the sites range from about 2 metres to more than 100 metres. In some cases, as at the west end of Little Lake Ridge, it is microtopography that determines the extent of a site. That is, flake clusters and scatter are present on slightly raised terrain but are absent, or are not observable, on lower flanking ground covered by muskeg, low vegetation and damp organic soil. Sites in such cases are naturally partitioned or delimited traces of cultural activity. Discounting the effects of the Utopia burn, the sites are covered with relatively sparse small trees, primarily aspen but also birch, spruce and alder, with an undercover of shrubs, sphagnum moss, cladonia and leaf litter. Most sites are simply present in the forest on slightly elevated flat places, benches, and knolls along the ridges. With the forest cover, only a few sites provide a good view of the surrounding terrain. During any periods of deforestation, though, most would command offer visual access to a broad environs. Sites RkIg-10 and RkIh-28, and minor flaking stations elsewhere including RkIg-17 located near the upland source, occupy topographically prominent locations which provide especially good views of surrounding terrain. Some sites are situated along the shores of small lakes, but such lakes and ponds, most no more than 1 km in extent, were not especially necessarily localizing factors. Specimens were picked up on the lake shore at Batzatiga in 1970 when the water was low, especially at an eroded site that literally had been rolled up by ice shove. The water there was too high for us to make a shore collection in 1971. Otherwise, shoreline erosion is not significant and is not a factor that can be exploited for site surveying.

The nonglacial soil of the ridges is sparse and contains considerable stone derived from local bedrock. Batzatiga is an exception where on the west and northwest flanks the matrix and substrate of several sites is colluvium and fine sediment. Local exposures of bedrock were seen only high on the slope at the southwest end of Batzatiga, along the Indian River, at Late 324, and in the upland source area, but microtopography and the exposure of abundant detrital stone elsewhere suggests that on the hills bedrock barely beneath the surface. Interlocked stones tied together by matted roots made testing difficult at some sites. A very substantial part of the archaeological material is exposed on the surface, but at several sites heavy flake concentrations extend into the rocky soil for approximately 10 cm. Sometimes these concentrations consisted of relatively pure lenses of massed flakes. At some sites the matrix is so stony that excavation consisted essentially of removing and stacking up rocks; elsewhere we attempted to excavate with trowels. No buried or stratified sites were found, but there was little incentive to make deep tests into the rubbly soil when material of apparently all ages occurred on the surface or at a superficial depth. In a few cases flakes appear to have been distributed by soil creep, and in other cases they have been concentrated in the depressed margins of frost boils, but there also are striking examples of apparently undisturbed flake concentrations. When archaeological material is present in frost involutions it may occur as much as 40 cm deep. At certain sites the flakes have sharp edges whereas at other sites not only are the edges nibbled and crushed (producing pseudo-artifacts) but the faces and ridges between flake scars are worn or abraded. These conditions suggest both an active soil layer in which the artifacts have been enclosed and an antiquity subjecting nibbled and abraded artifacts to more episodes of soil movement or freeze-thaw cycles than fresher appearing specimens.

Figure 1.17. "Little Lake Ridge" from the edge of the Koyukuk River flats (A ground view of the terrain in Figure 1.16.)

The sites do not present a totally homogeneous group. They vary greatly in size and shape, in implement content, flake size, obsidian cortex variety, in apparent surface disturbance through soil sorting and, taking Batzatiga into consideration, in soil matrix. Flakes collected from the shore of a lake at Batzatiga were two to six times larger than those excavated from sites at the same locality. No specific explanation is offered here for that observation, but the cause may be taphonomic. Sites vary considerably in the type and variety of artifacts recovered. Some evidently were living or camp sites; the majority were only flaking stations and yielded few or no finished implements among masses of flakes. Various periods or archaeological traditions are represented, and some sites may present a mixture of material from differing components.

Most sites are characterized by two factors which are detrimental to the interests of archaeologists. (a) The sites are primarily flaking stations, analogous to quarry sites though most are not located at the precise source of raw material. For that reason they yield a great amount of detritus and broken unfinished objects but few finished artifacts, and they produce little in the way of living site distributions and assemblages. (b) Due to poor development or loss of soil, frost action and other geomorphic processes, the sites are essentially surface assemblages. This, coupled with natural disturbances, has resulted in lack of component separation where more than one component is present, displacement of artifacts, and destruction of any features.

Each collection locality is listed in Table 1.2. The table provides the only description to appear in this report for a large number of sites. Some of those sites yielded large flake collections but only produced small implement assemblages which are not readily placed in terms of the periodization of succeeding chapters (They are included, however, in the tables in Appendix II). They vary from single flake clusters to sites of large or substantial undefined (limits not determined) dimensions. Batza Téna is located within the Melozitna map quadrangle. Site numbers may be created by prefixing the field number with the state and quadrangle code, 49-Mlz, according to the system proposed by West (1967a) which is employed in Alaska. The numbers used in this report, however are from the so-called Borden system, otherwise used exclusively for Canada except where adapted and extended to cover Canadian Museum of Civilization fieldwork elsewhere. Most site dimensions were paced, and then converted to English values and metric units. In some cases the converted dimensions may create a false sense of accuracy.

TABLE 1.2. ARCHAEOLOGICAL SITES

Field number	Date	Site number	Formal tools*	Details, Chapter reference**
1	1969	RkIg-1	20	Fluted point find, hydration study, Chap.2
2	" "	RkIg-2	1	C 12 m long, 2 flake clusters, uniface Pl.21 R, 8 kg flakes
3	" "	RkIg-3	2	Three flake clusters 0.6-1.4 m dia.; 11 m long; 2.21 kg flakes
4	" "	RkIg-4		Extension of RkIg-10, Chap. 2
5	" "	RkIg-5	6	Two flake clusters, separated by 2 m sterile terrain; one is 1 m in dia. and yielded less than 0.5 kg flakes (17 basalt, 337 obsidian) but had 6 end scrapers
6	" "	RkIg-6	0	Slightly larger than RkIg-5; 287 (0.8 kg) flakes
7	" "	RkIg-7	0	1.5 m dia. with nearby minor flake cluster; 111 (0.17 kg) flakes from the first, no implements
8	" "	RkIg-8	2	Areas 1.5x6 m extending downslope & 6x12 m yielded 177 and 109 (0.8 & 0.66 kg) flakes respectively, biface frags., end scraper
9	1969-71	RkIg-9	1	C 6 m long; 650 (1.25) kg flakes partial coll.; local areas trowelled, results poor, end scraper
10	1969-71	RkIg-10	21	Fluted point find, hydration study, Chap. 2
11	1969-70	RkIg-11	11	Sparse 60+ m long with local clusters; extends from sites 12 to 41; 1290 (2.8 kg) flakes + flakes not coll., bifaces
12	1969	RkIg-12	5	Six clusters in 3x14 m zone with wide scatter beyond; nearly merges with RkIg-11; 2556 (5.1 kg) flakes; Pl.22 O, bifaces
13	" "	RkIg-13	5	3x5 m; 1375 (1.75 kg) flakes, partial coll, biface
14	" "	RkIg-14	4	Main and minor cluster in 8 m linear zone; 680 (1.9 kg) flakes, bifaces

TABLE 1.2--continued

Field number	Date	Site number	Formal tools*	Details, Chapter reference**
15	" "	RkIg-15	0	5 or more large (3.5-5.5 m-dia.) clusters of flakes in 6x24 m area on slight bedrock bench partially exposed in forest; 840 (2.9 kg) flakes partial coll., core & roughout frags.
16	" "	RkIg-16	0	Scattered slope finds near 1045 summit, small area; 59 flakes, core
17	" "	RkIg-17	2	Unvegetated highland view point near source, at 1045 elev. summit, 20x50+ m; 718 (2.2 kg) flakes, partial coll. from lichen-covered ground, bladelike flake Pl. 22E
18	" "	RkIg-18	1	Sparse, intermittent for 60+ m linear; poorly exposed, 0.25 kg flakes, partial coll., Pl.22G
19	" "	RkIg-19	0	1.4 m dia., 60 cm central cluster; 1.1 kg flakes
20	" "	RkIg-20	0	Two clusters & scatter on knoll, c 22 m; 229 (0.9 kg) flakes, no implements
21	" "	RkIg-21	0	60 cm cluster; 6 m away is a loose cluster; scatter to 15 m; 553 (1.6 kg) flakes, Pl. 23B
22	1969-70	RkIg-22	8	Two clusters & scatter 8.2 m long; another flake cluster 25 m away. 4.7 kg flakes, Chap. 5
23	1969	RkIg-23	1	Areas of 12, 6 & 2.4 m dia. 7 m apart; flake scatters, 131 (0.9 kg) flakes, cores, biface
24	" "	RkIg-24	2	Scatter 14 m dia. with 1 & 0.5 m clusters; 786 (2.7 kg) flakes, biface, point base
25	1969-70	RkIg-25	0	Clusters in 27 m-long zone, scatter to 45 m; 2030 (8 kg) flakes from 7 clusters, no distinct implements
26	1969	RkIg-26	1	Two clusters 0.6 & 1 m, a flake scatter 8 m from the clusters; 161 (0.5 kg) flakes, biface
27	1969, 71	RkIg-27	2	Poorly defined clusters in 36x15 m area on high point of Little Lake ridge; 368 (1.6 kg) flakes partial surface coll., leafshaped basalt point
28	1969-71	RkIg-28	28	Basalt common, Chap. 3
29	" "	RkIg-29	8	Fluted point, Chap. 2
30	1969-71	RkIg-30	19	Fluted points, hydration study, Chap. 2
31	1969-71	RkIg-31	17	Fluted & sidenotched points, Chap. 2
32	1970-71	RkIh-32	23	Microblades, other, Chap. 4
33	1970	RkIh-33	5	Coll. from 145-m-long beach & muskeg forest at Batzatiga; 8.5 kg flakes, exposed items totally collected, point Pl. 6N has 3.4 microns hydration, bifaces, end scrapers, cores Pl. 23N, 24A
34	1970	RkIh-34	0	From 20-m-long beach at Batzatiga. 3.6 kg
35	1970-71	RkIh-35	1	Possibly Batza Téna Tuktu, Chap. 5
36	1970-71	RkIh-36	13	Batza Téna Tuktu, Chap. 5; 9.4 kg flakes from shore; excavation in 1971
37	1970	RkIh-37	9	Batza Téna Tuktu; 6.3 kg flakes, Chap. 5
38	1970-71	RkIh-38	4	Diffuse finds at a lake at Batzatiga; 0.2 kg dispersed flakes + 0.58 kg others; Chap. 5
39	1970	RkIh-39	0	Two flake loci at Batzatiga c 60 m apart found in random probes of forested area, extent of end-of-Batzatiga site not determined
40	1970	RkIh-40	0	From small submerged beach at Batzatiga, 0.4 kg flakes, core Pl. 23C
41	" "	RkIg-41	11	Discontinuous flakes in 18x6 m area; 1.6 kg flakes partial coll., bifaces, end scrapers

TABLE 1.2--continued

Field number	Date	Site number	Formal tools*	Details, Chapter reference**
42	" "	RkIg-42	2	Two small flake loci; 0.6 kg flakes, end scrapers
43	1970-71	RkIg-43	2	Fluted point find; 1.9 kg in 1970; Chap. 2
44	1970-71	RkIg-44	14	Fluted points & other; 6.9 kg in 1970; Chap. 2 1971 excavation, partial surface coll.
45	1970	RkIg-45	5	Scattered flakes in 12-m-dia area; 0.6 kg
46	" "	RkIg-46	1	Minor flake clusters in 36-m-long zone; 0.7 kg flakes + clusters, knife Pl. 22K
47	1970	RkIg-47	7	Microblades, Chap. 4
48	" "	RkIg-48	3	Complex topography next to Little Lake with discrete clusters & scatter; considerable exposure of flakes but few implements, 0.8 kg sample only, point, cores, bifaces (Pl. 21T)
49	" "	RkIg-49	1	Minor, c̲ 4 m long; 55 flakes, basalt common
50	1970	RkIg-50	3	Three small clusters & scatter within 3x6 m area; 0.7 kg flakes nearly complete coll.
51	1970-71	RkIg-51	4+	C 22 m dia., selective collection 1970; partial excavation in 1971, Appendix I
52	1970	RlIg-52	5	Includes Lake 324 complex, Chap. 7
53	1970	RlIg-53	0	Two small clusters, widely separated; 0.4 & 1 kg flakes, no implements
Up to this point site and field number numerics match.				
54	1970	----	0	No collection, not designated as site
55	1971	RlIg-33	6	Location of Lake 324 field camp, Chap. 9
56	1971	RlIg-34	0	60 m dia., 2 flake concentrations trowelled, 1 produced most of the 1 kg flakes, 2nd major & other minor clusters examined, not coll.
57	1971	RkIg-32	1	2.59 kg flakes, point frag., Chap. 2
58	1971	RkIg-33	1	1.12 kg flakes
59	1971	----	0	Not designated, observed but not collected
60	1071	RkIg-35	2	At E end a 1.5 m flake cluster, at W end an 8-m-long flake scatter on barren rocky ground; biface fragment Pl. 22P; 0.73 kg flakes E from cluster
61	1971	RkIg-36	1	Overlook on source highland; 1.03 kg flakes from cluster, others scattered by soil creep
62	1971	RlIg-35	4	Exposed clusters & scattered implements, some of chert, 5.8 kg flakes, Chap. 8
63	1971	RlIg-36	1	0.89 kg flakes from clusters at end of minor ridge that extends onto flats; Pl. 21D
64	1971	RlIg-37		Microblades, Chap. 4
65	1971	RlIg-38	2	2.67 kg flakes from 1 excavated cluster and a 4x6 m surface scatter on 19-m-dia site on slight ridge; core, point base Pl. 21F
66	1971	RlIg-39	0	30x12 m area + outliers, major 0.75x2.4 m cluster, minor clusters, flake scatter; 5.5 kg flakes, no implements
67	1971	RlIg-40	0	14x4.5 m, small clusters & dispersed flakes exposed on fractured ground, 0.73 kg sample
68	1971	RkIg-37	2	11x4.8 m + scatter beyond; 2.85 kg flakes from tight cluster, other clusters & scatter not collected, chert core, basalt biface
69	1971	RlIg-41	1	Tight 1x3 m cluster & dispersed 2x4.5 m cluster; excavated; 0.5 kg flakes totally collected, basalt flakes, point Pl. 21CT

TABLE 1.2--concluded

Field number	Date	Site number	Formal tools*	Details, Chapter reference**
70	1971	RkIg-38	1	4 small flake clusters in 6 m dia. area; 2nd lithic area 30 m N, 3rd area 5 m E, 4th area 12 m E, additional small clusters on site, most not coll., basalt point Pl. 21A found separate
71	1971	RlIg-42	1	2x4 m scatter & separate 1 m cluster; 0.4 kg
72	1971	RkIg-39	4	2 small clusters of basalt & obsidian flakes in 1.5x2 m & 2x3.6 m areas 10 m apart; 0.35 kg flakes, basalt & obsidian point bases
73	1971	RkIg-40	0	1.32 kg flakes from tight 75 cm-dia cluster on Little Lake ridge crest, additional partially exposed clusters present, 1 of which was exc. but not coll. as only flakes were present
74	1971	----	0	Massive flaking stations observed, no implements seen on surface, no collection
75	1971	RlIg-43	0	Cluster in 1.1x1.5 m area, minor clusters 25 m distant; 1.56 kg flakes, 2 biface frag.
76	1971	RlIg-44	2	3 clusters in only 3x4 m area & other scattered flakes, 2.1 kg flakes from 2 clusters, hammerstone, notched point Pl. 21N
77	1971	RlIg-45	1	Dispersed flake distribution for 35 m & 2 clusters on mini-ridge at edge of flats, from 1 coll. cluster & a tree-throw exposure 1.5 kg flakes, non-obsidian uniface Pl. 22B.
78	1971	RlIg-46	7+	Flakes litter c 90 m exposed area; partial flake coll.; inspected for implements, App. I
79	1971	RlIg-47		Fluted point & other, Chap. 2
80	1971	RlIg-48	1	2 clusters & scatter, most of 1 cluster coll., chert implement 2 m from it; 0.27 kg, biface Pl. 24I; partly obscured by forest
81	1971	RlIg-49	3	On knoll top 45+ m long (forest covers one end), 1.7 kg flakes from one cluster, point base Pl. 21I, end scrapers Pl. 20Q, coll. elsewhere; hasty examination in rain & failing light.
82	1971	RlIg-50	1	Lower adjunct a few 100 m west of RkIg-49; flakes present not collected; hasty examination in rain & failing light
83	1971	RkIg-53	0	Indian R overlook on bedrock bluff, 65x40 m; 7.7 kg flakes, no implements
84	1971	RlIg-51	0	200+ m long, 1.2 kg flakes, partially coll. from 60 cm of 4-m cluster; biface Pl. 21Q
85	1971	RkIh-27	0	Very large on hill crest, heavily vegetated, flakes trowelled out, not coll. Rock samples
86	1971	RkIh-28		Microblades, Chap. 4
87	1971	RkIh-29	0	3 TP in birch grove at edge of tundra; 3.63 kg flakes, site extent not determined
88	1971	RkIh-30	0	1.69 kg flakes and obsidian pebble sample from 1 m TP, shovel probes in vicinity pos., extent of this Batzatiga site not determined
89	1971	RkIh-31	0	5.43 kg pebbles geoarch. TP on Batzatiga

*   Formal tools exclude retouched flakes, bladelike flakes, flake cores, small fragments of bifacially flaked stone, unclassified point fragments, amorphous worked objects, and possible early stage biface roughouts and corelike objects.
** If no chapter is indicated, the site is not further described in this report.

CHAPTER 2: FLUTED POINTS AND SITES

Introduction

Fluted points were found at nine Batza Téna sites. The significance of these points lies in their probable relationship to fluted points found elsewhere in the New World and the place of the fluted point horizon or Clovis culture in Palaeo-Indian prehistory. This historical problem is discussed in the next paragraphs and in the concluding chapter. Each site, each fluted point, and associated artifacts are described in this chapter. To an undetermined degree, though, the collections are composed of mixed assemblages of diverse age and thus they do not necessarily define a valid technological complex. Earlier articles have presented statements on the dating of northern fluted points, their relationships, and their distribution (Clark 1984a 1984b; Clark and Clark 1975, 1980, 1983; see also West 1982). These arguments will not be reiterated in detail.

During the decade following publication of the discovery of the Folsom fluted points found associated with remains of extinct bison (Figgins 1927), which established an antiquity for people in the New World, archaeologists turned to Alaska for correlative evidence of early migration into the Americas. Fluted points were the earliest accepted evidence of Palaeo-Indians, and it was surmised that migrants trekking from Asia, via Alaska, brought with them this technology. This hypothesis was not new, but now archaeologists had an "index fossil" to follow in their search. The association of fluted points and Palaeo-Indians was reinforced within a few years by the discovery of Clovis fluted points with the remains of mammoths, predating Folsom, in the southwestern United States (Cotter 1937, Haury 1953).

By 1939 Rainey was able to report on several finds from the interior of Alaska which were thought to come from Pleistocene muck deposits (Rainey 1939, 1940). These did not include any fluted points but there were lanceolate points, suggestive of ones later designated as Plano points, and a polished bone point or rod similar to ones found farther south in Clovis Palaeo-Indian sites.

It was not until 1947 that the first recognized northern fluted point was found in Alaska by a Geological Survey party operating on the Utukok River (Thompson 1948). This small chert specimen, first identified as a Folsom point but perhaps better classified as a Clovis-related point, displays distinctive triple fluting on both faces. Soon after that discovery three or four additional fluted points and fragments were reported from western and northwestern Alaska (Giddings 1951, 1964; Solecki 1951). Earlier, however, Hibben had reported a specimen, from Circle north of Fairbanks, with apparent short triple flutes, which he called "Folsom-like" (Hibben 1943:Pl. XVd). Wormington (1957:109) classified this specimen as a Plainview point, and subsequently it attracted little notice in the archaeological literature. We would accommodate this point within the range of variation of northern fluted points.

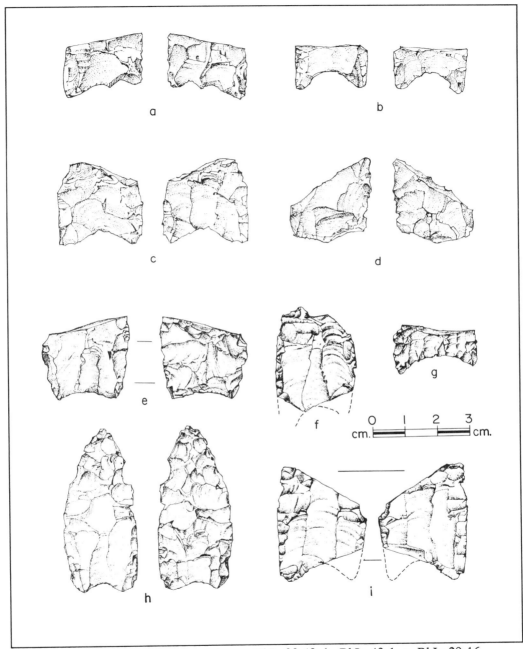

Figure 2.1. Drawings of fluted points. a. RkIg-30:42, b. RkIg-43:1, c. RkIg-29:16, d. RkIg-44:38, e. RkIg-31:15, f. RkIg-1:49. g, RkIg-28:9, h. RkIg-31:60, i. RkIg-10:36.

Thompson (1948:63) implicitly linked the Utukok discovery with the migration of Palaeo-Indians into the New World. Several years later, in discussing an enigmatic specimen from Cape Denbigh, Giddings (1964:235; see also Hall 1969) pointed out that two or three of the four then known Alaskan fluted points were associated, though not always conclusively, with the Denbigh Flint complex, and that no other association was known for any of these points. This introduced a non-Palaeo-Indian interpretation today indicating a relatively young age of little more than 4000 years. Before then Wormington had introduced another explanation, reversing the north to south migration hypothesis. Wormington (1957:210) proposed that "if the writer is correct in believing that the tradition of fluting developed in the Southwest or in the Plains, the fluted specimens found in the extreme north may represent the spread of a trait through diffusion or later northward movement of people who employed this technique." She also suggested that the north "may represent a peripheral area where, at a later period, there was a mingling of traits that were elsewhere, or at an earlier time, chronologically distinct" (1957:210). Her statement specifically accommodated the Denbigh Flint occurrence which at that time was thought to be much older than the age later established for this complex.

Thus, in the 1950s, Alaskan fluted points were considered as having been left there by any of the following: (a) Palaeo-Indian migrants who either brought the technology from Asia or developed it in Alaska, (b) by hunters of the Denbigh Flint complex; or (c) by hunters of any number of prehistoric peoples in northern Alaska who had received the trait from relatively late Palaeo-Indians that had migrated northward from the Plains. Instead of there having been northward Palaeo-Indian migration in the strict sense, the fluting trait could have diffused northward through an already extant population. (d) The possibility of independent invention, briefly noted by Hall (1969) also was not completely excluded. Today, even after considerably more northern data have become available, essentially all these explanations are still offered (cf. Clark 1984a). It may be significant to this problem, however, that recent research on the 11,000-year-old and older Nenana complex of interior Alaska has failed to recover any evidence of fluted points (Hoffecker, Powers and Goebel 1993, Powers and Hoffecker 1989).

After 1950 no additional points were found in the north until 1965-66 when attention was again directed to the Utukok River. Then Humphrey (1966) found bases of two triple fluted points and several possible unfinished fluted specimens together with artifacts thought by him to be validly associated. Humphrey (1966, 1969) proposed that this Driftwood Creek complex was of Eurasian origin and ancestral to the fluted point tradition in North America. By that time Haynes (1964 and later references) was proposing a similar hypothesis. Interest in the fluted point problem was rekindled (for contemporary statements see also Bryan 1979 with CA comments and Irving 1971). The recovery of fluted points and basally thinned points, considered by us to be part of the range of variation of a single type, quickened in 1969, 1970 and 1971 when numerous specimens, reported here, were recovered at Batza Téna (Fig. 2.1) and others were found at the Putu site in the Brooks Range (Alexander 1974, 1987; Cook ed 1970), as well as on a southern tributary of the South Fork of the Koyukuk River (Holmes 1971), and deep within the

Healy Lake sequence in the Tanana River valley (though thick and poorly fluted, J. P. Cook personal communications). This history takes us through the discovery of the points at Batza Téna. Subsequently, and continuing to the mid-1980s, several additional fluted points have been found through excavations on the ALYESKA pipeline right-of-way, especially in the Koyukuk drainage (Cook ed. 1977, Gal 1976), by various agency surveys undertaken in northwestern Alaska including the Brooks Range, and at the periphery of the Old Crow Flats in the northern Yukon Territory (J. Cinq-Mars personal communications, Irving and Cinq-Mars 1974:74). These later finds, together with earlier ones, have been listed and referenced elsewhere by the author (Clark 1984a). Recently, two possible examples were found at the Broken Mammoth site in the 9000-10,000-year-old middle component (D. Yesner personal communication to D. Clark, November 1992), though there is some uncertainty about their classification as fluted points.

For most persons, fluted points no longer hold the significance to New World prehistory that they did when they were essentially coeval with the designation "Palaeo-Indian" (exclusive of the Plano horizon). That is because there is a growing acceptance by archaeologists that fluted points were preceded by earlier Paleo-Indian occupation (Haynes 1969b). But the substantiation of earlier sites remains problematical and many archaeologists still believe that fluted points are indicators of the initial peopling of the New World. Alternative explanations, that, for instance recognize earlier occupation but often credit the first stone-tipped projectiles to Clovis, are but only slightly less significant to North American prehistory. Fluted points were developed during a period which saw the termination of the last glacial age, the extinction of Pleistocene megafauna, and the development of the first American cultural horizon to be characterized by highly distinctive wide-spread artifacts.

Fluted Point Sites

Fluted points were recovered from ten sites at Batza Téna:

RkIg-1	RkIg-43
RkIg-10	RkIg-44
RkIg-29	RlIg-46
RkIg-30	RlIg-47
RkIg-31	IM 9 reported by Reger and Reger
RkIg-32 (identification of point uncertain)	

Most of these sites are clustered at the east end of Little Lake Ridge (Fig. 2.2). Had it not been for the separation of lithic distributions provided by slight topographic dips mantled by soil and vegetation, the fluted point occurrences on Little Lake Ridge would have been grouped into two sites: RkIg-10 and the remaining RkIg sites. In addition, there is one site RkIg-1 on Basecamp Ridge and three sites up the Indian River. Each site and collection is described and assessed below. It is cautioned that in no case is it certain that pure assemblages are represented.

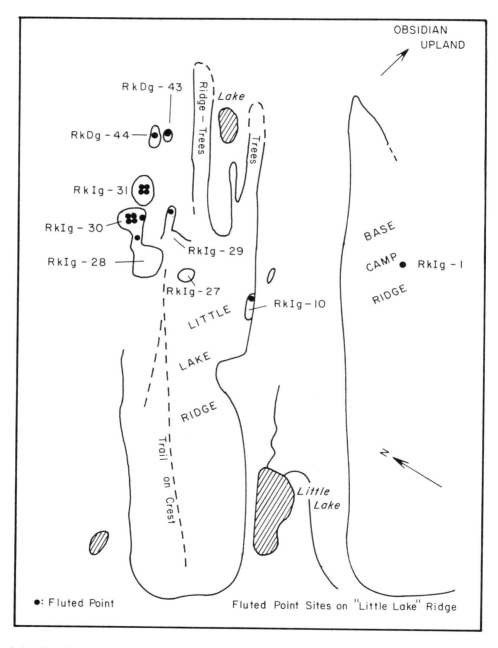

Figure 2.2. Sketch map of the location of fluted point sites at Batza Téna. The
distance from top to bottom is approximately 2 km.

Site RkIg-1

Surface collections were made at two loci in 1969; in 1970 further surface collections were made and the site was trowelled to a shallow depth at six locations.

The site (Figure 2.3) is located on undistinguished terrain along the crest of Basecamp Ridge near its eastern end. The site measures c 25 m in diameter. All flake loci represent, to a degree, flake clusters exposed at the surface, especially through burning of the organic litter, but it is possible to trowel out flakes from a shallow depth at almost any place on this site. Flakes were rarely found as deep as 10 cm. The flake clusters range from 70-cm-wide concentrations of flakes piled one on top of another to thinner and sometimes poorly delimited groups two or more m in extent. One cluster of small flakes partially collected in 1969 had a relatively narrow, linear distribution suggestive of a secondary concentration along a frost crack or involution. With the exception of locus E, the site was intensively burned over in 1968.

Collection

8.56 kg of flakes were collected, but at three loci only a partial pick up of flakes exposed on the surface was made. At another locus a flake concentration was brought together, examined, found to contain only non-utilized obsidian flakes, and was discarded on location. No implements were recognized at the site in 1969, but later examination of the flake lots revealed a biface blade fragment, an end scraper, and a fragment of a fluted point plus two probable utilized flakes. Presumed natural nibbling and attrition of flakes on the surface or in the soil has resulted in there being a large number of dubiously utilized flakes at this site. In some cases attrition is similar to the smooth edges often attributed to use, but such smoothed areas sometimes are found in positions on the artifact that lead to assigning their cause to natural agencies.

Only one locus collected in 1970, E, yielded a significant number of artifacts. The presence of a modest number of weathered bleached basalt flakes there attracted our notice. At E obsidian, chert and basalt flakes and implements were distributed in an area 2 m across. They occurred from the surface to a depth of 5 cm, very locally to 20 cm, in a difficult matrix of soil lodged within the interstices of stone rubble tightly bound together by roots. A six-foot section was excavated while less productive adjacent ground was probed or scratched with a trowel. The locus E collections include an indented-stem obsidian point (Pl. 19J) found on top of the moss at the periphery of the locus, an amorphous fragment of a basalt biface, ten end and convergent scrapers, three of which are chert, and a retouched flake (Pl. 19A-I). Fragments of calcined bone also were found in the soil at this locus in a restricted area less than 30 cm in diameter. Among other artifacts from RkIg-1 is a large V-shaped biface flake core (Pl. 24H). It is an isolated surface find not associated with any flake cluster. The RkIg-1 collections are listed below.

Fluted point, Table 2.10 (Pl. 1A, Fig. 2.1f)

Side-notched point, Locus E, Table 5.8 (Pl. 19J)

9 end scrapers (7 from Locus E), Table Append.I.3 (Pl. 19)

3 convergent end scrapers, Table Append. I.3 (Pl. 19)

4 bifacially worked fragments, all small and unfinished

Biface, No. 85, rough unfinished, low grade chert, Locus E, 40x57 mm

Bifacially edged basalt flake, roughly prepared on one edge only, 62 mm

2 retouched or utilized flakes, (may be naturals)

2 retouched bladelets (may be natural) 14 & 18 mm wide, 50 mm long

V-shaped bifacial core, fine, chopper-shaped, isolated find, 95x84 mm (Pl. 24H)

Other catalogued items consist of items of technological interest, bladelike flakes and equivocal
utilized flakes chipped and smoothed by soil processes.

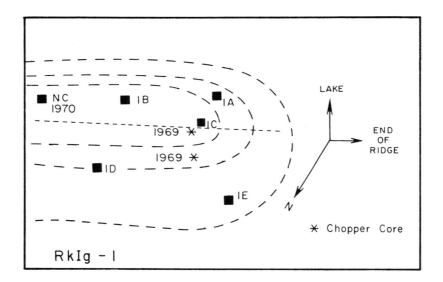

Figure 2.3. Sketch map of the collection loci at Site RkIg-1.

Assessment

Obsidian hydration measurements were made for a number of flakes collected in 1969, on the
fluted point and on three artifacts from Locus E. The data, calculated and collated by L. B.
Davis, Montana State University, are as follow in Table 2.1. "BP" refers to age at the time
hydration was measured, in the early 1970s. Three thin sections were made for certain artifacts.

These data show considerable variance. The 1969 collection locations had been intensively burned, and burning can erase hydration or create vague thick hydration layers (Clark 1984b and refs.). We nevertheless find that the hydration data tend to indicate more than one episode of prehistoric utilization. However, there is no convincing evidence that the fluted point is coeval with the rest of the RkIg-1 collection which on the basis of thinner hydration may be younger. Inasmuch as Locus E had been less subjected to the effects of burning, at least in 1968, we expected the results of hydration measurements there to be more reliable. The data nevertheless show an erratic spread between the end scraper and the other two specimens. There is strong reason to believe that this small discrete locus represents a single brief camp, and that the spread of hydration data are to be blamed to the history of hydration and other vagaries of hydration analysis. RkIg-1 probably is primarily a Northern Archaic camping area, utilized sometime between 5500 and 1500 years ago judging from the occurrence of a notched point. There may be traces of other occupations, one of which is responsible for the fluted point fragment.

TABLE 2.1.   OBSIDIAN HYDRATION DATA FROM RkIg-1

Specimen type	Specimen number	Hydration in microns	Hydration squared	Age BP Rate .82	Age BP R. 1.4
1969 Collection (from burned area)					
flake	S21*	none legible			
biface	S26	burned			
flake	S34	none legible			
flake	S24	0.65	0.4225	515	302
flake	S29	0.65	0.4225	515	302
flake	S30	0.75	0.5625	686	402
flake, ret.	S33	0.81	0.6561	800	469
flake	S35	0.89	0.7921	966	566
flake	S24	0.97	0.9409	1147	672
	" "	2.11			
flake	S31	1.02	1.0404	1269	743
flake	S32	1.03	1.0609	1294	758
flake	S27	1.28	1.6384	1998	1170
flake	S28	1.88	3.5344	4310	2525
flake	S22	2.13	4.5369	5533	3241
fluted pt.	RkIg-1:49	3.18	10.1124	12330	7223
" "	" "	3.38	11.4244	13930	8160
" "	" "	3.40	11.5600	14100	8257
flake	S23	4.34	18.8356	22970	13454
From Locus E					
end scraper	RkIg-1:65	2.01	4.0401	4927	2886
" "	" "	2.33 vague	5.4289	6620	3877
notch point	RkIg-1:53	0.80	0.6400	780	356
" "	" "	0.86	0.7396	901	411
" "	" "	0.85	0.7225	881	401
ret. flake	RkIg-1:55	1.02	1.0404	1268	577
" "	" "	0.98	0.9604	1171	530
" "	" "	4.04	16.3216	20000	11660

Site RkIg-10

A surface collection was made and Loci 1 and 2 were collected or excavated in 1969; Locus 3 was excavated and further work done at Locus 1 in 1970. In 1971 the surface was further examined and three additional small loci were trowelled, one of which (Locus 4) was collected and the others that produced only flakes were discarded at the site.

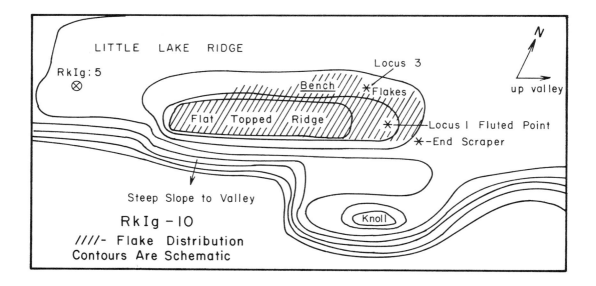

Figure. 2.4. Sketch map of Site RkIg-10.

RkIg-10 is situated on a forested bench near the top of the steep south flank of Little Lake Ridge (Fig. 2.4). Of the sites at Batza Téna it offers one of the best views of surrounding terrain. From the edge of the bench which the site occupies one can see the small valley between Base Camp and Little Lake Ridge, adjacent parts of the Koyukuk Flats, and distant country to the west as well as part of the upland to the east. The site has been traced for approximately 120 m along a well drained slightly raised relatively narrow strip of ground. It terminates at the east when the terrain it occupies plunges down the flank of the ridge. None of the flake concentrations was especially visible on the surface and it is possible that further concentrations exist at the site, though in 1971 a few shovel probes failed to locate additional flake clusters.

Locus 1 is of particular interest because the base of a large point with triple flutes was found there in 1969. It was primarily through this specimen that fluted points were first recognized at Batza Téna. Investigated in 1969 and 1970, Locus 1 is situated on the site axis in a relatively narrow raised area approximately 13 m west of the east end. Initially, an area of about 1.3 square m was excavated. Flakes were found in the leaf litter, the root mat, and in the thin layer of brown topsoil. The fluted point was found at a depth of approximately 5 cm in the brown soil. Further, deeper, excavation at that spot led into an area of very light grey clayey soil where flakes occurred highly concentrated between blocks of stone rubble evidently derived from local bedrock. In places the volume of obsidian flakes exceeded that of the soil matrix. The clayey soil tends to occur as lenses at a shallow depth, but deeper the lenses join. At increased depth, in a small contiguous test probe made in 1970, blocks of bedrock became the major component. When blocks of stone were removed it was found that obsidian flakes occurred in the clayey interstitial filling to a depth of 46 cm. They may be present at greater depth, but it was not practical to deepen the small 1970 test. The light clayey soil tended to occur along a slightly depressed linear microfeature, which may be a frost feature. A similar, apparently sorted, clayey artifact-bearing matrix also is found at other sites. The flake concentration described thus probably is secondary and drawn in from an original area approximately ten feet wide where there already had been a high concentration of debitage and artifacts. Flakes still found on or near the surface may have escaped this sorting process, or they may belong to a more recent component. Given the surmised history of frost sorting and the disposition of artifacts among blocks of bedrock, it is not surprising that many flakes from this cluster (as well as from Locus 2) have a trampled and haphazardly retouched appearance.

Locus 2 is situated near the center of the site. Its limits were not completely defined inasmuch as there was only a localized test here. Obsidian flakes were trowelled from a depth of 0 to 8 cm from beneath the moss cover.

Locus 3, collected in 1970, was found on a lower sub-bench nearly 15 m inland lateral to (away from Little Lake valley) from the crest of high ground that formed the principal part of the site. It is 6 m from the east end of the site. Flakes occurred here from the surface to a depth of approximately 15 cm in the depressed margins of frost boils, particularly at a Y where the margins of three frost hummocks met. This appears to be a relatively clear case of concentration through frost action.

Locus 4, trowelled in 1971, consists of two flake concentrations found 41 to 43 m west of Locus 3 . Artifacts were recovered to a depth of 15 cm in light colored clayey soil. The second flake cluster was situated 2 m farther west. It was totally excavated to yield 1.04 kg of flakes but no implements.

Collection

The only highly diagnostic artifact recovered from this site, in terms of cultural-historic indicators, is the fluted point fragment. Other implements include point and biface fragments, end scrapers and probable utilized flakes. Details of the collection are provided in Table 2.2.

Assessment

The fluted point (Pl. 1B), an end scraper (RkIg-10:156, Pl.6K), biface (10:157, Pl. 6M), a series of flakes and five rudimentary implements, were measured for obsidian hydration (Table 2.3; Clark 1984b). Exclusive of the first three implements noted above, the measurements, calculated and collated by Leslie B. Davis, average 2.60 microns, and at the exponential rate of 0.82 microns squared per 1000 years the resultant age is 8250 years. We vacillate between interpreting the five rudimentary items as implements or as fragments of unfinished bifaces altered by nature. These possible implements (RkIg-10:102, 103, 33, 26 and 104) have hydration measurements at 0.77, 2.19, 2.29, 2.36 and 2.40 microns respectively compared to slightly thicker hydration measured at 4.88-4.94, 2.55-3.85, and 3.30-3.33 microns for multiple sections from three definitive artifacts (the fluted point, end scraper and biface). All of these are within or close to the range of hydration for flakes from this site. The end scraper was found several metres from the fluted point. These data indicate at least moderate antiquity for Locus 1, as was expected from the presence of a fluted point, though given the vagaries and variances of hydration dating they neither prove nor disprove that Locus 1 consists of a single component. Given this uncertainty, the collection contributes little to the definition of an industrial complex associated with fluted points at this lookout workshop.

While, as noted, most of the artifacts indicate lithic workshop activity, the few end scrapers and well-finished point fragments, including the fluted point base, also suggest that there was camping at this location.

TABLE 2.2.   COLLECTIONS FROM SITE RkIg-10

Description	Locus 1	Other loci	Description
Flakes	9.1 kg	5.81 kg	Plus 170 flakes not weighed
Fluted point	1	0	Table 2.10 (Pl. 1B, Fig. 2.1i)
Other point fragments	2	0	a very thin, well prepared undistinguished midsection; b small rounded basalt base
Unfinished bifaces	2	2	Loc. 1, 53 & 90 mm long on large flakes
Biface, rough small	1	0	Asymmetrical x-section, scraper?
Biface frag., unfin.	7	10	
End scraper	2	3	One of chert (Pl. 6K-L)
Unfinished uniface	0	1	
Retouched or utilized flakes	3	5	2 from Loc. 1 including a 'spokeshave' & 2 from Loc. 2; retouch may be natural
Equivocal flakes	x	x	Utilized appearance probably is natural
Hinged edges	x	x	Fragments from unfinished bifaces
Biface fragments, tiny	x	x	Lesser fragments of unfinished bifaces
Flake core		1	
Unclassified	1	3	

TABLE 2.3.   OBSIDIAN HYDRATION DATA FROM RkIg-10

Specimen type	Specimen number	Hydration in microns	Hydration squared	Age BP Rate .82	Age BP R. 1.4
Flakes and Rudimentary Objects					
Flake	S3	no legible			
Flake	S17	no legible			
Flake	S14	0.72	0.5184	632	370
Flake, ret.	RkIg-10:102	0.76	0.5776	704	413
Flake	S18	0.77	0.5929	723	424
Flake	S2	1.38	1.9044	2322	1360
Flake	S20	1.95/2.16	3.8025	4637	2716
Flake	S9	2.15	4.6225	5637	3301
Uniface	RkIg-10:103	2.19	4.7961	5849	3426
Scraper?	RkIg-10:33	2.29	5.2441	6395	3746
Flake	S5	2.35	5.5225	6735	3945
Flake?	RkIg-10:26	2.36	5.5696	6792	3978
Biface	RkIg-10:104	2.40	5.7600	7024	4114
Flake	S1	2.40	5.7600	7024	4144
Flake	S16	2.94	8.6436	10540	6174
Flake	S8	2.95	8.7025	10613	6216
Flake	S15	3.33	11.0889	14401	7921
Flake	S7	3.79	14.3641	17517	10260
Flake	S12	3.80	14.4400	17610	10314
Flake	S4	3.85	14.8225	18076	10588
Flake	S13	4.17	17.3889	21206	12421
Flake	S6	4.17	17.3889	21206	12421
Flake	S19	4.75	22.5625	27515	16116
Implements (3 sections each)					
Fluted point	RkIg-10:36				
at edge		4.94 vague	24.4036	29760	17431
on flute		4.88 vague	23.3744	28505	16690
on flute		4.88	23.7744	28505	16690
End Scraper	RkIg-10:156	3.33	11.0889	13523	7920
		3.32	11.0226	13393	7874
		3.30	10.8900	13283	7778
Biface	RkIg-10:157	2.55	6.5025	7930	4645
at edge		3.36	11.2896	12547	8064
at edge		3.85	14.8225	18076	10588

Site RkIg-29

The site was discovered 1969; examined and test-probed in 1970; inspection in 1971 failed to find any promising areas for excavation.

RkIg-29 is located on a narrow, forested, east-west trending ridge located on the south side of the top of Little Lake Ridge 15 to 25 m south of RkIg 28 and RkIg-30. It is separated from those sites by a slightly depressed area that provides a metre or two of relief to the site.

Near the western end of the site there is a slight rise, little more than a metre high and a few metres across, where several flakes were exposed on the surface. The eastern locus of the site is 140 m distant, but the artifact distribution between these points probably is discontinuous. Artifacts were found on the surface at various locations. Only some of the flakes and generalized biface fragments seen exposed were collected.

The fluted point locus is 111 m from the west end of the site. There a fluted point base was found on the lightly burned surface among flakes distributed over an area approximately 3 to 4 m in diameter. From part of this locus in a 1.3 x 4.1 m (4 x 4.5 ft) area we excavated 1.2 kg of flakes, most of which were found at a depth of less than 3 cm.

Collection

The collection (Table 2.4) includes a fluted point base. Otherwise, at the fluted point locus there were only edge fragments from biface production and flakes.

Assessment

Considering its great linear extent, the site probably comprises more than one component of occupation. The small varied collection appears to indicate both hunting and camping or materials processing and obsidian reduction for biface or biface blank production. Only biface production is associated with the fluted point.

The point yielded a consistent set of three hydration measurements between 1.02 and 1.05 microns, a biface roughout outrepassé flake (RkIg-29:13) inconsistent measurements between 0.72 and 2.20 microns, and a flake (29:14) with utilized appearance (probably natural retouch) produced three consistent measurements between 3.46 and 3.71 microns. These three artifacts were found in proximity to one another. Clark has suggested (Clark 1984b) that hydration of the point, equivalent to an age in the order of 1000 years, probably measures renewed hydration that occurred after a past event had destroyed the previous hydration layer. The measurements on flake 29:14 conform with expectations for material from the Palaeo-Indian period.

TABLE 2.4.   COLLECTION FROM SITE RkIg-29

Identification	Location	Number
Fluted point	Fluted point locus	RkIg-29:16
Bipoint, 54 mm long, slightly assymetric	Middle one-third	RkIg-29:17 (Pl. 6J)
Biface fragment	1969 collection	RkIg-29:2
" " unfin.	East end	RkIg-29:6
" "	Fluted point locus	RkIg-29:21
" "	West one-third	RkIg-29:8 & :9
End scraper, chert	East end	RkIg-29:5
Retouched flake	Middle one-third	RkIg-29:25
" " large flat frag.	Middle one-third	RkIg-29:22
" " bifacial edge	Middle one-third	RkIg-29:25
Utilized flake?	1969 collection	RkIg-29:1
Utilized flake basaltic, 75 mm long	Western third	RkIg-29:7
Small biface frags.	Various locations	
Bladelike flakes	Various locations	Fig. 5.14g
Hinged biface edge fragments	Various locations	

Site RkIg-30

A minor surface collection was made in 1969; a test excavation made in 1970; and more extensive controlled excavation done in 1971.

RkIg-30 (Figures 2.5-2.10,2.13) is essentially contiguous with site RkIg-28 (Chapter 3) with which it is joined through a necked or constricted area 94 m long. The main area of RkIg-30 is approximately 300 m diameter. It is centered 151 m NE of the site RkIg-28 zero stake placed at the southwest end of the neck bridging the two sites (Fig. 2.5). The site is located a short distance north of the east end of fluted point site RkIg-29. Lithics, including fluted points, were found in both the neck and the main area. Like other sites on the flat upland top of Little Lake Ridge, RkIg-30 is situated on well drained, slightly elevated stony ground (Fig. 2.10, 2.13) These sites are separated from neighboring sites by areas of slightly lower terrain that supports growth of tundra vegetation. The sites are covered with an open forest of small aspen, birch and the rare small spruce tree. The forest cover probably has been opened up by forest fires, but it may always have been light on some of the stony sites.

One flake cluster and other selected flakes, amounting to 253 flakes (1.9 kg) were collected from among extensive exposed flake concentrations seen in 1969. In 1970 a 2 m area was excavated at the centre of the site. Two implements and a modest number of flakes were seen exposed on the surface there, and the excavation produced several additional implements and 2.1 kg of flakes from a superficial depth. The base of a fluted point was found on the surface in the constricted area bridging sites RkIg-28 and RkIg-30.

In 1971 we resumed excavation at the same location, including in our layout the 1970 test area. It was found that the previous year's excavation had recovered almost all of the implement cluster there. But through the excavation of 42 six-foot-square sections several fluted point fragments and more than 100 additional artifacts plus 63.2 kg of flakes were recovered from the top of the stony soil. Artifacts were seldom found more than 8 cm deep, and excavation consisted principally of removing the stony matrix. The distribution of excavated sections and certain artifact classes is shown in Figures 2.6-2.8.

The collection consists mainly of rough or unfinished biface fragments and biface processual debris including hinged edge fragments. Other items include finished bifaces, finished and unfinished fluted point fragments, other points or fragments, retouched flakes, flake core fragments and detritus. In addition to the obsidian artifacts, there are a small number of basalt specimens (Table 2.6). Numerous flakes were shaped dorsally, prior to detachment from the core, through retouch from the sides or from the sides and both ends. However, these are detrital products and should not be compared to Levallois flakes. Hundreds of flakes bear areas of edge and surficial retouch, but they are interpreted as products of natural trampling and other taphonomic processes.

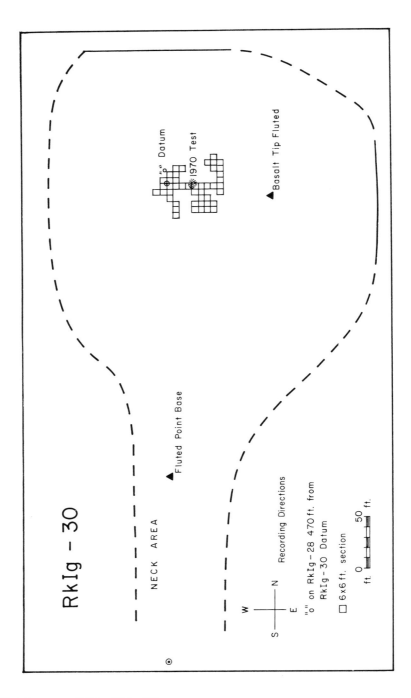

Figure 2.5. Sketch map of Site RkIg-30.

Collection

The collection from RkIg-30 is listed in Table 2.5 and is described in the paragraphs below.

Bifaces--The predominant lithic industry at RkIg-30 is biface implement production (Fig. 2.7), including projectile points. The only other common artifact class there consists of bevelled flakes, many of which may have been modified only along the edge through use. Unfinished bifaces vary in preparation from relatively early to advanced stages of knapping. Some show development from large flakes, especially cortical flakes. The reduction of split pebbles to form bifaces, which is apparent in some assemblages, is poorly illustrated by this collection. Complete or near complete unfinished bifaces, including roughouts, are relatively small. The largest specimen measures 94 by 53 mm, smaller ones approximately 50 by 30 mm. The average of the length of 14 unfinished complete obsidian bifaces, comprising the total collection in that class exclusive of two basalt specimens, is 55.9 mm and the average width is 33.7 mm. The two small unfinished basalt specimens, described in Table 2.7, fall within the same range of size and shapes. A series of these specimens is illustrated (Pl. 3). Shapes are more or less ovate pointed, elliptical and bipointed. One small unique specimen with concave base forms a crude approximation of a projectile point. Another small partially unifaced specimen is suggestive of a limace. Ovate-pointed and square-based to leafshaped pointed forms which often characterize biface collections from other sites are not common. Three of the unfinished obsidian bifaces were reconstructed from fragments. Considering the large number of fragments recovered (109 including fits but exclusive of hinged edge fragments) this is a relatively low ratio of fitting.

TABLE 2.5. COLLECTION FROM SITE RkIg-30

Identification	Description	Number	Plate
Fluted point fragments	Table 2.10	9	Pl. 1D–J, Fig. 1.13a, 2.1a
Point fragment	Not fluted, Tab. 2.10	10	Pl. 3C–D
Points, complete	Table 2.10	3	Pl. 3A–B
Biface, unfinished	Complete or nearly so	16	Pl. 3J–R
Biface, unfinished	Fragment	107	
Biface, unfinished	Hinged edge fragment	66+	
Biface, finished	Complete or nearly so Table 2.6	5	Pl. 3E–I
Biface, finished	Fragment, Table 2.6	14	
Flake uniface	See text	2	Pl. 4E
Discoidal uniface	Basalt	1	Pl. 4R
Graver spur	On quartz crystal	1	Pl. 4L
End scraper	See text	3+3	Pl. 4A–C
Rounded end scraper	Round to semipointed end	2	
Bevelled uniface frag.	From end scraper?	3	
Retouched flake	See text	36	Pl.3S–T, Pl. 4F–J
Flake cores	Uncommon		Pl.4K
Amorphous	Unfinished or fragments	11	
Equivocal utilized or retouched flakes and technologically interesting flakes		65	Pl. 4J,M
Bladelike flakes		20	
Frags. unclassified pointed and edged implements		6	

Complete finished or nearly finished bifaces may provide more accurate information on biface
forms than unfinished specimens. However, the six obsidian and basalt implements from RkIg-30
probably are two few for this to be the case. These pieces, each of which is described in Table
2.6 and is illustrated, tend to be small. In some cases this leads to questioning the distinction
between these items and other bifaces identified as projectile points. The rounded base, pointed
tip leafshaped form is present only in semifinished fragments. The basalt specimen with bevelled
inset margin (Pl. 4P) is unique. It is seen from the widths given in Table 2.6 that a relatively
small size also prevails among fragments.

TABLE 2.6.   **FINISHED AND SEMIFINISHED BIFACES AND FRAGMENTS FROM RkIg-30**
Exclusive of Projectile Points

Number	Length	Width	Shape	Description/Illustration
Complete or Nearly Complete				
RkIg-30:30	30+3	21	Pillow shape, was pointed at one end	On a flake, dorsal & partial ventral retouch (Pl. 3E)
RkIg-30:80 + 81	56	33	Lenticular, more pointed at one end	Incompletely finished (Pl. 3L)
RkIg-30:117	37	30	Tabular, pointed at one side	Thin, edges rough (Pl. 3H)
RkIg-30:154	46+	26	Lenticular, blunt rounded and obtuse pointed ends	(Pl. 3F) 1.71 microns hydration
RkIg-30:163 +167	60	30	Leafshaped, base straight, sharply rounded tip, asymmetrical	Each side near the base has been removed through flaking errors. Edge wear is natural? (Pl. 3J)
RkIg-30:139	81	34	Incurvate margin	Table 2.10 (Pl. 4P)
Fragments				
RkIg-30:24	--	28	Pointed tip	Incompletely finished
RkIg-30:43	--	28	Stemmed (Pl. 3I)	Tip missing; a point?, natural edge crushing
RkIg-30:84	--	--	Asymmet. pointed	On a flake blank
RkIg-30:98	--	--	Rounded end	On a flake blank
RkIg-30;115	--	45	Midsection	Thin, flat
RkIg-30:134	--	31	End rounded, sides nearly straight	Thin edges crushed naturally? (Pl. 3G)
RkIg-30:151	--	--	Semipointed	Small fragment
RkIg-30:188	--	27.5	Rounded end	Basal edge smoothed
RkIg-30:148	--	--	Bluntly pointed end	
RkIg-30:180	--	--	Pointed end	
RkIg-30:173	--	--	Very rounded edge	Fine, semiunifacial
RkIg-30:211	--	29	Very rounded end	1.25 microns hydration
RkIg-30:212	--	38	Rounded end	Incompletely finished
RkIg-30:234	--	--	Pointed end	Small fragment

Bevelled flakes and Utilized Flakes--A large number of battered, nibbled, crushed and
abraded flakes have been excluded from analysis because they appear to be natural. There
remains 35 reasonably certain utilized or bevelled flakes (Pl. 3 S-T, Pl. 4 D-J). Edge smoothing,
bluntness and bevelling together appear to indicate that most of these items were scrapers, though
there also are sharply edged bevelled flakes which may have been used as knife blades.

Criteria for accepting a specimen as having been intentionally produced or utilized include any or a combination of the following: presence of (a) a wide steep bevel, (b) series of both coarse and fine retouch flake scars, (c) a smoothed, even edge lacking sharp projections, (d) low angle bifacial retouch that produces a sharp edge (uncommon) (e) bevel or retouch confined to one face at any edge, in contrast to short runs of retouch that skip from one face to the other face, and (f) a form that fits the analyst's concepts of a tool type, a spokeshave for instance. These attributes may be expressed, more or less convincingly, to greater or lesser degrees.

End scrapers--Two definite and a number of possible end scrapers were recovered. Definite end scrapers include a small flake bevelled at the end in the manner characteristic of such scrapers (RkIg-30:409, Pl. 4C) and a large blunt-nosed specimen shaped and bevelled along the sides as well as at the working end (RkIg-30:100, Pl. 4A). In addition, there is a thick blunt-nosed uniface that probably is an end scraper (RkIg-30:321, Pl. 4B) and an end scraper fragment (lot 30:264). A double-ended specimen (RkIg-30:323/324) lacks wear traces and I am not convinced that the bevels were intentionally produced for scraping. Some of the items counted as bevelled flakes could have served as end scrapers. These include a large stemmed flake with 56-mm-broad roughly bevelled end suggestive of an end scraper, but which may be a "naturefact" (RkIg-30:79), and two thick steep-edged scrapers with rounded to semipointed working ends. Apparently, the purposes of end scrapers were served by other, evidently poorly formalized implements at RkIg-30 or scrapers simply were not used there to any notable extent.

Graver spur--The spur on a fragment of quartz crystal is unique among the Batza Téna collection (Pl. 4L). There is a unifacial notch on either side of the tiny short spur which itself is partially bifacial. Being incomplete as well as unique there is little basis for comparing this specimen with others of the same type.

Flake unifaces--There are two thin curved flakes unifacially retouched over the dorsal surface. One (RkIg-30:164) 59-mm-long item has not been prepared to a sufficient degree to remove all the cortex and may be unfinished. The other, more thoroughly prepared 51-mm-long specimen (Pl. 4E) has had the original flake margin significantly reduced through primary and secondary retouch. Nibbling and crushing of the edges may, however, include natural damage. One edge is relatively sharp edge. Some unfinished bifaces are to a certain extent unifaces but are notably thicker than the two specimens described above. The low incidence of this artifact type contributes to the picture of there being few finished tools at RkIg-30.

Projectile points--each point and fragment is described or listed below. Figure 2.8 shows their distribution.

A. Nonfluted Points

RkIg-30:44 (Pl. 3C). Tip missing, other end flaked to irregular, (damaged?) thinned termination. Edges of straight sides are heavily ground. Planoconvex cross-section. Classified as a point on the basis of size and ground edges. 17.2 mm wide, 6.6 mm thick.

RkIg-30:141 (Pl. 3A). Leafshaped/elliptical, tip damaged, base not completely finished, edges from middle to base are ground which is criterion for segregating from other small bifaces and identifying as point. 46.5 mm x 25 mm, 8 mm thick.

RkIg-30:130+131 (Pl. 3B). Leafshaped/lanceolate, narrow rounded base, widest above midpoint, edges below midpoint ground. 54 x 22.2 x 4.3 mm.

RkIg-30:205+206+213 (fitting fragments). Basalt knife or asymmetrical point, described in Table 2.7.

RkIg-30:312 (Pl. 3D). Basal fragment of small point, straight sides converge towards straight base, edges ground, lenticular cross section.

RkIg-30:147. Midsection fragment, 21.7 mm wide, 5.4 mm thick, 2.65 microns hydration.

RkIg-30:86, :140, :208, :217, :258+93. Five, tip, midsection/near tip, and midsection fragments.

B. Fluted Points and Related Items

RkIg-30:42, :220, :254, flake lot RkIg-30:291 (publ. as 30:321). Four finished and unfinished fluted point basal fragments, described in Table 2.10 (Fig. 2.1a, Pl. 1D-F, H).

RkIg-30:flake lot 306 (publ. as 30:323) (Pl. 1I). Basal portion of a thin nonfluted equivalent of a fluted point, described in Table 2.10.

RkIg-30:160. Basal fragment with trace of flutes (Pl. 1J).

RkIg-30:165. Tip fragment, hinged-off with end of channel flake.

RkIg-30:236. Basal ear with trace of one flute, edge ground.

RkIg-30:300 flake lot. Corner ear of fluted point, edges ground.

RkIg-30:247. Basalt point tip/midsection, shows apparent ends of shallow flutes on both faces (Pl. 1G). 26.1 mm wide, 6.7 mm thick.

The considerable number of fragments with ground edges suggests that people stopped at the site to replace broken points with new ones made on the site.

Basalt and nonobsidian industry--In addition to obsidian, three is a small series of basalt artifacts. These are included in the list of RkIg-30 collections in Table 2.5 and their distribution is shown in Figure 2. 9. For reference, the nonobsidian series is listed below in Table 2.7, and items not described above are described there. The most common material is basalt, which is the identification of flake RkIg-30:34 thinsectioned and analyzed by the Geological Survey of Canada. Evidently, a small number of basalt implements were produced on the site. On the basis of flake recovery, it appears that one item of coarse quartzite also was produced there. The slight number of flakes of other lithologies could be the result of reshaping implements brought in from elsewhere. The basalt likely is from cobbles found in gravel bars along Indian River.

The basalt implement and flake distribution is sufficiently broad that knapping of this material cannot be localized or segregated from that of obsidian, nor is this distribution likely to arise from a single encampment of a small group that utilized a less common or less preferred material. Evidence for relating the basalt industry to the occupation responsible for the fluted points includes recovery of an apparent tip end of a basalt fluted point and the fact that elsewhere in the Koyukuk drainage fluted points were produced from this material (Holmes 1971, 1973). However, at adjoining site RkIg-28 (Chapter 3) fluted points are absent from a more abundant basalt assemblage. Basalt flaking evidently is not exclusive to the fluted point component.

Assessment

Abundant waste from biface production indicates that RkIg-30 was a station for the primary reduction of obsidian nodules and production of biface preforms. There is a strong relationship between the quantity of waste material and products of failed biface production. For example, three excavation sections that produced flake lots of 5000 grams or more each yielded an average of 12 unfinished bifaces (most fragmentary) and hinged edge fragments; for the four sections with 2000-2500 grams of detritus the comparable biface average is 5.5 specimens; for the 11 sections each with less than 500 grams of detritus the biface average is 0.5 specimen (Fig. 2.7). Recovery of fragments of both finished and unfinished fluted points suggests that the bifacial reduction process was carried through to the production of points. None of the artifacts other than the fluted points is a diagnostic indicator of cultural placement. Recovery of fluted points on adjacent sites and their wide distribution over parts of RkIg-30 gives reason to expect the site assemblage to be part of a fluted point industrial complex.

With this expectation in mind, and especially with the interpretation that biface roughout production at RkIG-30 was part of the preparation of fluted points there, hydration measurements were taken on a set of unfinished biface hinged edge fragments and bifaces. The results, reported in Clark 1984b, unexpectedly fell into two hydration thickness clusters. In one of these the average hydration was 1.32 microns, which at the 0.82 nonlinear rate could account for an age in the order of 2000 years. The other discrete very consistent cluster had an average hydration thickness of 2.73 microns which, at the 0.82 exponential rate, accounts for an age in the order of 9000 years (closer to 6000 years at a faster rate). Measurements also were taken on three RkIg-30 fluted points. These came out to be: burned, no hydration; 0.92--1.08 microns (multiple

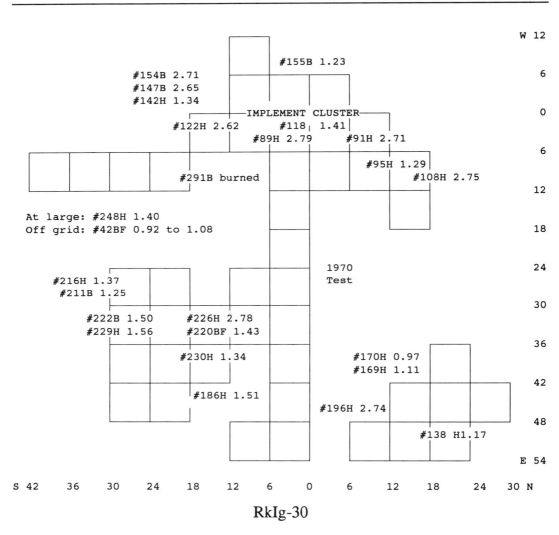

RkIg-30

OBSIDIAN HYDRATION MEASUREMENTS

Catalog Number
H: Hinged Biface Edge Flake
B: Biface, BF: Fluted point
Numeric: Hydration in Microns

Figure 2.6. Distribution of obsidian hydration measurements at RkIg-30.

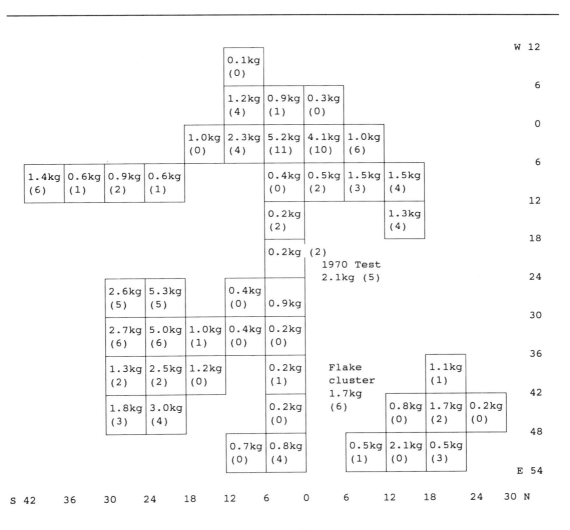

RkIg-30

RECOVERY OF FLAKES AND UNFINISHED BIFACES

Weight of flakes in kilograms; number of unfinished bifaces in parentheses.

Figure 2.7. Plot of gross distribution of flakes and unfinished bifaces, RkIg-30.

sections); and 1.43 microns (single section). Three interpretations are possible. The first is that the two measurement clusters (one tight, the other displaying greater variance) indicate multiple occupations one of which is plausible Paleo-Indian in age. The second is that one series of measurements (the thinner group) is invalid, probably because of the effects of forest fires, and that the single component hypothesis remains valid. The third is that both of the preceding conditions are present and it is difficult to form conclusions regarding the number and age of components. Thicker hydration readings tend to be localized in one area of the site, but not exclusively so (Fig. 2.6).

TABLE 2.7. NONOBSIDIAN ARTIFACT COLLECTION FROM SITE RkIg-30

Number	Material	Description
Various lots	Basalt	144 flakes, 3 largest may be utilized
Various lots	Quartzite	16 flakes, fine and coarse
Various lots	Chert, cherty mudstone	5 flakes, various subvarieties
Various lots	Other lithology	9 flakes
RkIg-30:97	Fine quartzite?	Tabular piece, roughly-flaked steep and low-angle bevels on opposite edges
RkIg-30:247	Basalt	Point tip/midsection, fluted?
RkIg-30:205+ 206+213	Basalt	Pointed biface, side asymmetrical, base straight, knife or damaged point, 77x33x7.8 mm, thinner at base (Pl. 4Q)
RkIg-30:139	Basalt	Biface tool, asymmetrical incurvate edge, one end thin and sharply rounded, other is nearly pointed incurvate edge is formed by a unifacial bevel, unique, unequivocal well formed, lenticular cross-section, 81x34 mm (Pl. 4P)
RkIg-30:159 :371,405	Basalt	Three biface pointed tip and rounded end fragments
RkIg-30:35	Basalt	Unfinished complete biface, elliptical, 63x37x15 mm (Pl. 4O)
RkIg-30:172	Basalt	Unfinished biface, nearly complete, one edge is curved asymmetrical, 44+mmx30x10.6 mm
RkIg-30:156	Basalt	Discoidal uniface on a flake blank. Secondary edge retouch is in part damage. 48-50x13.3 mm (Pl. 4R)
RkIg-30:33	Cherty mudstone?	Flake retouched on two adjacent edges, partly bifacial (Pl. 4N)
RkIg-30:244	Crystal	Graver spur (Pl. 4L)

Site RkIg-31

In 1969 and 1970 surface collections were made at RkIg-31, and in 1971 several test sections were excavated. The site is located immediately east-northeast of RkIg-30 with which it merges at its northwest corner through a forested zone (area of merging not exposed, not tested and not necessarily artifact bearing) (Fig. 2.10-2.11). The two sites occupy similar slightly elevated rocky terrain surrounded by lower zones of muskeg-tundra vegetation (Fig. 2.10-2.13). Fluted point site RkIg-44 lies a short distance farther east. The site is exposed in relatively open and barren area that occupies less than one-half of the slightly elevated terrain. The exposed area is 40 m long

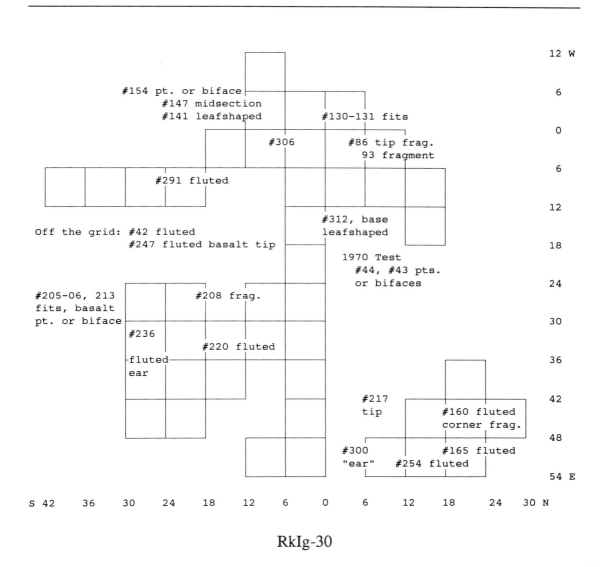

RkIg-30

DISTRIBUTION OF PROJECTILE POINTS

Figure 2.8. Plot of point distribution at RkIg-30.

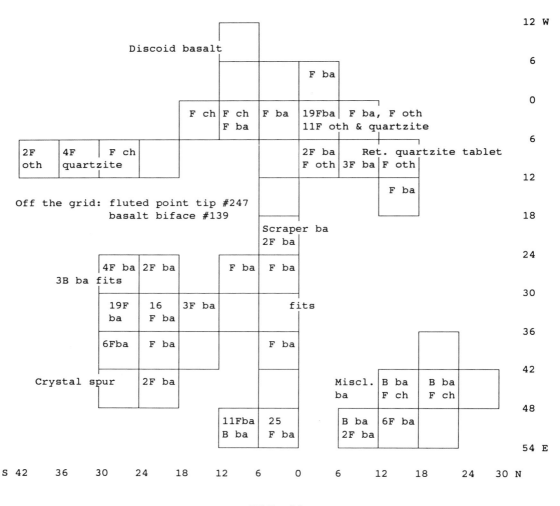

RkIg-30

DISTRIBUTION OF NON-OBSIDIAN LITHICS

B: Biface.   F: Flake.   ch: Chert.   ba: Basalt.   oth: Other
From at large within the section unless point-plotted.

Figure 2.9 Distribution plot of nonobsidian artifacts at RkIg-30.

Figure 2.10.
Low oblique
air views
extending from
Site RkIg-44
(barren lobe)
to RkIg-30.

and half that in width. Flakes also were found in the soil close to the surface in a lower forested area at the north flank of the site. Flakes occurred in clusters, but implements tended to occur separately at scattered locations.

In addition to the surface collections, one group of six six-foot-square sections was excavated in 1971. The location of this excavation, on exposed terrain, was selected because there were worked pieces of obsidian exposed on the surface near where a fluted point previously had been found. Only one of the six sections was very productive. It yielded biface fragments and the base of an unfinished fluted point. An additional fluted point base also was found on the surface of another adjacent section. The latter discovery, and excavation of the sixth section to incorporate the area around this find was done a week after the first five sections had been excavated. The point was observed plainly exposed on the surface when the 1971 crew was crossing the site on their way to another site. This find illustrates the often fortuitous nature of such discoveries. Flakes occurred to 8 cm depth in a stony matrix. In places excavation consisted largely of removing the surficial layer of rock. Test probes were made elsewhere on the site but failed to reveal artifact clusters, other than flakes. Two such clusters were excavated, but the collection from one, which yielded only flakes and two biface fragments was examined and discarded on location.

Collection

The collection is listed and described in Table 2.8. It consists primarily of notched and fluted points and biface fragments. The nonobsidian industry at RkIg-31 is limited to a sidenotched point, two very small point fragments and 12 flakes, all of cherty rock except one probable basalt flake and one quartzite flake. This use of chert contrasts with the predominance of basalt as the most common nonobsidian material on other fluted point sites at Batza Téna.

Assessment

There is no assurance that the surficial material from RkIg-30 belongs together as a coherent assemblage. The co-occurrence of sidenotched and fluted points especially may indicate mixed components. Hydration measurements have been of little help. For the single obsidian notched point exposed on the surface two measurements revealed no hydration and the third a thin 0.68 micron layer indicative of an age no greater than a few centuries. The likely age of sidenotched points is between 1000 and 5500 years. Fluted point RkIg-31:15, which also was exposed on the surface, similarly produced no hydration in two sections and a thin localized 0.92 micron segment of hydration in a third section. Hydration of the other two fluted points was not measured.

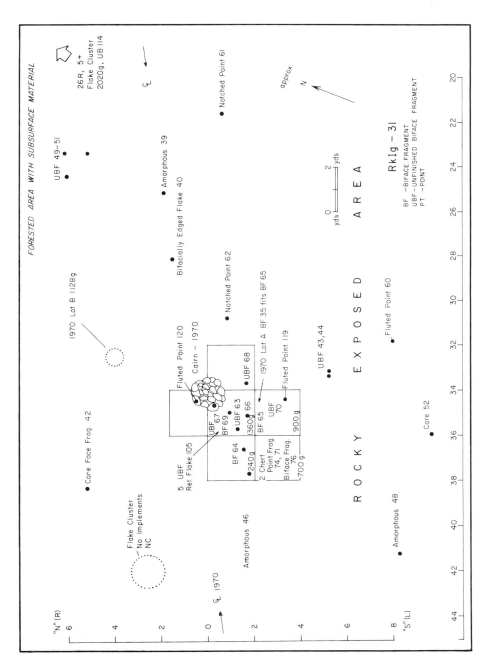

Figure 2.11. Plot of artifact distribution and excavation units at RkIg-31.

TABLE 2.8.   COLLECTION FROM SITE RkIg-31

No.	Identification	Description
4	Fluted points	Table 2.10 (Pl. 2A-C, Fig. 2.1e,h)
2	Sidenotched points	Table 5.8 (Pl. 6D-E, Fig. 1.13d)
5	Point/small biface fragments	3 obsidian, 2 chert, small, not definitive
1	Point/small biface midsection	26.4 mm wide, long axial flake scars are not definitive flutes
1	Biface end, finished	End with ground edges may be pointed base of knife or lance blade (Pl. 6B)
1	Biface fragment, large	Semifinished pointed tip 10.7 mm thick
2	Biface, complete unfinished	a) Advanced stage, 2 fitted fragments, 64 x 37 mm. b) Early stage, 2 refits, 64 x 41 mm which is the middle size range of fragments below
34	Unfinished biface fragments	Predominantly earlier stages. Ends semipointed to rounded (Pl.6A)
7	Retouched or bevelled flakes	(Pl 6C, G-H)
1	Unclassified bevelled flake	31:57 uniface on a flake; a flake that removed central part of the dorsum hinged inward and detached the distal end of specimen (Pl. 5C)
1	Flake core, multilateral	Rotated (Pl. 6F)
8	Hinged biface or core edge fragments	
11	Amorphous worked pieces	Most probably relate to biface roughout production
32	Possible bevelled, retouched or utilized flakes	Natural attrition in the rocky site is severe
2.8 kg	Flakes	Collected in 1969 and 1970
5.2 kg	Flakes	From sections excavated in 1971.

Site RkIg-43

A surface collection was made at RkIg-43 in 1970. The site is located adjacent to the east end of RkIg-44 (description follows), a little more than 100 metres southeast of RkIg-31 at the eastern end of the summit area of Little Lake Ridge. These three sites provide a good eastward-looking perspective of the middle reaches of the Indian River, but topography obscures closer terrain of the valley and the distance is too great for spotting game. RkIg-43 consists of a single large flake cluster plus scattered flakes located on the surface of a slight knoll measuring close to 2 m high, 10 m wide and 16 m long. Site RkIg-43 may be regarded as a topographically separated extension of larger RkIg-44. However, the distribution of flakes between the two is discontinuous, stopping before the end of RkIg-44 far short of RkIg-43. Flakes were clustered in a 2 m-long, 1 m-wide area that following the contour of the slope at the front (up-valley) edge of the knoll. At the time this site was examined most of the cladonia cover had been burned off and the surface was exposed for inspection. Portions of the site adjacent to RkIg-44 support a growth of birch trees.

Figure 2.12. Site RkIg-31 in 1971, showing the stone spoil pile and rocky surface.

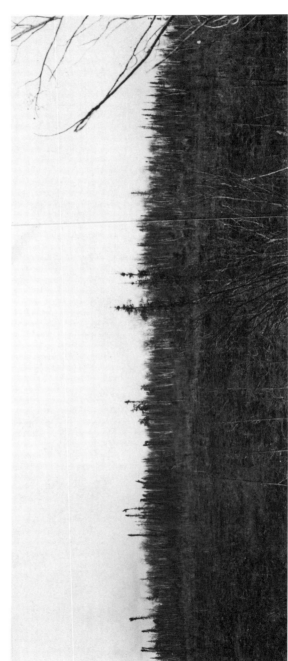

Figure 2.13. Front of Sites RkIg-31 and RkIg-30 seen from the south (position changed slightly between photographs).

Collection

Few distinctive implements were recovered. The collection includes the following:

1.9 kg flakes, exclusively obsidian, being most of those seen exposed.
Fluted point base (Table 2.10).
Biface, rough unfinished, flat cortical back, curved single edge, 63 mm.
Biface fragment.
Possibly utilized flake, 49 mm long.
Amorphous worked pieces, and unfinished biface edge fragment.

Assessment

A single fluted point base was recovered. Its association with the remaining artifacts may be coincidental, and it is problematic whether this collection should be combined with RkIg-44.

Site RkIg-44

A surface collection and testpit were made here in 1970. In 1971 a long shallow trench was excavated.

Figure 2.14.   Site RkIg-44 seen from the southeast. RkIg-43 is marked by taller trees immediately to the left of the barren lobe of RkIg-44.

The tested area of RkIg-44 is located nearly 100 meters east of RkIg-31 at a slightly lower elevation, though proximal parts of the two sites are much closer. The site is approximately 50 m long and occupies the greater portion of a slight knoll that rises, especially at its eastern end, 2-3 m above the adjacent tundra (Figures 2.14-2.15). It is comprised of two distinctive areas. The front (up-valley or eastern) third to one-half of RkIg-44 is a barren surface of finely fractured stone rubble supporting light lichen growth (Fig. 2.14). Few artifacts, noted as coming from Area 1, were found here. The remaining, contiguous, portion of the site, Area 2, located towards RkIg-31 is lightly forested. Where it is not obscured by vegetation, the surface of Area 2 was seen to intensively sprinkled with obsidian flakes.

Two flake samples were obtained from Area 2 in 1970. In one (Cluster A), which was excavated, 4.9 kg of flakes and numerous unfinished biface fragments were obtained from an area hardly more than half a metre square that was only partially collected. The area of this test was incorporated into the 1971 trench (The flake collection indicated in Figure 2.15 is for 1971). The other sample (B), from a somewhat larger excavation located laterally to the 1971 trench on its southwest side produced fewer flakes.

In 1971 a "trench" or alignment of thirteen six-foot-square sections was "excavated" along the longitudinal axis of Area 2 extending to the edge of Area 1 (Fig. 2.15). I refer to this "excavation" in quotes because of the very shallow thickness of deposits trowelled. Five major flake clusters were recognized in Area 2. Two were intersected by the trench, two lie to the right of the trench, and one which yielded the smaller sample in 1970 to the left. Only flakes and biface fragments, as recorded in Figure 2.15, were recovered from the shallow excavation. Most of this material was examined and discarded on location. A battered fluted point was found on the surface near the excavation.

Collections

Collections include blade and microblade cores from Area 1, fragments of unfinished bifaces from Area 2, and a battered incomplete fluted point and base of another, unfinished point from Area 2. The site produced a large number of flakes with chipped, crushed and seemingly utilized edges. Flakes also show attrition and scratches on the faces. Although in some circumstances these items would be identified as implements, here nearly all interpreted as "naturefacts."

The collections are described in Table 2.9, and the distinctive cores are discussed below. Items 1 through 41 were collected in 1970. Of these, 1-12, 16-34 and 39 are from Area 2 Cluster A; 14, 35 and 41 from Cluster B. Numbers 42 through 81 were obtained in 1971, all from or adjacent to the trench in Area 2 except No. 42 which is from Area 1 and 72-79 which are from various surface spots. Most of the complete bifaces have been reconstructed from fragments. Biface 44:47+49 was broken during detachment of a large flute-shaped thinning flake from the end. Similar longitudinal thinning flakes were detached from RkIg-44:2 and RkIg-44:3+48. Complete bifaces are relatively small, frequently between 70 and 76 mm long. All items listed

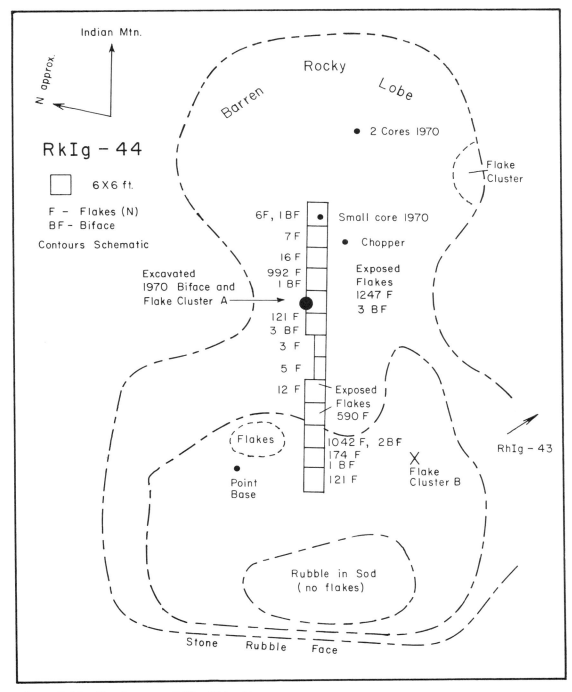

Figure 2.15. Sketch map of Site RkIg-44.

in Table 2.9 are from Area 2 with the exception of the four cores, described below, which are from Area 1 or, in the case of the microblade core No. 13, intermediate.

Core RkIg-44:40 (Pl. 5L) had been used for the production or attempted production of bladelike flakes. The top was detached obliquely from a rounded obsidian pebble somewhat more than 8 cm in length. This surface was to form a striking platform, but at an angle of 30-35 degrees to the axis of the pebble it evidently was too acute. The outer edge of the platform area accordingly was retouched, increasing the angle between the platform and the face of the core to approximately 45 degrees. A number of bladelike decortication flakes and possibly blades more than 75 mm long (not recovered archaeologically) were detached. Some blades broke short close to the platform and the core was discarded or lost. Key attributes in this core variety are (a) decapitation of a pebble at an oblique angle to its axis to provide a platform, and (b) adjustment of the platform angle through retouch.

Core RkIg-44:15 (Pl. 5I) is on a split pebble. The platform area is no smaller than that of the preceding core but the face is short (35 mm maximum) and the bladelet scars narrow. This core probably never was as high as core 44:40, but its height has been reduced to an undetermined extent through reflaking the platform. In its present condition the core has a flaked platform spanning the area between the core face and the original split surface that forms the back of the core. The angle between the platform and face is approximately 50 degrees. As in the preceding example, this core has been prepared at the platform, though hardly elsewhere, and the platform angles are of the same magnitude. But otherwise, both are poorly formalized.

TABLE 2.9. COLLECTIONS FROM SITE RkIg-44

Identification	Number	Details	
Fluted point	RkIg-44:	Table 2.10.	(Pl. 2G)
Point base	RkIg-44:38	Table 2.10.	(Pl. 2F, Fig. 2.1d)
Worked obsidian	RkIg-44:17+30	Initial stage biface	
Biface, unfinished,	RkIg-44:3+48	72 x 41 mm	(Pl. 5E)
complete	RkIg-44:6+53	76 x 38.5 mm	
" "	RkIg-44:11	66 x 36 mm	(Pl. 5D)
" "	RkIg-44:12	70 x 36 mm	(Pl. 5F)
" "	RkIg-44:46	44 x 26.5 mm	
" "	RkIg-44:47+49	71 x 45.5 mm	(Pl. 5A)
Biface, unfin. frag.	RkIg-44:...	15 items: 2, 4, 7, 10, 14, 32,	
	(Pl. 5B)	43-45, 50, 52, 61, 71, 74-75	
Bevelled flake	RkIg-44:1		(Pl. 22H)
Retouched or	RkIg-44:23	Sharp edge	
utilized flake	RkIg-44:79	Linear edge	
	RkIg-44:58	Bevelled	
Blade core	RkIg-44:40	See text	(Pl. 5L)
Bladelet core	RkIg-44:15	See text	(Pl. 5I)
Microblade core	RkIg-44:13	See text	(Pl. 5J)
Core object	RkIg-44:42	See text	
Chopper	RkIg-44:80	Split cobble, thick back, 123x90 (Pl. 5K)	
"Utilized flakes"	Many entries	Apparent use is due to natural attrition	
Biface edges	Many entries	Hinged-out edge fragments	
Bladelike flakes	Few entries		

RkIg-44:13 (Pl.5J) is a small core made on a segment of an obsidian pebble. There are two platforms. One platform was formed through retouching the edge of a large flake scar that forms one surface of the core, but none of the microblade-size flutes on the face originate from this old battered platform. Apparent microblades were struck from the opposite end of the core. The fluted face is highly curved and one attempted blade removal broke off a short distance below the platform--ample reason for discarding the core. The angle between the large flake scar that formed the top of the core and the curved face of the core is in the order of 35 degrees. That evidently was too acute and the platform was roughly retouched, increasing the angle to about 50 degrees. Here, as in other examples, the platform angle at a split pebble surface was increased through retouch.

RkIg-44:42 (Pl. 5H) is a split pebble core object. The angle between the split surface and the object face, where there have been several short wide flake removals, is approximately 30 degrees. However, the split surface (platform) has been extensively flaked, though coarsely, removing two-thirds of it and forming an angle with the face in the order of 50 degrees. This short, apparently unfinished core tool shows the same technological elements as the cores described above.

Assessment

The primary activity at this site, in Area 2, was the production of biface roughouts. The simple blade and microblade cores, which were recovered from Area 1 and the 1-2 border evidently are not part of this activity and do not necessarily derive from the same component of occupation. It is problematical whether there is any relationship between the fluted point, unfinished point base and cores and biface production discards. However, the highly battered condition of the fluted point is concordant with the battered and scratched condition of other items from Area 2. These specimens have had at least a long common experience in the natural environment of RkIg-44.

Site RlIg-46

A surface collection was made at RlIg-46 in 1970. The site (Fig. 2.16) is located on an elevation or topographic nose protruding from the flank of a hill, on the south side of Indian River south of Utopia. This location is several kilometres up the drainage east of the fluted point site cluster on Little Lake Ridge. Thousands of obsidian flakes (not collected) were observed in an area 32 m long situated within a larger denuded zone. Exposed implements of chert and obsidian (collected) were few and there was no close or physical association between any two implements.

Collection

Among the small varied lot of artifacts is the base of a fluted point (Pl. 2H). Other artifacts include a fine wedgeshaped microblade core, described in Chapter 4, and an unfluted lanceolate point (Pl. 6I) and other points described in Table App.II.4.

Assessment

Because of the wide separation of artifact find spots, the fluted point is treated as an isolated find. The unfluted lanceolate point could be from a related component.

Site RlIg-47

RlIg-47, surface collected in 1971, is situated on a sparsely vegetated topographic bench on the north side of Indian River approximately across from and slightly upstream from RlIg-46 (Figure 2.17). The sites are separated by intervening low terrain. Minor obsidian flake clusters and a small number of implements were found on the rubbly surface in an area ranging from less than 10 m to 20 m wide and 40 m long. Part of the surface is obscured by lichen and moss growth.

Collection

Recovered implements include two fluted points (Pl. 2 I-J), a retouched basalt flake (Pl. 22M), a notched point base and an end scraper, all of obsidian. The fluted points were located 10 m distant from one another, the sidenotched point fragment was approximately 13 m from the closest fluted point, and the end scraper 9.5 m from the same fluted point.

Assessment

The two fluted points can be related on the basis of technological attributes, but there is no basis for concluding that the remaining items do or do not belong with these points.

Site RkIg-32

This intensive surface showing of flakes was trowelled in 1971. The site is located on an eastward extension of Little Lake Ridge just north of a small pond. The area trowelled measures 1.5 by 3 m. Dimensions of the site were not determined. It was only moderately exposed and hardly had been burned in 1968.

Collection

The flake lot weighs 2.6 kg flakes. Artifacts were recovered from the general site area, not the flake cluster, and consist of the following.

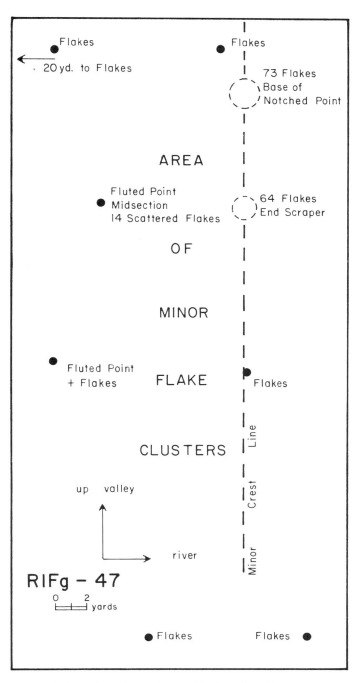

Figure 2.16. Sketch map of Site RlIg-47 showing collection locations.

Point midsection, obsidian, 25 mm wide, 4.4 mm thick   32:3
Biface fragment
Worked basalt fragment, biface roughout?   32:8
2 rudimentary biface roughout fragments and a hinged biface edge fragment.

The midsection incorporates the near-base area from which, on one side only, there are the flutes of 4 thinning flakes, and there is the trace upper portion of a basal "ear." This specimen could be a fluted point variant. On each edge there is a series of small notches or coarse serrations that appear to have been produced intentionally. For this attribute this specimen is unique at Batza Téna.

Other

A nonfluted, concave base, lanceolate **point from RkIh-33**, No. 7, located near Batzatiga produced three thick hydration readings of between 3.37 and 3.40 microns. Associated material is limited to flakes, rough or unfinished bifaces, flake cores, end scrapers and retouched flakes. The point had been washed out of the low-lying site into a small lake.

Figure 2.17. Terrain at the east end of Little Lake Ridge, where sites lack visibility, east of the cluster of fluted point sites.

Point base fragment RkIg-32:3 has four abruptly terminated narrow basal thinning flakes on one face. Although this obsidian specimen was found in the proximity of the fluted point site cluster on Little Lake Ridge, piece may not fall within the range of variation of fluted points.

Associated materials are few, consisting principally of unfinished biface fragments.

Description of Fluted Points from Batza Téna

Artifacts from each site have been listed in the preceding section. In this section we offer a more detailed unified description of the fluted points. Most of this information is conveyed through Table 2.10. The following paragraphs also provide a summary and processual description of fluted point knapping. In addition to the specimens described in Table 2.10, basal corner and tip fragments have been recovered from RkIg-30.

Two complete, damaged, points and many snapped bases were recovered as well as a midsection and minor fragments. All fluted points are made of obsidian with the exception of one apparently fluted basalt tip fragment. Other point forms, made of both basalt and obsidian and less often chert, were recovered from some of the fluted point sites. The complete fluted points are only 29.7 and 53 mm long, but several now fragmentary specimens in the fluted series were larger, judging from their width and thickness. Width ranges from 20 to 28.3 mm and appears to be at its maximum either close to or as much as one third the distance above the base. Thickness is in the order of 4 to 5 mm. The two measures of thickness in Table 2.10 were taken c 6 mm above the inside of the basal concavity and at the location of maximum thickness respectively.

Fluting usually consists of three shallow vertical thinning flake scars located on each face, but in some cases only one or two thinning flake removals are apparent. The smaller complete specimen is fluted on one side only, as also is one of the fragments. Although a flute often is a distinctive narrow channel bounded by adjacent parallel flutes, sometimes it may be obscured or largely removed by a subsequent thinning flake, particularly when the latter is wide or irregular.

Almost invariably, the medial flute follows the lateral flutes in the flaking sequence, although specimen RkIg-30:220 (Pl. 1E) presents an exception on both faces. The lateral flutes may be close to the edges and sometimes have been partially removed through subsequent retouch directed from the edges and base. They and probably also the first medial flute, and occasionally the second (obverse) medial flute, appear to have been formed from an essentially straight bevelled base which had become slightly concave by the time both faces were thinned. The concave base and ears were then formed through further retouch. The final medial flake on one face probably was not detached until the basal notch had been prepared or partially prepared. The base may have either a U-shaped or a V-shaped profile which varies in depth. No clear-cut dichotomy of basal shapes was seen in the Batza Téna points. Finally, the lower edges along the sides and around the base were blunted through grinding. We have not remarked on the initial forming and lateral retouch or shaping of the Batza Téna points inasmuch as these steps presently are inadequately understood. Some shaping retouch from the edges precedes fluting while further retouch succeeds it. Numerous small unfinished bifaces have been found on sites yielding fluted points, and such roughouts probably form a stage in the production of fluted and other points.

In some cases the blank evidently was a flat flake, the dorsal side of which was thinned through removal of long parallel flakes even before elementary shaping of the point was undertaken. This speculation is prompted by our finding many flakes and biface roughouts thinned in a manner approximating fluting, and by point fragments showing an early generation of flute-like thinning. Under opportune circumstances a thin flake may be shaped into an unfluted piece having the profile of a fluted point. The association of specimen RkIg-30:323 (Pl. 1I) with fluted points suggests that such points are a variant within the fluted point series. This specimen has basal notching, ear formation, and base and edge grinding but is not fluted, probably because the blank was already a thin 4-mm-thick flat smooth-faced flake.

A few additional details can be added to the description above, or specific examples cited. Bases were bevelled, probably twice, to form a platform for detaching the thinning flakes. The steps of manufacture are represented in several unfinished specimens. In the case of RkIg-44:38 (Pl. 2F) three or more flakes up to 13 mm long were struck from the edge of a narrow bevel. This, however, did not result in successful fluting. Previous to the bevelling, possible flutes or broad, large thinning flakes apparently had been removed from the obverse side, although this observation is equivocal due to irregularities in this specimen. RkIg-31:15 (Pl. 2A), which is triply fluted on one face, has a bifacial bevel. The principal bevel appears to have been formed to serve as a platform for planned but unconsummated fluting of the face opposite the one already fluted. In the preparation of this bevel, the proximal or bulbar area of the existing flutes was removed. RkIg-30:220 (Pl. 1E) has been fluted on both sides but basal preparation was not carried beyond that stage. Thus there is a bevel on one face which removed the base of antecedent flutes on the same face while two subsequent flutes on the observe face, detached from this bevel as a platform, still have their negative bulbar areas intact. These present conspicuous indentations in the bevelled platform. Finally, the basal notch and ears are formed as in RkIg-30:321 (Pl. 1H), which is fluted or thinned on both faces. In this case the edges along the sides are only roughly flaked and the lower edges have not been ground. Edge retouch and grinding probably are among the final steps of preparation.

Comparisons and Significance

The points described here differ from classic Clovis points in that the shallow medial flute of the classic point usually is larger and longer than the lateral flutes or "guide flakes" as they are called in that case. Detachment of the medial flute in the case of the Alaskan and Yukon points leaves the lateral flutes intact to a substantial degree, so that many of these points can properly be described as triply fluted or channelled. Many southern Palaeo-Indian sites, however, are characterized by points which in terms of their multiple fluting are not particularly different from the Alaskan specimens (cf. Fitting et al 1966), and this especially is the case for points from western Canada.

There is considerable variation in the size of specimens from various assemblages, but those from the north tend to be smaller than classic Clovis points. Various style and shape differences occur between several North American assemblages. To compare the Alaskan points with those from more southerly provenience in any comprehensive manner would entail detailed analysis which we do not intend to undertake for this report. But considering subcontinental style differences, the Alaska-Yukon fluted points cluster well with most Clovis points from regions within and west of the cordillera, though not all western fluted points conform to a single norm. This concordance includes many specimens from Nevada, California, western Alberta and British Columbia (cf Davis and Shutler 1969; Fladmark 1981: Fig. 43 a-b; Gryba 1985: Fig. 1-2; Tuohy 1969; Wilson 1987, 1989). Our immediate interest, in making comparisons with the south, thus can be focused on specimens from central to northern Alberta and northeastern British Columbia. As has been discussed in other publications (cited above), there remains more than one interpretation of how the northern fluted points relate to those found in western Canada south of Latitude 60 and those distributed farther south. To a large degree interpretations are governed by hypothetical models that are continental in scope.

We are alerted to the possibility that fluted points were produced in northern Alaska and the northern Yukon over an extended period, as much as a millennium or more, and that there may be temporally and historically significant variations in style. In the present sample, however, uniformity is more apparent than variability. The triple fluted format is well documented across the northern distribution (Clark 1984a). It is not possible at this time to assign any age difference to those that vary from this norm. We do find, though, increasing evidence that for the time range of approximately 7000 to 10,000 years ago there are points of lanceolate format with straight to concave bases, sometimes with slight basal thinning, which could be interpreted as a development out of more distinctively fluted points (cf. Kunz 1982, 1992 and ref. in Clark 1984a). Kunz, however, suggests the thick lanceolate points from Mesa and other sites are fundamentally different from fluted points, which are relatively thin, and thus two distinct Palaeo-Indian traditions appear to be represented (personal communication to D. Clark, April 1993). These and other leafshaped and lanceolate points in the north may illustrate an independent development paralleling that of Plano-style points in the south.

Critical to interpreting the significance of northern fluted points is the question of their age. This is not completely settled. For the southern approaches there is an unreliable radiocarbon date of approximately 9500 years from a fluted point component at Sibbald Creek, Alberta (Gryba 1983:122) and three closely clustered dates, averaging about 10,500 years, from the fluted point component of Charlie Lake Cave (Fladmark, Driver and Alexander 1988). For Alaska and the Yukon there is an increasing number of moderately old radiocarbon dates that could be associated with fluted points. These include a miniature tip fluted on one side recovered in the c 10,700-year-old Dry Creek II component (Powers, Guthrie and Hoffecker 1983), points and fragments (none conclusively good fluted points) from various lower depths of the Healy Lake site that probably date within the range 9000 to 11,000 years ago, a short basally-thinned point and fragment suggestive of the fluted point format from the 9500-10,500-year-Old middle component at the Broken Mammoth site (Yesner personal communication to D. Clark 1992), and Putu points which, with considerable uncertainty, date to the same early period (R. Reanier finds that the early Putu radiocarbon date more likely applies to a leafshaped point than to fluted points-- personal communication to D. Clark, April 1993). This evidence indicates a time frame in which the northern fluted points likely are related to southern ones, but much more information is needed for precise dating and to formulate a statement on origins and migrations. Where one might expect evidence for an early date there is little or none: recent investigation of 11,000-to 11,400-year-old Nenana Complex sites in Alaska has failed to produce any fluted points (Powers and Hoffecker 1989). This negative evidence suggests that the Alaskan points either date to yet an earlier period or to a later period, or that whatever their age they are so uncommon that they are not present in many site assemblages.

TABLE 2.10. BATZA TENA FLUTED POINTS

Object	Site and number	Ground on-Edge	Base	Width mm	Thickness mm	Flute details, each face length mm each flute
Base	RkIg-1:49	+	+	25	5.1-6.5	3 ea. face; 21+ 21 25+ irreg /18+ 32+ c27.5. Battered
Base	RkIg-10:36	+	+	28	4.4-5.5	3 ea. face; 21 28+ 12+ /9+ 24 31
Base	RkIg-28:9	-**	-**	26.3	3.6-4.2	None seen on 8 mm frag., basal retouch may obscure
Base	RkIg-29:16	+	+	26.3	3.7-5.9	3 one face, 1 on other face; c19 irreg./21+ 15 16
Base	RkIg-30:42	-**	-**	24.7	3.8-4.8	Damaged, 2 ea. face? 15 irreg. trace/5 15+ irreg.
Base unfin.	RkIg-30:220	-	-	23.8	3.5-5.8	3 ea. face; 31.4+ 31+ 28/20.5 27.4+
Base corner	RkIg-30:254	+	+	NR	4.1-4.9	2 or 3 one face only, frag., some observations obscured
Base unfin.	RkIg-30:321	-	-	28	3.8-5.0	3 one face, 9+ 22+/other has several thinning flakes
Base unfin	RkIg-31:15	-**	-**	22-27	4.6-5.6	3 on one face, plano-convex x-section, 21+ 17 25+
Whole	RkIg-31:60	+	+	20-24	3.5-5.0	3 ea. face; point 53 mm long; 9 22 irreg. 14/19 18 27
Near base	RkIg-31:119	-	-	27.2	4.0-4.6	2 ea. face, all 23+, side edges look unfinished
Base	RkIg-31:120	+	+	21-24.5	3.2-4.3	3/2 or 3 obscured, truncated 17.7+ to 21.5+
Base	RkIg-43:1	+	+	23.7	4.2	2 ea face truncated at 8 mm, obscure antecedent thinning?
Base unfin	RkIg-44:38	-**	-	24.8	5.1	Fluting attempted?
Near base	RkIg-44:81	+	NR	24.7	4.4-4.9	Battered, 3/2, 18? 17 irreg. 20.5+/12+ 23.5
Base	RlIg-46:62	+	+	20-22.2	4.4-6.5	Wide off-centre 18+ ea face, traces of 2nd & 3rd ea face
Whole point	RlIg-47:13	+	+	20.0	4.4-4.0	3 one face only; 19 main flute; point length 29.7
Mid-section	RlIg-47:4	+	NR	28.3	5.1-5.9	3 & 2 off-centre, truncated at base, L between 13+ & 30+

NR = Not Recordable (because of incompleteness).
*   A "+" value for flute length measurements indicates truncation at a broken edge and that the full length is grater than the value given.
**   (within "Ground" column entries). Accompanies a "-" or "not ground" entry and indicates that though not ground the edges are lightly crushed.

CHAPTER 3: SITE RkIg-TWENTY EIGHT

The Site and Collection

Site RkIg-28 is distinguished from all others at Batza Téna through its high incidence of basalt artifacts and the occurrence there of several round-based lanceolate points. Neither of these characteristics makes the site wholly unique, but they suggest a cultural-historic identification at least in part different from that of other Batza Téna sites. Additional basalt artifacts were found on adjacent sites.

Figure 3.1.   Surface collecting at RkIg-28 in 1970. Not all flake clusters are indicated.

The site encompasses several flake clusters, scattered flakes and artifacts found in an area 87 m long and 25 to 47 m wide (Fig. 3.1, 3.2). Its context is a sparsely vegetated flat area of stony soil in the upland apex part of Little Lake Ridge (Fig. 2.2). The lateral margins are largely coeval

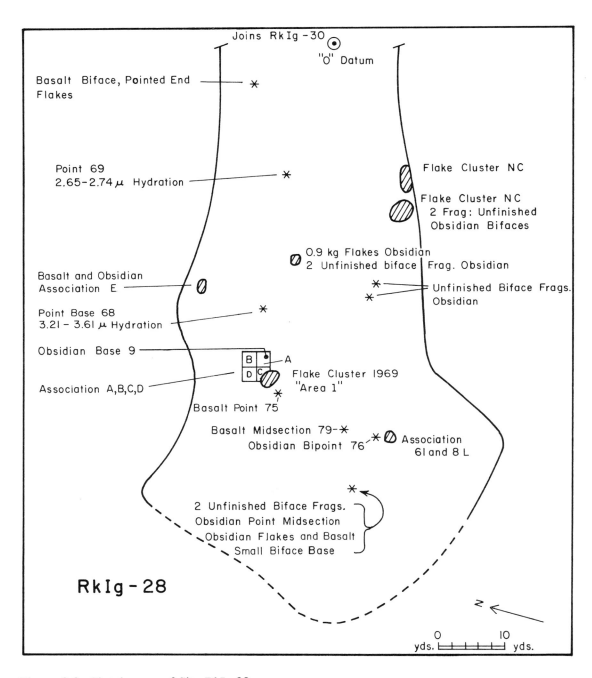

Figure 3.2. Sketch map of Site RkIg-28.

with slightly depressed areas covered with tundra vegetation and soil, but at its eastern end the site narrows and joins Site RkIg-30 through a slightly elevated neck of land. At its southwestern end the site is defined through the limit of flake occurrences instead of by topography. Most of the site had been intensively burned over in 1968, which permitted close inspection of the surface. From RkIg-28 it is possible to see many of the surrounding hills and distant flats, but close terrain is obscured by topography and the forest.

In 1969 most of one flake concentration was picked up and an additional small surface collection was made during a brief visit to the site. The surface was thoroughly inspected for artifacts in 1970 and one additional flake concentration was sampled. Several spectacular flake concentrations were seen on the surface, particularly at the eastern end of the site. These were examined, largely without disturbing them, were seen to lack implements in most cases, and were not collected. A flake cluster near the western end of the site was picked up and trowelled over, the flake collection was examined on location, was found to lack implements, and was left at the site of recovery. Most implements that were found on the site occurred as isolated finds or as minor clusters of associated specimens. Only a modest amount of flaking detritus was associated with the implement clusters. One group collected in 1970 contained five bifacial and unifacial knife blades--four of weathered basalt and one of obsidian. Basalt artifacts were seen to be distributed over the entire site but they usually were absent from the clusters of obsidian flakes.

In 1971 we returned to the site and trowelled four seven-foot-square sections at the location where the five bifacial artifacts had been recovered the previous year (sections A-D, D comprised largely the old excavation). One other area, E, where basalt and obsidian co-occurred was tested. These excavations produced only a small number of additional implements and flakes but helped defined the limits of two artifact clusters.

There are four modes of flake occurrence at RkIg-28: (a) sparse scatter, (b) moderate surficial cluster, (c) moderate surficial and shallow subsurface cluster, and (d) massed concentration (surrounded by many additional flakes). The first characterizes areas in which obsidian and basalt implements co-occur on the surface and at a shallow depth. Some large obsidian flake aggregates at the eastern end of the site appear to be totally surficial, although this evaluation needs confirmation inasmuch as none of these concentrations was tested. At a mode "c" cluster from which a 0.95 kilogram sample was collected in 1970 there was a moderate to strong show of flakes on the surface but an equal or greater amount of flakes also occurred relatively evenly distributed within the top 5 cm of stony soil. Finally, in the mode "d" massed flake concentration collected in 1969 there was a good surface exposure of flakes within an area 2 m in diameter, but most flakes were clustered in a small central area measuring 50 cm long and 15 cm wide. There flakes were piled on top of each other to a maximum thickness of 8-10 cm in a matrix of light-grey, clayey, frost-segregated soil. This type of soil was discussed earlier for Locus 1 at RkIg-10. Most of the 1969 collection of 578 flakes (2.5 kg) came from this cluster. Approximately 60%-70% of those present in the cluster were collected.

Artifacts

Projectile points, small symmetrical biface blades for knives or lances, asymmetrical knife blades, heavy unfinished biface fragments and bevelled and utilized flakes are the principal implements found at RkIg-28. The collection is listed in Table 3.1, while points and small bifaces are described in Table 3.2. End scrapers are limited to a single atypical specimen defined more on the basis of wear traces than on bevelling of the working edge. Large numbers of seemingly utilized or retouched flakes have not been counted as tools because of the likelihood that they were formed naturally within the stony soil matrix.

There were three principal clusters or associations of artifacts, in addition to the flake clusters (Fig. 3.1). These involve the co-occurrence of basalt and obsidian artifacts. The contents of each is listed here.

Cluster in Sections ABCD
Slender point or bipoint RkIg-28:75, basalt, 2-3 yards from main group
Leafshaped point or knife RkIg-28:40+93 (joined fragments), basalt
Incomplete leafshaped point RkIg-28:86, basalt
Point RkIg-28:43, damaged and missing ends, obsidian
Slender point or knife missing base, RkIg-28:91+92, basalt
Concave base of a point, RkIg-28:9, obsidian
Convergent, rounded point bases, RkIg-28:87 and 88, obsidian
Rounded end of small biface or point RkIg-28:44, obsidian
Retouched utilized flake RkIg-28:39, obsidian
Biface fragments, RkIg-28:41, 42 and 85 basalt
Worn flake used in the manner of an end scraper, RkIg-28:89
Small flake lots including some basalt flakes

The 1969 obsidian flake cluster identified as Area 1 overlaps this cluster in Section C and contained 5 or 6 hinged unfinished biface edge fragments, 2 unfinished biface fragments, 2 probable utilized or retouched flakes and a number of possible utilized flakes, all of obsidian.

Cluster E
Broad oblanceolate point, RkIg-28:81, obsidian
Biface fragment made on a flake, RkIg-28:80, large, obsidian
Biface fragment, RkIg-28:47, large well prepared, obsidian
Biface/uniface fragment, RkIg-28:83, unfinished, obsidian
Uniface fragment, RkIg-28:48, basalt
Thick bevelled uniface (scraper plane) RkIg-28:49 + fitted fragment from flake lot 104, volcanic rock, incomplete (Pl. 7S)
Utilized flake, RkIg-28:84, obsidian
A small lot of flakes, RkIg-28:104 including some basalt flakes

Cluster at Location 61 yards +, 8 yards L

Leafshaped point or knife with long stem/high shoulder, No. 71, basalt

Leafshaped point or knife, RkIg-28:72

Unifacial sideblade on a large flake, equivalent to a biface tool, RkIg-28:74, basalt (Pl. 7Q)

Double-edge, bevelled, pointed flake No. 73, large, pointed at end, basalt (Pl. 7O)

Ovoid biface, RkIg-28:70, irregular, unfinished?, obsidian, 3 hydration sections nil, 0.98 and 4.77 microns

Ovate-pointed   or bipointed obsidian point, RkIg-28:76, 2 m from centre of cluster.

TABLE 3.1.   COLLECTION FROM SITE RkIg-28

No.	Identification	Material	Description	
Point/Small Biface Series				
7	Complete	3 obsidian	Table 3.2	(Pl. 7)
		4 basalt	Table 3.2	(Pl. 7)
4	Base	Obsidian	Table 3.2	(Pl. 7)
2	Midsection	Obsidian	Nondescript	
		Basalt	Table 3.2	
1	Rounded end fragment	Obsidian	Table 3.2	
3	Pointed end fragment	Basalt	Nondescript	
Large or Unpointed Bifaces				
1	Complete, unfinished	Obsidian	Elliptical 49x27.5 mm	
5	Incomplete, finished or nearly finished	2 obsidian	i. Nearly square end, 28 mm wide; ii. pointed end, 40 mm wide	(Pl. 7R)
		3 basalt	Pointed & unpointed frags., edge smoothed	
14	Unfinished fragments	Obsidian	Ends rounded, slightly pointed, or cortical	
7	Hinged biface edges		From edges of roughouts	
Uniface Series				
2	Biface equivalents	Basalt	i. Frag.; ii. Complete asymmet., 74x32.3, some ventral retouch	(Pl. 7Q)
1	Thick tool fragment (scraper plane?)	Volcanic rock	Large, high bevel, 29 mm thick	(Pl. 7S)
1	End scraper	Obsidian	Worn edge largely natural	
1	Bevelled flake	Basalt	92x44, pointed at one end, knife?	(Pl. 7O)
7	Bevelled or utilized flake	Obsidian	5 have sharp edges, 1 possible spokeshave	
1	Split cobble	Obsidian		
149	Flakes	Basalt	Identified in thinsection	
x	Flakes	Obsidian	4.9 kg collected, some clusters not collected	
26	Segregated flakes	Obsidian	Of technological interest or with utilized appearance presumed due to natural causes	
2	Amorphous worked			

Assessment and Comparisons

The frequency of basalt and obsidian flakes indicate that implements of both materials were produced at the site. Nevertheless, the recovery of only 155 nonobsidian flakes in contrast to 15 implements, a ratio of 10-to-1, is out of proportion with the many thousands of obsidian flakes observed or collected. Furthermore, considering that there were only 35 obsidian implements (42 counting hinged unfinished biface edge fragments) it is evident that several hundred obsidian flakes occur for each obsidian implement. Most basalt or non-obsidian artifacts broken, lost or discarded here and subsequently recovered evidently were fashioned elsewhere, though there was some flaking or repair of these artifacts at RkIg-28. On the other hand, the site was a primary flaking station for obsidian tools. This situation is not unique to RkIg-28. A similar proportionate disparity between basalt flake/implement ratios and obsidian flake/implement ratios exists at RkIg-30. In only one case was a small possible core chunk of this material recovered, and there are few cortical flakes at either site. This reinforces my impression that preforming of basalt implements or core reduction was done elsewhere. There is no assurance that the basalt and obsidian industries are coeval at these sites aside from the approximate equation of point and biface forms. The lack of fabricating tools such as end scrapers, side scrapers and burins, viewed from the point of the obsidian industry, reinforces the impression the site is substantially a flaking and hunting station (broken finished bases imply the latter), but viewed from the basalt industry it is a hunting station only.

Broad, straight-based points and round-based points with converging stem margins and high shoulders are not as ubiquitous as leafshaped and lanceolate points. Nevertheless, they are not uncommon in northwestern Alaska and they do not necessarily definitive of a culture-historical entity. Poorly dated assemblages characterized by such points continue to pose problems for Alaskan archaeologists.

Similarities may be seen between Tuktu or Northern Archaic leafshaped and oblanceolate points and high shouldered or oblanceolate points of RkIg-28 (cf. Campbell 1961: Plate 1 7-8; Anderson 1988). Nevertheless, if RkIg-28 has yielded a representative assemblage, the lack of side-notched points, end scrapers, notched pebbles and chopping tools and microblades excludes affiliation with the Northern Archaic tradition, with sites that bear the characteristics of this tradition in combination with a microblade industry, and with the Palaeo-Arctic tradition or Denali complex.

A few specimens comparable to ones from RkIg-28 have been found at the Mesa site but by far the greater emphasis at Mesa is on concave base lanceolate points, of which there is only one fragmentary specimen from RkIg-28, and that readily distinguishes the two collections (Kunz 1982). Mesa and RkIg-28 could, however, be variants of a tradition-level entity. The single date 7620 ± 95 radiocarbon years age of Mesa would be acceptable to me as the age of RkIg-28.

Fragments of convergent stem, round-based points from the 10,700-year-old Dry Creek II Palaeo-Arctic occupation, and to some degree "small spatulate knives" and "elliptical knives" from the same component show general similarities to the RkIg-28 assemblage, although identity is lacking (Powers, Guthrie and Hoffecker 1983: Fig. 4.29, 4.30). But otherwise there is little similarity between the two site assemblages.

TABLE 3.2. POINTS AND SMALL BIFACES FROM RkIg-28

RkIg-	Part	Material	L	W	T	Edges*	Form
28:9	Base	Obsidian	--	26.5	9	Unsmoothed	Thinned concave base, outline is
							suggestive of fluted point, short fragment not definitive (Pl. 7K, Fig. 2.1G)
28:43	Midsection	Obsidian	--	17.5	6.6	Ground	All but the ends present, semi-
							lozenge cross-section; narrowest end is thinnest and ground at edges; bipointed? (Pl. 7E)
28:44	End	Obsidian	--	20	4.7	Unsmoothed	Round-based point or small biface fragment (Pl. 7J)
28:63	Midsection	Obsidian	--	26	5	Unsmoothed	Not definitive, unfinished?
28:68	Base	Obsidian		25	5.7	Unsmoothed?	Lanceolate point frag?; straight
							base slightly angled (damaged?); slight smoothing (natural?) on faces; 3 vague hydration sections 3.21 to 3.61 microns (Pl. 7G)
28:69	Complete	Obsidian	50	29.7	8.4	Unsmoothed?	Asymmetrical, stubby, broad-base
							lanceolate, weakly concave base is angled, natural attrition obscures edges. 2.65-2.74 microns of hydration in 3 sections (Pl. 7B)
28:71	Complete	Basalt	67	30.6	10	Smoothed	Oblanceolate, straight lower edges
							converge to rounded base, widest above midpoint; short thin blade element above widest point appears reshaped (Pl. 7L)
28:72	Complete	Basalt	78	30	7	Smoothed	Leafshaped, excurvate,
							rounded base, widest at midpoint, edge grinding largely limited to one edge. High points on one face smoothed (Pl. 7P)
28:75	Complete	Basalt	60	19	6.8	Unsmoothed	Symmetrical slender bipoint
							(end damaged), sides excurvate, widest at midpoint, ends not differentiated (Pl. 7C)
28:76	Complete	Obsidian	55	24.7	7.2	Smoothed	Very excurvate sides, leafshaped
							bipointed, widest near damaged or unfinished base (Pl. 7F)
28:79	Midsection	Basalt	--	29	7.1	Ground	Near straight sides taper towards end presumed to be base
28:81	Complete	Obsidian	53	30.8	8.4	Ground	Slightly curved sides of wide oblanceolate
							point converge from point of greatest width above midpoint to narrow rounded base; edges ground below wide point but not at the very base (Pl. 7A, Fig. 1.13b)
28:86	Tip & midsection	Basalt	--	22.3	8.4	Unsmoothed	Slender (Pl. 7D)

TABLE 3.2--concluded

RkIg-	Part	Material	L	W	T	Edges*	Form
28:87	Base	Obsidian	--	27+	7+	Ground	Slightly curved sides converge towards
		narrow slightly rounded base. Base damaged (Pl. 7H)					
28:88	Base	Obsidian	--	26+	8+	Ground	Curved sides converge towards
		narrow slightly concave base (reshaped?). Form similar to No. 87. High areas on one face ground (Pl. 7I)					
28:91 +92	Point & midsection	Basalt	--	27.8	7	Unsmoothed?	Asymmetrical knife/ sideblade, (Pl. 7N)
28:93 +40	Complete	Basalt	66	28	9.2	Unsmoothed?	Leafshaped, ends rounded, base found
		separately is highly weathered (Pl. 7M).					

Similar artifacts from adjacent Batza Téna sites merit mentioning. They include the following: (a) RkIg-27:18, located next to RkIg-28, high shouldered basalt point with nearly straight, edge-ground stem convergent towards the missing (presume rounded) base; (b) RkIg-39, located a short distance east of RkIg-28, three base fragments (2 basalt, 1 obsidian) of convergent-stem round-based points, ground on the edges; (c) RlIg-41, basalt knife or misshapen point, slightly convex ground edges converge from point of greatest width towards damaged base; (d) RlIg-52:174 located at Lake elevation 324, basalt point. The highly pointed end of this specimen is the base judging from the placement of edge grinding, and the greatest width above the midpoint. Possibly, during the course of several generations, the same people who camped at RkIg-28 stopped at other places in the vicinity.

A plausible, though tentative, placement of RkIg-28 is that is predates the Northern Archaic tradition and that it also predates the later microblade industries not of typical Palaeo-Arctic or early Denali format. It likely postdates or is coeval with the latter. It may be an aspect of the same culture responsible for the fluted point fragments left on several adjacent sites, which according to the tentative Western Subarctic sequence we favor would make it either earlier than or coeval with the Palaeo-Arctic tradition.

CHAPTER 4: MICROBLADE SITES

Introduction

With one exception, assemblages which have produced evidence for microblade production, particularly cores and microblades, are described in this chapter. The exception is for the Batza Téna Tuktu (Northern Archaic) complex assemblages (Chapter 5) which are distinctive from any of those described here and in which the microblade industry is a very minor component. Those described in this chapter evidently date to various periods and may be specialized activity sites of cultures otherwise assignable to recognized or proposed cultural traditions. The latest assemblage likely is contemporary with or only slightly older than Batza Téna Tuktu to which it may be related.

Questions surrounding this kind of material in Alaska (Fig. 4.1a-b) center on the age and temporal range and the co-occurrence of differing forms of microblade cores, and the types of associated implements. The present sites shed some information on these questions. Although some sites evidently are late in time and more recent than others, there is no clear dichotomy between late and early or Palaeo-Arctic microblade phases at Batza Téna. Possibly only late and middle time-range sites have been collected, to the exclusion of any classic Palaeo-Arctic component, but dating of these sites is tentative. The following are the principal sites described in this chapter:

Site RkIh-28, a probable middle time-range site, illustrates the co-occurrence of microblade and blade production. The only microblade core recovered here is based on an unformalized preform, a pebble with selected natural shape.

Microblade production at RlIg-37 is based on more formalized cores with bifaced wedge element. Only fragments of these cores were recovered. The single associated implement is a fragment of a small sidenotched point. A relatively late date is indicated by a series of obsidian hydration measurements.

At RkIg-47 the microblade cores are based on unformalized preforms. Platform rejuvenation tablets were found at this site and the preceding two. Evidently this trait is common to both formalized and unformalized cores. Equally fine microblades are associated with both core forms.

Two core types--prepared wedgeshaped and nonwedge (or semiwedge based on the form of the natural pebble blank)--are found together at RkIh-32 associated with a varied assemblage of tools. At this eroded site, component mixture is suspected. The recovery of a late-appearing adze blade there nevertheless is not necessarily out of line with microblade technology inasmuch as first

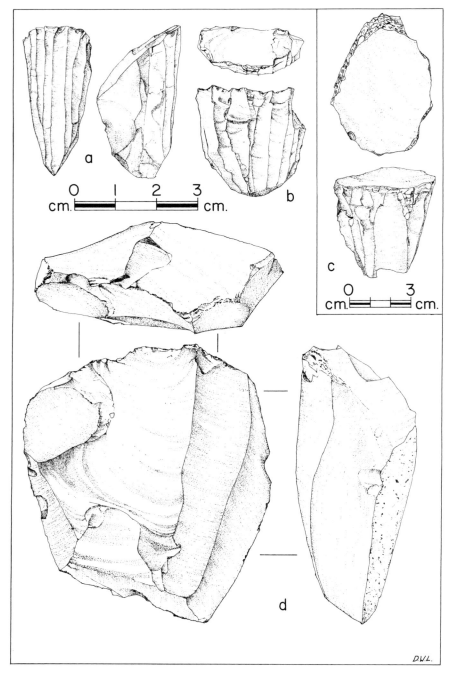

Figure 4.1.   Microblade cores from RkIh-32 and RkIh-47, flatfaced blade or
flake core RkIg-x:27, and (in box) platformed flake core RkIh-34.

millennium A.D. dates have been proposed for proposed for some Alaskan microblade
components, including the Batza Téna Tuktu phase. An additional type of microblade core made
on a biface will be reported in Chapter 5, and, further complicating analysis, there are a number
of specimens, some of which are described in the present chapter, that appear to show
intergradation between microblade cores and flake cores.

As was done in previous chapters, each site and its collection is described separately. Only
very brief conclusions will be offered here. The question of the significance of microblade
industries and the presence of various core types in northwest Alaskan prehistory is discussed in
the concluding chapter.

The Sites

Site RkIh-28

RkIh-28 (Fig. 4.2) is located at the northern tip of a low, broad hill situated southwest of
Batzatiga. Five km of tundra flats and two small, sluggish, deep streams separate the two hills.
At its southern end and eastern side this hill looses elevation and merges with surrounding terrain,
but at the north end and on the northwestern side it drops off rapidly forming a distinct
prominence rising about 25 m above the bottom land flats. The crest, where blocks of vesicular
volcanic rock outcrop, is forested with birch trees while tundra vegetation, including scrub spruce,
mantle the eastern slope. The surface was examined and two areas were tested in 1971.
Scattered flakes and minor flake clusters (not collected) also were seen for approximately 100 m
along the local crest.

Two clusters of lithic material were found on a relatively flat area or bench at the northern
tip, between the steep rise from the bottom-land and the ridge that forms the spine of the hill
(Fig. 4.2). Area A, which was closest to the crest and within the forest, was trowelled to yield 3
kg of obsidian flakes (plus 5 other flakes) and several unfinished biface fragments. This material
occurred at a shallow depth in the organic litter and rootmat zone and in underlying brown soil.
Cluster A appears to be unrelated to the microblade locus, Cluster B, and is not discussed further.

Cluster B was found closer to the edge of the hill, at a plausible overlook. Excavation
followed the distribution of blade, microblades and abundant flakes (8.6 kg) and formed an
irregular area. It would have been desirable to excavate and test more extensively at RkIh-28 and
on the hill, but by the time this amount work had been done we had largely exhausted our energy.

Soils at area B are as follows:
1. Litter and live root mat. Contained many flakes and at least 3 microblades.
2. Yellow-brown soil. Contained many flakes and most microblades and bifaces.
3. Partially decomposed volcanic bedrock in red soil, starting $\underline{c}$ 20 cm below the surface.

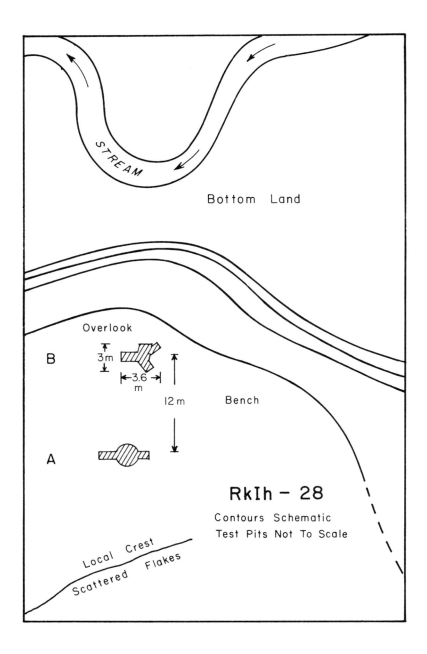

Figure 4.2. Sketch map of Site RkIh-28.

Locally this soil contained flakes, and at the top of this layer a biface and unfinished uniface.
  4. Grey frost involution soil, localized, extending into red soil. Contained many flakes.

I doubt if this soil sequence is significance to the chronology of archaeological components; e.g.,
artifacts from a single occupation now appear throughout the sequence. For instance, one biface
was recovered in three well separated fragments distributed through the soil column.

Collection

   The Cluster B collection consists primarily of microblades and byproducts of microblade and
macroblade production.   As well, there are several unfinished bifaces, end scrapers and other
items as are listed in Table 4.1. The occurrence also of a macroblade industry is significant,
although it is represented by only core processing debris, an end scraper and reject fragments of
macroblades.   The recovery of two or three broad, ovoid bifaces also is noteworthy.   At other
Batza Téna sites bifaces tend to be leafshaped or occur in more elongate forms.

   Many Cluster B implements and flakes have been altered extensively through burning.
Burning destroys the glassy lustre of the surface. Except for rare items, this condition was found
elsewhere at Batza Téna only in one area of Batzatiga site RkIh-36 (Chapter 5). But between
the two sites, only at RkIh-36 does the burned obsidian display fracture patterns similar to that
occurring in fractured tempered glass. These specimens, from both sites, appear to have been
subjected to intense or prolonged heat that evidently rarely results from forest fires. The fire at
RkIh-28 must have been localized, as was the case at RkIh-36, inasmuch as burned and unburned
fragments were recovered from the same RkIh-28 biface. Further description of selected artifacts
is provided below and in Table 4.1.

   Cores--Each core is described below, exclusive of amorphous flake cores or fragments. Some
obsidian microblades and core preparation spalls do not match in colour any of the cores
described here. This points to the use of additional cores at the site.

Core-shaped object RkIg-28:36 has the form of a wedgeshaped core with a triangular cross-section
in the horizontal plane.   It cannot, however, be identified as a microblade core.   Either
modifications have removed all traces of microblade flutes, or it is a preform or fortuitously
shaped object.

Spent (?) blade core RkIh-28:35 (Pl. 8N) is roughly rectangular in horizontal section and tapers
towards its base. It measures 30 x 33 mm at the platform and is 50 mm high. Broad, bladelike
flakes have been removed from three faces. The fourth face shows two incomplete flake scars
that originate from the direction of the present crushed base, suggesting that the core has been
rotated.   Alternatively, it may be a preform.   The platform is uneven, approximately horizontal
and minimally prepared.

Unformalized blade or bladelike-flake core RkIh-28:15 (Pl. 8M). An obsidian pebble was decapitated, and then, using the resultant flake scar as the striking platform, several large flakes and linear flakes were detached from the core face. The core starts to assume a wedge shape. The platform measures 40 x 47 mm (close to original width of pebble) and the longest face is 67 mm high. This face forms an angle of c̱ 65 degrees with the platform but elsewhere the angle between the platform and sides of the core shifts to an obtuse one.

TABLE 4.1. COLLECTION FROM SITE RkIh-28, CLUSTER B

No.	Identification	Description, Dimensions mm
Bifacial Series		
1	Point fragment RkIh-28:34	Obsidian, pointed but edge heavily ground, probable base, 8.3 mm thick, 2.61 microns hydration (Pl. 8D)
3	Biface, un-finished, complete	i. Pointed elongate, largely uniface formed on hinged sideblow flake, 85x32 ii. Broadly ovoid 60x49x10 (Pl. 8E) iii. Irregular discoid 63x55x12 (Pl. 8F)
4	Biface, un-finished fragments	i. Straight/curved sides meet at acute angle, nearly finished ii. Highly rounded end or curved edge, broad facial flakes, nearly finished (Pl. 8G) iii. Nondescript chert and obsidian (1 each)
1	Worked pebble	Flaked and battered around perimeter without complete cortex removal from either face
2+	Biface edge	Hinged biface roughout edge fragments & the spalled or struck-off edge of an unfinished biface
Uniface Series		
6	End scrapers	Obsidian, Pl. 8L made on blade segment, several have some dorsal preparation, (Table 9.4, Pl.8L,P)
1	Side scraper	Steep bevel along side & at end of 59x41 mm, partly cortical, thick flake
2+	Utilized flake	i. Sharp fine retouch along side, 51x30, partly cortical ii. Thick fluted bladelike spall from core has crushing retouch along one edge iii. 3, possibly utilized, crushed or nibbled edges
2	Amorphous	Irreg. dorsal edge retouch around 3/4 of perimeter of 42x38 discoidal cortical flake, & worked frag. of uniface
3	Single-edged uniface	Steep, broad, rough bevel along side of thick flake, triangular or trapezoidal cross-section (Pl. K)
Blade and Microblade Industry		
3-4	Cores	Described in text (Pl. 8A, M-N)
3	Platform tablets	Described in text ((Pl. 8O)
+	Core fragments	Fragments & large flakes from unformalized cores showing blade/bladelike flake technology
17++	Blades, blade-like flakes	Imperfect blades, some derived from forming cores, most wider than 12 mm. One retouched along side, the retouch truncated by subsequent blade removal (Pl. 8B, H-J)
++	Microbladelike flakes	Imperfect microblades and small spalls as above but under 12 mm wide
38	Microblades	In Table 4.2, all but 3 are obsidian (Pl. 8C)
1	Sandstone pebble	Barshaped 127x37x27 mm, natural wedge-shape ends, some flaking at one end but no battering or grinding although the shape is suggestive of an implement.

TABLE 4.2. MICROBLADES FROM SITE RkIh-28

Segment	L	W	T	Arrises	Remarks
PMD	34	6.9	1.8	1	Tapered, W taken at midpoint
PMD	34	6.2	1.6	1	
PMD	30	7.0	1.6	2	Tapered, W&T taken medially
PMD	33	8.4	1.6	1-2	Hydration series #f, tapered reject
PM	21	7.4	1.7	3	
PM	36	10.5	2.0	2	Fine specimen
PM	36	7.1	1.7	2	Fine, tapered, W taken at midpoint
PM	30	5.8	1.6	2	Wavy, W&T avoid extremes
PM	30	8.7	1.6	1-2	T&W taken medially
PM	--	5.5	2.5	1	Laterally curved
PM	26	7.4	1.8	1	
PM	27	7.3	1.8	1	Hydration series #v, poor example
PM	28	9.7	2.5+	1	Hydration series #o, humped ridge
PM	31	8.1	2.0	1	Hydration series #p, expanding
P	20	7.7	2.0	2-3	Defective, T varies
P	23	10.8	1.8	2	
P	16	8.6	1.7	2	
P	18	9.2	2.1	2	Hydration series #k
P	23	8.8	1.8	2	Hydration series #q
P	23	7.1	1.6	1-2	W is maximum
P	19	8.4	1.7	1	
MD	31	8.6	2.0	3	W&T taken at break
MD	31	7.0	1.5	2	T varies
MD	29	8.2	1.6	2	Tapered defective, WT taken at break
M	32	6.7	1.8	2-3	Very fine
M	25	9.6	2.2	2	Tapered, W taken medially
M	21	6.7	1.5	2	
M	17	9.2	1.2	2	W is maximum
M	19	5.2	1.44	2	W&T taken at wide end
M	17	9.4	2.0	2	Not obsidian
M	15	6.6	1.4	2	Not obsidian
M	24	5.2	1.6	2-3	Not obsidian, fine
M	--	8.8	2.0	2	
M	--	7.2	3.0	1	T varies
M	19	5.6	1.6	1	
M	24	8.3	1.7	1	Hydration series #u
M	34	10+	3.0	1	Hydration series #i, wavy
M	--	8.8	1.9	1	Feathered, W&T taken at thick end
Means	--	7.83	1.80		For all 38 specimens
	--	7.64	2.07		For 13 single arrise specimens
	--	7.94	1.66		For 25 double/triple arrise specimens

P = proximal, M = medial, D = distal.
All specimens are from lot RkIg-20:27. One series was lettered for hydration measurements. Most from that series are not recorded in this table because they are highly imperfect (better specimens were not sacrificed for sectioning).

Microblade core RkIh-28:23 (Pl. 8A). The history of this core is relatively clear. An obsidian pebble was decapitated and the resultant flake scar served as the platform for bladelet removal. First, however, the sides were formed through removal of large flakes from the base of the core nodule. Cortical surface remains on the upper part of the back of the core. Four or five short microblades were removed from the face. Two complete microblade flutes are in the order of 7 mm wide and 28-34 mm long. The specimen measures 28 mm wide, 21 mm thick and 38 mm high. The platform angle is c̲ 60 degrees. It was beginning to assume a wedge shape.

Microblade core platform tablets--There are two objects in this category.

Obsidian tablet RkIh-28:28 removed most of the top of the core but failed to removed one lateral edge of the platform. It appears to have been detached from the rear of the core. Five fluted facets are present but they probably do not represent the entire face edge of the tablet. It measures 45 (face to rear)x26x6 mm.

The faceted front edge of the platform has been removed from tablet RkIh-28:18a by means of laterally directed spalling or flaking. This feature may be due to 90 degree core rotation, platform edge rejuvenation or other causes. The tablet presently measures 39x31 mm.

Nonobsidian specimen RkIh-28:18b (Pl. 8O) encompasses an entire platform surface which measures 19 mm deep by 23 mm wide (maximum depth of the top of the core from its front to back extends beyond the platform area and is 25 mm). The scalloped edge with traces of microblade facets in places is irregular and extends two thirds the distance around the perimeter of the tablet. Tablet removal was through a blow directed to the front or side of the core.

Single-edged unifaces--The one complete specimen is on a thick flake 54 mm long with cortex at each end. One additional, fragmental, specimen (Pl. 8K) appears to be made on a blade, but primary retouch of its bevelled side may have been done on the core, prior to formation of two dorsal blade facets and removal of this piece from the core. After it was detached there was further retouch and crushing of the edge.

Assessment and Interpretation

The elevation at RkIh-28 probably attracted people throughout prehistory, and therefore there is no particular reason that all the finds there should represent a single prehistoric component. Technologically, the industries in Clusters A and B differ from one another, but within Cluster B there is technological coherence in the microblade/blade industry. At least one end scraper and one uniface recovered there are formed on products of the blade industry. Cluster B thus belongs essentially to a single component, the only possible uncertainty being the bifaces, and they were closely associated with specimens of the blade/microblade industry.

Abundant debitage, unfinished bifaces, and byproducts of core preparation show that RkIh-28 was a flaking station. The site also could have served as a lookout. It may have been sufficiently close to potential kill locations to serve also as a camp site, as finds of end scrapers, side scrapers and two point bases suggest. Other camp locations in the vicinity might have been at nearby small lakes that we did not examine.

While obsidian cores were and utilized on the site, others not of obsidian were used to some extent but not exhausted, and apparently were taken away when people left. Evidence for this consists of the three nonobsidian microblades (and one microblade reject) and core platform tablet. Each microblade is of a different lithology, showing production from different cores. The platform tablet provides evidence that at least one core, other than those of obsidian, had been in the hands of the occupants (microblades only do not demonstrate this, because they could have been brought into the site alone from elsewhere). Less than 20 flakes not of obsidian were recovered. One can envision that a small group arrived from beyond Batza Téna with chert implements and at least one microblade core. They renewed their raw material with an abundant supply of Batza Téna obsidian from which they proceeded to make number of cores, microblades and bifaces. And then they moved on.

Inasmuch as blade industries or combined blade and microblade industries tend to be uncommon and early in Alaska--Akmak (Anderson 1970b) is and example--a relatively early age is possible for RkIh-28. Obsidian hydration measurements form a highly variable series, with a Coefficient of Variation of 40.4 (Clark 1984:97) even though the measures specimens came from a subsurface context. This makes me less than confident of the suitability of estimating the age of this assemblage on the basis of the average of the hydration series which is 2.02 microns. That hydration normally would indicate an age of 5000 years at a 0.82 microns squared geometric rate, less at a faster rate. These are mid- or late mid-range dates compared to the earliest dated microblade assemblages from Alaska. Large spear or lance blades with pointed bases may have chronological significance, though it is not clear that such points are restricted to a single period, and as yet Alaskan contexts of this style point are poorly dated. Specimen RkIh-28:34, the single item in the hydration series that is not a microblade, has a hydration measurement of 2.61 microns or an equivalent age of about 8000 years which meets my expectations for the age of the industry. But hydration dating on the basis of single specimens is unreliable, and the 0.82 micron rate may be too slow (cf. Kunz 1984).

Site RlIg-37

RlIg-37 (Fig. 4.3) is located on incipiently raised ground on flat land one km southeast of Lake 324, near the edge of a very small pond. The 1968 Utopia burn had killed the small stand of birch trees at the site and had consumed much of the organic litter and rootmat there (Fig. 4.3). This exposed a small area of flakes and microblades. Through trowelling we recovered additional specimens, in 1971, to a depth of as much as 15 cm in the underlying soil. The distribution of artifacts within this 4-m-square plot was somewhat T-shaped (e.g.,two corners were barren). The site is very inconspicuous and it would not have been investigated had it not been on one of our reconnaissance routes. The collection should represent a single component created within the space of no more than a few days. Therefore, it is interesting to note that soil processes had redistributed the artifacts vertically through 15 cm of soil although material was concentrated at the soil/organic mat interface due, presumably, to the conjoint effects of frost sorting and frost disturbance. Many specimens sectioned for hydration dating showed effects of burning. Some of these produced usable hydration readings but others showed no hydration.

Collection

The collection represents various aspects of microblade and core production from obsidian.
There also the base of a notched point and a select chert flake fragment (Table 4.3). Core form
(a variety of wedge core) and exclusive devotion of knapping to one industry distinguish RlIg-37
from other local sites with microblades.   The cores, as determined from the examination of
fragments, had elongate to elliptical platforms (Pl. 9H), were roughly bifaced and pointed at the
back, and initially there was a bifacially prepared edge at the front from which microblades
subsequently were detached. Platforms were formed or trimmed through retouch directed from
both sides and the front of the core. Platform renewal through platform tablet removal also was
practised.   However, this was done in a cruder manner than is the case for typical Palaeo-Arctic
tradition cores.   Possibly, though, the sample is biased through its small size.   A further
consideration is that greater crushing and shattering of obsidian, compared to chert, during
preparation and renewal makes these core fragments less definitive than otherwise comparable
chert specimens. A noteworthy attribute seen on several platform tablets or fragments, is crushing
and grinding of the edge of the platform. This variety of microblade core contrasts with those in
which there is little preparation other than to decapitate a pebble in order to obtain a platform
and for which the pebble itself served as a blank without any need for further shaping (cf. RkIh-28
microblade core and three specimens from RkIh-32). These are wedgeshaped cores, though as
commented on above they are not Palaeo-Arctic (Denali or Campus) cores. The two principal
fragments upon which this assessment is based are described below.

TABLE 4.3.   COLLECTION FROM SITE RlIg-37

No.	Identification	Description
1	Notched point frag.	Obsidian, basal fragment, concave base well pre-pared, edges smoothed; 14.7 mm across the notch
7	Platform tablets & probable fragments	Obsidian
1	Core fragment	Described in the text, 20 mm high
152	Microblades	Microblades, attempted microblades, rejects and elongate core preparation flakes; Table 4.4
x	Flakes	1240 g

Core tablet RlIg-37:223 (Pl. 9H) includes the complete platform and top part of the core
minus most of one side. From this specimen the following attributes are recorded:
Platform shape: elliptical, pointed at the back.
Platform preparation: various generations of flake scars; at fluted face edge there is one medium
and several small flake scars originating from the front of the core.
Platform-to-face angle: approximately 90°.
Platform (core) width: 18.7 mm.

Platform depth (length front to back): 22 mm (which is 2 mm less than core length). Direction of tablet removal: from front of core.

Back of core: acute, bifacially flaked in rough, random manner.

Sides: large flakes removed from platform edge (observed on one side).

TABLE 4.4.   MICROBLADES FROM SITE RlIg-37

No.	Segment	L	W	T	Arrises	Remarks
RlIg-37:...						
62	M	18	7.1	1.6	1-2	
63	P	20	7.45	3.0	3	
66	PM	23	8.25	2.8	2	
67	M	19	6.9	3.1	1-2	Near distal, uneven
73	M	22	4.9	1.9	2-3	
81	P	20	8.25	2.1	1	
82	PM	30	8.2	2.0	2	Relatively good
83	PM	28	10.1	2.3	2	Feather-edged reject? hydration meas.
95	M	24	7.1	2.1	1-2	Humped, tapered, T&W at wide end
102	P	14	5.8	2.0	2	
103	PM	22	6.0	2.0	1	
110	PM	27	5.4	2.0	2	Better specimen, not perfect
111	P	20	13.3	2.6	2	Possibly a feathered-edge reject; hydration measured
115	M	13	9.9	2.6	1	
121	P	16	5.8	2.02	1-2	
124	M	16	7.1	2.7	2	
137	M	15	5.7	1.04	2	
138	M	15	8.6	2.04	2	Expands, T&W taken at wide end
140	P	15	6.4	1.6	2	Width expands
152	M	11	7.0	1.65	1	
179	P	20	9.15	2.9	2	Hydration measured
182	M	17	7.04	1.44	2-3	
183	MD	27	7.6	2.8	2	Tapers, W&T taken at wide end
184	PM	22	6.6	1.9	1-2	Tapers, W&T taken at wide end
185	PM	26	9.9	2.1	2	Relatively good
186	M	25	6.8	2.2	2	Curved and tapered
187	PM	21	6.7	2.0	1	
189	PM	25	8.6	2.0	3-4	Defective beyond midpoint
198	M	15	6.14	1.9	1	
204	M	12	5.1	1.88	1-2	
206	PM	16	4.78	1.05	1	Probably undersize reject
Means, mm			7.34	2.11	1.8	N = 31

Core fragment RlIg-37:221 lacks the front or fluted face but it again exhibits a roughly bifaced back or dorsum and preparation of one side through removal, from the platform, of two elongate flakes or oversize microblades. The platform is narrow, 9 mm wide, and the fragment is up to 11 mm wide. The platform is formed by part of a large negative flake scar that originated from the side of the core during an earlier stage of shaping.

Among 152 microblade segments, attempted   microblades and related spalls there are 7 specimens that have a bifacially prepared ridge. Often the flaking on one side of the ridge is finer than that on the other side. These are the first spalls removed from the bifacially-trimmed front of the core. Although both the front and back of the core was bifacially shaped, there is no evidence that the core preform was a biface or that the platform was formed through removal of so-called ski spalls.

Part of the lateral surface of the core is present on 23 microblades. Occasionally this consists of cortex or broad irregular flake scars on one facet, but usually it consists of medium-size horizontally oriented flake scars. Such flake scars originate from the bifacial retouch at the front of the core that was not completely removed by the first ridged flake.

Virtually the entire microblade collection consists of rejects, attempted removals and products of processual stages. Evidently, better microblades were carefully garnered and taken away from the knapping site. A series of less-flawed specimens is described in Table 4.4.

Assessment and Interpretation

With the exception of three chert pieces, all specimens from this site are of obsidian. The only identified use for the obsidian is the production of microblades. The chert pieces are two flakes (possibly implement fragments) and a broken point base. In view of the inconspicuousness of this site location we would expect only one occupation there. The chert items probably were brought into the site from beyond Batza Téna and left there by the same people who produced the microblades. The type and amount of debitage present and other artifacts show that both core preparation and subsequent production of microblades took place at this location.

A series of 16 microblades or microblade-related flakes was measured to obtain an obsidian hydration date for the assemblage (Clark 1984b). The average hydration of 1.49 microns is equivalent to an age of 2666 years (before 1984) at the 0.82 microns squared rate. When burned specimens that show no hydration are excluded, this series has a relatively low Coefficient of Variation at 15.1. Relative to the temporal range of microblade industries in the north, this assemblage and its prepared cores (see below) is relatively late. On the basis of this dating, the single industry focus, and the presence of a sidenotched point fragment it is suggested that this site is a specialized activity area the same cultural tradition as Batza Téna Tuktu (Chapter 5), though it may be several centuries earlier than BT Tuktu.

RkIg-47

Four clustered lots of microblade industry debitage were found on the northwestern flank of Basecamp Ridge, near its outer end, in 1970. Site RkIg-47 occurs in mixed forest near the front edge of a relatively undistinguished flat area. It covers a linear extent of 26 m though most material occurred in half that area. The matrix is very stony soil.

Figure 4.3. Collecting from the surface of site RlIg-37.

Some of the lithic clusters showed poorly on the surface and one (D) was discovered only upon reexamination of the site. But others were well exposed on the surface and all material present was confined to a very shallow depth of no greater than 3 cm within the soil. Each flake cluster ranged from slightly less than 1 m to nearly 2 m in diameter. A sparse scatter of flakes and implements also was found distributed over the site elsewhere. Cluster A consisted of a massive concentration of flakes weighing 1.4 kg. Although this debitage is weak in linear flakes and attempted microblades expected from the preforming and use of microblade cores, one core and two platform tablets actually were recovered among the flakes, and bifacial trimming flakes are absent. The latter, would have indicated biface production. Cluster A thus appears to illustrate very wasteful use of raw material to produce microblade cores. The remaining three clusters had less debitage, weighing 0.6 kg in total, but were more strongly oriented towards microblade production.

Collection

The collection consists of microblade cores, microblades, core and microblade production byproducts including core tablets, and an scraper and hammerstone (Table 4.5-4.8). Recovered microblades are grossly defective. The less defective specimens, though still rejects, and short segments are described in Table 4.6. No means are calculated for the measurements because we do no consider this to be a representative collection. The cores are characterized by their small size, lack of preforming (but see below comment), and extensive areas of cortex remaining on the sides, back and base. Core tablets, described in Table 4.8, are larger than the platforms of the four recovered cores. One flake from the retouched front of a core is 52 mm long which is considerably greater than the height of the face of any recovered core. This evidence for larger cores suggests that the present specimens are reduced remnants. Retouch on three facial or ridged spalls shows that there was some preforming or retouch of the front area to become the fluted face. Flakes and microbladelike spalls from the sides of the cores nevertheless lack the scars of horizontally-directed flakes such as were found to be common on flakes and on primary (first course) microblades from the preformed cores of site RlIg-37. Evidently, very different core technologies were used at the two sites. Those from RkIg-47 are not wedgeshaped.

Discussion and Dating

With the exception of the endscraper, the assemblage is technologically coherent and single-focused. All loci can be assigned to a single component of occupation because the site location is relatively obscure. Whether or not the several clusters and scatter of lithic material were each left by different knappers, from a band that had visited the obsidian source, or all are the waste piles of a single person left successively during a short time span is a mute question. There are no fits of material linking different clusters.

An attempt was made to estimate the age of RkIg-47 through obsidian hydration measurements. Two good slides from Cluster D showed no hydration; three slides from two Cluster C specimens gave 0.94 to 1.02 microns hydration; and two slides from a Cluster B core face fragment gave 0.84 and 1.09 microns. The four positive values when averaged indicate an age of about 1100 years at the 0.82 microns squared rate, or less at a faster rate. Later, a series of slides from Cluster B flakes from a single obsidian nodule was measured (Clark 1984b:102). This nodule, partially refitted from several flakes, appears with reasonable certainty to be the source of the core from which the sectioned Cluster B core face flake was derived. The objective surface for 5000 years without being disseminated. At a moderately faster rate of hydration, though, 2.03 microns of hydration would result in a date within the younger range of known was to test the homogeneity of hydration of flakes from the same nodule. Average hydration in this case is 2.03 microns, which is equivalent to an age of about 5000 years at the slow geometric rate. These results are discordant and fail to provide very satisfactory age estimates for RkIg-47. It is unlikely that competent microblade technology still existed in the area as recently as 1100 years ago, or later if one, with reason, calibrates the obsidian with a rate faster than 0.82 microns.

TABLE 4.5. ARTIFACTS FROM SITE RkIg-47

Identification and Description	A	B	C	D	X	Total
Retouched flake, roughly bifaced						
unfinished edge on cortical flake					1	1
End scraper, see Table 9.4					1	1
Hammerstone, flat, circular quartzite						
62x57x30, lightly crushed (Pl.9I)					1	1
Possible utilized flakes, side scrapers		3	1			4
Microblade cores, Table 4.7 (Pl. 9A-C)	1		2		1	4
Platform tablet (Pl. 9J-K)	3	1	1	1		6
Possible platform rejuvenation flakes			3			3
Core face flake (Pl. 9G)		3	1			4
Bifaced ridged flake					1	1
Unifaced ridged flake		1			1	2
Blade, small, single arrise		1			1	2
Microbladelike flake with cortex or						
irreg. flaking from side of core		8	5	4	1	14
Clean-facet microblades & rejects	4	11	10	10	6	41

Column X: Finds at large.

TABLE 4.6. MICROBLADES FROM SITE RkIg-47

No.	Location	Segment	L	W	T	Arrises
6	A	P	19	8.8	2.0	1-2
7	A	P	13	9.9	2.2	2
---	A	PM	24	8.4	3.3	1
18	B	PM	29	10.8	2.5	2
21	B	P	25	10.6	2.8	2
23	B	P reject	24	12.5	2.4-4	1
26	B	P	19	10.0	2.1	2
27	B	P poor	18	8.5	2.3	2
31	B	M	20	6.6	1.6	
42	C	PM reject	27	11.5	1.5-2.7	1
49	C	PM	26	8.5	2.1	2
51	C	M	19	6.3	1.6	2-3
58+62	C	P	19	9.2	2.3	2
60	C	M	13	6.3	1.6	2
61	C	P	13	5.8	1.5	2
69	D	M	16	9.1	1.5	2+
74	D	D	13	7.05	1.4	2
78	D	M	--	7.3	1.94	2
79	D	P	12	6.2	1.3	2
81	D	M	--	5.42	1.04	1
92	General	P	17	6.2	1.1	1-2
105	General	M	22	10.1	2.7	2
107	General	M poor	12	7.0	1.2	1-2
108	General	P reject	16	6.3	1.8	1

TABLE 4.7. MICROBLADE CORES FROM SITE RkIg-47

No.	H	W	D	Sides	Back	Base	Platform	Angle
RkIg-47:...								
10	26.4	21.0	16.4*	Fluted face,	Single	Cortex	Small flakes	67°
	26.4	21.0	17	linear scars	flake scar		from front	
	Almost cylindrical (Pl. 9C).							
47	22+	14	20+	Cortex/	Cortex/	Missing	Flakes from	90°
				missing	missing		side	
	Incomplete, cortical surfaces, no shaping of preform (Pl. 9B).							
93	28	24	12.2	Cortex	Cortex	Cortex &	2 flakes from	66°
	30	28	25			2 flakes	front & side	
	Made on unpreformed irregular pebble. Flutes arch (not illus.).							
110	25.4	22	10.2	Fluted face,	Single	Cortex	Single dished	67°
	24	26.5	11.8	wide flake	flake &		flake from	
				& cortex	cortex		face	
	Remnant? (Pl. 9A, Fig. 4.1b)							

*   Measurements on the upper line are (H) height of the fluted face as seen in the longest microblade removal flute, (W) platform width and (D) distance from front to back of the core without regard to the orientation of the platform; lower line values are the maximum height, width and length of the core mass with the platform oriented horizontally.

TABLE 4.8. CORE PLATFORM TABLETS FROM SITE RkIg-47

No.	W	D	T	Description
RkIg-47:...				
4	47	34+*	13.8-0	Original platform is a large flake scar with fine edge retouch. Removed by front oblique blow. Scalloped edge scars are small blade width (Pl. 9K)
5	26.2	25.5+	5	Front blow removal. Fluted edge poorly represented and tablet identification is uncertain.
A	39	32+	5	Front blow removal. Original platform formed by fine & medium retouch from the front (Pl. 9J).
B	34	27+	4-5	Incomplete, width-depth orientation uncertain.
C	31	27+	7-0	Front blow removal. Original platform irregularly flaked from the front.
65+	35	26	4-6	Front or rear blow removal; edges damaged, fluted
66				face not identified; original platform flaked from several sides. Similar to uncataloged Loc. B. tablet.

*The "+" indicates that the tablet fails to encompass the entire platform.
A, B and C are uncataloged specimens in the flake lots.

On the other hand, one might question how flake clusters could exist on the microblade production. The core type found at RkIg-47 differs from that of the preceding two sites discussed in this chapter, for which ages between 2000 and 5000 years are proposed. Inasmuch as the present site probably dates within the same time span as the other two, probably near the earlier end, this situation brings up the question of whether there was rapid changes in core types or whether the various microblade cores at Batza Téna are coeval.

Site RkIh-32

Several sites were found around the shores of <u>Batzatimunket</u> (Obsidian Hill Lake, but possibly in error for <u>Toban Naka-ish Todlioden</u>). Two of these sites, from which the Batza Téna Tuktu assemblage comes, will be described in the next chapter. The cultural placement of the present site is uncertain, and possibly more than one component is represented. Nevertheless, the collection deserves notice here on the basis of a series of microblade cores. Site RkIh-32 is located on the west side of the lake, farthest from the base of Batzatiga and closest to the Koyukuk River. A meander of the Koyukuk swings within 2 km of the site and there are old swales showing that the river once was closer. However, the topography and superficial sediments at the site and in its immediate vicinity are not those of the Koyukuk River flats but appear to be more local and are similar to those found around the flanks of Batzatiga. The site lies on a low isthmus between two small lakes. Essentially, the only relief it has is a very narrow ice-shove ridge which incorporates archaeological material (Fig. 4.4). Excepting a notched pebble and some obsidian flakes recovered from the ice-shove ridge, all the collections from RkIh-32 were found scattered over a 100-m-long strip of sandy beach.

In 1971 we revisited the site, following surface collecting in 1970, and made an effort to understand its origin. Obsidian flakes were found from the surface of the ice shove ridge to a depth of 15 cm, and in one place were 30 cm deep (or more if one compensates for the fact that erosion has removed the original surface). The flakes tended to cluster at the back edge of the narrow ridge which immediately drops away to low ground little or no higher than the lake shore. Large spruce trees growing upright on the ridge show that this feature did not develop only during the last few decades. Nevertheless, in places the ice-shove ridge has an overhang at its back edge which should have collapsed or settled if it was a very ancient feature. The site probably was formed on relatively low ground and then shoved up and partially incorporated or rolled up into the ridge. Ice-shove ridges usually are narrow, and subsequent erosion has further reduced the width of this one. It now is too narrow for any excavation sections larger than one metre to be placed there. Presumably, erosion has resulted in the redeposition of many artifacts on the shore, though it is possible that the artifacts on the shore are not derived from the same context as those in the ice-shove. No further beach collection was recovered in 1971. Most of the flakes on the ridge were not associated with any implements and were discarded there.

Collection

All flakes found on the beach, amounting to 8 kg, were collected in 1970. We failed to recover any additional material by wading through the higher level water in 1971. The flakes generally are large and somewhat abraded, evidently as a result of their erosional history. Although several bladelike flake and microblade cores were found, few core preparation flakes and microblades were recovered. This may be because of an erosional history that favors recovery of large flakes in surface collections. A varied artifact assemblage was found, including,

Figure 4.4.   Two views of the front of Site RkIh-32, taken when the water level
               was low in May 1970.

in addition to the microblade industry, an adze, two types of scrapers, a point, notched pebble and an abrader fragment (Table 4.9). Several items are of material other than obsidian. RkIh-32 is the only Batza Téna site to have a ground adze. It was disappointing to find that a site with this range of lithic raw material and suite of implements was not excavatable.

TABLE 4.9. COLLECTION FROM SITE RkIh-32

No.	Identification	Description
1	Point	Tip-medial section, chert knife or point (Pl.10G)
2	Bifaces, complete	Unfinished, ovoid, each has cortex at each end; a:53x37x10, b: 57x42x13.8 mm
7	Biface fragments	Unfinished, at a rudimentary stage
4	Biface hinged edge frag.	
5	End scrapers	In Table 9.4. One is chert (Pl. 10I-K)
6	Bevelled/utilized flakes or fragments	Formats vary, some distinctly bevelled, 1 has convex edge and V-shaped notch, 4 not obsidian include a chert bladelike flake (Pl. 10H).
3	Possible bevelled/ flakes	Retouch may be natural but format is suggestive of knives and scrapers
3	Microblade cores	Described in text (Pl. 10F, Fig. 4.1a)
1	Small bladelet core	Described in text (Pl. 10D-E)
3	Bladelike flake core	Described in text
3	Flake cores	Nondescript & flatfaced (Pl. 10 A-B, 24B)
2	Microblades	Hydration measured; good, one has single arrise
1	Adze	Pecked and ground, well formed, acute edge, nearly symmetrical bit profile, 103x53x21 mm, impure nephrite (Pl. 10L)
1	Whetstone fragment?	Chip of granular stone, parts of 2 intersecting ground facets present
1	Notched pebble	On 2 sides, flat 68x48 (Pl. 10M)

A series of microblade and bladelike flake cores is described below. Further details of the collection are given in Table 4.9.

Cores--There is one prepared wedgeshaped microblade core and several cores that intergrade between unformalized microblade cores and flake cores. A series of these cores appears to demonstrate continuity between and sameness of flake and microblade production techniques. Some cores are fresh appearing. Others are not, but they have suffered erosion on the lake shore; thus condition is not likely to indicate differences in age. Each core is described below, where appropriate in a progression from microblade cores to flake cores. Key data appear in Table 4.10.

RkIh-32:25 (Pl. 10F, Fig. 4.1a) has a roughly bifaced wedge element. The lateral faces, between the wedge and fluted face, are relatively even though narrow, and were prepared from both the top and base of the core. The elliptical platform is pointed at the rear. Originally it may have been formed as a single flake or fracture surface but it has been retouched and adjusted to a more obtuse angle through relatively fine flaking directed from both sides of the platform edge. The last course of microblades detached from this core was narrow: 3.4 mm and 3.9 mm wide for complete flutes and less for laterally truncated flutes.

TABLE 4.10.   RkIh-32 CORES

No.	Type	H*	Face L	Platform D	W	Platform to face angle**
RkIh-32:...						
25	Preformed microblade	30	40	29	17	55 degrees
48	Microblade	54	54	39	24	90+ degrees
24	Microblade-like flake	40	44	25	35	67 degrees
	Fluted face is lateral, hence platform D & W are switched					
21	Aborted small flake?	54	--	37	20	Oblique
	Platform oblique to all axes, measurements are for core mass without reference to platform orientation					
17	Linear flake	65	55	33	55	Like #24
	Face is lateral, hence functional platform D & W are switched					

*   Height (H) is measured perpendicular to the plane of the platform. This height often is shorter than the length (L) of the fluted face.
** Face here refers to the fluted face or front.

RkIh-32:48 (Pl. 10E) is on a pebble which has been decapitated, by a blow to the side that later became the fluted face, in order to provide a smooth, single flake scar surface platform. Several long, straight, wide microblades and small blades were detached forming a fluted face that wraps part way around the core. The rest of the perimeter is in cortex. Relative complete blade scars are 6 to 10 mm wide exclusive of a 19-mm-wide decortication spall. This specimen has assumed a tongue shape that may have been determined by the original shape of the pebble blank.

Core RkIh-32:24 (Pl. 10D) is formed on a split or decapitated pebble. Short narrow blades have been detached from one side of the core, hence the long dimension of the platform is essentially coeval with the width of the fluted face (descriptive terms for wedgeshaped cores apply poorly). The flutes run obliquely down the face of the core. Bladelet scars are broad and uneven, ranging in the order of 7 to 13 mm width for three relatively complete ones. The lateral margins and back of the core are formed by a combination of large flake scars originating from various surfaces and cortex. One margin is truncated by breakage.

RkIh-32:21 (Pl. 10C) is a small obsidian pebble decapitated to provide a smooth striking platform. The width was reduced through coarse flaking or fracturing of one side. Several flakes, none of them very long, were removed from that part of the core. I interpret this piece as a setup for an unformalized core from which attempted bladelet removal failed to meet requirements. Probably for that reason the core was discarded.

RkIh-32:17 (Pl. 10B) is a large version of RkIh-23:24. The shape of the core mass, platform to face angle, platform shape, mode of platform preparation (smooth scar left from pebble decapitation, bulb to the left), location of fluted face (on the side) and even the fact that the axis of the principal flake removal scar is oblique are attributes similarly expressed in both cores. Half or more of the perimeter of the present core is in cortex. The core may not have reached the stage of preparation where it could be exploited successfully. The two cores compared--the larger one (No. 17) a flake core setup, the smaller one (No. 24) a bladelet core or inexpertly used microblade core--appear to demonstrate continuity and sameness of production techniques.

RkIh-32:15 (Pl. 23K) is basically similar to and comparable in size to RkIh-32:17 but it represents a more advanced stage of trimming or exploitation for flake production. One side was removed or is broken. This specimen complements some observations reported above.

RkIh-32:20 (Pl. 10A) differs from all the preceding, at least in its apparently spent form. The flat face is formed primarily by three large flake scars. Evidence for a flatfaced flake core variety, to which this specimen might be attributed, is discussed in Chapter 9.

Assessment and Dating

Recovery of a range of tool types at RkIh-32, as well as obsidian flaking detritus, may indicate that this site was a base camp rather than simply a way station on the route to batza and a stopping point where craftsmen reduce their load by preforming obsidian implements on the way home. Even if mixed components are present, this assessment may characterize the overall focus of occupation there. Nevertheless, access to obsidian probably was the controlling reason for people being in the immediate area. RkIh-32 may have been a gateway camp for western access via the Koyukuk River or from regions located farther west. Evidence of this lies in the fact that seven nonobsidian (mostly chert) flaked items were recovered but all except one of the numerous flakes found are obsidian. The chert tools obviously were brought in from elsewhere. A similar situation occurs at the two nearby Batza Téna Tuktu sites (Chapter 5) where several nonobsidian artifacts were recovered.

For dating the site three artifact types have potential chronological value. (a) Notched pebbles appear in the Northern Archaic horizon, rarely also in the Denbigh Flint complex but they occur within a broad time range of as little as 1000 or 2000 years to as much as 6000 years ago. (b) The adze has its most common counterpart in Neoeskimo specimens of the last 1000 years, but the form also is reasonably common in sites of the Norton tradition which are as much as 2500 years old. Older ground adzes are known in the north, but tend to differ in format from the present specimen and possibly are not found at all in interior Alaska, Denbigh Flint complex specimens from Onion Portage excepted (Anderson 1988: Pl. 37). The RkIh-32 adze is made from material resembling very impure jade, in which case a Kobuk source and the more recent dating is probable, though there also are uncommon occurrences of jade in earlier Kobuk River components, again Onion Portage Denbigh for instance (Anderson 1988). Because of the fineness of this specimen, inexplicably lost by its prehistoric owner, we do not intend to undertake any analysis that will damage it. (c) Microblade cores more or less of wedge-shaped format with oval to elliptical platforms but not of the classic Palaeo-Arctic or Campus-Denali format occur through

Figure 4.5.   The other side of Site RkIh-32, seen from across a small lake
looking eastward with Batzatiga in the background.

a broad temporal and spatial range in Alaska. They particularly have a focus in northwestern
Alaska, where they are found in Onion Portage Denbigh (Anderson 1988: Fig. 91e), the Tuktu
complex (Campbell 1961), Girls' Hill in the Koyukuk Drainage (Gal 1976) and at Kurupa Lake
on the north side of the Brooks Range (Schoenberg 1985). Most of these sites appear to date
within the range of 3000 to 4500 years ago, but this type of core also comes from younger dating
site RlIg-37 described earlier in this chapter. But it is not possible to draw clear culture-historical
conclusions on the basis of the distribution of this core form since in many sites it co-occurs with
other varieties of microblade cores including tabular or Tuktu cores and classical wedge-shaped
cores of the Palaeo-Arctic tradition. The last are known to be as much as 10,700 years old
(Powers, Guthrie and Hoffecker 1983) and as recent as 1500 years old (Holmes 1988). The finest
wedgeshaped example from the site presently under consideration is generally similar to a Denali,
though it is thicker than the norm, but it lacks the distinctive Palaeo-Arctic modes of platform and
rejuvenation. The final piece of evidence leans on the fact that the microblade industry at the
Batza Téna Tuktu sites is about 2000 years old (Chapter 5). These factors together suggest a
plausible age for RkIh-32 in the order of 2000-3000 years provided that all the artifacts there are
essentially coeval. If they are not, we could have a basket of material dating from as recently as
500 years ago to 5000 years ago.

Triple hydration measurements   taken on the two RkIh-32 microblades suggest a somewhat greater age (unpublished data prepared by L. B. Davis).   Measurements   on one specimen are between 1.94 and 2.1 microns, those on the other microblade between 2.34 and 2.71 microns.   If the 0.82 geometric rate is applied, these yield average ages of approximately 4800 and 8000 years. A faster hydration rate may be preferred, and this would draw the hydration age down to the date range estimated above, but application of a faster rate to microblade assemblages already dated to the first millennium A.D. on the basis of the slow rate would make those other sites too recent. The small series of hydration measurements presents an enigma and may not satisfactorily date the site.

Finds From Other Sites

RlIg-46.   Core RlIg-46 (Pl. 9D) is a fine but exhausted wedgeshaped core. There remains an evenly retouched, competently bifaced dorsal element, a small platform area, and the face with six complete or partial microblade flutes. The platform remnant is formed from a series of small flake scars. Probably because of the small size of the remnant platform, it is not apparent that the core ever was rejuvenated through tablet removal. The longest microblade flute is 51.3 mm, which is the hight of the core now and probably also that of the original core in a less spent condition.   However, the original width was greater than the remnant 11.5 mm width. I am uncertain whether this specimen was entirely formed from a biface preform, for which category there is only specimen, RkIh-36:123, which is an otherwise basically different type. Probably only the dorsal element   and the now exhausted basal wedge were bifacially prepared, as is characteristic of wedgeshaped cores. Flaking of the dorsal edge is much finer than that seen on any other wedgeshaped core from Batza Téna. Other implements were recovered from RlIg-46 (cf. fluted point in Chapter 2) but they were widely dispersed and none were associated with the core. Only poorly formed or equivocal microblades came from this site.

Specimen RkIn-1 (Pl. 9E) is a typical well prepared wedgeshaped chert core. Possibly it is of the Campus or Palaeo-Arctic variety although this is not readily apparent because of the irregularly flaked platform. It measures 29 mm high, 27 mm from front to back, and 11.5 mm wide near the front of the platform. The platform was roughly trimmed from the sides and back. In its present condition it carries no evidence of rejuvenation through tablet removal. The roughly bifaced dorsal ridge curves under the core forming the wedgeshaped keel element. Two fluted arcs, one apparently being removed by the other, meet at the face at an approximate right angle, an attribute common in Palaeo-Arctic cores. This specimen was purchased at Huslia where it and a chert flake had been found in a shallow sand exposure within the present village. No further material was seen there by the writer although Huslia residents occasionally have found stone implements within the settlement.

RkIh-36 cores (Batza Téna Tuktu) (Pl. 11). Here we may briefly note the evidence for a microblade industry in the Batza Téna Tuktu phase. This information is presented in more detail in Chapter 5. Two microblade cores and a number of bladelike flake cores from this site represent three core types. A small number of microblades and bifaced ridged flakes from cores also were recovered. The cores for bladelike and microbladelike flakes show that there is formal and presumably technological blurring of the distinction between microblade technology and the production of flakes.

Specimen RkIh-36:454 is the fragmentary lower part of a microblade core. The keel and back appear to have been very roughly shaped in the bifacial mode. It apparently is comparable to the preformed wedgeshaped core RkIh-32:25 discussed above.

A very different type of core from RkIh-36, No. 123, is made on a small biface. It is rounded at one end. The highly acute angled fluted face and platform presently form the other end. The platform was produced through removal of part of the biface edge by a blow comparable to burination directed from the end of the preform. This is the only core of this rare type from Batza Téna. More common core with similar attributes found in Japan are called Oshoroko core burins (M. Yoshizaki personal communication).

SaEw-1, Sithlemenkat Lake (Pl. 9F). The top edge of a chert microblade core, minus a small portion, together with part of the face, are represented by tablet SaEw-1:1. The platform is ovoid, measuring 29 by 21.5 mm. Microblade facets are present around two thirds of the circumference, the remaining third being unobservable (largely missing). The flat platform consists of varied-scale retouch directed from all sides of the platform edge, though the finest trimming is devoted largely to one end of the platform. Judging from the distribution of platform retouch, the fluted face accounted for one half the perimeter of the core and platform tablet detachment was from the rear. The platform to face angle is slightly obtuse, approximately 100 degrees. This core probably was of the wedge to semiwedge, oval to elliptical platform, non-Denali type noted previously as common to northwestern Alaska

Core XI-E:41 (Pl. 23I). This bladelet core illustrates the intergradation between unformalized flake cores and microblade cores. Further examples are RkIh-34:14 described in Chapter 5 and several RkIh-32 cores described in the preceding section. Had the flake scars been more regular and narrower, the present example would have been classified as an unequivocal microblade core. This core forms a scalene trianguloid mass 38 mm high (platform held horizontal). The original height was greater before the base was removed along with the largest flake from the perimeter. It is 44 mm wide across the platform and 34 mm from front to the back of the platform. Several bladelet scars extend down the fluted face which occupies half the perimeter. The back of the core, which is roughly formed and includes an area of cortex, is nearly vertical while the fluted face forms an angle of c 60 degrees with the platform. The platform is a broad oval shaped area largely formed from a single flake scar. This red obsidian specimen was found on hillside of Batzatiga behind site RkIh-36.

Conclusions: Discussion of Core Varieties

Classification

Several formal categories of microblade cores are present in the Batza Téna collections, the absence of classic Campus and Tuktu cores notwithstanding. These are summarized below. Some core forms intergrade and the technological attributes of cores can occur in various combinations. These date should be approached in the format of an attribute analysis, but for the convenience of discussion here known attribute combinations will be treated as core types. The following statement, however, is not meant to be a classification of Alaskan cores. There are two broad categories: (A) wedgeshaped cores and (B) cores that are not wedgeshaped. The latter may be roughly conical, cylindrical, formalized tabular or flat faced (Tuktu) and imperfectly or unformalized flat faced. Some Class B cores imperfect share attributes of the base and back, e.g., taper or wedging, with wedgeshaped cores.

A1. Classic Campus or Denali (Palaeo-Arctic) wedgeshaped cores (Pl. 9E). Though these are defined as wedgeshaped cores, they are distinguished on the basis of their narrow shape, platform preparation from the side and rejuvenation through tablet removal directed from the front (fluted face). Although the keel and back are to varying degrees trimmed bifacially, the core blank is not a biface. This type apparently has not been recovered from Batza Téna (sometimes a particular specimen is not definitive) but has been reported from the Bonanza Creek tributary of the South Fork by Holmes (1971) from Girls' Hill in the upper drainage (Gal 1976) and may be the type of the core from Huslia noted above.

---. Core or burin. In some cases archaeologists have difficulty distinguishing between burin and very narrow wedgeshaped cores made on flake blanks. One of the Minchumina cores can be taken as an example (Holmes 1986: Fig. 41 a). Anderson recognizes a Choris burin spall core at Onion Portage (Anderson 1988). Present in Kobuk-Alatna headwaters (Clark 1974b, Kunz 1984) but probably not at Batza Téna.

A2. Core blank is a roughly bifaced discoid. An uncommon type. After the discoid has been prepared it is split or a portion is removed to make way for the platform. Further preparation and use (rejuvenation) follow the classic Campus or Palaeo-Arctic mode and the microblade cores may not be distinguishable from form A1. Not recognized at Batza Téna.

A3. Prepared wedgeshaped cores lacking Campus-Denali platform attributes (Pl. 8A, 9H, 10F). These are prepared wedgeshaped cores with more randomly flaked platforms that lack the mode of rejuvenation and other attributes of Denali platform preparation. More than one variety may be present; some were rejuvenated through tablet removal, some--Denbigh Flint cores for instance--were not. Platforms tend to be elliptical (ranging from oval to a very broad ellipse) and are wider than Campus Palaeo-Arctic cores. The more circular form (in plan, subcylindrical in profile) grades into the B series. Present at Batza Téna. Microblade flutes tend to carry farther over onto the sides than is the case with classic Palaeo-Arctic cores.

A4. Core made from a well prepared elongate or leafshaped biface (Pl. 11 O). The platform is prepared through detachment of a ridged spall or edge of the biface (Yubetsu technique). One specimen was recovered in Batza Téna Tuktu. This is a rare microblade core type in Alaska, hence the sample base for description is small. However, the biface blank format probably continues to characterize the appearance of the core throughout its use.

A5. Fortuitous wedgeshaped cores (Pl. 10E). These microblade cores on unprepared blanks (thus the distinction between them and form A3) assume a wedge shape through use or from careful selection of the flake or pebble blank. This passive type intergrades with flake and blade cores of the B series. Present at Batza Téna, as at RkIh-32.

B1. Subcylindrical cores with prepared platforms (Pl. 9C). This form grades into and carries over some attributes of from A3 wedgeshaped cores. These microblade cores are only roughly cylindrical. There is sufficient differentiation between areas of the core for fluted faces, sometimes sides, and backs to be distinguished. They may taper slightly towards the base, which possibly increases through use, that gives the face profile a slight wedge shape. The fluted face extends onto the sides of the core. Platform rejuvenation is through tablet removal. A variant in northwestern Canada tends to be rectangular. Present at Batza Téna.

B2. Cylindrical to conical cores lacking platform preparation. These cores are B1 except they are less formalized and more variable. Some assume a wedge shape and intergrade with or become part of the formal rance of the A5 cores. The microblade cores intergrade with flake cores. Present at Batza Téna.

B3. Tuktu tabular cores. This is a very straight or flat-faced tabular core with formalized preparation of the sides and flat back. Platforms are flaked from the front of the core and are not rejuvenated through detachment of platform tablets. Absent at Batza Téna.

B4. Unformalized flat faced cores (Pl. 9B, 9A may be a B3/B4 intergrade). These cores depart from the ideal controlled or formalized format of the Tuktu core and being a passive type they exhibit considerable variation. There are both microblade cores and blade cores, though on the latter there may be only 2 or 3 flutes on the face. Fluted faces may be less than perfectly flat. Broad, spent A3 cores may resemble this type. In their simplest form these are pebbles that have hade bladelets detached from one surface, though usually the platform is retouched (to adjust the platform angle?). Present at Batza Téna.

Wedgeshaped Cores

A distinction can be made between wedgeshaped cores for which the blank is a biface and the striking platform was formed by the detachment of part of the biface edge or so-called ski spalls (starting with a triangular ridged spall), and wedgeshaped cores fashioned in other ways. Only one example of the first variety was found at Batza Téna, core RkIh-36:123 noted above. This mode of initial platform preparation is uncommon in Northwestern North America. However, one may be led to such expectations by earlier, widespread comparisons with microblade industries of Japan employing the Yubetsu technique (Hadleigh-West 1967a) together with the identification of a form of this technique at Bezya in Alberta (Le Blanc and Ives 1986) and the perhaps erroneous attribution of many North American cores to this production system by Smith (1971, 1974). Moreover, North American wedgeshaped cores often are identified with the Dyuktai cores of Siberia, though clearly the Dyuktai platform preparation sequence determined by Flenniken (1987), which entails detachment of triangular ridged spalls, and secondarily, flat ski spalls, differs from the common Campus or Palaeo-Arctic core technique. Evidently, Dyuktai utilized more than one mode of platform preparation or core subvariety.

Excluding the core type just discussed, wedgeshaped cores can be categorized as those which were more or less formally shaped at the blank or preform stage, and those which assumed a wedge or tongue shape as microblade production ensued. These two categories probably intergrade, but it is the cores produced on prepared blanks that receive sophisticated or specialized platform preparation and rejuvenation. Examples of cores not based on formally shaped wedge preforms include RkIh-36:57 which is an unfinished microblade core preform or a linear flake core (Chapter 5) and some RkIh-32 specimens, while RkIh-28 specimen 23 is an intergrade.

In the more formalized preparation of wedgeshaped cores, the back of the core often is roughly bifaced, though sometimes it is left unprepared, while more attention goes into shaping the base or wedge element. This bifacial preforming may be applied to a pebble, split pebble or flake blank or, far less frequently to a rough discoid biface blank. The latter is illustrated by one or more specimens from site KbTx-2 located in the Yukon territory (Clark 1992) while the former is very widespread. Within this group there are differences in the mode of platform preparation and rejuvenation. It has not been determined, though, that these differences have any particular cultural and historical significance. One mode, the Campus or Denali set of attributes, is characteristic of early Palaeo-Arctic assemblages, Dry Creek for instance, although it also is present in assemblages of very modest age, at 4600-year-Old Otter Falls (Cook 1968) and in probably more recent Minchumina Lake occupations (Holmes 1986)

On Campus-Denali cores, the platform is prepared through removing flakes transversely (Hayashi 1968 uses the term "latitudinal") across the platform from one of its edges, e.g., originating from the side of the core. Preparation sometimes did not extend entirely across the top of the piece to the back of the core which was left more elevated and more roughly fashioned than the platform. Powers, Guthrie and Hoffecker (1983:85) refer to this feature as a hook or spur. At this stage the platform often is inclined obliquely to the plane of the core, The leading or high edge of the platform usually is crushed, apparently as a deliberate step in preparing the core. During microblade production, platforms were rejuvenated or adjusted in the following ways. The front of the platform was trimmed by removing small rejuvenation flakes or a short platform tablet. The blow by which this was done was directed to the very front of the face of the core. Platforms also were renewed or further shaped by removing a longer platform tablet or thin slice from the entire top of the core, the blow directed as previously noted. Often the cores that receive this treatment have narrow long platforms. This procedure contrasts with the mode of tablet removal often seen on wide or subcylindrical cores, in which the blow is, instead, directed to the side of the platform, and initial platform preparation appears to have followed more varied procedures.

None of the Batza Téna wedgeshaped cores clearly shows the classic A1 mode of platform preparation and rejuvenation described above (though some have been rejuvenated) and tend to have a broader ovoid shape in plan. This leads me to believe that the modes or attribute combinations discussed above have some historical-cultural distinctiveness, typological intergradation and the coeval occurrence of some types notwithstanding. It may be noted, though that Campus or classic Palaeo-Arctic cores are found at sites located in every direction from Batza Téna, for instance, at Onion Portage, at Bonanza Creek a tributary of the Koyukuk (Holmes 1971, 1973), possibly at Huslia not far to the south (this chapter), and at Lake Minchumina (Holmes 1986), though some cases are not clear where description has not focused on specific defining attributes. Its absence thus far at Batza Téna may be fortuitous.

The prepared wedgeshaped core variety A3 that is represented in the present Batza Téna collections and possibly the Sithylemenkat Lake specimen (this chapter) is one that is well prepared and in most respects is a classic wedgeshaped core but it tends to be relatively broad in the platform and lacks traces of the specialized mode of platform preparation and rejuvenation described above. This variety may be coeval with the Campus type, and in that case it would range in age from early to late. Many assemblages feature only the classic A1 type, but in some cases both the classic and the less specialized (A3) cores are present in the same assemblage, though this is not always clear on the basis of published illustrations.

Cores not of Wedgeshaped Format

These cores generally lack preparation of the blank except at the platform. Platforms are formed on fracture or single flake scar surfaces and show further shaping or retouch from the front, presumably done to adjust the platform angle. This group includes microblade cores, small blade cores and flake cores. One series of cores, individually differing in overall morphology but nearly identical in technological attributes, has been described for site RkIg-44. Production tends to be from a single face of the core. If this face is relatively flat, the core is somewhat like a Tuktu core (RkIg-47:93 and RkIg-47:110 for instance). If nearly exhausted, these cores become thin and tabular. It may be noted, though, that the Tuktu-type cores from Healy Lake (specimens examined at the Archaeological Survey of Canada) show formal, careful preparation of the sides and back, a feature absent in the Batza Téna specimens.

The fluted face may wrap around the sides of the core, giving it a semi-cylindrical to subconical shape. On RkIg-47:10 the fluted surface envelopes about 80 percent of the core perimeter, but this core does have a distinct back formed by a fracture surface and, at the base, by cortex. There are some platform rejuvenation tablets from cores with very broad roughly circular platforms, and this evidence reinforces the evidence provided by fragmentary cores of semicylindrical to subconical format from Batza Téna. Cores of this format are common at Lake Minchumina where they co-occur with frontal wedgeshaped cores (Holmes 1986:71-76). The bladelet core XI-E could be described as subconical, though it does have a distinct back and also could be classified as a very "fat" core of assumed wedge shape.

In pointing out that these cores do have a certain degree of asymmetry inclined towards a broad wedge format, attention is drawn also to the intergrades that assume more or less a wedge format not through shaping but through selection of the blank. These intergrades lack the specialized modes of platform preparation and rejuvenation described for many core types in the A series. Further comparative analysis is required to determine whether the cores in group B particularly differ in age from the group A wedgeshaped series. There is a distinct possibility that the latter are older though on the basis of a single radiocarbon date that applies to a heterogeneous series of rough cores from the Gallagher Flint station (Dixon 1975) it appears that more than one type of core was being used in Alaska between 10,000 and 11,000 years ago. Anderson (1980), Ackerman (1979, 1986) and Mochanov (Dolitsky 1985:367 and references) have suggested that the more or less cylindrical to conical microblade cores owe their existence in western Alaska, sometime after the appearance of Palaeo-Arctic wedgeshaped cores, to influence from the Sumnagin culture of eastern Siberia. I would suggest, however, that these relatively simple or passive cores represent a case of parallel development and are not evidence for further migration or diffusion across Bering Strait. Present data also suggest that the co-occurrence of several core varieties is the norm although one may hope that patterns will emerge when more well dated components are available for comparison and possible cases of mixed components are eliminated.

Microblades from Broad and Narrow Cores

Researchers have pointed to the respective existence of wide and narrow microblades (cf. Cook 1968:Fig. 1; Owen 1988; Workman 1978). Large size clearly distinguishes Denbigh Flint complex collections from many interior microblade assemblages. Within the interior region, however, both are present and sortation between wide and narrow microblades at this time does not clearly lead to distinct cultural traditions. Some persons have noted though, that broad cores tend to produce broad microblades. This is clearly shown by the selected data presented below in Table 4.11. In some attributes microblades mirror cores. It appears that in some cases microblade information can serve as a proxy indicator of core form: narrow blades indicating

TABLE 4.11. MICROBLADE WIDTH CORRELATED WITH CORE TYPE

Site	Microblade width mm	Core width	Notes
Associated With Classic Campus/Denali Cores			
Dry Creek	3.8	14 (10-18)	Large sample out of 1772 collected
KbTx-2, Yukon	4.1	12 (9-17)	N=243, from fine-screened SE locus
Otter Falls, Yukon	4.4	8*	N=150, c 4500 BP 14C date
Donnelly Ridge	4.8	10.6	N=286, Denali type site
Campus	5.0		N=239, Campus/Denali type site
Akmak	5.6		N=28
Associated with Broad Cores not of Classic Campus Type			
MiRi-2 Horton L.	7.2	11,32,35	N=56, W is for each of the 3 cores
RlIg-37 Batza T.	7.3	10, 18.7	N=31, W is for 2 core fragments
O.P. Denbigh	7.3		N=300
MgRr-1 Colville L.	7.6	21 (13-28)	N=27, for 4 cores
O.P. Proto Denbigh	7.7		N=102
RkIh-28 Batza T.	7.8	28	N=38, W is for one complete core
Norutak Lake	7.9	25 (21-33)	N=173, for 4 cores
Others			
Bezya	4.6	10.5 (9-12)	N=83, 3990+170 BP, 5 cores
Bonanza Creek K25	5.5		N=122
Minchumina MMK-4	6.5	Both	N=203
Kobuk Complex	7.1		N=49, 1 wedge core
Pointed Mountain	7.3	c 12-24	N=80, NW Microblade Trad. type site
Little Arm, Yukon	7.2		N=363, Level 5 JiVs-1, 11 cores

*Chord distance (4.3--11.4 mm) across fluted end may be slightly less than core maximum thickness, for 5 specimens mainly from Otter Falls (Workman 1978:243).

Sources: Dry Creek: Powers, Guthrie and Hoffecker 1983; Akmak: KbTx-2: Clark 1991, a collection from the same site that was not screened was 4.8 mm.; Otter Falls: Workman 1978, see also Cook 1968; Akmak: Anderson 1970; Donnelly Ridge: West 1967; Campus: Holmes 1971 on collections by West and others; MiRi-2 and MgRr-1: Clark 1975, the sites located inland north of Great Bear Lake may be affiliated with the Northwest Microblade Tradition or with the Arctic Small Tool tradition. RlIg-37 and RkIh-28: this report; Onion Portage Denbigh and Kobuk complex: Anderson 1970, 1978; Bezya: Leblanc and Ives 1986, Table 5 recalculated to exclude distal segments; Bonanza Creek: Holmes 1971; Minchumina: Holmes 1988; Pointed Mountain: Holmes 1971, microblade core width scaled from drawings of four cores in Morrison 1987; Little Arm: Workman 1978. Some collections have been studied by more than one person, thus slightly variant data may be available.narrow and especially classic Palaeo-Arctic cores, wide microblades indicating wider oval platforms and other broad cores. For intermediate width blades, however, there are three possibilities. These may indicating assemblages with both cores, or mixed components, or a core form from which production is intermediate size microblades. A 4-mm-wide microblade is a very delicate item compared to one 7 to 8 mm wide. I would not be surprised is there were cultural and historical differences in the mode of their utilization. Gal (1981a:77) discusses the problems of correlating microblade width with historiography. He states that "the clustering of microblade collections [by certain size attributes]...can probably best be explained by the exigencies of blade manufacture than by common cultural norms." In one sense, Gal's comments point to the same conclusion stated above, that microblade width correlates with core width. Nevertheless there may be cultural norms that at the outset determined whether wide or narrow blades would be produced.

The group "others" in Table 4.11 is a mixed bag and requires comments as follows:
1. The Bezya cores, which I have examined in casts, are not classic Campus-Denali cores, but one could ask whether there is any underlying significance to the Bezya people elected to produce narrow microblades which evidently required that the cores be narrow.

2. Minchumina contains both Campus-type and broader subcylindrical cores. The intermediate average value of microblade width reflects this nicely.

3. Wide microblades in the Kobuk complex, a late Palaeo-Arctic tradition component (Anderson 1970, 1988) may indicate that the cores differed from Akmak or other classic Palaeo-Arctic cores.

4. Pointed Mountain, located in the southwest corner of the Northwest Territories, is a type site for MacNeish's Northwest Microblade tradition, and Little Arm is an important Yukon member of that tradition. Microblade production was based primarily if not exclusively on wedgeshaped cores. This interior tradition also differs markedly from its presumed progenitor, the Palaeo-Arctic tradition and from KbTx-2 and Otter Falls to which it is thought to be closely related. Microblade width is similar to that in the unrelated Denbigh component.

5. For Bonanza Creek K25 Holmes (1971) notes the recovery of four cores of both Campus and Tuktu format, but we do not have any pure sample of microblades from tabular or Tuktu-type cores to judge how those from that type differ from microblades from Campus cores.

CHAPTER 5:

BATZA TÉNA TUKTU AND THE NORTHERN ARCHAIC

Chapter 5 describes the Batza Téna Tuktu site cluster. Also described here are a small number of other sites which, though not properly Batza Téna Tuktu, represent the more encompassing Northern Archaic tradition. In order to avoid blurring possibly distinct individual assemblages, and to bring the RkIh-36 occupation area into focus, separate descriptions are provided for each site and assemblage. However, the main collection, from RkIh-36 and the next principal collection, from RkIh-35, are cross-referenced and are listed conjointly in the tables accompanying RkIh-36. The two sites form a discontinuous cluster broken by a low area between RkIh-35 and RkIh-36. Two lesser sites also are included here because these shore-zone collection areas, RkIh-34 and RkIh-37, are proximal to the designated Batza Téna Tuktu sites. Finally, one additional collection, from a site (RkIh-32) located at Batzatiga like the preceding ones, and one from Basecamp Ridge (RkIg-22) are described here, though their relationship to Batza Téna Tuktu probably is at the more general level of the Northern Archaic tradition.

This culture was briefly summarized in Chapter 1. It may be helpful to repeat the main points. Batza Téna Tuktu approximates the Tuktu complex of Anaktuvuk Pass (Campbell 1961) or the combined Palisades and Portage (Northern Archaic) complexes of Onion Portage (Anderson 1988). At RkIh-35 widely spaced sections were excavated, revealing, evidently, artifacts from numerous camping episodes. At RkIh-36, however, an apparent tightly focused prehistoric camp is indicated by the distribution, in a continuous excavation layout, of more than 40 end scrapers plus other implements. Microblades are rare and only two microblade cores were recovered. Other artifacts include sidenotched points and leafshaped points, neither of which are common; numerous bifaces, many of them unfinished; a retouched hide scraping stone; a notched pebble axe, notched and roughened pebble sinkers or weights and pebble hammerstones; flake cores; linear ridged flakes that sometimes are like prismatic blades; a copper awl; and a burinated chert blade. No intact features were uncovered.

Sites and Collections

Site RkIh-36

The shore area of RKIh-36 (Figures 5.1-5.9) was surface collected in the spring of 1970 when the water was low. Test probes were made then at the top of the site. Work at the site in 1971 focused on excavating an occupation area at the top of the low rise inland from the shore of

Obsidian Hill Lake (Batzatimunket) (Fig. 5.1-5.3). The intervening slope was only casually probed. The slope appears to be impinging on the shore through the process of soil creep, thus the original location of the shore-zone artifacts could have been several metres upslope.

Figure 5.1.　The forested terrain of RkIh-35 (higher on the right) and RkIh-36 on the left along the far shore of the lake.

Description

Shore zone. Beginning 82 m (paced) northeast of a prominent beaver house, located in front of Site RkIh-35, there is a sparse distribution of obsidian flakes for 80 m (paced). These were not collected. This interval was followed, continuing northeastward, by 91 m of shore with a more intensive artifact litter. Excepting several whole and split obsidian pebbles, which were left there, all exposed artifacts were collected. These include 9.4 kg of flakes and shatter. Separate lots were collected by sector, but because of the small number of implements recovered sectors have been pooled. The 1971 excavation locus lies behind the southwestern part of the shore zone.

Benchtop zone. Viewed from the front, especially from the opposite shore of the lake, RkIh-36 appears as a slight rise, as an elevation not as large and as high as the adjacent hill where site RkIh-35 is located. From the rear, though, the site terrain is seen as being an area where a nearly flat tundra meadow breaks into a slope that runs down to the lake. The change in slope evidently improved the drainage and this has promoted a dense growth of small spruce. The stand of taller spruce trees at the top of the site provides much of the appearance of higher elevation there. Obsidian detritus occurred within and extended beyond the apparent occupation locus here, defined by an implement cluster dominated by end scrapers.

Figure 5.2. Laying out the baseline on RkIh-36.

<u>Soils.</u> Most sections had a well developed rootmat and organic litter layer. Once the roots of shrubs had been severed this turf layer could be rolled up, in some sections exposing in the bottom of the peaty layer a virtual pavement of obsidian flakes. This concentration of flakes at the turf-soil interface may be secondary--a result of soil or frost sorting--though I am not aware of studies demonstrating this to be the case.

Artifacts also were found several cm into the underlying brown soil. The brown soil grades downward into a greenish yellow-brown soil which also contained artifacts, especially end scrapers. The latter soil in turn graded into the grey-green sandy soil of the substrate. If there is any difference in age between soil and rootmat contexts, it can be noted that some artifacts which ought to be early on the basis of type, notably microblades, were found within the organic rootmat.

The third context for artifacts consists of frost involutions. There the soil is more clayey, light to medium grey in appearance. Artifacts, particularly flakes, sometimes are concentrated in this matrix and occur to relatively considerable depths, up to 30 cm. They often are oriented on edge (vertically).

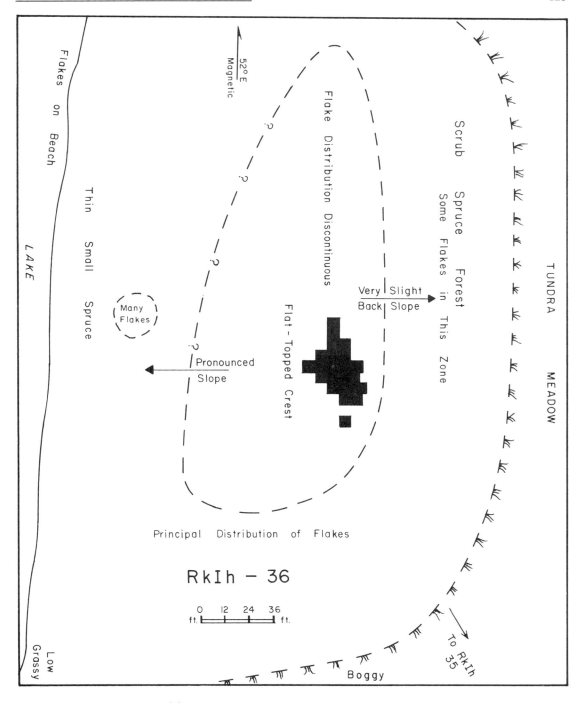

Figure 5.3. Map of RkIh-36.

The distribution of flakes and implements varied considerably from location to location. In some cases they were mainly in the rootmat and were rare in the underlying soil. In certain other places they were scarce everywhere. Elsewhere they sometimes occurred in all soils, bit there also were sections where they were abundant only in frost involutions where they evidently had been redeposited.

We can note here observations on the substrate deposit at adjacent RkIh-35 which probably are applicable to an area that extends beyond these sites. It is suggested elsewhere that these sites are located on an ancient alluvial feature elevated slightly above the Koyukuk flats. In section N48-54, W48-58 of RkIh-35 a pit was dug down to 75 cm depth, at which point frozen ground was reached. At and just above this depth there is clean washed sand, as also was encountered in a pit at the sloping front of the site. The rest of the soil column is sandy but not as clean. On the flat bench there are exposures that break through the tundra cover. Only fine sediment consisting of poorly washed sand was observed at these exposures. No pebbles are exposed on the surface, though at the foot of or on the slopes of the hill Batzatiga there is a pebbly soil matrix.

Features and Distribution Analysis

The implement distribution extending somewhat irregularly for about eight metres defines an apparent camp locus. The distribution of artifacts at RkIh-36 is plotted in Figures 5.4 through 5.9. Figure 5.4 shows the extent of the uncovered occupation location as it is defined on the basis of scrapers (which are plotted in Figure 5.5) and extended slightly to include the full distribution of the microblade industry (Fig. 5.6) and miscellaneous implements (Fig. 5.4). There is a close fit between the distribution of scrapers, microblades and miscellaneous artifacts.

Rock (Fig. 5.7) probably served as maul heads, flaking hammers, boiling stones, and may have been kept on hand for future use inasmuch as the nearest source is the Koyukuk River. Thus, its presence is pertinent to both domestic camp activity and lithic knapping.

Together, any of the rock utilized for flaking hammers, flakes and cores (Fig. 5.8), and various core and lithic reduction products (Fig. 5.9) such as pieces amorphously worked in the bifacial mode, roughed out and unfinished bifaces, and biface edge overpass (outrepassé) flakes, and also linear flakes (Fig. 5.6) reflect use of the site as a flaking station. It is readily seen that the site was used extensively in that manner. Recovery of up to 12 kg flakes per section compares with recovery of up to 11 kg at adjacent RkIh-35 and up to 5 kg flakes per section at RkIg-30, both of which are thought to be combination camp sites-flaking stations. A pressing question is whether the site was concurrently a flaking station and camp, or whether there was some spatial and/or temporal differentiation between these activities.

Data from figures 5.5 to 5.9 are collated in Table 5.2. Between categories of the reduction industry there is no particularly strong correlation; e.g., a section with tremendous quantities of

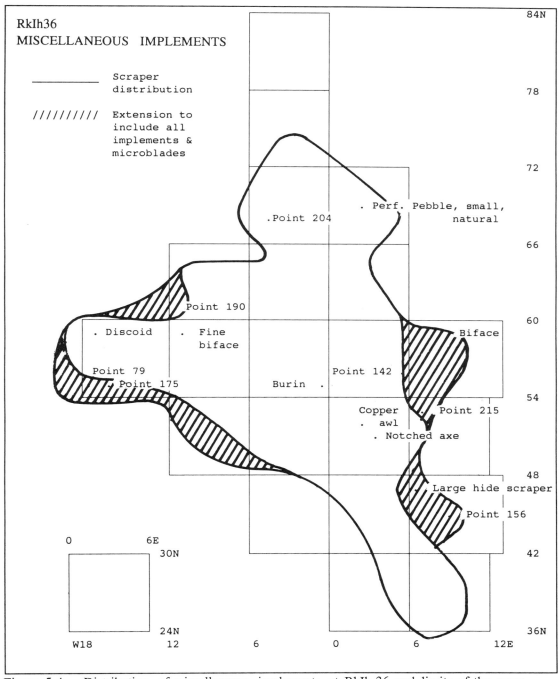

Figure 5.4. Distribution of miscellaneous implements at RkIh-36 and limits of the camp
locus as determined by artifact distributions.

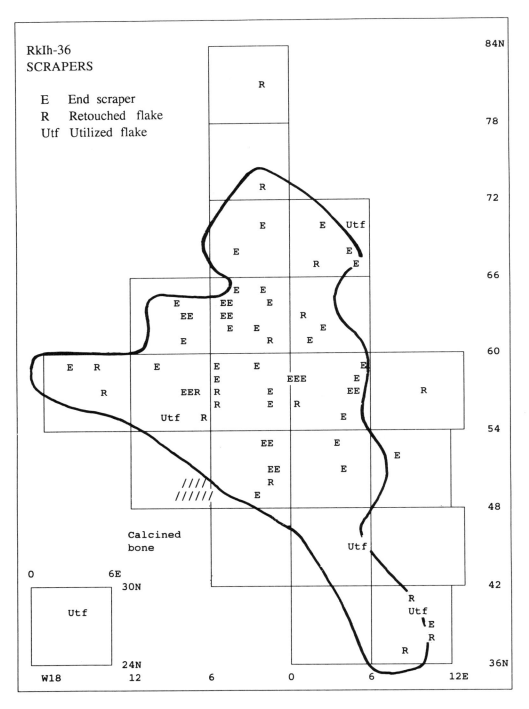

Figure 5.5. Distribution of scrapers at RkIh-36.

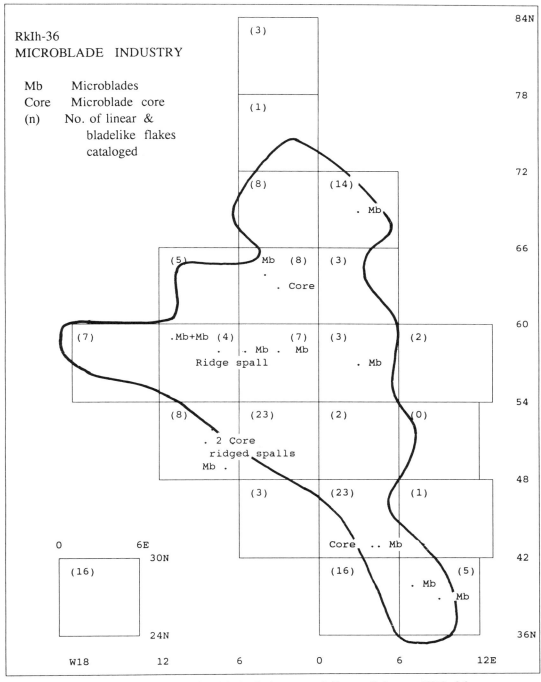

Figure 5.6. Distribution of the microblade industry and linear flakes at RkIh-36.

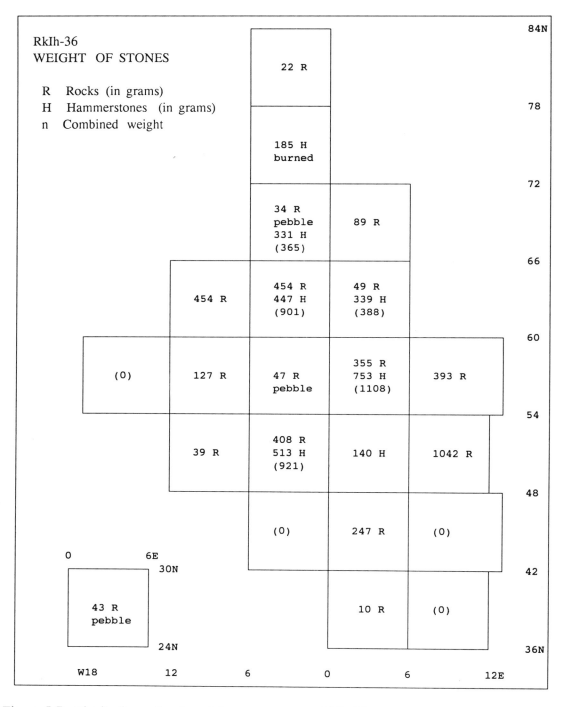

Figure 5.7. Distribution of rock and hammerstones at RkIh-36.

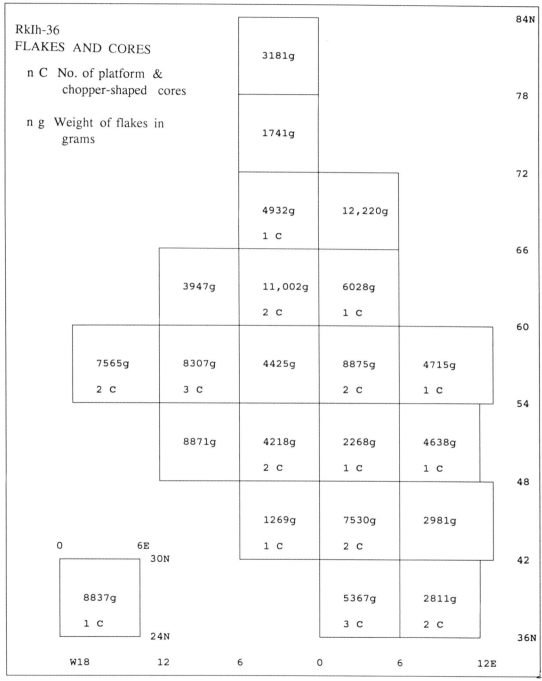

Figure 5.8. Distribution of flakes and cores at RkIh-36.

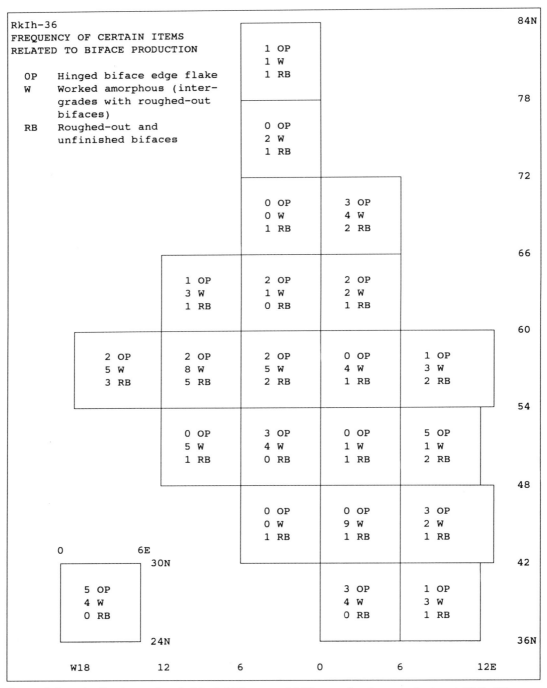

Figure 5.9. Distribution of unfinished bifaces and biface reduction products at RkIh-36.

flakes and shatter does not necessarily have a large number of cores, nor does it necessarily have many unfinished bifaces or linear flakes. In some sections there is an apparent correlation, in others there is none. If there were more consistency, it would be possible to model the results, for instance, in terms of periodic disposal of detritus away from the work setting as knapping progressed to various stages or operations. We are left, then, for interpretation the gross occurrence of lithic waste.

It also is helpful to have models upon which to base interpretation of the overall distribution. The following are proposed:

1.   Limited use of the site as a flaking station will result in clusters of detritus, as are seen on many Batza Téna sites.

2.   Extensive, continuing use of the site as a flaking station will result in merged clusters and a high density scatter of flakes.

3.   If the camp and flaking station aspects of site utilization are not concurrent, the camp will be superimposed on (within, or underlie) the flaking station distribution.

4.   If they are concurrent, it is expected that an accommodation will have been made so that the sharp detritus will be disposed of in localized dumps, either within or peripheral to the camp area.

The figure plots show that although flakes, cores and roughouts are not evenly distributed, they are abundant everywhere, especially flakes which range from 1.3 kg to 12.2 kg per section. Extensive use of the site as a flaking station during several episodes is indicated. It is difficult, though, to assign a time span to this activity. A few decades or several thousand years could be involved. Hydration data (below) suggest a briefer rather than a longer duration.

Insufficient sections were excavated outside the camp locus to clearly contrast that area with the rest of the site. Evidently, though, a high incidence of debitage occurs in some areas beyond the camp locus as well as within the camp area. There is no particular differentiation of lithic concentrations vis-à-vis the implement locus. The camp thus appears to be superimposed on (or within) a larger flaking station. We noted that the flaking station probably reflects several episodes of site use. However, the tight clustering of scrapers and other implements suggests that a single camp is responsible for their occurrence. Possibly, though, this camp was visited several times, over the span of a few years. The growth of vegetation may have been a parameter that tended to restrict people to this spot.

Within the camp location there are two distributions or occurrences that can be termed features, though neither was discretely bounded. One consists of finely fragmented calcined bone mixed with the soil of a frost involution, found in an area measuring 15 by 60 cm. It probably is the disturbed remains of an unformalized hearth, in archaeological jargon an "incineration area." Calcined bone first appeared at one spot in the organic rootmat, and then its distribution spread out into a lens lying beneath the principal brown soil and overlying green-brown soil. Only a few small obsidian flakes were directly mixed in with the bone fragments. Elsewhere a trace of calcined bone and red sand (presume fire reddened) appeared in the excavation but this did not develop to an extent sufficient to justify its identification as a hearth.

The other feature consists of a somewhat broader distribution of burned or heat altered obsidian. With due allowance for disturbance from frost action and tree growth, the heated obsidian appears to be in place, but no heat treating hearth or other feature that could account for burning the obsidian was recognized. Only one other case of burned obsidian was seen at Batza Téna, that from microblade site RkIh-28 (Chapter 4) although forest fires are frequent in the Koyukuk region. Circumstantial evidence from RkIh-28, in particular the conjoining of burned and unburned implement fragments, suggests that the obsidian was not intentionally burned there, for instance, to process it for flaking. The type of artifact affected (and not affected) at RkIh-36 was examined to see if this information would provide any relevant clues or pattern. The items are as follows:

Some cobbles (not obsidian, possibly burned from use as boiling stones, not
   related to the area of burned obsidian).
1 retouched flake (natural retouch?), shows granular fracturing.
4 biface roughouts (1 complete, 3 fragments). They variously show
   granular fracturing with retained glassy lustre, or a dull surface
   and slight development of wavy fractures attributable to heating; or
   heavy frosting. There also are a few additional apparent roughout
   fragments with curved fractures. They are badly broken up because of
   these fracture lines.
1 aberrant end scraper or retouched flake, eroded and burned.

Items not burned:

No other end scraper out of 48 specimens.
No finished or semifinished bifaces.
No catalogued hinged biface edge fragments.
No microblades nor the two microblade cores.
No linear or bladelike flakes out of catalogued items.
No recognized core (but some cores may have fractured and disintegrated
   due to heating and thus have not been recognized).

It is difficult to draw conclusions from these data. Primarily roughouts or unfinished implements are affected, but that kind of material is the most common sort on the site. At least one functional tool was burned, but the most numerous artifact classes largely escaped. A plausible explanation is that the burning was not intentional, or it was not directed towards certain kinds of artifacts or raw material. It evidently took place in such a small area of the site that by chance artifacts of only a few types were affected. Fetter and Shinkwin (1978:32) suggest that some material at the K-9 site, on the Middle Fork of the Koyukuk, was heat treated and cite changes an the killer of the artifacts and fused phenocrysts as evidence. But their discussion is too brief to indicate that these are not the result of wildfire at the side or that the artifacts had not been discarded into or overlain by hearths.

Collection

Artifacts from site RkIh-36 are listed in Table 5.1 together with those from related assemblages. Except where stated otherwise, all flaked specimens are of obsidian. Only obsidian was knapped at these sites, but a few implements of chert and other material, which evidently had been produced elsewhere, were recovered.

Specimens collected in 1970 are catalogued as RkIh-36:1 through 59. Of these, 1-5, 34-37 and flake lot 59 come from Test Pit 1, located in the area excavated in 1971. The remainder are from the beach. The beach was collected in sectors, numbered Areas 2 through 5 but the distinctive artifacts are too few for any differences to be noted between sectors. Collections from the 1971 excavations were catalogued RkIh-36:60 through 714. Later, several items extracted from the flake lots also were given individual numbers. Not all these are implements. A large number are bladelike flakes and core chunks, or are flakes singled out for further examination.

Cores and Flakes. The attempt to sort and classify flake cores was complicated by the presence of apparent core-biface tools and worked obsidian pebbles, largely in the roughout or even less advanced stages. The task is complicated further by the incidence of rotated, unformalized and fragmentary cores. In addition, there are numerous pebbles that seemingly were "tried out" but evidently were discarded when they split in the wrong manner or after only one or two flakes had been detached. The number of cores catalogued and counted in Table 5.1 easily could be doubled by including additional cores observed in the flake lots. The actual number present is somewhat indeterminate and depends upon counting and classifying fragments. Batza Téna flake cores are discussed further in Chapter 9 and are illustrated primarily in Plates 23 and 24.

Chopping-tool-shaped cores (Pl. 13H, Pl. 23E-F). Chopping-tool-shaped core objects are pebbles roughly bifaced along one edge. Coarse flaking originates from one edge, which may the end, side or oblique edge, occasionally too from parts of adjacent edges, and extends to varying degrees down the face of the pebble. There may be lesser chipping at a secondary location. Such objects usually are notably wider than they are thick. Chopping-tool-shaped cores may be flake cores, stages in the production of core-biface tools, or chopping tools. Some are less developed or less worked-down than others. They may be several applications, especially considering the wide range in size, from objects as small as 27 mm to 76 mm wide measured perpendicular to the flaked edge.

Multilateral cores (Pl. 24C-D) are an entirely different form in which there is no

TABLE 5.1.   COLLECTIONS FROM BATZA TENA TUKTU COMPONENTS

Identification	RkIh-36 excavated	shore	RkIh-35	RkIh -34	RkIh -37
Cores without platform distinct from faces					
Chopper-shaped	7	3	1		2
Multilateral		2	1		1
Cores with flat platform distinct from face					
Form A	8		8	3	9
Form B	1	4			
Form C	1				
Residual cores	15+	1	7		6
Flakes	126 kg	9.4 kg	87 kg	3.6 kg	6.3 kg
Linear flakes, bladelike flakes	146+	2+	11	4	3
Hinged bifacial and platformed edges, mostly outrepassé, & spalled biface roughout edges	43+		29	1	
Uniface study series (various forms, some roughouts)	7	3	2		
Rudimentary pieces (early stage biface roughouts & rejects?)	17+	3	12	1	5
Roughly bifaced objects	69	13	28	2	4
complete	(12)*	(9)	(23)	2	
fragments	(57)	(4)	(5)		
Biface, unfinished	17	3	8		4
Biface, finished or nearly so	6		5		
Points (most for projectiles)	7	1	3		
Retouched/utilized flakes	32	2	25	1	1
conclusive	(18)		(17)		
uncertain, some natural	(14)	(2)	(8)		
End scrapers	49		7		2
Burinated blade	1				
Microblade cores	2				
Microblades, some poor	20		8		1?
Retouched ridge spalls from microblade cores	3				
Awl, copper	1				
Notched chopper	1				
Notched cobble, no worked edge			1		
Other nonobsidian chopper/scraper	1	2	1		
Hammerstones (not obsidian)	11		5		
Unmodified cobbles & pebbles (not obsidian)	Several		7		
Unmodified obsidian pebbles	23	+ **		1	
Obliquely split obsidian pebbles	Present	+ **		3	

* Items in parentheses are counted in a preceding inclusive category.
**Not collected.

morphological distinction between face and platform elements except vis-à-vis the derivation of individual flakes. These cores, which are more common than the single clear example from RkIh-36 would suggest, have five or more relatively flat faces, each face usually formed by a single flake scar. The edge of one face served as the platform for forming (detaching a flake from) an adjacent face. There also are three examples in the flake lots which retain some cortical surface although each core also has several faces formed through detaching flakes.

TABLE 5.2.   ARTIFACT RECOVERY, RkIh-36, BY SECTION

Section	Rock g*	Flakes g**	Cores ***	OP#	Amorphous ##	Biface roughout	Linear flakes	Microblades @	End scr. @@	Other impl.
24N,6E	43	8837	1	5	4	0	16	0	0	1
36N,12E	0	2811	2	1	3	1	5	2	1	4
36N,6E	10	5367	3	3	4	0	16	0	0	0
42N,13E	0	2981	0	3	2	1	1	0	0	2
42N,6E	247	7530	2	0	9	1	23	2	0	1
42N,0W	0	1269	1	0	0	1	8	0	0	0
48N,12E	1042	4638	1	5	1	2	0	0	1	1
48N,6E	140	2268	1	0	1	1	2	0	2	2
48N,0W	921	4218	2	3	4	0	23	0	5	2
48N,6W	39	8871	0	0	5	1	8	3	0	0
54N,13E	373	4715	1	1	3	2	2	0	0	2
54N,6E	1108	8875	2	0	4	1	3	1	4	2
54N,0W	47	4425	0	2	5	2	7	2	8	3
54N,6W	127	8307	3	2	8	5	4	2	2	5
54N,12W	0	7565	2	2	5	3	7	0	1	5
60N,6E	388	6028	1	2	2	1	3	0	2	0
60N,0W	901	11002	2	2	1	0	8	2	9	2
60N,6W	454	3947	1	1	3	1	5	0	4	1
66N,6E	89	12220	0	3	4	2	14	1	3	2
66N,0W	365	4932	1	0	0	1	8	0	2	1
72N,0W	185	1641	0	0	2	1	1	0	0	1
74N,0W	22	3181	0	1	1	1	3	0	0	1
Total			26	36	71	27	146	15	44	37

* Boiling stones, hammerstones, large pebbles and fragments.
** Here, as is the case throughout this volume, the weight of flakes does not include a number of catalogued items that in the final analysis are not considered to be implements, nor, in the present case, does it include the linear flakes and the OP flakes.
***Does not include a number of minor fragments.
\#   OP = biface edge overpass or outrepassé flakes.
\#\# Intergrades into biface roughouts. Table 5.1 reports 110 uniface roughouts, rudimentary pieces, roughly bifaced objects and unfinished bifaces among which are included the total of 99 amorphous worked objects and roughed-out and unfinished bifaces reported in Table 5.2.
@ Includes 2 cores and 3 fine-scale bifacially retouched ridge spalls.
@@ End scrapers. There are 23 other scrapers or side-scrapers among the "Other Implements"; a total of 67 scrapers of end and side scraper format are reported in Table 5.1 though the breakdown between Tables 5.1 and 5.2 varies slightly.

Biface cores. Another type of core recognized at Batza Téna but uncommon and not verified in the present collection is the rough biface or core biface which instead of being a stage in the preparation of a large biface implement served instead as a source of flakes. No attempt was made to segregate these possible cores from roughly bifaced objects and fragments. A special case is the relatively flat semidiscoidal biface roughout or core of which two were catalogued and two more were observed among the flake lots. It is not clear that discoidal flake cores actually were used at Batza Téna.

Cores with flat platform (platform core, Pl. 23 shows specimens from other sites). The basic flake core with distinct or separate striking platform (Form A) is a pebble or cobble from which one end has been detached. The resultant flat surface then served as a platform from which flakes were struck off the sides or face of the core. A variation (B) occurs when the platform is shaped through removal of several flakes, sometimes localized near the platform edge. One example from the lake shore (Pl. 23J) (RkIh-36:57) of red-brown obsidian shows several small blade removals and may be either a poorly formalized small blade core or a microblade core preform. As best as I can define it from the single example, a third core form (C) is basically the same thing but it is based on a quadrilateral chunk of material instead of a rounded pebble. These cores become complicated or less obvious through rotation, breakage or when the core nears exhaustion (the last is referred to as the "residual form"). There also are examples where a flat area of cortex, or even a curved cortical surface, has served as the platform. (D) Some platform cores have very flat faces, though not any from RkIh-36, and are designated as "flatfaced" cores (see RkIh-37 specimen in Pl. 24J).

Core No. 36:23, which evidently did not advance to the production stage, is roughly bifaced along one edge. One may query whether this piece was not first intended for a bifaced or chopping-tool-shaped core. Another possibility is that it was being preformed for a microblade core with roughly prepared wedge element.

The numerous residual form category consists of otherwise unclassified fragments, spent and rotated flat platformed cores, broken cores lacking the platform area, probable pieces of quadrilateral cores, and large amorphous intergrading pieces of material. This group also includes the basal portions of cores from RkIh-36 that have flake scars which originate from two faces and meet at the bottom of the core at an acute angle. Few complete cores with the last configuration were recovered from any Batza téna site.

In the context of cores there can be noted numerous split obsidian pebbles and fragments of pebbles (collected among flake lots). Some of these are entered in Table 5.1 as "obliquely split pebbles." These were rejected pieces, tried out for platformed cores, or surplus material, but in many cases similar pieces evidently served as the basis of tools produced by a core reduction technique.

Twenty-three wholly unaltered obsidian pebbles were excavated. I am uncertain whether these were naturally present or had been carried into the site with raw material lots. Most are small and may have been discarded for that reason. Test pits outside the flaking station area could show whether or not the pebbles occur naturally in the soil at the site as they do a few hundred metres distant on the flanks of Batzatiga.

Linear flakes and bladelike flakes (Pl. 13A-G). Several hundred linear, ridged and bladelike flakes (200 of which were catalogued) were examined for evidence of a formalized blade industry. Such evidence is hardly forthcoming. Some of these items should be called blades, but I do not use that term here because I do not want to imply the degree of formalization and technological focus that a blade industry implies. Examples of these flakes are illustrated.   RkIh-36:85 (Pl. 13G), which is barely outside the microblade size range, is the only specimen not of obsidian.

Retouch at the proximal end of No. 76 (Pl. 13C) shaped this piece into a semblance of a small end scraper, but I am not convinced that this retouch was generated with the intention of forming a tool. No. 685 is part of the face of a small core displaying three bladelet facets. Superficially, No. 14 has the morphology of a prismatic blade, but antecedent flake removals from the core, as expressed in the dorsal facets of this specimen, resulted from blows struck from various directions. RkIh-552 (Pl. 11S), on which one of the two dorsal facets is retouched, is difficult to explain except as a blade that detached the front (face) edge of a core that had been retouched to adjust the straightness of the face. No. 596 removed the entire lower end of a core from which a number of linear flakes already had been detached. No. 596 terminates in an area of cortex present at the base of a core and shows on its dorsal surface scars from two shorter antecedent flake removals. Many of the bladelike flakes seem to be retouched, but in most cases this condition is ascribed to damage and natural attrition taking place in the ground or underfoot.

Flakes. Flakes were inordinately numerous in most excavated sections. Their distribution by weight is shown in Figure 5.8. The 121 kg of flakes collected averages 5.34 kg per six-foot section or 148 g per square foot (almost $1.6 \, kg/m^2$). Interpretation of this area of the site as a living area, defined by the occurrence of domestic tools, appears to be in conflict with an alternative identification as a manufactory or flaking station suggested by the incidence of flakes, inasmuch as an intense litter of sharp flakes would have posed a hazard to occupation. We can safely assign the majority of flakes to a summer or open season occupation between early May and the end of September inasmuch as ready access to a large supply of obsidian nodules is required for intensive knapping. So much obsidian was wasted at the site that gathering this raw material and flaking it must have been essentially concurrent activities. In that case, was the domestic occupation a separate winter activity at this site? An alternative explanations is that domestic occupation was later after the sharp chips had been absorbed into the vegetation mat.

Cortical flakes are numerous and by weight constitute the overwhelming majority of flakes. Split or broken obsidian pebbles, large flakes which might be prized in areas where obsidian is scarce, and fragments of cores are numerous. Some flakes have altered surfaces (in addition to dirty residue) which may be attributable to burning and/or chemical alteration succeeding heating. In addition, a large number of flakes and worked fragments, largely from one area of the site, show a granular fracture pattern that probably is due to heating and chilling.

Virtually all flakes are obsidian. The small number of flakes not obsidian consist of the following:

3 tiny glassy flakes. Neutron activation analysis of one shows it to be identical to Keele River fused tuff from the Mackenzie Valley in the Northwest Territories (Cinq-Mars 1973 and personal communication). This is the only reported Alaskan occurrence of the unique fused tuff.

9 small chert flakes, mostly red coloured, some possibly are chips from implements.

4 flakes of grey stone, clustered in a single excavation unit.

1 very large basalt flake (36:559) with trace of a serrate edge; a damaged implement?

Microblade Industry. The microblade industry is described as a specialized type of flake industry.

Microblade cores (Pl. 11). Two microblade cores were recovered. One was made on a completely bifaced preform; the other is incomplete but probably was a wedge-shaped core with a roughly bifaced keel.

The core on a biface (Pl. 11 O) measures 45.5 mm long from front to back by 23.8 mm high (equivalent to biface length and width). The length is slightly reduced from the original size of the biface blank through use or shaping of the fluted facet. Biface thickness, e.g. core width, is inconsistent and ranges between 8 and 10.5 mm. A 19-mm-long platform was formed through removal of part of one lateral edge by detaching a ridged spall by means of a blow directed to one end of the blank. The outer part of the platform was further retouched from the end. Microblades or intended microblades were detached from the end of the core. At 40 degrees, the angle between the platform and fluted face is especially acute. Three fluted scars, the longest 29 mm in length, form the facetted end or fluted face of the core. Final attempted microblade removal was unsuccessful, resulting in a short, hinged-out flake. Cores of this type are formed in the manner of burins, which has given rise to their designation by such terms, in Japan for instance, as Oshorokko core-burins.

The platform, the greater part of one side and the back of the second core are missing (Pl. 11P). Sufficient remains, however, of the fluted face, sides and lower end to identify a roughly keeled wedge-shaped core. At its broken margins, one concave and one convex edge are retouched and crushed, possibly from use as a scraper.

TABLE 5.3. MICROBLADES FROM RkIh-36

No.	Seg.	L	W	T	Arris	Notes
RkIh-36:						
60	M	26	6.5	2.16	1	Thin, curves
110a	M	22	8+	3.1+	1	Thickness tapers, side flares
116	P	20	--	1.82	1-2	Irregular
124	PM	20	3.9	1.38	2	Malformed
137	PM	29	5.9	1.71	2	
192	PM	24	9.0	1.40	2-3	
197	P	18	--	1.53	2	Edges uneven
262	M	17	9.0	1.70	1	Damaged or irregular
281	P	15	8.0	2.00	1	Arrise is irregular
322	P	21	10.6	1.8	2	One edge feathered
344	M	16	6.6	1.7+	1	Thickness tapers, side flares
379	PM	26	7.4	1.85	2	Arrises irregular
386	PMD	23	9.3	1.3	0-1	Malformed
387	M?	12	12.6	1.64	2	Identification uncertain
439	M	19	18+	2.1+	1-2	Malformed
441	PM	23	8.0	1.53	1	Malformed
458	PM	23	7.5	1.98	1	Malformed
641	M	20	8.3	1.68	2	One edge is uneven
663	D	17	10.8	2.59	1	Lacks very end
716	D	--	--	--	2	Irregular, ex flake lot

Retouched ridged flakes (Pl. 11L-M). Three ridged flakes, triangular in cross-section, appear to be spalls that were detached from the edge of a bifaced blank to form a platform, as was done in the case with the first core described above. These spalls are more or less equally retouched on both sides of the dorsal ridge, though the ridge is slightly off-centre. The ventral surface is an unretouched flake surface. At their proximal end the spalls are pointed, reflecting the edge profile of the biface blank. They terminate in hinge fractures (1 case) or combination hinges and breaks. Length is 27.2 to 38.4 mm; width is 6-6.3 mm for the two larger specimens and 4.6 mm for the shorter spall; and thickness is 3-3.7 mm for the larger two and 2.7 for the smaller one.

Microblades (Pl. 11N). The microblades are typical microblades. Only obsidian specimens are present. None is retouched. Twenty specimens are listed in Table 5.3, but nearly all are highly defective, obvious rejects, and for this reason no summary metric description is provided. Seven additional microblade-related spalls have one edge or facet surface formed of cortex or which is flaked to varying degrees. These come from the sides of the core at their juncture with the fluted face

Biface Industry. Four points of reference are recognized here in the relatively continuous process of biface production. First (a), in amorphous reduction there are fractured or very coarsely flaked chunks of stone amorphously reduced on two or more faces. They are identified as part of a bifacial industry or early stage roughouts largely through reference to the abundance of co-occurring more advanced bifacial artifacts. Some specimens, however, may be cores and one has the attributes of a wedge (pièce esquilée). Next (b) are roughly bifaced objects or roughouts. These items variously display extremely coarse flaking and have unfinished edges with thick areas of flat platform and cortex. Then (c), in series, come the unfinished bifaces, a later stage of production in which coarse flaking continues and portions of unretouched or cortical edge remain, though not to such an extent and degree of coarseness as found in the preceding group. Finally (d), there are the finished and nearly finished bifaces. Bifaced points are described as a separate category. Not only is this an intergradational series, but zones along the edge of a single artifact may be at different stages. Classificatory problems and assumptions arise in this kind of scheme which attempts to take into account more than morphology.

Biface roughouts (Pl. 12, Pl. 23A). One quarter of the biface roughouts are complete or nearly so. Most of the fragments are either rounded end pieces--largely unworked or in cortex--or otherwise have not been flaked to any distinctive form. Among the rounded end fragments and smaller complete roughouts with thick cortical edge there are several especially narrow specimens. These range in width between 20 and 32 mm. For this small size there are no equivalent counterparts among finished bifaces, exclusive of points, and there is only a single example so narrow among unfinished bifaces. We find thus, even at the very rudimentary roughout stage bifaces as small as the smallest recovered finished specimens (which are the points). Complete biface roughouts and unfinished bifaces are described in Table 5.3.

Unfinished bifaces (Pl. 12). The four nearly complete unfinished bifaces from RkIh-36 range from rounded (and in cortex) to pointed at the ends. They show little variation in length, which is 62.5 to 67.5 mm long, but otherwise no two are alike. Additional forms are present among the unfinished fragments and finished bifaces. RkIh-36:73 (Pl. 12E) gradually tapers from its thick roughed out cortical butt to a thin tip. The other complete specimens are illustrated. Fragments represent the rounded to pointed ends of biface blades, especially ones of larger format. Two of these are 56 mm wide. This width is exceeded by only a few specimens found on other sites.

Finished bifaces (Pl. 11). Five serviceably edged (not fully finished?) to finely finished biface blades were recovered in addition to a pointed basalt blade fragment and the projectile points.

TABLE 5.4.   COMPLETE UNFINISHED BIFACES AND BIFACE ROUGHOUTS, SITE RkIh-36

No. RkIh-36:	L	W	T	Form
Unfinished Bifaces				
10	63	35.8	13	Planoconvex, symmetrical, lenticular in plan
73	63.4	28	14	Width and T taper to tip, described in text
111	62.5	25+	8.5	Ovoid, rounded ends, side removed by outrepassé flake, made on flake blank
196	66.5	38.3	10.2	Flat base, pointed end, nearly a roughout
Roughouts or Implements with Single Edge (width measured from back to edge)				
121	81	55	23	Ends sharp semipointed & thick with cortex
226	68+	50.5	23	Cortical back extends across intact end
364	79	34.7	15	Extremely rudimentary, unformed cortical & pointed ends, cortex forms back
Roughouts with two Parallel or Parallel-convergent Edges				
From lake shore				
13	79	36.5	24	Thick, planoconvex, largely unifacial, on split pebble, cortex at pointed end
15	60+	37.7	16.8	Roughly ovoid elongate; some cortex on faces
16	77	32.3	15	Roughly slug-shaped, on sideblow flake or split pebble, ends pointed, arched
17	68	46+	16	Roughly elliptical, trace cortex at edge
20	71	42.3	27	Thick planoconvex, triangular cross-section, cortex at rounded ends
32	76+	43	20.5	Rudimentary, one edge thick flat, cortex on rounded end
56	71	45	14.5	Irregular tending ovoid, cortex at end
From excavation				
77	68	60	14	Square tabular, 2 edges remain as cortex (Pl.12J)
99	57	25.6	18.3	Linear semiunifacial on thick flake, some cortex remains on back and one end
136	68	25.6	12	Elongate parallel sided, semipointed ends, cortex remains on one face
151	78	62	19	Rudimentary, roughly elliptical, no shaped edge,
177	59+	47	19	Thick, subrectangular, on split pebble, cortex at rounded end and along one side
207	61.2	37.4	19.4	Planoconvex, lenticular in plan, one sharply rounded end retains some cortex
216	80	42.6	12.6	Elongate elliptical, cortex at ends (Pl. 12K)
233	54.6	33	16	Irregular tending to planoconvex ovoid
292	55.5	31.3	18	Ends pointed and round in cortex
383	78	62	19	Very rudimentary, one end pointed

Some of the points and the basalt fragment comprise the only nonobsidian specimens in the biface industry. No two specimens are alike. Nevertheless, the variety of biface tools is meagre. The bifaces include a thin well-finished blade fragment (Pl. 11H), an ovoid or nearly discoidal implement (Pl. 12B), and a thicker leafshaped blade Pl. 11I). The latter two implements are extensively smoothed at the edges and on the ridges between flake scars. Such smoothing, found also on other excavated specimens from RkIh-36, is credited to natural agencies or attrition in the soil context. Another possible explanation is that these pieces were recycled into the site from elsewhere already in their "worn" condition. The massive blade illustrated in Plate 12L shows patches of unmodified cortex at each end at the edges. Although this condition might be a criterion of unfinished work, natural cortical ends also are common on biface blades from other sites. It is entirely possible therefore that these implements are as finished as was intended to be the case and that the unfinished ends suited their mode of hafting. This RkIh-36 tool is the longest obsidian artifact from any Batza Téna site. Natural obsidian cobbles of its length (134 mm) evidently are rare.

Points (Pl. 11). The term "point" usually infers projectile point. One specimen from RkIh-36 with notched base is of such wide proportions that its identification as a point must be questioned seriously. It is incomplete but identification as a hafted knife is likely. The points are of side notched or indented, leafshaped, and indeterminate stemmed (incomplete) varieties and are made from obsidian, basalt and cherts. Each is described in Table 5.5. Four of the seven excavated points are of material other than obsidian, which is noteworthy considering the low incidence of other flaked nonobsidian artifacts and the complete absence of evidence for any knapping at the site other than obsidian flaking. Several exotic points evidently were brought to the location by people who came from beyond Batza Téna.

Unifacial Industry. This industry consists of bevelled or retouched flakes and end scrapers, plus a few other objects shaped on one surface or face.

End scrapers (Pl. 13). The end scrapers commonly are flakes with one edge bevelled on the dorsal surface, usually at the distal end in terms of flake orientation. Occasionally the two adjacent edges or sides of the scraper are bevelled, but this usually was done to shape the piece, and rarely to form additional scraping edges, e.g.,a convergent scraper (Pl. 13S). Otherwise, the scrapers retain the form of the original flake blank. There are one or two exceptions, RkIh-36:59 and to some extent 36:89 (Pl. 13Q-R). On these specimens the entire dorsal surface is shaped through flaking directed from both lateral edges. Two scrapers also have been trimmed to a petal shape (Pl. 13M-N). Frequently the dorsal surface is wholly or partially cortical (Pl. 13 O-P). This reflects an emphasis on the selection of primary and secondary decortication flakes for scraper blanks. On some, though, the dorsum bears negative flake scars and ridges carried over from the parent core from which the flake blank was detached. Chert specimens often have a flat dorsum due to this attribute. There appears to have been no preshaping of the dorsal surface on the core or selection of flake blanks for particular attributes such as double or single dorsal ridges, flat or tabular profiles, fan-shaped plan, etc., though all these and other attributes are present in the

TABLE 5.5.   POINTS FROM SITES RkIh-36 AND RkIh-35

No.	Type	Material	L	W	T	Description
RkIh-36:...						
19	Side indented	Obsidian	37+	c26	7.7	Beach rolled, base concave, stem c20 mm wide, expands slightly
142	Side indented	Obsidian	49.3	29	8.3	Stem 17.8 mm wide, base convex, base & notch edges ground (Pl.11D)
156	Long-stemmed	Obsidian	45.6+	23.2	9.3	Stem tapers from barely offset shoulders to broken base; edges ground (Pl. 11B)
175	Side/base notched	Light-grey chert	--	42	7.2	16.5 mm wide inside notches, convex base, not projectile point? Edges of base & notch ground (Pl. 11G)
179	Side indented	Grey chert	34.5	c23.5	7.6	Stem 16.7 mm wide, base convex (Pl. 11F)
190	--	Obsidian	--	27+	5.6	Damaged fragment, nearly straight base
204	--	Basalt	--	c22	c5	Apparent midsection of stemmed point
215	Leaf-shaped	Basalt	53.5	23.3	6.2	Excurvate sides converge towards rounded base (Pl. 11 A)
RkIh-35:...						
9	Stemmed	Dark chert	41+	18.9	6.2	Stem broken, less than 14 mm wide; blade asymmetrical, no edge smoothing (Pl 11C)
62	Stemmed-side/base indented	Obsidian	59	26.8	6.0	Well flaked, sharp tip, symmetrical, stem 20 mm wide (Pl. 11E)

assemblage. The end scrapers are not always longer than they are wide.

Ventral surfaces always are unretouched and retain the longitudinal profile of the flake blank. Thus, they usually are flat, though a few are arched at the bevelled end. This characteristic is pronounced in the two largest specimens, which are the ones noted with flaked dorsum. Generally, corners are rounded rather than sharply cornered or spurred. No one or two attributes or attribute combinations alone characterize the collection. Nevertheless, all scraper bits come from a single delimited site area and a very few persons probably are responsible for producing the entire lot. Compared with the obsidian scrapers, the small sample of five nonobsidian end scrapers shows a relatively greater frequency of bevelled lateral margins and flat, predominately single flake dorsal surfaces. Each specimen is described in Table 5.6. The average length and width, of 37.9 and 31.5 mm respectively, is seen to be more or less similar to that of scrapers from other Batza Téna sites (in Table Append.II.3), an exception being the large 60.1 by 36.2 mm specimens from the Lake 324 complex (RlIg-52, Chapter 6).

Trial uniface group (not illustrated). A series of unifacially flaked objects was segregated and examined for evidence of reoccurring unifacial tool types. It appears that most of these items are

TABLE 5.6.   END SCRAPERS FROM SITES RkIh-36 AND RkIh-35

No.	Material	L	W*	T	Dorsum; Notes**
RkIh-36:					
1	Obsidian	36.4	30.3	9	Cortex/flake; notched side
2	Not obsidian	32+	32 (17 edge)	8	Natural fracture; 2 retouched edges, both functional?
3	Obsidian	41.6	26	8.8	Cortex; some ventral flaking
68	Chert	41	35.2	9.4	Single flake, sharp corner, also has major side bevel
70	Obsidian	29.9	28.5	8.1	Flaked; sharp corner; hydration measure
71	Obsidian	28	34.8	10	Cortex; ventral face irregular
83	Obsidian	34	39.8	8.3	Flaked; sharp corner; hydration measure
88	Chert	24	28.1	8.2	Flake scar; 3 bevels, 2 or all of which are functional edges, rectangular
89	Obsidian	67	39.5	12.7	Cortex & retouch; crushed retouched sides also are scraping edges?
92	Nonobsidian	38.1	28.6	7.8	Flat seam; sides well bevelled
95	Obsidian	38.3	28.2	7.3	Flake scars; red colour
97	Obsidian	29.2	31.4	6.6	Flake, cortex; hydration measured
98	Obsidian	34.9	31.8	7.3	Cortex; hydration measured
113	Obsidian	48	29.4	8	Cortex, flake; sharp corner
126	Obsidian	45.6	39.2	7.9	Flake, cortex; trimming bevel on side, well worn
129	Obsidian	36.9	36.2	7.6	Flake, cortex; sharp corner
133	Obsidian	31.9	34.8	9.5	Flake scar
139	Obsidian	26+	19.6	6.1	Cortex; hydration measured
140	Obsidian	37.9	27.7	10.1	Cortex; on side-blow flake
141	Obsidian	32.8	33.5	9.7	Cortex; 3 sides bevelled and crushed at edge
143	Obsidian	29	30.4	6.5	Flake; concave sides bevelled
145	Chert	43.1	31.6	8.2	Flake scars; fits 642-643
159	Obsidian	73	28.7	12.3	Dorsum shaped from the sides; end worn, side edges crushed, unique format
182	Obsidian	42.6	36.3	6.9	Flake scar; sides bevelled and crushed at edges but only end is worn smooth
187	Obsidian	37.2	30.2	5.3	Cortex; hydration measured
194	Obsidian	46.5	35.3	10.3	Flakes; thin side also bevelled
195	Obsidian	36	37.5	10.6	Cortex; flake scar
205	Obsidian	22+	31.7	6.5	Cortex; hydration measured
206	Obsidian	35	34.4	6.9	Flake scar; uneven bit edge
211	Obsidian	26.5	34	9.2	Cortex; one side also bevelled
217	Obsidian	38	35	10	Flake scar; edge 29 mm wide
238	Obsidian	40.5	36.2	11.2	Flake scars, cortex; very thin
239	Obsidian	26	28	9.1	Cortex, flake; short side worn, convergent edges
287	Obsidian	47	29	8.8	Cortex; spatulate stemmed, end scraper or combination tool, burned and eroded
353	Obsidian	43.8	24	7.5	Thin sharp 19.5 mm working edge
373	Obsidian	frag.	30.3	6	Flake, cortex; hydration measured
374	Obsidian	24+	25.2	3.8	Atypically thin
391	Obsidian	31.2	19.7	4.8	Cortex; hydration measured
392	Obsidian	30.3	28	6.8	Mostly cortex; edge well worn
421	Obsidian	33.4	24.5	8.6	All cortex
447	Obsidian	33	29.6	9.6	All cortex
493	Obsidian	31.4	32	5	All cortex; irregular edge
494	Obsidian	44.8	32.5	7	Largely single flake scar
495	Obsidian	39.8	39.2	5-7	All cortex; hydration measured
497	Obsidian	36.3	36.6	9.6	All cortex
571	Obsidian	39	25.1	8.3	Largely cortex
613	Obsidian	c35	c42	9.2	Irreg. flake back; edge irregular
672	Obsidian	35.3	34.5	8	Cortex; from flake lot
705	Obsidian	--	29.3	11.3	On end fragment of bladelike flake from flake lot

TABLE 5.6--concluded

No.	Material	L	W*	T	Dorsum; Notes**
RkIh-36 all		43	49	49	Sample size in calculation
		38	31.5*	8	Average
RkIh-35:					
24	Obsidian	34	38	8.0	Flaked surface; edge worn
51	Obsidian	43	36	12.3	Single cortex surface; curved edge
107	Obsidian	34.3	36.5	9	Flake scar; convergent bevels; butt ground/worn ventrally
150	Obsidian	41.9	28	10.4	Single cortex surface; curved edge
149	Black chert	30	25	6.4	Flake scars; also 1 side bevel
184	Obsidian	31.8	29	5.1	Cortex surface; very worn
188	Obsidian	34.9	22.1	5.0	Flake & cortex; delicate
RkIh-35 average		36	31	8	

*Length of the working edge sometimes is less than the maximum width of the specimen. The average working edge W (N=47) is 30 mm.
**The first observation describes the back of the scraper.

exceptional cases involving unfinished tools normally expressed in the bifacial mode. Most appear to be in the roughout stage and have little diagnostic value. No. 36:606, however, is an finished uniface in the form of a thick flake completely retouched over the dorsal surface. It is broken and, probably for that reason, lacks a functional edge.

Bevelled and/or utilized flakes. These flakes, many of them fragments, are divided into two groups. Those in one group have been intentionally bevelled or bear retouch or wear (edge smoothing and crushing) resulting from their use as tools. The other group contains the more dubious specimens in which wear and retouch very likely is the result of trampling and natural attrition in the soil. It is not always clear in which category a specimen should be placed. Selected examples are described briefly below.

RkIh-36:67 is an irregular flake with a worn curved thick bevelled edge.
No. 199 is a large, thin, linear basalt flake with a low-angle dorsal bevel extending along one edge and extending around the curved end of the flake.
No. 236+407 is a small nonobsidian flake with a consistent narrow steep bevel along one concave margin.
No. 128 (incomplete) is a flat flake on which both margins are retouched on the dorsal face.
No. 198 is a very broad flake bearing an edge that either was intentionally bevelled or is chipped from heavy use as a scraper.
No. 232 is a flat flake bearing dorsal retouch around the entire perimeter. The edges converge to a sharply pointed tip.
No. 253, which measures 22 x 44 mm, bears dorsal retouch and has a crushed edge at the rounded distal end of the flake blank. This end is similar to but thinner than the edge of an end scraper.

Burin (laterally burinated flake) (Pl. 11K). A linear chert flake 61+ mm long (incomplete) is finely retouched on the dorsal surface along one lateral edge and evidently also was retouched on the opposite margin. Most of the latter edge has been superseded by a 42-mm-long burin facet. The facet terminates in a jagged step fracture. It originates at a crushed platform edge where there is a slight negative bulb of percussion on the facet. Because of these attributes, I interpret this to be a true burin facet. Additional narrow linear flakes also had been detached from the back of the flake.

Other Objects

Notched cobble chopper (Pl. 14B). A small, flat, alluvial cobble, 22 mm thick and approximately 100 mm wide, was bifacially flaked across one end to produce a straight, blunt 75-mm-long edge. Two small opposed notches were placed on the lateral edges near the poll end of the implement and two broader smoothed or blunted indentations were formed adjacent to the retouched edge.

Large, flat flake uniface and other Large Tabular Objects. A nonobsidian implement (Pl. 14G) stands apart from all others due to its size: 95 by 81 by 13 mm thick. The ventral surface is nearly flat and evidently was formed when a cobble was split to form the blank flake. Unlike split cobble implements and chitho hide scrapers, it has been completely retouched over the dorsal surface through removal of several large flat flakes and through bevelling of the margin. The broad bevel is limited largely to one edge. The opposite edge is retouched primarily through removal of flat flakes from the ventral surface, and the edge at the end is flat and thick. All edges are smoothed, but this condition probably can be attributed to weathering and natural attrition in the ground.

Two additional large tabular cobble spalls were recovered from the beach. One is a split schist shingle (broken and incomplete). It bears unifacial retouch on the cortical surface at the intact broad end. Tabular chitho hide scrapers commonly are made on split shingles, but unlike the present specimen chithos usually have a battered bifacial edge retouch. The second specimen from the beach also is a split cobble shingle broken and bevelled along one edge. It is thoroughly water-rolled and the retouch modification may be natural, predating the time of water-rolling. However, in the area where this piece was found the soils of the site and substrate contain no stone other than obsidian and cobbles brought in by the occupants and thus the item appears to be an implement.

Hammerstones (Pl. 14). Hammerstones are alluvial cobbles that show areas of impact, e.g. crushing or pecking derived from use. Each specimen is described in Table 5.7. Hammerstones were more numerous at RkIh-36 than at any other Batza Téna site. Hard hammers might occur at most sites where there was primary processing of obsidian nodules, especially to produce biface roughouts. However, except at RkIh-36 they are rare. Selected or favored hammers, collected from stream beds often more than one kilometre distant, may have been retained or curated and for that reason seldom are found at the flaking stations. Those from RkIh-36 probably served in some cases as maul heads or for purposes other than obsidian knapping. Additional cobbles and fragments were recovered. Many of the latter appear to be heat altered and probably were boiling stones. A few of the hammerstones also appear to be heat altered.

TABLE 5.7. HAMMERSTONES FROM SITES RkIh-36 AND RkIh-35

No.	Weight grams	L & W mm	Description
RkIh-36:			
102	420	211x71	Light crushing at various locations (Pl.14E)
130	141	112x57x16	Thin, elongate, side edges battered (Pl.14D)
135	140	78x51	Pecked along one edge and at end
185	398	80x62	Burned?, battered at each end (Pl. 14J)
208	107	88x58x16	Thin, lateral edges battered
210	232	80x52	Quartz, pointed end and corners of rounded end are battered
231	185+	70x?	Incomplete, burned, subspherical, battered areas present
357	513	91x66	Angular, impacted at end corners
371	306	71x66	Subrectangular, middle of end battered
553	120	67x55	Slightly pecked (and eroded?)
577	331	116x50	Trianguloid section, crushing & battering at pointed ends, use traces elsewhere
RkIh-35			
21	156	65x50x36	Subconical-subrectangular pebble, ends battered
37	235	71x50+	Subconical pebble, mainly small end battered, fits hand nicely
38	610	146x45x52	Ends & one side battered or shaped, rectangular cross section (Pl. 14H)
39	327	94x72x42	Angular pebble, slight battering at ends
92	364	117x61x36	Elongate river cobble, crushed and battered at both ends (Pl. 14I)
123	133	56x51	Small pebble, not definitely used

Copper awl (Pl. 11J). The widespread subarctic copper working techniques of hammering and folding (Franklin et al 1981) are plainly visible on a 62.5-mm-long awl. This is the only native metal specimen recovered from Batza Téna. It tapers gradually from a somewhat irregular rectangular butt, measuring 8 by 2.5 mm in section, to a very sharp tip. There is no trace of the tip having been sharpened through grinding, though heavy patination may obscure evidence of the mode of finishing.

Dating and Assessment

The RkIh-36 settlement locus, as defined from the distribution of end scrapers and other implements, is set within a considerably larger site that was primarily a flaking station or merged cluster of flaking stations. Inasmuch as for the flaking station aspect, finished implements seem to be relatively uncommon (occurring in low frequency in the shore-zone collection and outside the boundary of the occupation locus drawn in Figure 5.4), we can assume that the implement cluster represents primarily a single occupation. Possibly, though, some people camped there at other times and left a few additional tools.

Calcined bone from the unformalized hearth feature context described above yielded a radiocarbon date of 1355 ± 260 years (S-976) or A.D. 625. At one sigma error, but without MASCA or true age correction and without adjustment for the dated material being calcined bone (which could increase it by 15%), the date falls between A.D. 885 and A.D. 365. The radiocarbon date thus provides a very blunt measure of the age of the site. Moreover, we cannot be certain that it does not apply to a flaking station episode rather than the occupation responsible for the implement accumulation. Recovery of a microblade industry indicates that an earlier age is possible and in fact is likely. Northern Archaic and Tuktu components at Onion Portage (Anderson 1968) and Anaktuvuk Pass (Campbell 1961) are dated between 4200 and 6500 years ago, but the Onion Portage occupation is truncated and in the case of the Anaktuvuk Tuktu other, younger, dates are available (Gal 1982). The impulse to assign early dates to notched points that prevailed three decades ago has been tempered by the realization that similar points, and also microblades, can date to a relatively late period. Accordingly, the RkIh-36 radiocarbon date cannot be dismissed as being fundamentally too recent, although, as is discussed in the next chapter, it may be adjusted to a slightly older date because the dated material is calcined bone. This adjustment of approximately three centuries is not critical to the present discussion.

To examine this feasibility of the date, and the possibility that different technologies represented by the collection come from components of occupation widely separated in time, obsidian hydration measurements were taken on four categories of artifacts: bladelike flakes, end scrapers, biface outrepassé flakes, and microblades (Clark 1984). The hinged biface outrepassé edge flakes and bladelike flakes were intended to represent the flaking station aspect, the end scrapers the main camp occupation, and the microblades foreseeably would represent an earlier occupation if multiple components are present. All sets produced average hydration values sufficiently close that there is no basis for concluding that they do not belong to closely spaced occupations by people of a single cultural tradition, if not to a single occupation. If more than one occupation is involved the age differences are not great and grouping into a single culture phase remains justifiable. Instead of being the oldest artifacts, there is a weak basis for concluding that the microblades are the youngest ones, and the mean hydration of the biface flakes and bladelike flakes falls on either side of that of the end scrapers. Significantly, in all cases the thickness of hydration was sufficiently low to be comparable with the age indicated by the radiocarbon date. The hydration measurements actually are uncomfortably low, requiring a hydration rate somewhat slower than was anticipated for the site in order to give equivalent dates that are not altogether too young for a microblade industry.

There is a basis for accepting the presence of microblades in western interior Alaska as late as near the end of the first millennium A.D. (Holmes 1986:153 ff). It is difficult, though, to set an exact time when the last microblades were produced. While it has become necessary, but possible, to accommodate a late date for the microblades, which also could fit into an earlier time frame, there is one artifact for which it is difficult to accept any other than a late date. This is the copper awl. Most native copper in sites of Western Subarctic of Alaska and the Yukon is derived from sources in the Copper River drainage or peripheral to the Wrangell Range and dates to the last centuries of the second millennium A.D. Early second millennium dates are possible in a few cases. The RkIh-36 specimen appears to be either precocious or is derived from later use of the site. The possibility that this piece might have been traded to North America along with iron of Asian origin also might be considered in the light of the fact that an Asian iron bit was found at in a first millennium A.D. Hahanudan Lake house (Chapter 6).

Site RkIh-37

This is a shore-zone collection of undetermined affiliation recovered adjacent to the principal Batza Téna Tuktu site. Material was collected from the narrow strip of shore exposed during low-water early in 1970. The site is on a northeastern extension of the shoreline that runs along the face of Site RkIh-36. It is separated from the latter by a strip of lake shore covered with a surficial layer of soft comminuted organic detritus. This litter cover prevented us from determining whether the distribution of flakes between the two sites is continuous. The collection came from a 65-m-long strip of washed sandy beach. The shore here is angled to the north and departs from the trend of the front of RkIh-36. Terrain behind the shore strip is a low bank that supports a growth of tussocks. It was not an inviting locale for test excavation. Relatively large obsidian flakes and artifacts were found on surface and within the sand on the upper part of the beach, but none were observed in the underlying more compact, unwashed clayey or soily sand.

Collections consists of 6.3 kg of flakes and 53 catalogued items. These are classified in Table 5.1. Some uncataloged cores (Pl 23M, see also Pl. 23J, 24J) are from the flake lots while several items originally catalogued have been demoted to the status of flakes. Certain distinctive artifacts are discussed below.

There are 5 pieces of chert and basaltic rock. These are a chip, a "winged" flake (a type often derived from lateral trimming of wedgeshaped microblade core platforms), a flake bevelled on two sides that probably is an end scraper fragment, a rough biface fragment, and an apparent sideblade knife. The latter (Pl. 22L) is made on a large side-blow flake. The broad, single, cutting edge is bifacially retouched. The dorsal surface of this flake also bears some coarser flaking, probably reflecting shaping on the core prior to detachment. An obsidian microblade is irregular and it is not certain that it came from a prepared microblade core.

One of the finished bifaces (Pl. 20P) can be compared with a Kayuk knife or "double-edged side scraper (Campbell 1959, 1962 Pl. 2-16; see discussion of the Kayak problem in Chapter 6). The faces are formed through parallel oblique flaking, a Kayuk characteristic. The blunt, slightly rounded ends have been left in cortex. This feature also is found on a more delicate specimen of this type from another Batza Téna site, and thus is not taken to indicate that the implement is unfinished. Nevertheless, the present specimen may not have been an altogether satisfactory tool inasmuch as most of one edge is very thick and blunt.

This assemblage is neither clearly part of the Batza Téna Tuktu phase, nor can it be excluded on the basis of the few distinctive implements recovered. The modestly high incidence of artifacts made of material other than obsidian is one point of concordance, but there also is a relatively high frequency of nonobsidian items at RkIh-32 (Chapter 4). However, aside from the fact that RkIh-32 could be related to Batza Téna Tuktu, the occurrence of nonobsidian items in the sites at Batzatiga could be credited to their being gateway sites for people who came from the west to exploit the obsidian source.

Site RkIh-35 "Beaver Knoll"

This site (Figures 5.10-5.12) provided the second principal Batza Téna Tuktu collection. In 1970 nine quick shovel probes and two small test pits revealed a wide distribution of obsidian detritus. A number of widely-spaced sections were excavated in 1971. These were positioned in relation to a rectangular baseline laid out over the site (Fig. 5.12).

The site occupies the top of a prominent low knoll or bench that supports a mixed forest of spruce, birch and shrubs (Fig. 5.10, 5.11). By 1970 the front slope was largely deforested by beavers who had been extirpated by trappers a few years earlier. A large beaver house remained just off shore in front of the site gives the site its name "Beaver Knoll." As seen from across the lake, the site terrain is a distinctive hill, though apparent relief is enhanced by the taller forest growth here as compared to elsewhere in the immediate vicinity. But, like the adjacent terrain on which smaller site RkIh-36 is located, from other directions, especially from the flat tundra at rear of the site between it and Batzatiga, the elevation is less pronounced. Drainage provided by the slope to the front encourages the forest growth that distinguishes the knoll from the tundra. The forest root network made excavation very difficult in some sections.

Flakes and artifacts occur from the surface (in the rootmat) to, for instance, a depth of 13 cm in one test and 17 cm in another test. The artifacts were found in association with various soils which in places, evidently due to frost action, display a complex or irregular pattern.

Artifacts also were collected from the shore in front of the knoll and were recorded under the site designation RkIh-34. The slope near the shore appears to contain little archaeological material. Shovel tests and a substantial pit dug into the sandy deposits in that area for the field party's "refrigerator" were negative, hence the attribution of the shore and knoll collections to different sites.

Collection

Artifact recovery from RkIh-35 suggests that activities there were similar to those at adjacent RkIh-36. Cobble artifacts include a notched cobble, a bevelled shingle, hammerstones and burned rock. There are rare microblades, two stemmed points (one is broken and could have been notched), numerous obsidian cores and bifacially worked items, a few end scrapers, and eleven nonobsidian flaked implements and fragments. In comparing the two sites, it may be noted that the collection from RkIh-35 comes from separated excavation units no two of which are likely to yield material from the same camping incident, while there is a certain distributional and typological coherence to the RkIh-36 excavated assemblage.

Including flake lots, there are 250 catalogue entries for RkIh-35. All but the first five are for the 1971 excavations. The assemblage is listed in Table 5.1 and other tables jointly with RkIh-36 artifacts. Descriptions of selected artifacts are provided below. The RkIh-35 collection was studied four years after the RkIh-36 collection was analyzed. In the event that my criteria for classification may have changed during that time, some key criteria used for defining RkIh-35 artifact classes will be restated.

Cores. Three of the numerous obsidian cores merit comment. Two, one a platform core, the other the residual face of a core, are essentially exhausted but display the fluted traces left after removal of bladelike flakes (Pl. 23 O). The flake scars are up to 70 mm long. The third core, RkIh-35:55 (Pl. 23H), has a subconical form, imparted through the shape of the original split cobble blank and detachment of flakes from around the perimeter. Flake removal had not progressed to the extend of removing all the cortex. Fissure flaws are present in the stone, and the core may have been discarded for this reason. If that had not been the case this piece probably would have become very similar to a conical microblade core.

Rudimentary or amorphous reduction. These objects are worked but are so rough and rudimentary that they are not obviously either bifaces or cores. Most probably are early stage rejects from the biface industry. Counted here among these pieces also is a small chert nubbin. This quadrilateral, 22 by 22 by 12 mm piece is reduced on all sides and edges. Unlike the case for pièces esquillées, which usually are thinner, there is no crushing on the edges or traces or burin or microblade-like spalling.

Roughouts (Pl. 12A,C). These objects are shaped through bifacial techniques, but are very rough or coarse and unformed over much of the surface, some of which is still in cortex. The final shape intended is not obvious. The five complete roughouts tend to have rounded ends, excurvate sides, and are 52 to 68 mm long and 25 to 51 mm wide (or 57 mm counting fragments).

Bifaces, unfinished. Objects in this class are clearly unfinished, but are believed to reflect the form of the intended finished object. They are more finely prepared than the roughouts with which they intergrade. Three fragments may be ends of broad, ovoid pointed bifaces.

Specimen RkIh-35:26+31 (Pl. 12I) is shaped like an adze blade, 67 mm long and 47 mm wide. The similarity in shapes, featuring a thin straight transverse edge at one end opposite a thick rounded end, may be coincidental.

Figure 5.10. RkIh-35 as seen from across Batzati Lake.

Figure 5.11. RkIh-35, looking westward, as seen from the flat between the site and the hill Batzatiga (1971 R2 F15).

Specimen RkIh-35:81 may be an unfinished point, notched along one edge, abandoned when efforts to thin the other edge of the 56-mm-long piece failed. The latter edge consists of a large flat area, highly crushed along one side.

The remaining specimens are a small subrectangular object measuring 45 by 35 mm, a pear-shaped biface measuring 61 by 47 mm, and an illustrated fragment (Pl. 12M).

Bifaces, nearly finished. None of the bifaces, other than the points (below) is fully or finely finished, but some items may be as finished as their maker had intended them to be. In this group there is a midsection fragment no wider than a projectile point but thicker, two incomplete relatively broad bifaces (Pl. 12G-H), and two leafshaped specimens--one complete and one incomplete. The smaller one of the last two (RkIh-35:43, Pl. 12D)) shows wear or attrition on the flake ridges of the faces and has ground edges in the area of the apparent broken stem. The larger, complete, finely proportioned symmetrical blade, RkIh-35:63 (Pl. 12F), is 85 mm long, 36.5 wide and up to 11 mm thick.

Points. RkIh-35:62 (Pl. 11E) is a finely flaked, 59-mm-long, 27-mm-wide obsidian point. It has a waisted stem, slightly concave along the sides and across the base and separated from the blade portion by gently sloping shoulders.

Chert point RkIh-35:9 (Pl. 11C) also has sloping shoulders terminated by a stem break. The form of the base is not readily apparent. The relatively narrow 19-mm-wide blade is not as well proportioned and prepared as the preceding point. The third specimen is a nondiagnostic tip fragment

Retouched/utilized flakes. There are 17 reasonably certain bevelled implements plus 8 examples for which I am not convinced that the bevelling and edge crushing was not produced incidentally (not through use) or through natural agencies. Some of the latter have prepared edges, but the preparation probably was to serve as a flaking platform and not as an implement edge. Numerous additional very dubiously retouched specimens have not been counted.

One retouched flake (Pl. 11R) has a bifacially prepared edge. A straight break on the flake blank forms the back of this probable knife sideblade.

The others have dorsal surface edge bevels of varying degrees of steepness. In many cases the bevels may be the result of use rather than intentional retouch or shaping. One bevelled edge is slightly notched, and in a few cases bevelling or use has straightened an edge to some degree. The basic form, however, is that of the decortication flake blank. In most instances there is some smoothing of the edge through wear, evidently from use as scrapers. A few specimens are sufficiently sharp, though, that they could be cutting tools.

Four retouched flakes are of black chert or other nonobsidian lithology. Two of them have

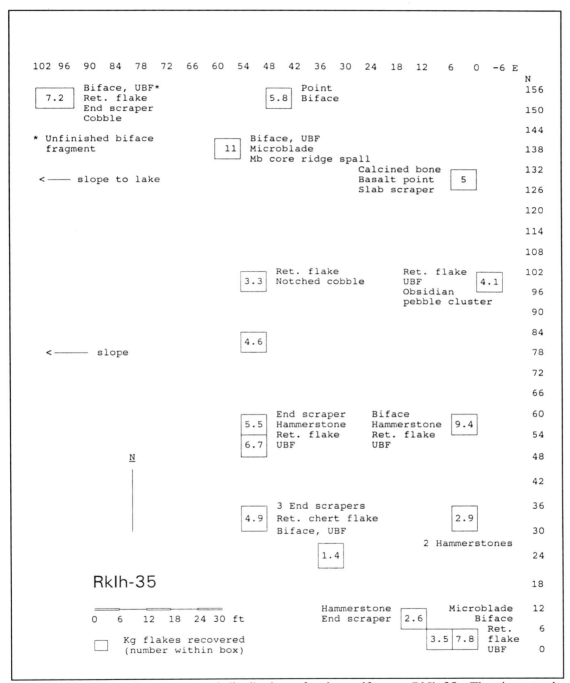

Figure. 5.12. Excavation Layout and distribution of major artifacts at RkIh-35. The site extends
<u>c</u> 100 feet farther along the NS axis and 50 feet along the EW axis.

extremely fine edge retouch. Among this group is the largest retouched flake from RkIh-35 (Pl. 14C). This 66-mm-wide flake has a single 77-mm-long bevelled edge, and once it may have been longer as the flake blank was broken at some stage of its history.

End scrapers. Two of the seven end scraper blades (Table 5.6) have highly arcuate bevelled ends. One group of artifacts found closely associated is comprised of the two end scrapers just noted which are on obsidian cortical flakes, a well-formed black chert end scraper, a utilized red obsidian flake, and a fragment of a small prismatic blade of chert.

Flat notched cobble (Pl. 14A). A large flat notched cobble is unlike the few others from Batza Téna, which either are small or are retouched, but it is similar to ones credited to the Northern Archaic tradition from Alaska and the Yukon.

Retouched split shingle or cobble spall (Pl. 14F). This broken object is 10 cm wide across the break and expanding. It is suggestive of the chitho or stone slab hide working stone except that chithos usually have battered or bifacial retouch. The present specimen has a well prepared unifacial bevel. A smaller unifacially bevelled split shingle came from the RkIh-36 shore area.

Hammerstones. The hammerstones, pitted from impact, include both small cobbles that can be grasped by the fingers and two elongate maul-shaped hammers.

Assessment and Dating

No date is available for this site. There are several cross-ties with RkIh-36. These include a notched alluvial pebble and other utilized pebbles, a notched point, cores for bladelike flakes, a like incidence of artifacts not of obsidian, and rare microblades. Together with the lack of any evidence suggesting otherwise, this assemblage is considered to be closely related to the main Batza Téna Tuktu component.

Site RkIh-34

Material was collected from a narrow strip of shore at RkIh-34, exposed during low-water in 1970. The site consists only of the shore strip located in front of RkIh-35. Test probes failed to reveal any archaeological material on the lower slopes of "Beaver Knoll" between RkIh-34 and RkIh-35. For 20 m the shore here was strewn with relatively large obsidian flakes. Only 14 individual items of low characterization were catalogued. These contribute little to our understanding of the Batza Téna Tuktu complex and do not necessarily belong with it.

The collection consists of 3.6 kg of flakes, several platformed cores and core fragments, a trimmed split pebble, a few bladelike flakes, and a subrectangular biface fragment. A fine-appearing platformed core (Pl. 23G, Fig. 4.1c) has several parallel flute scars suggestive of blade removal, but the distribution of cortex and imperfections in the piece suggest that is unlikely that little more than decortication flakes had been removed. One bladelike decortication flake shows heavy utilization on the sharp concave edge.

Site RkIh-38

Collections and test probes were made here in 1970, and in 1971 when a memorable incident occurred. Our party of four persons was charged then by a very determined small black bear. The bear rushed, then slowly closed the distance to about 5 metres, and with much hesitation finally turned and fled after we raised a great din banging with trowels (which was to its benefit because we were prepared to shoot it).

The site is situated on the northwest side of an unnamed lake or Hellodilithta Lake (local name), approximately one km from the main Batza Téna Tuktu component described above. Finds of lithic material here were sparse and dispersed although several bank exposures were examined. High ground on the outlying side of the lake (away from Batzatiga) was probed with a metal ice chisel in 1971 but no site was found away from the bank along the lake. Minor flake clusters were found along the bank for a considerable (unmeasured) distance and one was collected.

Only 0.2 kg of flakes were found in 1970 along various parts of the site. Clusters found in 1971 were localized at the edge of the bank and through trowelling 5.8 kg flakes and a few artifacts were collected.

Core (Pl. 24F)	38:8
Biface roughout fragment, rudimentary	38:9
Biface fragments, small, unfinished	38:1, 38:4
Single-notched pebble	38:2
Planoconvex implement on a long, arched flake, half the ventrum is flattened through flaking, is dorsally flaked from both edges unfinished, closest format is a slug-shaped uniface, relatively unique to Batza Téna (Pl. 22F)	38:10
Retouched flake, large, low-angle unifacial retouch along one edge, cortex other edge, 73 mm long, irregular but an unequivocal implement, possibly knife sideblade	38:3
Chert flake proximal fragment, thin, both edges retouched	38:5

The notched pebble is a type characteristic of Batza Téna Tuktu.

Site RkIg-22

This site, located near the west end of the south flank of "Basecamp Ridge" was surface collected and a localized trowel probe was made in 1969. It was revisited in 1970 when three implements were collected from the surface but the few exposed flakes seen were not collected and no testing was done. It is the only component described in this chapter that is not part of the site cluster at Batzatiga. RIIg-22 consists essentially of two areas of flake concentration (Fig. 5.13). One area was divided for collection and called Area 2 and 4. There is some flake scatter beyond and between clusters.

Area 1 has an irregular-shaped flake cluster averaging 60 cm in diameter. Several large flakes and chunks of obsidian, some of them located under the surface were collected.
Area 2, about 1.3 m across, yielded a number of artifacts.
Several flakes occurred relatively sparsely distributed in a zone barely 2 m in diameter, adjacent to Area 2, designated as Area 4.
Area 3 is separated from Area 2 by a zone about 23 m broad in which there were few, and in most places no flakes. No implements were found there.

From Area 1 there are 128 flakes (1.5 kg). The pitted cortex predominates, although fissured also is prominent. The fissured and a fine or semi-smooth textured cortex predominate among the 750 flakes (2.1 kg) collected from Area 2. Area 4 yielded 84 flakes and no implements. From Area 4 there are 160 (.04 kg) flakes with cortex similar to Area 1.

Core, unclassified amorphous (Area 1)	22:3
Rough biface pebble chopper or core (Area 1)	22:2
Kayuk-style knife or scraper (isolated, position in Fig. 5.13)	
70x31 x10.5mm; hydration was measured (Pl. 20 O,Fig. 5.14c)	22:29
Biface, damaged, irregular (Area 2)	22:11
Biface fragment (Area 1)	22:5
End scraper, 1 not obsidian (Area 2). Hydration measured for 22:7.	22:7, 22:27
Retouched flake scrapers (Areas 1 & 2; Pl.22I, Fig. 5.14d)	22:12, 22:14
No. 12 is a thick chert uniface steeply retouched along one edge.	
The form of the complete tool is not certain.	
Utilized flake, concave (Area 1, Pl. 22J)	22:1
Large notched mattock or axe (Area 2, Pl. 18B)	22:13
Boulder flake, weathered, scraper?	22.28
Hammerstone, large alluvial cobble, ovoid	NC

Other items catalogued, or noteworthy but not catalogued: 7 amorphous or fragmentary core fragments, many dubious utilized flakes, 3 hinged biface edge fragments (Area 2).

Some of these items may indicate affiliation with the Northern Archaic tradition. Figure 5.14 shows the kayuk-style knife together with several artifacts from minor sites of undetermined cultural affiliation, described briefly in Table 1.2. The kayuk-style knife produced inconsistent hydration readings that give equivalent ages of 1319 and 18,549 years at the 0.82 nonlinear rate. End scraper 22:7 produced three consistent hydration measurements of between 2.10 and 2.23 microns for which the equivalent age is between 3150 and 3552 years at the 1.4 rate and 5533 and

6065 years at the 0.82 rate. The third object sectioned for this site is the apparent unfinished botched biface fragment RkIg-22:11. There was one low reading of 0.91 microns and two thicker readings of 2.25 and 2.27 microns. The latter are practically stated the same as those on the end scraper and yield an equivalent age of about 6200 years at the 0.82 rate. On the basis of typology, any age between about 2000 years and 6000 years is probable for this material. Hydration suggests that the site dates to the earlier part of this range.

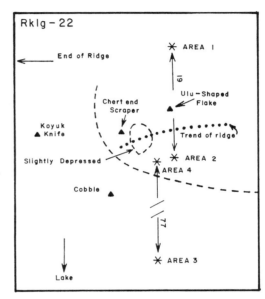

Figure 5.13. Sketch map of site RkIg-22.

Notched Points

Notched points are associated primarily with the Northern Archaic tradition of which Tuktu is a part. It may be appropriate to list here, in Table 5.8, other notched points from Batza Téna not in the RkIh-35/36 cluster. Two of these specimens come from fluted point site RkIg-31 which is described in Chapter 2. Another small notched point base is from fluted point site RlIg-47 while one from RkIg-1 is distantly and presumably coincidentally associated with a fluted point. The RkIg-1 notched point is associated with a cluster of end scrapers in Locus E. Hydration measurements on RkIg-1 specimens indicate a wide range of possible dates (Table 2.1) but the point may be no more than 800 years old. Three hydration measurements on the RkIg-31 specimen showed an absence of hydration except at one location where a measurement of 0.68 microns was obtained. This would indicate an age of less than 600 years at the slow 0.82 exponential hydration rate. Possibly, though there had been previous hydration that was obliterated and the is older. Three of the points listed in Table 5.8 were found clustered at site RlIg-33. The small, apparently late collection from this site is described in Chapter 8.

TABLE 5.8.   NOTCHED POINTS

Number	Material	Length mm	Width mm	Notch width	Details
RkIg-1:53	Obsidian	32+	27.5	13.0	Notch, base edges ground (Pl.19J)
RkIg-31:61	Chert	42	25	18.1	Base concave, notch edges ground, asymmetrical, 18-mm-long thinning flake off one face (Pl. 6E)
RkIg-31:55	Obsidian	34	25	18.2	Notch & base edges ground locally base slightly convex (Pl. 6D)
RkIg-x:37	Obsidian	41.2	29.8	21.7	Notches smoothed, base concave, 0.73 & 0.8 m hydration (Pl. 21M)
RkIh-37:	Obsidian	--	--	c14	Concave base frag., all edges smoothed, base width 20.4 mm (Pl. 21N)
RlIg-33:8	Obsidian	34	25.1	16.5	Corner notched, well proportioned triangular, base near straight, smoothed by attrition in the ground, 6.6 mm thick (Pl. 19Q)
RlIg-33:9	Obsidian	40.5	24.5	17.2	Well formed, notch & base edges smoothed, base slightly convex, 7.6 mm thick, (Pl. 19 O)
RlIg-33:10	Obsidian	33+	26.3	16.9	Poorly formed, smoothed by attrition in soil, straight base, 8 mm thick (Pl. 19S)
RlIg-33:11	Chert	37	24.4	17.2	Tip missing, c 40 long; 2 sets of ground notches
RlIg-37:168	Chert	---	20.5 at base	14.7	Edges smoothed, concave base, well formed
RlIg-44:3	Obsidian	48.7	27.9	21.8	Notches & base edges ground, well proportioned
RlIg-47:2	Obsidian	---	18+	12.8	Notch & base edges ground, thinning flake runs length of fragment

Tuktu and Batza Téna Tuktu

Two topics complement and conclude the foregoing presentation of data. One concerns the relationships of Batza Téna Tuktu within its northwest Alaskan context. The other topic is of broader scope and deals with the place of Batza Téna Tuktu within the Northern Archaic tradition and with the nature of that tradition and its place in prehistory. The first is the subject of the present section, the second topic will be discussed in the concluding chapter.

The reason why we chose to call this phase Batza Téna Tuktu instead of B.T. Northern Archaic is because the first is more specific and local. As well, that in 1971 the Northern Archaic was a new construct (Anderson 1968), Tuktu an old one (Campbell 1961), and the Northern Archaic had been defined as lacking a microblade industry while Tuktu had one. The Northern Archaic is a very broad, loose construct with considerable regional and temporal variety. To reach an understanding of it, it is important to build on the base of firmly established temporally delimited regional phases.

In western and northwestern Alaska there are three local sequences to which Batza Téna profitably can be compared: Anaktuvuk Pass to the north in the Brooks Range, Onion Portage to the west on the Kobuk River, and Lake Minchumina to the south. Anaktuvuk pass is nearly 300 km distant, Onion Portage about 230 km, and Lake Minchumina also is 230 km distant. However, in some cases lack of temporal control for comparisons introduces an element of uncertainty if not impossibility. I have accepted an early first millennium A.D. date for the Batza Téna site, but if the radiocarbon date and obsidian hydration dates are seriously in error the age of that phase could be up to several millennia older. At Onion Portage the Northern Archaic sequence is finely periodized but it is truncated about 2200 B.C. by the succeeding Denbigh Flint (Arctic Small Tool tradition) occupation. A date of 6510±610 years is widely cited for the Tuktu complex of Anaktuvuk Pass. This date seemingly places Tuktu outside the practical range for comparison with B.T. Tuktu. However, there are younger dates evidently from the same site of 5700 to 2600 years ago (Gal 1982). The Minchumina sequence has been finely subdivided, but in the absence of natural stratigraphic separation periodization has required the adroit use of radiocarbon and obsidian hydration dates (Holmes 1986). Finally, the basis for comparisons given in Table 5.9 is not wholly equal inasmuch as except for the site at Batza Téna it has been necessary to rely on published reports, in one case a summary report. Some artifacts of a ubiquitous nature have been left off the list, retouched flakes for instance, as are some types that may have been produced unintentionally, like the uncommon Itkillik pièces esquillées.

It would be attractive to collate these data and calculate coefficients of similarity, but that would create a false sense of scientific rigor. This kind of list is easily manipulated through selective inclusion and exclusions, and it does not take into account to any notable degree the quantitative factor. For instance, the microblade industry is weakly represented in Batza Téna Tuktu and in this respect that phase may be more closely related to those at Onion Portage than it is to Tuktu or Lake Minchumina, but for this trait the table makes a statement to the opposite effect. As well, some assemblages may be the product of only a few person's work, and the collections are not controlled for season of site occupation or ecological differences. These factors may be responsible for differences in individual assemblages of closely related peoples.

Of the two Onion Portage complexes, Portage represents a brief interval, Palisades more than a millennium, but most artifact types present in Palisades make their first appearance early there so the differences in duration may be of little consequence. At Minchumina Lake the Cranberry phase is more likely to crossdate with Batza Téna Tuktu than the later Raspberry phase.

Correlations between B.T. Tuktu and Minchumina are weak in respect to both quantity and typology or qualitative aspects. Qualitatively, there are many classes of tools present at Lake Minchumina, though some are not common, that B.T. Tuktu lacks. Conversely, certain B.T. Tuktu implements, and, importantly, ones which are shared with Onion Portage or Anaktuvuk Pass, are absent at Lake Minchumina. Major quantitative differences appear for burins and for the microblade industry. There are Batza Téna-Minchumina cross-ties reflecting a relationship at the level of the Northern Archaic tradition but there is no apparent closer relationship. Two different archaeological phases are represented even in my practice of defining a phase as a very broad entity just below the order of a tradition.

Batza Téna Tuktu, the Tuktu assemblage from Anaktuvuk Pass, and those from Onion Portage share many points of similarity. One of the few things Tuktu (Anaktuvuk) lacks that might be expected on the basis of the three-way comparison is rough heavy tools made on boulder spalls and slabs of rock. The stronger representation of a microblade industry in Tuktu also is a major element of difference.

For Onion Portage we have included in Table 5.9 the Itkillik complex which is radiocarbondated to the period immediately after the middle of the first millennium, about A.D. 500. Some archaeologists consider it to be a very late phase of the Northern Archaic, and its date is close to the one from B.T. Tuktu. However, Itkillik lacks many implements diagnostic of Batza Téna Tuktu, and conversely it has several styles of points and low-frequency implements found in neither B.T. Tuktu nor the other assemblages with which it is compared. Between the other two Onion Portage complexes and Batza Téna Tuktu, it actually is the earliest one from Onion Portage Palisades, that has the greatest number of features in common with B.T. Tuktu. It may be noted, though, that later Palisades is only slightly older than the Portage complex.

We noted above that there are reasons why we should not necessarily expect identity between the various assemblages compared. Proximity to the obsidian source is an especially strong environmental factor that accounts for the mass of obsidian detritus, cores, biface roughouts and bladelike flakes at the Batza Téna component. We could examine major differences that exist in some artifact frequencies but this would not be particularly worthwhile unless these data are thought to have some particular historical significance. A higher frequency of projectile points at Anaktuvuk Pass, for instance, could simply mean that the site there was primarily a hunting station. All these implied or stated factors considered, though, we are reluctant to combine Tuktu (Anaktuvuk), Batza Téna, and Onion Portage into a single megaphase or subtradition of the Northern Archaic. The main reason for this is uncertainty regarding the age of two components. There could be tremendous differences in age between some of them. Nevertheless, these components or complexes constitute a distinctive subset within the Northern Archaic tradition.

TABLE 5.9. COMPARISONS, BATZA TÉNA TUKTU

	B.T. Tuktu	Onion Portage Portage	Portage Pal.	N. Archaic Itkillik	Anaktuvuk Tuktu	Lake Raspberry	Minchumina Cran.
Microblades	X	O	O	O*	X	X	X
Tuktu tabular cores	O	O	O	O*	X	O	O
Other microbl. cores	X	O	O	O*	X	X	X
Sidenotched points	X	O	X	O	X	X	RARE
Asymmetrical notched points or knife	X	O	X	O	X	O?	O?
Long waist points	X	O	X		X	O	O
Short lanceol. point	X	X	X	X	X	X	X
Large lance blades	O	O	O	X	O	X	X
Point with long tapered stem	O	O	O	X	O	O	O
Large bipoint	O	O	O	X	O	O	O
Square-stemmed point	O	O	O	X	O	O	O
Parallel flaking	RARE	O	O	RARE	O	O?	X
Notched pebbles	X	X	X	X	X	O	O
Notched pebble chopper or axe	X	X?	O	O	X	O	O
Chopper, no notches	O	O	X	O	X	O	O
Whetstone	O	X	X	X	X	X	X
Grooved abrader	O	O	O	O	O	X	X
Endscrapers	X	X	X	X	X	X	X
" " numerous/and with cortical dorsum	XX	XX	XX	XX	X/?	X/?	X/?
Convergent scrapers	X	RARE	X		X	?	?
Burins	RARE	O	O	O	O	X	X
Large, elongate 2-edged bifaces	X	O	X	X	X	X	X
Native copper	RARE	O	O	O	O	O	O
"Ulu" bifaces	RARE	O	X	X	?	X	O
Prismatic blades/ bladelike flakes	X	O	X	X	X	O	O
Boulder spall tools	X	O	X	X	O	X	X
Drill	O	O	O	X	O	O	X

* Prismatic bladelike flakes and microflakes are numerous in Itkillik. There appears to have been an industry devoted to their production.

**Raspberry is the younger of the two phases. Together, they extend for approximately the entire first millennium A.D. but with the intrusion of a Norton-related occupation.

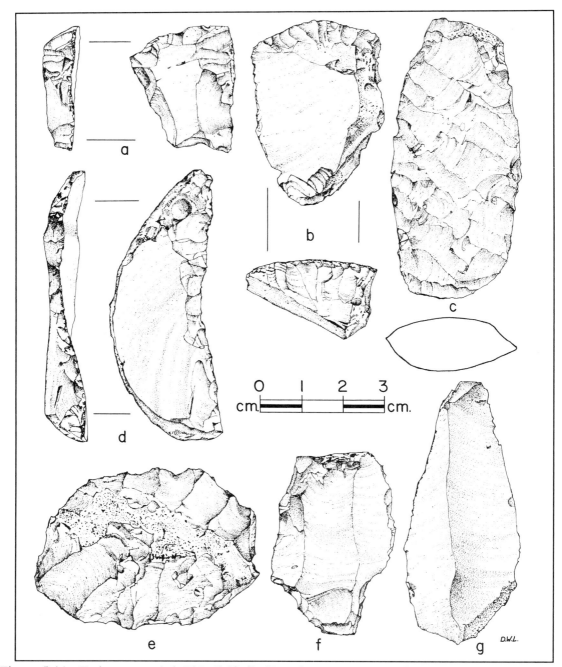

Figure 5.14. End scrapers (a,b RkIg-5:10, 9), "Kayuk scraper" (c RkIg-22:29), retouched flake (d
          RkIg-22:14), uniface (e RkIg-18:1) and bladelike flakes, (f,g RkIg-13:14, RkIg-29:4);
          unassigned.

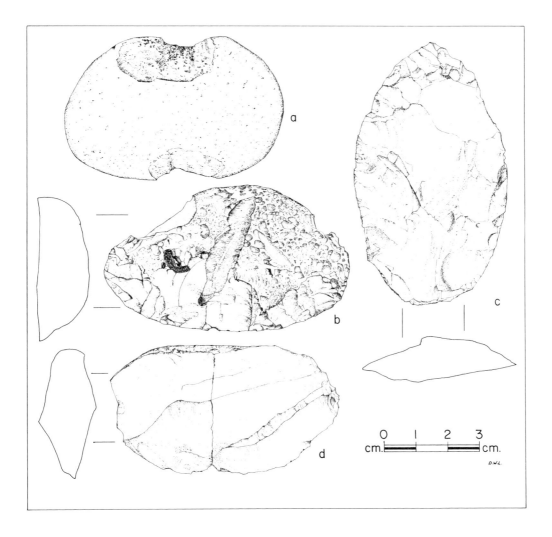

Figure 5.15. Drawings of a notched pebble (a RkIh-32), unifaces (b,c RkIg-46:12, RkIg-29:9) and a biface roughout (d RkIg-12:18). Unassigned.

CHAPTER 6: HAHANUDAN

STACKED CHRONOLOGY AND CLEAVED SPACE

Description

The inland occupation at Hahanudan Lake by late Palaeo-Eskimos of the Norton-Ipiutak tradition has been described elsewhere (Clark 1975, 1978). The site of these finds is only 72 km southwest of Batza Téna. Failure to recover traces of this occupation at Batza Téna may be the chance result of archaeological sampling, or there may have been a sharp ethnic boundary just south of that locality. Even in the latter case, it is likely that the inhabitants of the two areas were in mutual contact, that they had similar contacts with outsiders, and that events impacting on one area probably also affected the other area. In this chapter we will summarize the Hahanudan Lake occupation and discuss it with reference to Batza Téna and the greater region.

When we refer to Hahanudan as being related to Ipiutak, we view Ipiutak as a geographically and temporally restricted subset or phase of the Norton culture or tradition. On the basis of comparisons with artifacts illustrated for the Ipiutak site at Point Hope (Larsen and Rainey 1948) and the Norton site at Cape Denbigh (Giddings 1964) it appears that although many distinctive Ipiutak types were absent at Hahanudan, those present in the houses are inclined towards the Ipiutak assemblage. When Hahanudan was published, the Onion portage analysis (Anderson 1988) had not been published. That report now provides the opportunity for comparison with an interior assemblage from a location much closer to Hahanudan Lake than the coastal sites. These relationships will be discussed later in this chapter.

Discoveries at Hahanudan Lake pertinent to the present chapter include two housepit sites and a small open site. Radiocarbon dates on two houses each at the two sites indicate that one site was occupied sometime between A.D. 440 and A.D. 640, and the other sometime between A.D. 570 and A.D. 820, corrected radiocarbon age (Table 1.1). These dates are in accord with ones from late Norton and Ipiutak sites on the Bering and Chukchi Sea coast. The central values of the dates indicate that one site may be approximately 150 years older than the other. This difference is supported by obsidian hydration measurements.

Both assemblages are similar, but the case is otherwise for the small open site RkIk-4. Artifacts there differ from those of the housepit sites, though some key items have close counterparts in Norton culture sites. On that basis a date a few centuries earlier than the houses is proposed for portions of the open site collection. Because increments from other occupations appear to be present, and because of its large error factor the date of A.D. 1185±455 years for this site is of uncertain applicability and little use. Its MASCA-corrected date range is A.D. 780

to A.D. 1600. The material dated is calcined bone. It has been proposed that a 15 percent correction factor be added to the age of calcined bone dates. This would make the date approximately 150 years older but would not make it much more useful. There is no necessary reason either to accept or reject it as pertaining to Norton or Ipiutak: it covers a great range of possibilities. Interpretation of this component at Hahanudan must be based on style analysis.

The main basis for identifying the Houses as related to Norton or Ipiutak lies in the recovery of numerous bifaced discoidal scrapers--a hallmark of these cultures. Less numerous items that support the same conclusion include a ground burin, certain bevelled flake knives and a small asymmetrical lateral inset blade. Other items proper to but not necessarily unique to Norton or Ipiutak are present and include adze bits, abraders in various formats, knife side blades, leafshaped spear points and an iron carving tool bit. One peculiar feature of the housepit assemblage is the deliberate destruction of well-made adze bits through their use as cores. This element also is found in the Norton-Ipiutak related occupation at Lake Minchumina (Holmes 1988) but has not attracted notice in the analysis of coastal collections. For the open site, if we exclude items of uncertain affiliation, there is a cache of delicate end blades and very slender grooved unbarbed bone points (calcined and extremely fragmented). The points unequivocally link this site to Norton or Ipiutak although neither they nor any other artifact from the open site has a close counterpart in the housepit collection.

TABLE 6.1.   ARTIFACTS FROM HAHANUDAN HOUSEPIT SITES

Description	Frequency
Retouched &/or utilized flakes, unifacial	150
Retouched flake, bifacially edged	4
Flared or hookshaped implements	2
Unifaces	2
Bifaced scrapers	85
End scraper, conventional format	1?
Side blades, medium to large (knife blades?)	15
Large, broad biface knife, fragment	1
Points	15
Lateral inset blades, small	6
Fragments, points or small lateral insets	10
Drill bit	1
Other flaked stone (cores, unclassifiable fragments, hinged biface edge fragments, amorphous worked not implements)	99
Abraders, various types, mostly fragments which may cause frequency to exceed original number	24
Hammerstone	1
Ground burin	1
Adzes	11
Ground chips (mostly from adzes)	c50
Slender bone point, unbarbed	1
Amorphous worked bone	3
Beaver incisors	4
Iron chisel or burin bit	1
Beaver incisors	4
Total, flaked stone	391
Total, lithic artifacts	428
Total, all artifacts	438

For a more complete summary, the collections from the two house sites are listed in Table 6.1. That from the open site, without the minor cache pit component at the same site (see Chap. 8), is listed in Table 6.2. Three artifacts, the first from the open site and two from the houses, are illustrated in Figure 1.13e-g.

TABLE 6.2.   HAHANUDAN RkIk-4 OPEN AREA ARTIFACTS

Description	Frequency
Ceramics, plain 4.6 to 13.3 mm thick, hard	11
Sidenotched spear point, obsidian	1
Endblades, small lanceolate, Ipiutak style	10
Bone points, unbarbed, slender grooved, 27 tiny fragments	4?
Biface, obsidian, broad, pointed double edged	1
End scrapers, convergent snubnosed & thin single bevel	2
Bevelled or utilized flakes	4
Pebble or chitho fragment with red stain	1
Flake core, obsidian pebble	1
Flakes (13 are of obsidian)	54
Cracked rock, fragments, cobbles estimated	2
Fauna, calcined bone, muskrat, large & small mammals, nearly all expended for C14 date, fragments	c300

Comparisons

Minchumina Lake

The Dogwood phase at Lake Minchumina is identified as an intrusive deep interior Alaska Norton/Ipiutak occupation (Holmes 1988). Holmes estimates that this phase dates from about A.D. 550 to A.D. 850, which makes it coeval with the combined occupation of the two house sites at Hahanudan. A link between Minchumina and Batza Téna is suggested by the high incidence of Group B or 2 obsidian in the Dogwood phase (Holmes 1988:158). Characteristic Dogwood implements include bifaced discoidal scrapers, arrow points in stemmed, pentagonal and miniature leafshaped to lanceolate format, larger lanceolate points, small lateral inset side blades, knife-size sideblades, finely polished adzes, drills, various whetstones, and small retouched flake sideblades. All these types are present in the Hahanudan houses except the Hahanudan drill is not like the Minchumina drill, and the three varieties (10 specimens) of arrow points are only weakly represented at Hahanudan (where, however, most of the small points are difficult-to-classify fragments).   Holmes sees Dogwood as most like Hahanudan to the exclusion of other Norton/Ipiutak assemblages. On the basis of Lake Minchumina, Hahanudan is brought into focus as part of a substantial interior occupation and not as a local incursion of coastal people.

Onion Portage Norton/Ipiutak

The Norton-Ipiutak occupation at Onion Portage dates mainly, if not totally, between A.D.

300 and A.D, 500 or 550 (Anderson 1988:11). It was preceded by an hiatus at the site and was followed immediately by the Itkillik occupation. This dating places Onion Portage Ipiutak in an earlier period than Hahanudan, though there may have been temporal overlap between the end of the Onion Portage phase and the beginning of the Hahanudan occupation. Anderson points out that the flaked artifacts at Onion Portage are ubiquitous to both Norton and Ipiutak. Rather than leaning on the radiocarbon dating of this component to assign an exclusively Ipiutak affiliation, he leaves open the question of Norton and Ipiutak interrelationships in the interior region by applying the term "Norton-Ipiutak." A Norton-Ipiutak identity of Hahanudan is readily recognized on the basis of Onion Portage comparisons. There are, as might be expected, differences in the occurrence of uncommon artifact types, accented by the fact that the size of the Onion Portage assemblage (as measured by implements identified by type) is about four times the size of that from Hahanudan Lake.

Considering the difference in age between Hahanudan and Onion Portage, and the question still to be addressed of the age of the endblades from RkIk-4, Anderson's comments on possible early Ipiutak style trends are pertinent. Style attributes of the base of end blades seen in the RkIk-4 specimens tend to be early in Onion Portage Norton-Ipiutak. Early adze blades at Onion Portage are small and rectangular or triangular in plan; later ones tend to be more elongate and rectangular in profile. Hahanudan adzes thus find their closest counterpart in the latter which are more distinctive to Ipiutak than to Norton. Burin-like ground implements, of which there is one from Hahanudan, are found in the more recent Onion Portage Norton-Ipiutak levels. The Hahanudan house assemblages relate best to these later Onion Portage levels, which is in keeping with the fact that the Hahanudan sites are not as old as the early Ipiutak Onion Portage.

Since no delicate end blades like those from RkIk-4 were found in the Ipiutak houses at Hahanudan, it is surmised that these tips date to periods either preceding or postdating the houses. The former option, of preceding the houses, accords with the fact that style attributes of these points tend to be early in the Onion Portage Norton-Ipiutak sequence. The end blades and the two house sites at Hahanudan appear to represent three separate points in time during a Norton-Ipiutak occupation that must have been of several centuries duration. Although there is no present evidence that the Norton-Ipiutak domain included Batza Téna, the long-term presence of an Eskimoan people in the vicinity must have been a significant factor in the history of the obsidian source.

Cultures Tightly Packed in Space and Time

Hahanudan and Itkillik

These comparisons confirm that the dating of Hahanudan between A.D. 440 and A.D. 820 is essentially correct. As we have noted, the Norton-Ipiutak occupation at Onion Portage largely predated Hahanudan, though there could be temporal overlap around the middle of the millennium. But after about A.D. 550 when Ipiutak-related people were living in the inland region, at Hahanudan, they were replaced at Onion Portage by the Itkillik people. Itkillik stone tools are a radical departure from Ipiutak, and Itkillik appears to have no relationship with either coastal Palaeo-Eskimos or with the Neoeskimos who were beginning to make their appearance at Bering Strait about this time. It was the latter, called the Arctic Woodland culture in the local context, that succeeded Itkillik at Onion Portage after an hiatus of a few centuries.

Anderson (1970, 1988) identifies Itkillik as an intrusive Athapaskan occupation, and this is reasonable considering that it has no coastal counterpart and breaks into a sequence that does. This sequence presents a switch vis-à-vis the Koyukuk drainage: when a traditionally Eskimo area becomes Indian, an adjacent traditionally Indian area becomes Eskimo. Knowledge of this scenario presently is restricted, however, by the fact that Itkillik is unique to Onion Portage and has no reported close counterpart in the deeper interior region from which it might be expect to be derived. It may be worthwhile to examine the Onion Portage data for any clues that can shed light on Itkillik origins and relationships.

One clue is the recovery of three discoidal scrapers in Itkillik--an Ipiutak type of implement. Anderson (1988:130) concluded that these specimens are not intrusive. They probably indicate contact with Ipiutakers, though whether with those of the coast or those of the Koyukuk region is not apparent. One strong line of evidence suggests the latter. This is the occurrence of a black obsidian, opaque except in microscopic thin section, that presently is known to be distinct to only two archaeological assemblages: Itkillik and the earlier of the two Hahanudan house sites. This is the Hahanudan site that best cross-dates with Itkillik. The obsidian is a variety that does not come from the Little Indian River source at Batza Téna described by Patten and Miller (1970; see Chapter 1 here). Its origin is not known but I anticipate a bedrock source in the Koyukuk region not far from Batza Téna and Hahanudan Lake. We queried several persons at Huslia, Hughes and Allakaket regarding source locations and received many statements that the only place where batza occurs is in the Indian-Little Indian River area. It was stated that none occurs west of the Koyukuk River (though one person stated he had seen obsidian on a hill there while bear hunting, a probable archaeological occurrence). Evidently, Itkillik obtained their obsidian from the Hahanudan Lake people who exploited a source in the vicinity, or both independently exploited the same source. In the latter case the source likely is located west of Hahanudan towards the Kobuk River. Another option is that the two groups traded for their material with a third party probably living between the Koyukuk and Kobuk River. Hahanudan people also utilized Batza Téna obsidian extensively. At one house site 93.8 percent of the flaked artifacts are made from obsidian, 100 percent of which is Batza Téna in origin. At the other house site 84.9 percent of the flaked artifacts are made from obsidian, 63.7 percent of which is the opaque type discussed above. In Itkillik 45.4 percent of the artifacts (most of which are flaked) are of obsidian, but Anderson's data do not break down the obsidian into source groups or varieties. For comparison, the comparable figure for Norton-Ipiutak at Onion Portage is 18 percent obsidian artifacts, or approximately 23 percent obsidian flaked implements.

A third point indicative of possible relationships is the generalized resemblance between some Itkillik and Hahanudan projectile points (compare Anderson 1988: Fig. 127, Fig. 126a, Fig. 126b, Fig. 126e with Clark 1971: Pl. 5b, Pl. 7d, Pl. 8a and Pl. 3a respectively). However, throughout the prehistory of the greater region, point forms tend to recur and only very general relationships or functional parallels may be represented.

In relation to Batza Téna, both Itkillik and Hahanudan present enigmas. Why are they absent in the vicinity of the obsidian source? A logical answer to half the problem is that the Itkillik and Hahanudan were mutually exclusive, that the presence of one excluded the other. But even that might not fully be the case inasmuch as there likely was some temporal offlap between these cultures. Occupation of Batza Téna by a third group, B.T. Tuktu in particular, may be invoked. Itkillik, Hahanudan and B.T. Tuktu radiocarbon dates all overlap widely. If, however, a proposed 19 percent correction (Holmes 1986:124) is applied to the Batza Téna calcined bone date, this date is moved three centuries earlier and does not compete with Itkillik and with Hahanudan (except for the RkIk-4 end blades) for a position in the time column. Nevertheless, culture history cannot be handled in this manner without invoking the intervention of migrations or abrupt succession. Batza Téna Tuktu is a phase that had persisted, in comparable form elsewhere if not on the Koyukuk River, for a long duration. It cannot be turned off and out to make way for another culture unless there is firm evidence of ethnic succession. (Sometime before the end of the first millennium it was "turned off", but that is another problem in the culture history of the region that I will not attempt to tie to the present discussion.)

Earlier, one of us had suggested that Batza Téna Tuktu and Hahanudan were coeval and that a sharp ethnic boundary existed between the two just southwest of Batza Téna (Clark 1973, 1977). Assignment of an earlier date to B.T. Tuktu does not obviate the fact that the inland Ipiutak occupation did not extend indefinitely into the interior and to Batza Téna and northeastward up the Koyukuk drainage. Archaeological surveys and excavations on the east side of the middle and upper drainage, from the headwaters of the Kanuti River northward, as well as at Batza Téna have failed to find any trace of it (Cook 1970, 1971, 1977; Fetter and Shinkwin 1978; Holmes 1971, 1973). As knowledge of the prehistory of Batza Téna and the greater area becomes more detailed in the future, we can expect to determine where the boundary lies.

Kayuk

The Kayuk complex was found at Anaktuvuk pass, mixed locally with an Ipiutak component (Campbell 1961:42). It is characterized by parallel ribbon flaking on long narrow lance points and by a few broader biface knives and barshaped double-edged scrapers also exhibiting the same flaking techniques. Kayuk is largely unique to Anaktuvuk pass and the distinctive artifacts noted do not occur in Norton or Ipiutak elsewhere although at one time several archaeologists suggested that Kayuk and Anaktuvuk Ipiutak could be part of a single entity closely related to Ipiutak. Later recovery of assemblages from inland Norton-Ipiutak sites has failed to yield Kayak-like implements, thus from these data Kayak cannot be dismissed on the basis that it lacks integrity as a separate entity. Fetter and Shinkwin (1978) identify the undated Cathedral Mountain K-9 site in the upper Koyukuk drainage as a second Koyukuk component, but on a typological basis the correlation is weak. They provide valuable discussion of other possible Kayuk components in northwestern Alaska, and expand the inventory of the Kayuk complex. Some Lake Minchumina lance points, dated to the first millennium A.D. show parallel flaking more or less comparable with the Kayak style (Holmes 1986: Fig. 17-19) but they occur within a sequence otherwise lacking a Kayak phase complexion.

From Batza Téna there are two barshaped scrapers or thick knives of Kayuk type. One was found on the shore next to the Batza Téna Tuktu site (Chapter 5). The other was found on a minor site, also described in Chapter 5, where, some distance away, there was a notched cobble chopper or axe--an artifact that occurs elsewhere in the Northern Archaic tradition and hence, in the local context, could belong with B.T. Tuktu.

At another Batza Téna site, RIIg-35, there is a slender elongate round-based point which, among other possibilities (e.g., a relationship to the Minchumina Type 6 points noted above), is closely comparable to Kayuk points with parallel ripple flaking. This site, RIIg-35, is located on the west side of the outlet of Lake 324 on very slightly raised colluvial or broken up bedrock deposits. Two moderately dense flake clusters, about 1.5 m in diameter, were recognized within a 33-m-long zone of sparser flake and artifact distribution. Only Cluster A was excavated, yielding 3.6 kg of flakes, though an additional 2.2 kg comes from the general site surface.

The following implements were collected from various, well separated locations along the extent of RIIg-35:

Elongate chert point, 86+mm (tip missing) x24 mm, good parallel, slightly oblique collateral flaking on one side, no edge grinding (Pl. 20H)	35.5
Chert point fragment, too tiny for details to be determined	35:6
Chert point fragment, stem converges to narrow thin base; edges ground (Pl. 20G)	35:7
Chert end scraper fragment	35:12
Biface, ovoid, obsidian, traces of cortex at ends, edges unfinished 72x55 mm (Pl. 20F)	35:8
Bevelled obsidian blade midsection; dorsal bevels along both edges; flaked in the bifacial mode but the format is tabular	35:9

The point similar to No. 35.5, and to Kayuk points, recovered from Lake Minchumina MMK-4 is estimated to date between A.D. 1 and A.D. 550 (Holmes 1986:cover drawing).

A fundamental problem in dealing with this material is that we do not know to what extent Kayak is a valid entity, to what period it dates, and what artifact classes are proper to it. Until these questions are answered it would be dubious to force any Batza Téna artifacts into that taxon. The issue has been raised, though, to point out this possibility and document typologically comparable specimens.

Figure 6.1 diagrams the close temporal and spatial packing of archaeological phases at Batza Téna and in adjacent areas.

DATE	BATZA TÉNA	AREAS SW OF BATZA TÉNA	AREAS WEST OF BATZA TÉNA
AD 1200			
1100	Lake 327 Complex		Arctic Woodland Eskimo
1000			-------------------
900	?		
800		-------------------	hiatus
700	Hahanudan Ipiutak		-------------------
600	Houses		Itkillik
500		-------------------	-------------------
400	Batza Téna Tuktu	Hahanudan Endblades	Norton- Ipiutak
300	(& Kayak- style	(open site)	hiatus
200	flaking?)		
100			
AD/BC			
100	Late Microblade Sites		
200	(tentative dating)		

Figure. 6.1. First Millennium A.D. Sequences.

CHAPTER 7: THE LAKE 324 COMPLEX

Introduction

This unique complex or phase is defined and is exclusively represented at Batza Téna by the collection from one locus of site RlIg-52. It is highly uncertain that the entire site RlIg-52, described at the end of this chapter, belongs to the Lake 324 complex. The relatively large site is located along the shore of a small, unnamed lake which is situated at the south edge of the Little Indian River flats, a lesser arm of the Koyukuk flats (Fig. 7.1, 7.2). The lake, found 9.2 km east of the confluence of the Indian and the Koyukuk River, is partially surrounded by low ridges lying northwest of the obsidian source highland. Topographic maps note it's elevation as 324±ft., hence the designation "Lake 324 complex."

At the time of discovery, during a brief air stop in 1970, and when it was investigated in 1971 the site was largely devoid of living vegetation. There were, however, numerous deadfalls and standing trees that had been killed during the burn of 1968. The site consists essentially of a clustered group of flaking stations (Fig. 7.3). Exposed lithic concentrations were examined, and two flake clusters and parts of some others were trowelled. Except at one of them, few implements, almost none of them finished, were recovered. Flaking detritus was collected at one of these clusters in addition to the one which defines the Lake 324 complex (Fig. 7.4), and limited flake samples were taken elsewhere from the site. Other flakes were examined and left where they occurred. The most common matrix at the 324 complex locus is roots, thin brown soil and rock derived from the local bedrock which outcrops briefly in the bank towards the lake.

The 324 complex locus yielded various categories of implements. The assemblage has a high degree of coherence on the basis of artifact clustering and technological attributes. Technologically, little from elsewhere on site RlIg-52 appears to belong with this assemblage. As well, the Lake 324 assemblage differs from others found at Batza Téna.

Assessment, Integrity and Temporal Placement

A late date is proposed for this complex on the basis of the near absence of artifacts in styles dated elsewhere to an early period, the recovery of hide scraping stones of a format that usually is late, and a late radiocarbon date, though of uncertain reliability. However, a Lake 324-type flake point is reported from the Chindadn or Nenana Complex component at Healy Lake (Hoffecker, Powers and Goebel 1993 Fig. 3J).

Little found on other parts of site RlIg-52, coprising few distinctive implements, is assigned to the Lake 324 complex. A case in point is a flake dump located at the edge of the site between the shore and the zone from which the Lake 324 artifacts were collected (Fig. 7.3).

A more serious consideration is the need to insure that extraneous or unrelated material is not included with the Lake 324 complex. Possibly the broad biface blade (No. 88) and a small leafshaped point (No. 89) found with a small number of flakes nearly 30 m northwest of the main artifact distribution should not be included. Otherwise, the varied obsidian implements and the smaller collection of chert artifacts show a strong degree of coherence on the basis of technology displayed by elongate flake blanks. Most implements not made from obsidian are localized within the distribution of obsidian implements of the Lake 324 complex (Fig. 7.4), and there is one nonobsidian "flake point," a common implement form of the Lake 324 complex, linking tools of two materials to a single component. I am less certain about including the coarse stone industry. These consist of a pestle and four hide working stones of tabular "chitho" and boulder flake format. They cannot be tied to the others on the basis of technological attributes. Their spatial distribution is partially disjunct, to one side of the flaking locus, but that would be expected if there was differentiation of work areas within a camp.

The relationship to the Lake 324 complex occupation of the dated calcined bone and a charcoal-rich soil streak also are matters for concern. Although it was not continuous, the charcoal-rich soil was widespread and extended beyond the artifact locus even to the bank at the shore of the lake. In places it was exposed on the surface where it supported a thin moss growth, evidently as a result of its water-holding capability. This layer is thought to be natural, due to an earlier forest fire which also resulted in some artifacts being "burned." Initially it together with the calcined bone noted below were thought to be part of a hearth, but this evidently is not the case, although the charcoal-stained layer could obscure the presence of hearths within the same area. Scattered bits of calcined bone were found in a relatively large area, at least 3 m wide, within the area of artifact distribution. They occurred from the surface to a depth of 5 cm in the site matrix of brown soil and rock as well as locally in the charcoal-rich soil. Prior to the 1968 forest fire there may have been a turf laver over this part of the site that covered the artifacts, but this is not certain. The calcined bone probably is derived from a poorly defined hearth, though it possibly is derived only from originally unburned faunal refuse that subsequently was calcined when the site was swept by a forest fire, perhaps long preceding the 1968 burn. The fragmented state of this material suggests the passage of sufficient time for natural agencies to fragment it. A couple larger pieces of unburned (not calcined) bone also were recovered. The radiocarbon date obtained on a portion of this bone is A.D. 1065 (885±80 years; S-920). Discounting the vagaries of the radiocarbon dating method, especially when calcined bone is used, the date reasonably indicates a time of human activity at the site. A suggested correction of 15 percent applied to calcined bone (Holmes 1986) would move the date back to A.D. 897, an adjustment that does not appear to create problems, though it is surprising that there are no strong crossties with Itkillik of Onion Portage, which is only a few centuries younger, or with late Inland Norton-Ipiutak. Comparisons indicate that this age is not too old for the pestle and hide working stones, but whether those artifacts and the date actually belong to the Lake 324 complex is open to discussion. Considering that no good alternative date or correlation is proposed for

Figure 7.1.   Site RlIg-52 from the air. This view cuts off the east (right) end of
                 the site. The Lake 324 complex locus is central immediately to the right
                 of the light colored strip of grass growing at the edge of the water.

Figure 7.2. Site RlIg-52 as seen from Site RlIg-33, looking northeast.

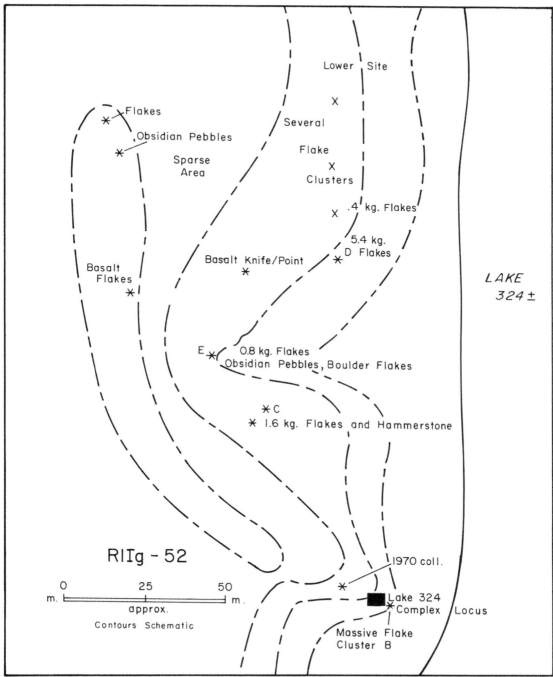

Lower Site

X

Flakes

Obsidian Pebbles

Sparse Area

Several

Flake

Clusters

X

X .4 kg. Flakes

5.4 kg.
D Flakes

Basalt Knife/Point

Basalt Flakes

LAKE 324±

E 0.8 kg. Flakes
Obsidian Pebbles, Boulder Flakes

C
1.6 kg. Flakes and Hammerstone

RIIg - 52

0   25   50
m.   m.
approx.
Contours Schematic

1970 coll.

Lake 324
Complex Locus

Massive Flake
Cluster B

Figure 7.3.   Sketch map of RlIg-52 showing the position of artifact and flake clusters. Contours are schematic.

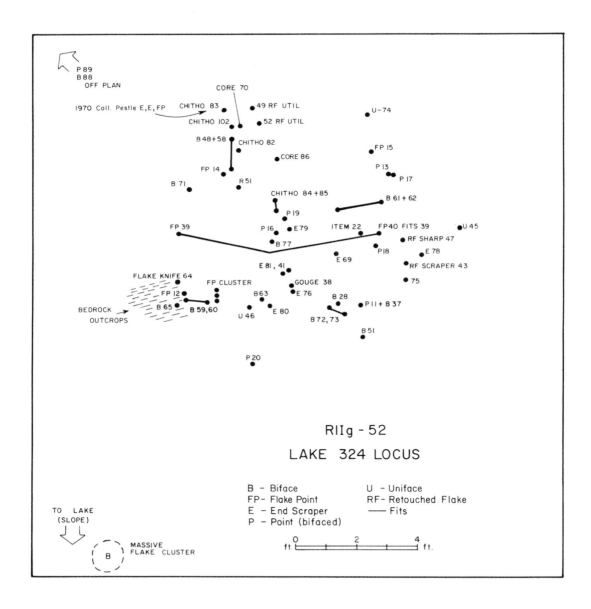

Figure 7.4. Implement distribution at the Lake 324 complex locus at RlIg-52.

the flaked artifacts, that the Lake 324 complex lacks artifacts such as notched points and microblades that would indicate an earlier date, and that it lacks small stemmed arrow points characteristic of a very late period, a terminal first millennium A.D. or beginning second millennium radiocarbon date (uncalibrated) is feasible.

Implement Description

The primary characteristic of the Lake 324 complex is that the implements consist mainly of modified flakes. Obsidian predominates but there also are a small number of dark chert artifacts. Several sharply pointed retouched flakes or "flake points" were recovered, the majority in a single tight cluster or presumed cache. Similar but broader flakes were used for scrapers. End scrapers are especially large and are completely unlike those of the Northern Archaic tradition and Norton-Ipiutak culture which are thought to date only slightly earlier than the Lake 324 complex. Some bear flaking preparation over the whole dorsal surface, an attribute that characterizes very few end scrapers from Batza Téna. As well, the size of these scrapers is outside the range of any other assemblage of end scrapers from Batza Téna (Appendix II Table 3). Bifaces bearing incomplete facial retouch show traces of their flake blank history. Four hide scraping stones (chithos) and a pestle found at one edge of the implement locus complete the assemblage. Negative attributes, especially the lack of a microblade industry, of fluted points, lanceolate points and side-notched points further distinguish the Lake 324 complex from other phases or complexes defined at Batza Téna.

Implements of the Lake 324 complex are listed in Table 7.1 and are described below. These objects come from a single RlIg-52 locus with the exception of a point and large biface blade found in an adjacent area and a uniface of unrecorded provenience that typologically appears to be part of the complex. Elsewhere from RlIg-52, as is noted in Chapter 9, there are two points, including a basalt projectile point or knife, eleven fragments of unfinished bifaces, one complete small unfinished biface, an end scraper, a chert and an obsidian retouched or utilized flake, a small boulder chip (chitho), an unformalized dark chert flake core, and a narrow elongate dark chert uniface on a thick ridged flake. With the possible exception of the two dark chert pieces these objects do not appear to belong to the Lake 324 complex.

Points. The small pointed bifaces are thought to be primarily tips for projectiles, but some of them may have served as small knife blades. There are four complete or nearly complete specimens of varied format, all made from obsidian. These include the following: (a) A presumed lanceolate or bipoint with broken base (Pl. 15B). One edge near the missing base is ground, the opposite edge is damaged. (b) A narrow roughly prepared, and also damaged, leafshaped point with relatively straight sides and a slightly rounded unfinished base (Pl. 15A). There is slight grinding on one edge near the base. This specimen is 66 mm long which is approximately the length of the preceding point when it was complete. (c) The third point is a stubby, 32.4-mm-long, 7.8-mm-thick pentagonal specimen (Pl. 15C). Its shape may be the result of refashioning a once longer more or less convergent straight stemmed point. The lateral edges of the stem are heavily ground. (d) A thin small leafshaped point, measuring 43.5 mm long and 4.3 mm thick, was found peripherally to the Lake 324 complex locus. The specimen (Pl. 15D) now is somewhat irregular due to edge damage. Fragments RlIg-52:11, 17-19 are not illustrated.

TABLE 7.1.   IMPLEMENTS OF THE LAKE 324 COMPLEX

No.	Identification	Description
8	Points	Mostly projectile points & fragments; 5 obsidian, 3 chert (Table 7.2, App.II.4; Pl. 15)
7	Biface blades	Finished or nearly finished, commonly asymmetrical sideblades; obsidian (Pl. 17A-D, F)
11	Biface in progress	Unfinished fragments & 1 complete; 6 obsidian, 5 dark chert
16	"Flake points"	Trimmed at edges, usually bifacially; 15 obsidian 1 other (Fig. 1.13i, Pl. 15)
2	Large "Flake points"	Apparent large version of above, sample too small for type definition; obsidian (Pl. 15Q-R)
6	Unfinished unifaces	Extensive dorsal flaking, some also have ventral retouch at edge, variable lot, obsidian and 2 dark chert (Pl. 15G-H, Pl. 16M-O)
2	Unifaces type B	Presume unfinished, not further classified; obsidian
10	End scrapers	Obsidian, includes 1 aberrant short & 1 unfinished or not end scraper (Pl. 16A-I)
8	Retouched/utilized flakes type A	Blunt, bevelled, usually thick edges (scraper?); 7 obsidian, 1 dark chert (Pl. 16J-L)
2	Retouched/utilized flakes type B	Sharp edge, flat retouch (knife); obsidian, (Pl. 16P-Q)
4	Retouched/utilized flakes type C	Bears probable use retouch; obsidian
18	Retouched/utilized flakes type D	Bears retouch of uncertain origin, possibly natural
4	Cores	Chunks of obsidian and spent flake cores
8	Unclassified flaked	Undistinguished items or small fragments
x	Flakes	4.9 kg incl. large unmodified obsidian pebble, tr. of dark chert and basalt, remainder obsidian
1	Pestle	(Pl. 17G)
1	Abrasive stone	Fragment
4	Hide scraping stones	1 boulder flake, 3 of tabular format (Pl. 17H-I)

Finished or nearly finished biface blades. Five specimens in this group are complete. There are two shape categories, ovoid to lenticular symmetrical and lenticular asymmetrical on the long axis. Individual specimens are as follow: (a) Lenticular with thickened, unfinished, bluntly edged ends, 74.4 mm long (Pl. 17C). This may be an unfinished implement or the ends may have been left thick and blunt intentionally. (b) This 76-mm-long ovoid specimen (Pl. 17F) is edged at one end to essentially the same degree as the lateral edges. The other end is unfinished, blunt and contains a small portion of cortical surface at the edge. This blade is better finished than the preceding one, though part of one lateral edge is unfinished. The reason why one end was left blunt remains open to interpretation.

The remaining three blades tend to be symmetrical on either side of their width axis (e.g. at each end) but one lateral edge is notably more convex than the other edge. Such blades appear to be for side-hafted knifes. (c) The smallest specimen, a 55.3-mm-long, 7-mm-thick piece, is roughly or opportunistically flaked on the underside (Pl. 17D). The entire perimeter is sharp, though the more highly curved long edge has, so-to-speak, the edge. (d) Preparation of the large, 94-mm-long specimen shown in Plate 17B focused on the edges, both of which are equally sharp. A tiny unfinished area of cortex remains on the edge at the pointed end of this blade. (d) The remaining blade (Pl. 17A), a massive 93.6-mm-long specimen, is more coarsely prepared than the preceding one. The more convex edge, though damaged, bears somewhat finer retouch than the opposite one and apparently was the cutting edge. This blade also has an unfinished end with cortex at the edge.

Bifaces in progress (unfinished) (not illustrated). Pieces in this group consist largely of fragments. Those of obsidian often bear thick areas of cortex on the edge. There are two nearly complete roughly bifaced pieces of black chert, each in the order of 52 mm long, 29 mm wide and 12 mm thick. Possibly they had been intended for finishing into points, but the black chert appears to be a very refractory material and these pieces may have been discarded as being impossible to process. Two non-fitting dark chert fragments appear to describe a single leafshaped biface (minus the midsection) in the order of 80-95 mm long and 30 mm wide. It may have been intended for use as a knife or lance blade or for further finishing as a projectile point. This pointed biface format is not recognized among the obsidian specimens except in the smaller biface identified in most cases as projectile points. The catalog numbers are: (chert) RlIg-52:28, 37, 51, 77, 113, (obsidian) 71, 72+73, 120, 122, 125, 132.

Flake points (Pl. 15). The flake points are elongate flakes that have been pointed and edged. Commonly both edges are retouched, and this retouch may appear on both faces or may be limited to one face. In some cases thick areas at the base of the flake points are thinned. Locally, retouch may be very extensive. Dorsal surfaces, where not retouched, display various flake surface characteristics, including (i) multiple flake scars originating from various directions on the core, (ii) a single arrise, (iii) planar (no arrise or an arrise at the very edge). Cortex is rarely present, being limited to one equivocal incomplete specimen and a small area on one of the two large series flake points. The pointed end, which usually is the distal end of the flake blank but sometimes is the proximal end, owes its format in varying degrees to the combined natural pointedness of the flakes and retouch. Several specimens were fitted together from fragments, some are whole, but others remain incomplete.

Most of the flake points were found in a single cluster, "cache" or "bag lot." A few were found elsewhere in the Lake 324 locus, however, so the presence of this artifact is not dependent on the one find. These items do not appear to be blanks or unfinished points. Considerable effort was taken to edge the flakes. Sometimes this entailed retouching the total perimeter or otherwise extensive localized bifacial flaking. All the tip ends are finished insofar as pointedness is involved. Complete specimens are described in Table 7.2.

TABLE 7.2. DESCRIPTION OF COMPLETE "FLAKE POINTS"

No.	Length mm	Width mm	Thickness at midpoint	Comments	Illustration
RlIg-52					
9	76	30	7.4	Retouch is slight	(Pl. 15N)
12	66	32.4	4.6	2 mm added for missing part of base, broad	(Pl. 15I)
14	59	24.1	8.0		(Pl. 15P)
23+24	69	28.1	5.1		(Pl. 15J)
31	64	25	6.6	Proximal end pointed	(Pl. 15O)
33	60.5	20.3	4.8	Very regular shape	(Pl. 15L)
34	79	24	4.8	Slender, thin	(Pl. 15K)
42	47	19.3	5.7	Not obsidian, sideblow flake	(Pl. 15E)
66+67	71	32	7.2	Half of dorsum flaked	(Pl. 15M)
15, 21, 22, 30, 32, 35, 37				Fragments	(Pl. 15F)
Large series					
64	89	37	8.0	On sideblow flake, poorly fits the type	(Pl. 15Q)
39+40	Size approx. as No. 64			Incomplete, fits the type	(Pl. 15R)

Unifaces. The unifaces are flakes moderately to extensively flaked over the dorsal surface, sometimes also with ventral retouch at the edges. The original outline shape of the flake blank may or may not be retained. The dark chert specimens (Pl. 16M) are fragments, and two others are incomplete or unfinished. Exclusive of the end scrapers (below) this leaves four specimens for description. (a) The first flake uniface is a thin specimen, 7.4 mm thick, flaked over the dorsum except for one area of cortex, and retouched around the perimeter on the ventral surface (Pl. 16N). The ventral retouch is similar to that seen on the Flake Point series, though the present specimen is less acutely pointed and relatively broader than a flake point. The edges are sharp, the most excurvate edge more so than the opposite edge. This 75-mm-long blade may be functionally equivalent to the bifaced sideblade knives described earlier. (b) The same function is proposed for the second uniface (Pl. 16 O), a sideblow flake, with one straight and one excurvate edge, measuring 60 mm long at the maximum. There is complete dorsal flaking except for a small area of cortex at each end, and localized ventral chipping which evidently was done to thin one area along the straight edge and to sharpen the excurvate edge. The latter appears to have been a cutting edge, although parts of the specimen are only haphazardly finished. (c) (c) The third specimen (Pl. 15G) is a gouge-shaped tool 68.6 mm long, 19 mm wide at the maximum and 7.6 mm thick. Although it is totally shaped in the dorsal aspect and retouched on the ventrum to such an extent that it is nearly a biface, this specimen still displays the longitudinal arching of the original flake blank. The edge at the butt end is coarsely ground or worn. The tip is crushed and blunted, and a long facet comparable to a burin facet forms one edge there. There is no wear on this facet which probably was formed unintentionally during use of the implement. (d) The specimen in Plate 15H was collected from the surface away from the Lake 324 locus, but it appears to be a tool of the types produced by Lake 324 people. It is a very well prepared uniface, retaining the curvature of the flake blank. The edges at the pointed termination are worn smooth. The butt end is damaged, either through use, through platform crushing when the flake blank was detached, or through taphonomic processes.

End scrapers (Pl. 16A-I). Measurements for the end scrapers are given in Table 9.4. The RkIg-52 Lake 324 complex end scrapers average larger than those of any other site at Batza Téna, and this is one of the defining characteristics of the Lake 324 complex. Another characteristic found on some specimens is total retouch or shaping of the dorsal surface. This is not the coarse random shaping or the broad linear (proximal to distal end) flake scars formed on the core that often make the dorsal surface of scrapers, but is flaking originating from the lateral edges of the scraper and done after the flake blank had been detached from its core. Three specimens made on relatively thinner elongate flakes highlight the Lake 324 motif of implement production on large or elongate flakes.

Bluntly-edged bevelled flakes (Retouched/utilized flake A). Flakes bearing relatively even or consistent steeply bevelled edges are interpreted as scrapers. The single complete specimen is a 61-mm-long cortical flake dorsally bevelled along one entire long margin and also retouched on the opposite shorter edge, leaving an intervening (adjacent) edge unretouched (Pl. 16K). The remaining specimens are all fragments, mostly cortical or partially cortical flakes, with dorsal bevels variously located on opposite edges, on convergent (joining) edges or on a single edge (Pl. 16L). The rectangular specimen with convergent bevels in Plate 16J with is nearly complete.

Sharply-edged bevelled flakes (Retouched/utilized flake B). One of the two complete specimens in this thin-edged group is a secondary cortical flake; that is, part of the dorsum is cortex and part is the scar from the adjacent antecedent flake removal (Pl. 16Q). On this 80-mm-long blade the edge along the cortical surface is unmodified while the opposite convex edge bears somewhat uneven relatively flat bifacial retouch. The specimen might have served very well as a knife side blade and is functionally equivalent to some uniface and biface blades described earlier. The second specimen (Pl. 16P) is a 58-mm-long flake that was partially shaped on the core. Two opposite long margins are retouched dorsally to form concave and convex edges respectively. The convex edge also bears a trace of ventral damage or nibbling.

Utilized flakes (Retouched/utilized flakes C and D) (not illustrated). It is proposed that the fine retouch on these flakes is not the intentional result of tool preparation but is use damage or attrition. Furthermore there are a number of seemingly utilized flakes where retouch may be natural damage that occurs due to human and animal trampling (several moose were seen near the site) and from frost action within a stony context. To distinguish between these two categories is an arbitrary process subject to varying degrees of conservatism, but not without governing criteria. Retouch that is intermittent, varying in intensity (or size of retouch scars), that wanders or shifts suddenly between ventral and dorsal surfaces, or occurs in very unlikely places usually results in a specimen being assigned by me to the natural category. Wear or smoothing is an acceptable criteria only if it is confined to probable working edges. To complicate matters, retouch of more than one origin may be present on a single specimen. We have accepted few specimens in the utilized category without reservation. Specimen RlIg-52:128 has extremely fine but very even and consistent retouch around the perimeter. RlIg-52:52 has relatively continuous nibbling on both ventral and dorsal sides along the concave edge. Convex edge appears to show a combination of use and natural retouch. The large but incomplete flake No. 49 shows continuous dorsal retouch along its slightly concave margin. The opposite highly concave edge is not retouched but there appears to have been some shaping of the edge outside the zone of concavity where the flake margin again becomes convex. Neither these nor the more numerous equivocal utilized flakes are formalized implements, but the working edges usually are sharp and not uncommonly are concave. This morphology suggests to me light-duty cutting and fine "shaving" functions rather than heavy cutting and scraping. The fourth Type C specimen is No. 140. Type D includes the following items: RlIg-52:5, 25-27, 50, 54, 56, 91, 92, 99, 104, 105, 115, 118, 119, 121, 123, 126 and 134.

Cores (not illustrated). Although the production of large sometimes bladelike flakes was an important activity for technicians of the Lake 324 complex, there are inadequate f flake cores to document this activity. Two small, rough chopper-shaped cores, a type described in Chapter 9, were found. One of these measures only 48 mm in its greatest dimension. A small bifacially-worked nubbin 37 mm in diameter and up to 19 mm thick may be a core remnant but more likely it is a core-tool reject--a piece of obsidian that could not be satisfactory reduced to the intended object. More in line with expectations, there is one large flake, measuring 62 mm long, 44 mm wide and 16 mm thick which displays two large linear fake scars on its dorsal surface. This piece can be interpreted as either a fragment of a core or a blank intended for further shaping. The catalog numbers for these objects are RlIg-52:70, 86, 103 and 134.

Abrasive stone (not illustrated). There is one fragment of a sandstone or fine grained greywacke cobble with a worn, smoothed and striated, slightly dished surface (RlIg-52:100). Two additional fragments of similar stone do not display any worn or cortical surfaces.

Pestle (Pl. 17G). This 19-cm-long object probably owes its slender, tapered-cone shape to a select shape of the cobble blank from which it was made, although the whole surface appears to have been pecked to impart the final shape. The wide end is pounded or work flat, the narrow or pointed end slightly flattened at the top, and two narrow grooves run the length of one side. A large spall is missing from along the other side, presumably the result of impact damage, and this may obscure the former presence of additional grooves. Two small smooth areas appear to be part of the original cobble cortex but one of these is flat and striated and thus evidently is a ground facet. Areas of red discoloration on this find from the surface of the site probably are due to heating. The object is made of a gritty stone, possibly a volcanic greywacke.

Hide scraping stones. These four objects are all large ovoid tabular hide scrapers or chithos (the Athapaskan term, occurring with variations, for such implements) made of a stone, like greywacke, common to the local area. One (Pl. 17H) is on a thick boulder spall 19 mm thick and 120 mm long. It is very bluntly edged. The others are more tabular. Plate 17I is from a slab split from the centre of a cobble and measures 11 mm thick and 130 mm long. It is carefully trimmed around the perimeter in the bifacial mode except for a small area of the back that has been left thick and untrimmed. Incomplete specimen RlIg-52:84-85 is almost exactly the same size and was prepared in the same manner, but from a finer grained stone. No. 102 is a fragment. It is only 7 mm thick but was of the same order of size as the others. The edges of all specimens are smoothed, evidently largely from use though intentional blunting was part of the preparation of this type of tool and there may have been further smoothing due to weathering.

Comparisons

Oval chitho hide scrapers are a characteristic Athapaskan tool of the second millennium A.D., though this type of implement appears in various shapes earlier. Comparable scrapers were found in most levels at Lake Minchumina (Holmes 1986). They also are present in Itkillik, where, however, stone slab implements are less prominent (Anderson 1988). One 9.6-cm-long hammerstone found in the first millennium B.C. component at Lake Minchumina is comparable to the pestle, though it is smaller (Holmes 1986: Fig. 42a). This type of implement is not especially common on interior Alaska flaking stations, but comparable pestles have been recovered in the Yukon, at the Klo-kut site on the Porcupine River (Morlan 1972: Plate 10) where they are assigned to a period of 600 to 1200 years ago.

Thus far, aside from the generally widespread occurrence of biface knife sideblades and leafshaped points, the lithic industry of the Lake 324 complex in its more specialized aspects is without parallel at Batza Téna and in northwestern interior Alaska. In particular, this characterization refers to the reliance on and treatment of flake blanks and the large size of the end scrapers. However, large dorsally prepared end scrapers have been reported for the Cathedral Mountain K-9 site (Fetter and Shinkwin 1978: Pl. 8) along with smaller end scrapers. Within the context of Batza Téna, the use of dark-grey chert to any notable extent (most of the 11 nonobsidian Lake 324 complex artifacts) is peculiar to Site RlIg-52. This, however, may indicate idiosyncratic lithic sourcing by a single small group that probably camped there, perhaps only once.

Site RlIg-52

As has been discussed above, one area of this site produced the Lake 324 complex. Here a description of the whole site will be provided and collections other than the Lake 324 complex are described. Aside from the Lake 324 locus, the site was more thoroughly examined, probed by shovel, and some flake clusters were trowelled and collected in 1971.

The site presented a ghost forest in 1971--a large burned over area with most of the trees still standing. The surface had been cleared by wild fire, though the burn was not so intense as to consume all shrubs and eliminate the turf. This very large site is nearly 200 m long. It is bounded behind by tundra flats, in front by the lake, at one end by an unproductive zone of forested terrain between it and RlIg-33, and at the other end by another unproductive zone before a group of minor sites along the lake outlet is reached. Considerable portions of the rocky soil were exposed, however, and this allowed us to locate and check many flake clusters and to collect unassociated items. Bedrock outcrops in one area at the front of the site in the area where the Lake 324 complex was recovered, and elsewhere it probably is not far below the stony soil. Figure 7.3 shows the location of various flake clusters and find spots.

Collections. Considering the amount of material exposed on the surface and examined, (outside of the Lake 324 complex) implement recovery from the site is low. Most of the flake clusters exposed at the surface were seen not to contain any implements and were not collected. Specimens 1 through 10 were collected in 1970, the others in 1971. Out of these, items 5 through 89, 107 and 110 through 141 belong to the Lake 324 complex. The following items were not found with the Lake 324 complex.

Projectile points, surface finds, 174 found with flake 176	52:173, 52:174
No. 173 is rough as if unfinished but edges are smoothed;	
No. 174 is a narrow stem fragment, basalt, 62x27.x8.3mm (Pl. 21E)	
Unformalized small biface, unfinished point?, 43 mm long	52:155
Core, amorphous spent, and rotated platform or multilateral,	
fragment, Area D	52:161, 52:163
Core, large flake with portion of core	52:171
Core, dark chert, damaged or rotated platform, 45 mm high,	
unassociated, material relates to Lake 324 complex	52:180
Biface, unfinished, small, Cluster D	52:155
Biface fragment, unfinished, in SE end flake cluster	52:182
Biface roughout fragments, Cluster D	52:166, 52:167, 52:178
Biface roughout fragments	52:177, 52:189
Hinged biface roughout edge fragment, Cluster D	52:157, 52:164, 52:165, 52:170
Hinged biface roughout end fragment, with minor flake group	52:185
Biface chopper-shaped core or roughout, unassociated	52:188
Uniface, incomplete flakeknife, dorsally shaped, elongate, black chert,	
technology & material relate to Lake 324 complex, unassociated	52:181
Giant end scraper, 76 mm wide, unassociated	52:186
End scraper, poorly formed, coarse ventral flaking	52:3
Retouched flake, 2 edges, in plan shaped like end scraper,	
lateral edge is the most retouched and worn	52:1
Utilized flake, large thin, basalt or dark chert, the thin	
edge, most of which is missing, finely retouched	52:176
Cobble spall scraper, with edge retouch, Cluster E	
could relate to Lake 324 complex chithos (Pl. 17E)	52:151
Blade or bladelike flake, single arrise, notches probably not intentional	52:172

Also collected: numerous amorphous or rudimentarily worked obsidian core and early-stage roughout fragments, and 11.916 kg flakes exclusive of the Lake 324 locus.

CHAPTER 8: LATER PREHISTORY AND EARLY HISTORY

The Lake 324 complex fails to articulate with the ethnographic present, when Europeans first contacted the Koyukon, by at least several centuries and possibly by as much as nearly 1000 years. The later prehistory and contact period history of the Koyukuk region is poorly represented in the archaeological record, and hardly is represented at all at Batza Téna. There are, however, scattered finds from the length of the Koyukuk drainage which provide some data for this period, while historic archaeology and ethnographic information contain clues that may guide the search for a later prehistory and early history.

Batza Téna

Some items from Batza Téna regarding which reservations were noted in previous discussions may belong within a late time frame. The copper awl from the main Batza Téna Tuktu component (Chapter 5) especially seems to be precocious in that context. A middle to late second millennium date would be reasonable for this artifact. From across the lake at Batzatiga, there is a jade adze (Chapter 4). According to Giddings (1952:112) jade (nephrite) tools did not become common on the Kobuk River, in the area where this raw material originates, until after A.D. 1400, though uncommon earlier use is recorded at Onion Portage (Anderson 1988). Site RlIg-33 not only was one of our campsites in 1971 but had attracted campers earlier on more than one occasion. Several notched points were found clustered in frost-churned soil at one edge of the site. These probably are more than 1000 years old and can be referred to the Northern Archaic tradition. More pertinent to the present discussion is the small series of artifacts recovered from the main site area. These include two items that on the basis of type or style demand a late date: a small, stemmed variant of a Kavik arrow point and a fragment of a large flat grinding slab (Pl. 18A). Also recovered there, but not necessarily late in age, is a scraper, possibly a variant of the chitho type, made on the edge of a flat pebble. The complete assemblage is described below.

Site RlIg-33

The first 1971 field camp, at unnamed lake elevation 324, was located on this site (Fig. 1.12, 8.1). The Lake 324 complex was found on a nearby site. Portions of RlIg-33 were trowelled, other areas surface inspected. This site had not attracted our interest until while we were examining the evidence of recent historic camping there (which consisted of sheet metal, a fork, and a small spruce cut off at 1 to 2.5 m height) I saw two pieces of obsidian in the depressed area several metres to the northwest of the cook tent. These turned out to be a sidenotched point and a roughly worked piece of obsidian. Further scraping of that area (A) turned up three more notched points, and amorphous worked obsidian associated with a small number of flakes, and adjacent to these, a larger cluster of flakes. These artifacts were located at the surface to a depth of 5 cm in moss and scant soil on top of disintegrating bedrock. This area was isolated from other parts of RlIg-33 by a surrounding non-productive zone. However, these finds stimulated John Nobleman and William Peacock to trowel the floor of their tent. John found a fragment of a small fluted biface (though probably not a fluted point fragment). Earlier, an end scraper had been found in the floor area of another tent.

Description.   The site is located on a bedrock bench at the edge of Lake 324. The inner periphery of the site has more soil or frost churned colluvium than does the outer edge.

The following flake clusters were noted (Fig 8.1):

A. The "frost boil" cluster (yielded notched points), located near the bottom of the low area which runs parallel to the site on its northwest side. It produced 2.72 kg of flakes.

B. A flake cluster weighing 0.97 kg in moss and scant soil.

C. A minor, somewhat dispersed cluster that was trowelled out. It contained no implements but yielded a piece of chert and 0.32 kg of flakes.

D. An intensive concentration of many small and larger flakes, most packed into an area no more than 30 cm in diameter and the whole group within an area 1 m in diameter. It was totally collected except for the many very tiny flakes. Definitive implements were recognized. The 0.75 kg of flakes occurred at a superficial depth on top of disintegrated bedrock.

E. This medium size cluster also was totally collected. It appears to form the southwest end of the site and is just off the central high ridge, onto its southeast flank. The 0.5 kg of flakes were recovered from an area measuring slightly less than 2 by 3 m, but most were concentrated into a much smaller area. They were superficial in a soily rocky matrix. Some pieces have a worked appearance.

F. Cluster F is a massed concentration of large and small flakes in the moss and scant soil found on top of broken bedrock in an area measuring about 25 by 30 cm with little scatter beyond. It is similar to Cluster D. An attempt was made to collect all the smaller flakes so the collection would be of suitable for the analysis of flaking technology. The flakes weigh 1.21 kg.

Collections

Bifacially reduced & crushed roughout, Area A	33:21
Shouldered, stemmed point, obsidian, 38.5x14.6x4.5(Pl. 19N)	33:13
Side/corner notched point, obsidian, near Cluster C (Pl. 19Q)	33:8
Side-notched point, obsidian, Cluster A (Pl. 19 O-S)	33:9, 33:10
Side-notched point, chert or basalt, near Cluster C (Pl. 19R)	33:11
Biface, small ovoid unfinished, Cluster E 39.5x50	33:26
Biface, unfinished, fragment, Cluster E	33:28
End scraper (Pl. 19K)	33:17, 33:18
Retouched flake (side scraper), near Cluster C (Pl. 19L)	33:16
Bevelled flake fragment, low angle edge, Cluster E	33:25
Flat tabular flake with bifacial flaking, suggestive of a poorly	

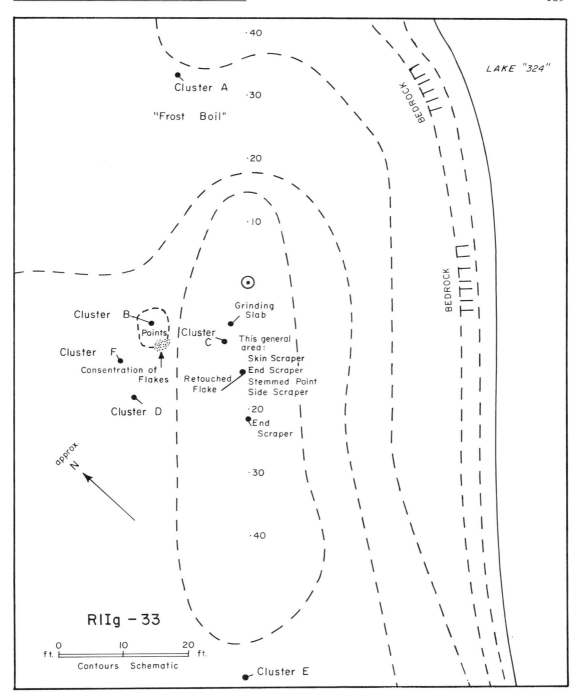

Figure 8.1. Sketch map of Site RlIg-33.

proportioned fluted point fragment, hydration measured   33:15
Pointed retouched flake, dorsally flaked to a point at bulbar end and along
one edge, Lake 324 complex style (Pl. 19M)   33:14
Edged pebble shingle, two opposite edges bifacially retouched in the manner
of a chitho scraper 96x62x10.4 (Pl. 19P)   33:19
Grinding slab, sandstone, 137x228x16, incomplete (some edges have
secondary breaks); red stain on face may be from fire (Pl. 18A)   33:29
Other items catalogued: hinged roughout edge fragment and 2 rudimentary biface roughouts or
amorphously worked pieces.

Three of these items--the stemmed point, the edge retouched shingle, and the grinding slab
suggest a late prehistoric age. The side-notched spear points could be somewhat earlier.

Lake Todatonten

Lake Todatonten is located northeast of Batza Téna but is sufficiently close that the same
Todatonten-Kanuti band could have exploited both vicinities. The outlet of this lake and the
upper part of Lake Creek or Mentanontli is a traditional area of camps, old houses and fish traps.
Our survey there, in 1968, was especially disappointing. On the south side of the stream we found
only a few pieces of fire-cracked rock. On the north site, one obsidian flake, three more pieces
of fire-cracked rock, tiny particles of calcined bone, and a few extremely tiny fragments of fibre
tempered pottery were found exposed in a clump of caved bank. Excavation back for two feet
from the edge of the bank at that location produced only a couple more fragments of burned
rock. A test 4 m back from the edge, if one can call clawing through the tough mat of shrub roots
a test, revealed numerous minute particles of calcined bone. This is the nature of the record at
an optimum site location.

Hahanudan Lake

Hahanudan Lake, southwest of Batza Téna, is another traditionally utilized area, and we
found traces of late prehistoric activity there (Clark 1977). These include several cache pits and
one very minor site. At RkIk-1, on a small sandy elevation next to the lake, burned bone was
found in an ash-like matrix under the sod, sewn birch bark and fish scales in the sod and cut wood
on the surface. A metre-square test pit and numerous shovel probes failed to find any buried
artifacts or lithic flakes in what obviously was a camp location in early historic and possibly late
prehistoric times. Twelve metres inland there was a rectangular cache pit. It contained only
sheets of rotten birchbark and a few muskrat bones.

Not far inland from this site an undistinguished location contained a small lot of bones, flakes
and implements exposed by wildfire. Among the weathered bones minimally representing several
species were a beaver cranium a fragment of a bird sternum, and fragments of a scapula, rib and

innominate from large and very large mammals, probably caribou and moose. The collection consists of two obsidian flakes, a bar-shaped sandstone pebble, fragments of cracked rock (from three stones obviously brought in from elsewhere for stone boiling or use as sinkers, and a net sinker made from a flat plate of large mammal bone. Two rectangular holes had been cut into the sinker, evidently by a metal tool. This would indicate that the site, RkIh-2 postdates European contact on the Yukon River or along the Bering Sea coast in the 1830s.

Four cache pits located adjacent to the Ipiutak-related houses at Site RkIk-5 were excavated. A potsherd and an obsidian chip were found in the fill over the roof of Pit A. Within, there was an obsidian chip, an articulated group of caribou vertebrae, and three loon bones. The relatively good condition of birchbark sheets within the pit suggests that this feature is not especially old. That is born out by the radiocarbon date of 285 ± 95 years or A.D. 1665 (A.D. 1460-A.D.1650 MASCA corrected range). The artifacts may be coincidentally present, and of an older age, derived from soil utilized to bank to pit cover. Pit B also was lined with intact birchbark sheets, probably from the caved cover. It contained only an obsidian flake and a utilized pebble. Cache Pit C has the poorest preservation of wood and birchbark, though it was the deepest one, and presumably it is older than the other two. It yielded a toothed end-of-the-bone flesher, a single duck humerus, and bone fragments from various parts of a large mammal, apparently caribou. Small Pit D produced a few obsidian flakes. These observations indicate that cache pits generally were not reutilized as refuse pits, provide information on the pits as late prehistoric artifacts, and indicate continued utilization of obsidian during the late-prehistoric period.

Open Site RkIk-4 was noted in Chapter 6. Adjacent to this site there are three rectangular cache pits, one of which was excavated (Clark 1977). No artifacts were contained within the pit proper, except decayed wood and birchbark from the structure, but charcoal stained refuse and a few artifacts were found spilling into one corner of the pit. This represents either a disturbed hearth deposit or material cleaned out of a hearth and dumped here. The hearth component would postdate the pit but possibly by only a few decades. Wood and bark preservation within the pit suggests that it is not as old as the Ipiutak-related house sites. It is uncertain whether any of the small collection of artifacts from the open area of RkIk-4 are coeval with the lot from the edge of the cache pit and whether the A.D. 1185 ± 455 radiocarbon date from the open area has any relevance to this lot. The cache pit lip lot included an eclectic collection of small, largely calcined fragments of muskrat, large unidentified cervid, probably beaver, other small mammal bones, a fish vertebra and three bird bones. Other items recovered from the sooty soil are small plain feather tempered ceramic sherds, a fragment of a pebble hone, a small rod-shaped pebble, two small obsidian flakes, fragments of three or four pebbles that have disintegrated due to heating, and four fragments of cut or grooved bone, now calcined. Here again use of ceramics and obsidian appear to be coeval. The collections from the adjacent open area (Table 6.2) are older of mixed age and include Norton-Ipiutak end blades and plain ceramics of undetermined affiliation.

Contact Period Houses

Houses dating to the period of European or American contact have been excavated in the vicinity of Allakaket (A. Clark 1991) and Kateel on the lower Koyukuk River (de Laguna 1947). Aside from providing information on semisubterranean house construction which would not be obtainable from older decayed structures, these sites have yielded a small number of artifacts representing indigenous continuities. The latter is less true in the case of the houses near Allakaket, which appear to date to the 1880s, than it is for Kateel where the occupation represented is about two decades earlier. Indigenous precontact-type artifacts from the houses, primarily from Kateel, include plain pottery, trimmed slab and boulder flake hide scraping stones (chithos), a snowshoe netting needle, red paint pigment stone and a large cobble mixing basin, whetstones, large sandstone grinding slabs, antler wedge, an antler comb, slender barbed and unbarbed arrow heads, birchbark basket trays, and skewer sticks for cooking.

The late prehistory also has an anecdotal presence founded in oral tradition and the memories of the oldest inhabitants of the region: for instance, the story of seeing a small tree growing up through a clay pot near Batza Téna, a locality near Huslia named what one might call, in English, "Clay Pot Lake"; a stone splitting adze found near the mouth of the Alatna River; a barbed bone arrow point found within the village of Huslia; a jade knife blade found in the bank at Alatna and a stone lamp found near "Steamboat" a short distance up the Alatna River, both possibly brought in by historic Kobuk Eskimos.

It is not known how far into the past the occupation of semisubterranean houses can be traced. Those excavated in the Koyukuk drainage are all historic, but prehistoric houses have been excavated at many localities elsewhere in interior Alaska. Some have yielded scant collections. Nevertheless house pits serve as easily identified targets in the search for late prehistoric sites towards which future archaeological work may be directed.

Early Historic Settlement and Utilization of Batza Téna and Vicinity

Overview

The present-day gateway to Batza Téna (Baats'a Tina [1]*)is the village of Hughes, located on the Koyukuk River a short distance to the northwest. Another modern point of entry is the Utopia airstrip, nestled at the base of Indian Mountain east of Hughes within the area of obsidian flaking stations (Reger and Reger 1972).

According to Orth (1967, after Stuck 1917), the town of Hughes was established in 1910 as

---

[1]Spellings in Koyukon orthography marked by an asterisk have been corrected by Eliza Jones, University of Alaska, Fairbanks. Others are approximate renditions of Koyukon place names.

a riverboat landing and "port of supply" for the Indian River (Utopia) placer gold mines. A store was established and after about 1915, when mining activity had subsided, it became a Koyukon village. In 1917 Hudson Stuck saw little future for the settlement:

> The life of Hughes City was brief even for a placer-mining town.
> Started in 1910, it was almost deserted in 1915, though in 1917 a
> little store still languishes; presently the natives attracted hither
> will return to their old haunts with some half-breed children and some
> chronic diseases, and the wilderness will resume its own (Stuck 1917).

But Stuck misjudged the case. The village persisted as a small settlement of two or three score persons. Its population has increased in size during the last three decades.

Nucleation of the Koyukon along the middle to upper river in towns like Hughes and Allakaket is essentially a 20th century development, beginning immediately after the 1898-99 Koyukuk gold rush. However, on the lower river, from not far above Huslia down to the confluence of the Koyukuk with the Yukon, there were substantial earlier indigenous winter communities during the middle and late 19th century, at Kateel and Dalby for instance.

During the period of village nucleation, and to about 1940, many families also had cabins along the Koyukuk River or on major tributaries where they spent the major part of the year. For Christmas and other occasions they went "to town" where they stayed with friends or maintained a second home. In addition, there was spring dispersal to "rat" (muskrat hunting) camps, summer moves to salmon fishing camps, autumn hunting and fishing on the tributaries and in the hinterlands, and winter trapping. The dispersed cabins along the river, the spring camps, and the trapping camps more closely approximate the precontact settlement pattern than do the present-day small towns. Although for precontact times the importance of winter fur trapping has to be deemphasised, there was prehistoric exchange of furs and other items from the area, and muskrat and beaver, possibly also lynx, were important sources of food as well as fur. During much of the 20th century numerous salmon fishing camps provided the most obvious sign of subsistence activity, but individualistic one- or two-family net fishing camps do not accurately reflect precontact settlement patterns. Earlier, people congregated around a smaller number of fish trap and weir installations.

The record of early historic settlement in the vicinity of Batza Téna appears to have deficiencies which may be interpreted as reflecting either partial abandonment of the area during the 19th century or that the area never did have a permanent population base. Most families presently living at Hughes trace their origins to other parts of the Koyukuk drainage. The forbearers of most people came from down river, from the region between the Hogatza and Dalbi River, though they first lived at various places before settling at Hughes. Local opinion acknowledges that the area is a good one in which to make a living from the land, but states that formerly "people just passed through Hughes [e.g.,they settled there for a while then moved on]

...No one is really from Batza Téna--Chief Johnny was there for a while [probably in 1880s, see below]...No one used to live at Hughes before about 1906 [when, following a dispute with Chief Moses, Old Atla moved down river and established a home just above and across from Hughes] (Edwin Simon)."

Possibly this area had permanent inhabitants at an earlier time, prior to the 1880s, but recollections about these families may have been lost because they have no living descendants on the Koyukuk River today. We found that many Koyukuk people could provide detailed genealogical information for their antecedents and local relatives, but knew little about families that had moved away, to the Yukon for instance, or which had died out.

A. Clark (1971:Fig. 1) had concluded that the Hughes-Indian River area originally was part of the band area of the people who lived around Lake Todatonten and the lower Kanuti River. By the time Allen saw them in their home territory this band was reduced to a small community camped near the confluence of Lake Creek and the Kanuti tributary of the Koyukuk. One route across the hills south of this settlement leads into the Melozitna River drainage, another to the headwaters of Indian River and Batza Téna. This band area might have extended almost as far west as the mouth of the Hogatza River, but by the 1880s the lower and middle Koyukuk population was undergoing shifts and realignment. Then there appears to have been a small nucleus of people at Batzaténa or Batzakakat which, however, failed to develop into a new band. The Indian River-Hughes region appears to have most of the economic requisites for supporting a resident group--upland hunting territories, tributary and main river fishing sites, lowland flats and lacustrine beaver, otter and muskrat habitats--but the area alone may have been too small to support a population of band size.

In either case, the area likely supported some families perpetually. Evidence of this should exist in the form of the remains of winter houses. Presently, prehistoric sites of this type have not been reported, but archaeological exploration of the lowlands near Batza Téna is inadequate by a large degree.

The discussion of historic camps which follows may provide an indication of the mode of prehistoric subsistence at Batza Téna. A keyed list of toponyms accompanies Figure 1.9.

Winter Occupation during the Contact Period

The earliest retrospective account is of Batzaténa Village, a settlement reportedly at the outlet of Batzaténa (Baats'a Tina*) Lake, located a short distance below Mathews Slough and the southern tip of Huggins Island. Baats'a Tina* (by some persons pronounced batza-ta-tena) means "obsidian trail." Reconnaissance in 1971 failed to locate this village but insufficient surveying rather than the veracity of accounts can be faulted.

In 1885, Lt. Allen passed the Batzakakat (Baats'akkaakk'at--batza river mouth) summer camp

and then went to a fish cache on an island one mile below the camp (Allen 1887). There were
ten persons in the settlement--men, women and children. The location reported by Allen on the
east bank of the Koyukuk just above the lower end of Huggins Island is close to the reported site
of Batzaténa village, although he apparently saw the summer fishing camp aspect, or as Fickett
(n.d.) stated, two tents, whereas traditional cold-season houses were reported to us. "Batzakaket"
is not to be confused with Bear Creek or Batza River as it appears on the U.S.G.S. Melozitna
quadrangle and on earlier maps. There is some question in our mind whether the map location
given by Allen is that of the fishcamp he visited or of a reported permanent settlement. Cause
for raising this question stems from the fact that while the map location is shown on the left bank
of the river, in a text table Allen states that the settlement was on the right side of the river. We
do know from the context of his publication that Allen frequently reported and named
topographic features and gave locations of settlements he did not visit on the basis of local,
Koyukon information and, further, that Allen correctly used the locational terms "right"and "left"
in relation to the direction of the current.

At the village there were four small single family "igloos" or semisubterranean houses
occupied by Old Paul, Old Thomas, Leon and Chief John or Old Isaac. The first three were born
in 1850, 1871 and 1863 respectively and were still young when they lived at Baat'sa Tina. Old
Isaac was an adult by 1851 when he participated in the Nulato Raid, and Chief John, said to be
Leon's uncle, may not have been much younger. They had moved upriver from the Huslia-Dalby
area, evidently at different dates, in response to the aftermath of a homicide, epidemics and poor
hunting conditions. (Not all information sources are wholly in accord. Edwin Simon dated Old
Thomas' move up the river to 1895 and did not associate him with Baat'sa Tina.) Chief John's
parents died when he was a boy living at Chakee or Willow Lake on Dalby Slough. He walked
out to a settlement near Cutoff on the Koyukuk. When he was still young he married and moved
to the Hughes area, it is thought before white men reached that part of the Koyukuk, and became
boss of the Batzaténa group. Reportedly, others had lived there before him. These were winter
houses, at Batzaténa, but the families also went together to a salmon fishing camp above Hughes
and to spring camps at Batzaténa Lake until Leon left the group, at an undetermined date prior
to 1907, and moved up river to Allakaket. Old Isaac (whose house may have been separate--see
below) and others from Batzaténa moved also farther up river, to Konamunket in the Kanuti
Flats, about 1895-96. This may have set the abandonment of Batzaténa. Chief John moved to
the Yukon River where he lived many years before returning to Hughes to lead a further eventful
life from which he departed at camp in 1941. Again, he had a cabin at or near Batzaténa Lake
(Arundale and Jones 1984:31).

There is a semisubterranean naklukno house on the west bank of the Koyukuk about 17 m
up the bluff and c 1.5 km above the lower end of Huggins Island. There is a graveyard a few
metres below the house site. According to Lee Simon, a former resident of Hughes and
Allakaket, the house was occupied by Old Isaac who came from down river near Huslia, when his
daughter (probably Sinaat'onh, Lucy, born before 1868) was young. The age for this settlement
thus would be about the same as Batzaténa, or slightly earlier. Arundale and Jones (1984:31,Map.

Ref. W-8) place these "igloos" below Huggins Island on the left bank of the Koyukuk at the location we identify as Batzatena Lake. Old Isaac's, next house was near the tip of the lower end of Huggins Island (Lee Simon). It was occupied before Old Isaac went to live in the upper Kanuti drainage at Kanuti Lake in the 1890s.

More recent winter season occupation, dating to the early 20th century, was at Rock Island Point, and Eight Mile Cabin where there also were summer salmon fishing camps. The forest location, at the juncture of a hill and high river banks with the lowlands, appears to be favorably situated for old settlement sites, but nothing indicative of earlier occupation was seen by us in riverbank exposures or on the adjacent hill slope.

The hills and lakes close to the obsidian source may not have been occupied by families during the winter. One local resident who had trapped in the area said he had not seen any old house pits there. However, Sarah Koyukuk Simon of Allakaket reported that there are traditions of an old naklukno (semisubterranean) house camp in the hills at the divide crossing to the Melozitna River (from the Batza Téna area). She also reported that there were old house pits at Tik'yeet a large lake southeast of Hughes (map location or identification in our notes is uncertain) as well as in the area south of Little Indian River and southeast of Batzaténa.

There is a source for iron-rich nodules used to produce red pigment at chida-dilthden or chih-ditzl-lithden or "Rock Paint Point" on the Indian River not far from the bedrock source of obsidian. Fred Bifeldt, who had lived at Rock Island Point, recalled that his grandmother told of stopping there, when travelling through the region (probably from the Melozitna to the Koyukuk), to dig through the snow with snowshoes to get pieces of red paint stone from the river bar near the "Rock Paint Point." Pressed on the question when people likely would have obtained obsidian from the same vicinity, though, he said that that would have been in the summer [because the obsidian is more dispersed?]. At the suggestion that this activity would have been combined with hunting, he said caribou and bear, and noted that there used to be caribou in the source-area uplands and hills south of the Little Indian River that did not migrate back north.

Eskimos used to come to the Koyukuk at two points near Batza Téna, to a hill on the west side of the Koyukuk between Forty Mile Slough and Matthew Slough, and, farther up the river, to a hill across from Rock Island Point. They signalled their presence by building a fire (SK Simon). We were not able to obtain specific information about their activities, other than the fact that they ate (with the Koyukon), but can presume that the visit was primarily for trading, and that this activity occurred prior to European contact on the Yukon River.

Spring Muskrat Camps and Fishing Camps

About 1920, people living in the vicinity Hughes went to spring camps in an area of small lakes and flats that extended along the east side of the Koyukuk River below Indian River. The base camps along the Koyukuk River were located primarily at Batzaténa Lake (an oxbow lake below Huggins Island), Kk'eeyh Lake (another oxbow lake said to be 9 km above Batzaténa Lake with which it may be confused in our accounts) where Mary John (died 1963 at age 90) and others before her, camped, Tutaholwelakta (not identified on map) where Billy Bergman and Little Sammie went, and Too Ghoy K'its'ilooyh Dinh*. Tak'badza hullanten or Taha-badza-hulantna and other small lakes between Matthew Slough and the upland obsidian source also were spring camp places, particularly suitable for beaver. None of these local names are identified on published topographic maps. There was not a large choice of suitable locations. Lee Simon indicated a spring trapping and hunting route leading inland and southward from Batzaténa or Keekh (Kk'eeyh*) Lake spring camp to a series of small ponds and lakes terminating in Kitsel hhakhten (lake) "we kill something" and adjacent ponds located close to the southern edge of the Melozitna D-4 map sheet. At spring camp the men caught muskrats and shot beaver. The women used two sizes of nets to catch little whitefish, which are called herring, larger whitefish, pike and sucker as well as some grayling.

Lavine Williams said that once when he camped in the country southeast of Batzaténa Lake he found a ceramic pot "mud bucket" or klatz-ul-tlok which had a small tree growing up through it (de Laguna 1947 describes the pottery used on the lower Koyukuk and adjacent Yukon River).

During high water in the spring it is possible to go up Indian River for about 15 km by canoe. In the old days, though, one was more likely to descend Indian River at that time. Abraham Oldman recalled that he had come down Indian River twice in the spring with his father Johnnie Oldman from a spring camp located near Utopia (probably in the Lake Creek drainage, a tributary of the Kanuti River). They had gone to camp overland from Hughes when there was still snow on the ground, and then came down the river shooting beaver and muskrat.

Summer Fishing Camps

Few reports were obtained of summer fishing traps near Batza Téna. Possibly this is because we obtained most of our information on the topic at Allakaket from people whose knowledge pertained mainly to reaches of the river located above Hughes. Old Beattus had a fish trap across from Rock Island Point, but this was an early 20th century operation. Allen obtained dried salmon (Fig. 1.5) from a cache near Batza Téna, and it can be assumed that there was a trap installation and summer community in the vicinity. Later, in the present century there have been a number of smaller gill netting camps in this region. The history of one camp located near the Batza Téna settlement, Twentyfive Mile Cabin as designated on the U.S.G.S. Melozitna quadrangle, has been traced to the late 19th century.

Autumn Activity

Two or three families stayed at the mouth of the Indian River in the autumn. They fished there with traps (Fig. 1.6). This probably was during the 20th century soon after Hughes was established (Lee Simon). Inspection of the high banks at the confluence of Indian River and

Figure 8.2. Split salmon drying along the banks of the Koyukuk River at Alatna.

Matthew Slough did not reveal any traces of structures.   Hughes people also went to other locations in the autumn.   The Indian River carries a reasonably heavy run of chum salmon during the summer months.

There was a caribou fence about 45 km behind Hughes at Badzazihi Mountain, an isolated pointed peak a short distance east of the obsidian source or the hills south of Little Indian River according to two differing sources.   The fence ran in a straight line all over the hill and across a low area between hills for a distance of about 12 or 15 km.   It was owned by a rich man Batu'tzah who built it with the help of others.   He may have been the grandfather of Happy Johnny (c 1885), both of whom bore the name Baku'tzah.

Figure 8.3.   Fish trap made of split spruce strips, used at Lake Creek near its confluence with the Kanuti River. This type of trap was placed in small streams during the spring and autumn.

CHAPTER 9: LITHIC SOURCE ARCHAEOLOGY

This chapter deals with Batza Téna holistically, as a single entity. Attributes of the lithic material found at flaking stations and other sites and its distribution are discussed as a reflection of utilization of the geologic source, especially in terms of a lithic reduction zone.

Review of Lithic Sources

Geologic sources exploited for lithic material have been reported across the Arctic and Subarctic. A single, large erratic quartzite boulder attracted campers and knappers to the edge of the barrens at Acasta Lake, located a short distance east of Great Bear Lake (Noble 1971). To the north, on the Arctic coast at Cape Bathurst, and along adjacent reaches of the Anderson and Horton Rivers, so-called burning cliffs (bocannes) created a clinker-like rock that was desired in the area for flaked artifacts (Clark 1975; Le Blanc 1991). Nearly every site in the local region shows use of this material for artifacts (Le Blanc 1991:Fig. 4), but the actual clinker outcrops lack evidence of quarrying or workshop activity. The latter situation can be laid largely to the occurrence of the outcrops along actively eroding riverbanks and shorelines. Not far from the outcrops, however, Le Blanc notes the presence of a base camp and numerous short-term lithic reduction sites that contained few finished implements. This situation appears to parallel Batza Téna except that a greater amount of lithic material (about 26 percent) other than clinker, e.g. other than that from the signal source, was flaked at these sites.

Pilon has reported a quarry/workshop associated with siliceous argillite outcrops on the lower Mackenzie River at the mouth of the Thunder River (Pilon:1990). Material from this source appears in interior archaeological sites located to the east of the outcrop and in Eskimo sites of the Mackenzie Delta, but diminishes to a few specimens around Great Bear Lake and the lakes to the north of it such as Colville Lake. Pilon draws attention to the fact that at the source and associated workshops people focused on lithic reduction with the objective of producing blanks, while at more distant sites Thunder River material appears largely as finished implements.

One of the most distinctive and widely disseminated materials from the Subarctic region is a glass-like welded tuff that comes from a unique geologic source located on the west side of the Mackenzie Valley southwest of Fort Norman (Cinq-Mars 1973). This stone is found in small quantities nearly everywhere in the western half of the District of Mackenzie and appears also in northern Alberta and the Yukon. There are two flakes of it at Batza Téna identified on the basis of physical appearance and Instrumental Neutron Activation analysis. Cinq-Mars notes that sites near outcrops, where the rock evidently was quarried, and near mountain streams where cobbles of it could be picked up, "yielded a relatively large quantity of chipping detritus which suggests a rather free use of the raw material.... It is possible to visualize the sites themselves as raw material processing stations...they cannot be regarded only as quarry sites" (Cinq-Mars 1973b:E14). This assessment fits the concept of a lithic reduction zone that forms a basis for interpreting Batza-Téna.

The major published northwestern North American lithic source, of either obsidian or chert, is Mt. Edziza, located in northwestern British Columbia where several obsidian flows are reported (Fladmark 1985). We will have occasion later to refer to Fladmark's analysis. An additional obsidian source has been discovered in the St. Elias Mountains of the Coastal Ranges in the southwest Yukon at Hoodoo Mountain (Stevenson 1982). The source occurs in rugged terrain and, perhaps for that reason, appears to have been only of local importance. Stevensen reports extensive lithic scatters within 1.2 km of both the primary outcrop and secondary stream source, consisting mainly of reduction products such as core fragments, core reduction flakes, biface reduction flakes and biface fragments.

Characteristics of Lithic Debris at Batza Téna and at a Distance

Site Types

Batza Téna is primarily a lithic reduction zone centered on a raw material source. Secondarily, Batza Téna was a hunting ground and an east-west route through uplands, as will be discussed later. In this section we will discuss the reduction zone aspect and the characteristics this imparts to the lithics. This zone consists of workshops where the raw material was reduced to roughouts and possibly blanks (conceptually these are two different things), especially biface roughouts. Some finished implements also were produced. This situation is comparable to the association seen between workshop sites and quarry sites.

We will refer to several types of sites. In his study of Mt. Edziza and vicinity Fladmark (1985:83 ff) notes the following site types: a) quarry sites, b) lithic workshops where, in Fladmark's words, "secondary lithic reduction was the principle archaeologically visible activity;" c) camps "where normal domestic processing and maintenance tasks dominate the artifact assemblage;" and d) intermediate or multi-purpose sites which both camp and lithic reduction station functions. He notes that the camps encompass a wide range of possibilities but are characterized by artifact diversity (1985:101). It is necessary, though, to recognize that very little is left at most camps represented in the prehistoric record of the Subarctic, thus the criterion of artifact diversity will not apply in the case of many sites. This is a case of negative or no evidence which for purposes of interpretation tends to be very labile. For that reason, I hesitate to propose additional site types, but recognize that there are minor aspects of the camp site category (and also of lithic reduction sites). To complete the record of prehistoric activity there also are isolated finds.

Thus far, no actual quarry sites have been reported at Batza Téna. Possibly the obsidian occurred in so many contexts, more or less disseminated as on river bars, that there was no occasion for quarry sites to develop. There is no quarry at the primary outcrop reported by Patton and Miller (1970). We were told by local persons that large quantities of obsidian occurred on the upland surface about 4.5 km east of Patton and Miller's outcrop. A reliable source referred to flakes, whereas another person mentioned large cobbles of obsidian. Our surveys by foot did not adequately explore that area, and may not have reached it at all.

The strategy of reducing obsidian nodules to blanks, or of producing implements on location saved people from having to pack heavy loads of raw material long distances, only for most of it to be discarded as flaking debitage. But, apparently, some whole nodules also were exported or carried away judging from the occurrence of cortical flakes at distant sites (Holmes 1986:134). At Huslia we also were told of a cluster of obsidian cobbles seen at a hill location several km northeast of the village--seemingly an obsidian trader or knapper's pack lot.

Since Batza Téna is a regionally unique source, flaking stations cluster there in contrast to the situation often found elsewhere, in which local materials or eclectic sourcing are drawn upon and flaking stations are dispersed among living sites or occur at multipurpose sites (cf. Bowers 1982). Extensive flake scatters, massive flake concentrations and an abundance of broken biface roughouts or preforms reflect this aspect. There are as well, a few sites with obviously utilized implements that reflect the camping or multipurpose land-use aspect.

Proportion of Implements to Debitage

Pertinent to this discussion is the relative frequency of debitage and implements. The frequencies of the two main classes of flaked implements (points and end scrapers) and debitage are compared in Table 9.1. In the Batzatiga sector, where parts of two multipurpose sites were excavated and all exposed debitage was collected from other sites, there are 3.9 kg flakes for each implement in the two tool classes noted. In the other areas the incidence of debitage drops, though it remains high, but the figures are biased towards the lower values because of selective surface collecting emphasising recovery of implements whereas many clusters of flakes were only examined for the presence of implements and were not collected (even an extensive excavated collection was abandoned at one site). It may be advisable to add microblade cores to the quotient of selected artifacts used for these comparisons inasmuch as microblades evidently were used to edge composite projectile points. The proportion of points, end scrapers and microblade cores to debitage at Batza Téna thus is one tool per 2.32 kg of flakes.

Published statistics fully suited for comparisons, consisting of debitage weight, separate data for obsidian exclusive of other lithic material, and information on the incidence of cortex are scattered or incomplete. One of the most useful sets of data is for two sites at Lake Minchumina (Holmes 1986). There are 214 artifacts in the point, end scraper and microblade classes for site MMK-4 (our calculation using Holmes 1986:Table 4). Excluding large sandstone chips, the flakes

TABLE 9.1.   COLLATION OF POINTS, END SCRAPERS AND DEBITAGE

Sector	Points	End scrapers	Flakes kg	Flakes/Points+Scrapers all	obsidian	Area sq km
Basecamp Ridge	6 (0)	26 (6)	57.2	1.79	2.2	2.9
Little Lake Ridge	76 (14)	18 (5)	117.6	1.22	1.57	3.9**
Lake 324	22 (8) +16 (1)	14 (1)	43.6	1.21 0.84	1.50 0.99	4.2
Obsidian highlands	0	0	7.7	---	--	c13
Middle Indian River	8 (2)	5 (1)	3.7	Most flakes seen were not collected		c10
Batzatiga	15 (7)	70 (8)	272.2	3.2	3.89	9.1
Total	127* +16	133*	502	1.93	2.48***	43.2

* 36 points and 21 end scrapers (figures in parentheses) are not of obsidian.
** Area calculated to include main ridge and east end sub-sectors but to exclude Lake Takbatzahullanten and highland northwest of the ridge.
*** Including also the 15 microblade cores and fragments, the value is 2.3 kg.

from that site weigh 4.426 kg or 0.0207 kg per artifact, in contrast to 2.32 kg at Batza Téna. This illustrates, perhaps more vividly than is required, that at flaking stations and around lithic sources there is a lot of debitage per implement.

Size of Flakes

A complementary expectation is that away from the source, as the utilization of raw material becomes more conservative and as there is greater emphasis on finishing blanks and repairing or recycling artifacts, flake size will become smaller. Limited data on flake numbers and lot weight were recorded for the Batza Téna collections, primarily for the 1969 collections (Appendix I Table 2) (most later collections were weighed only). Though not complete, these data show the average size of flakes, expressed as weight. The average of all lots in Appendix I Table 2 is 3.22 g per flake. Examples from various areas and sites are as follows.

Weight per flake:
Fluted & notched point site RkIg-1, Basecamp Ridge	2.5 g
Fluted point site Rkig-10, Little Lake Ridge	3.7 g
RkIg-28 (Chap. 3), first year collection	4.3 g
RkIg-30 (Chap. 2), preliminary (shows surface collection bias)	7.5 g
RkIg-19, a site with flakes piled on top of one another	2.2 g
RkIg-51, 1971 data, site with unfinished points, excavated test	0.75 g

The characteristics or attributes of the raw material, such as the size, shape and fracture or cleavage characteristics of cores or blocks of material, influence the size of flakes to such a degree that comparisons of unlike materials have limited validity. Nevertheless the following comparisons are offered.

Weight per flake:

Minchumina MMK-12 (Holmes 1986:Table 15, 16)
   N chert = 282   2.2 g
   N obsidian = 193   0.34 g

Minchumina MMK-4 Level 1
   biface thinning flakes, obsidian   0.20 g
   cortex flakes, obsidian   0.82 g

Minchumina MMK-4, range of 18 data cells, obsidian   0.06 to 0.95 g

SeIg-2, Norutak Lake between Koyukuk and Kobuk, 301 flakes
   (113 obsidian) pooled chert & obsidian (Clark 1974b)   0.78 g

SeIg-4, Norutak Lake Pit 4, mostly chert   0.25 g

Cathedral Mtn. K-9 (Fetter and Shinkwin 1978:Table 3),
   large multipurpose site and workshop, not obsidian
   Area 1-3   0.94 g
   Area 4   0.99 g

MfRd-4, Great Bear Lake, multipurpose site, chert common   2.25 g

MdPr-3 (Clark 1987) Great Bear Lake, definitive small workshop
   440 flakes/2129 g, no points or scrapers, microblades present   4.8 g

These data show a tendency for workshop flakes to be large (K-9 possibly the chert at Minchumina, Great Bear Lake sites) while nonworkshop flakes, including chert at Norutak Lake and obsidian at locations distant from the source, tend to be small.

Presence of Cortex

The proportion of cortical to noncortical flakes also is thought to be pertinent for distinguishing workshop activity (cf Le Blanc 1984:96 citations). Where only preforms that have been roughed-out elsewhere are processed, and broken tools are repaired, the occurrence of cortical flakes should be low.

Based on the 1969 collection, the ratio of cortical to noncortical flakes at Batza Téna ranges from 0.26 to 1.54, or about 20 percent to 60 percent cortical (Appendix II Table 2). For the total flake lots in Table 9.2 cortex is present on 42 percent of the flakes.

Holmes found an abundance of obsidian cortex flakes at Lake Minchumina: 30 percent of the obsidian flakes from MMK-12; 19.4 percent from MMK-4 (Holmes 1986, MMK-4 data calculated by the author from Holmes' Table 14). He feels that there are sufficient cortical flakes at MMK-12 to indicate that whole pebbles were imported into the site. The percentage of obsidian cortex flakes there is in fact high when compared with occurrences for flakes of other lithologies. Other comparisons include 8.8 percent cortex, basically not obsidian, in the large collection from Kurupa Lake site KIR-124 in northwestern Alaska (Schoenberg 1985) and 18.5 percent for a flake sample (from which shatter has been excluded) from Rat Indian Creek in the northern Yukon (Le Blanc 1984:Table 19. The average occurrence of cortex at Batza Téna of 42 percent, compared to 30 and 19 percent for obsidian at Minchumina and 18.5 percent at Rat Indian Creek (large not obsidian, but where in fact there was a lot of workshop activity but utilizing cherts) generally supports the opening proposition to this section.

Gross Area Frequency of Debitage

One measure expected to distinguish a lithic reduction zone is a higher gross occurrence of flaking detritus compared to other areas. This may be difficult to determine without intensive archaeological surveys, but such surveys could be accomplished with moderate effort in sparsely vegetated areas where much of the archaeological material is visible on the surface. Data from Batza Téna are insufficient to undertake this examination, but by working part way through the procedure we will show what we intend.

The Batza Téna area that was intensively surveyed is about 42 square km in extent (Table 9.1). For purposes of calculating the area represented by the archaeological remains we should not selectively exclude lakes and flats. Both are habitats exploited by the inhabitants of the area for hunting and fishing. The area bounded by the Koyukuk River on the west, the peak "cone" on the east and latitudinally extending from 2 km north of Indian River to 2 km south of Little Indian River and including all the area around Batzatiga is approximately 443 square km. Future work may show that the area should be expanded, especially eastward. The collection of 507 kilograms of flakes (502 in Table 1.1 plus the additional collected from the subarea northwest of Little Lake Ridge) represents this area. Approximately half the flakes observed were collected, and those observed likely account for something between one-tenth and five-tenths the total present. If these data were more precise it would be possible to calculate an estimated frequency by weight per unit area. Comparable calculations could be made for other areas more or less of similar size, determined either by natural features or by dividing the land into sections, each containing terrain suitable for camp sites and for finding archaeological remains. As flaking stations or lithic reduction sites utilizing local materials would be almost universally present, comparisons among the data would indicate primarily the relative importance of the major source/lithic reduction zone relative to scattered local flaking stations.

The Parameters of Batza Téna: Space and Function

Defining Batza Téna and its Spatial Limits

Batza Téna is the zone of obsidian flaking stations, including also multipurpose sites, surrounding the Indian River obsidian source. Some obsidian was traded or carried to distant locations, but it can be expected that the flaking station aspect of those sites will be subordinate to their camp aspect. Also, at more distant combination sites other materials are likely to share and even dominate the lithic supply. An additional parameter, lithology, thus can be introduced. The lithic reduction site type, which is determined by lithic reduction characteristics predominating among the debitage and lack of "camp" implement associations, coupled with the predominance of obsidian, are the defining features of Batza Téna. Other features such as the presence of multiple use sites and artifacts of basalt and chert are incidental and not a part of the definition of the lithic reduction zone. Nevertheless, they figure importantly in our attempt to understand how the source was utilized and the area was controlled.

Our surveys did not adequately delimit the extent of Batza Téna. On the west, it is likely that the Koyukuk River and its sloughs and flats set one limit. The hills south of the Little Indian River were not surveyed. Considering that these hills virtually abut the geological outcrop, it is likely that obsidian flaking stations will be found there. It is especially important that at least the lowest flanks of these hills be examined. It seems doubtful, though, that the cluster of flaking stations extends very far south and up the hill slopes because of the terrain and because most travel in the immediate area probably was in an east-west direction.

For the northern limit of Batza Téna there is some information on which to base an estimate. A short survey along the tractor road leading eastward from Hughes was negative, although surface exposure in that area is poor. Shovel probes on the Hill at Rock Island Point also were negative. Closer yet to the source is the large unnamed lake and a smaller lake on the north side of the Indian River flats. Two visits to this area revealed only one weak site (RlIg-53) and a few scattered flakes. Survey in the middle Indian River valley almost as far east as a point opposite the hill "cone" revealed a cluster of sites on the south side of the river but only one site and some minor flake clusters and scatters on the north side.

The country east of the source is largely unsurveyed. In the northeast corner, in the headwaters of the Indian River near the Utopia airstrip, Reger found a cluster of minor flaking stations and isolated finds (Reger and Reger 1972). Sites or finds also have been reported by other geologists: one north of Utopia in the Kanuti watershed (Thomas Hamilton communication to D. Clark) and one directly east of the southern fork of the Indian River headwaters (Edwin Hall communication to D. Clark). It is likely that because of the lower terrain on the east side of the Indian Mountains, and prehistoric travel between the Kanuti and Indian River watershed, that a northeastward lobe or outlier of Batza Téna is present in that area. However, the area around and east of the hill "cone", or generally from the obsidian outcrop directly eastward, is almost completely unknown at the present time. Historic travel, hunting and trapping is reported between the Koyukuk (Indian and Little Indian River) drainage and the Melozitna. We expect that there was similar land use and routes of communication during prehistoric time and that the Batza Téna lithic reduction zone will be found to extend eastward of the geologic source. It can be noted that because of its southeast-northwest trend the Koyukuk River is not a good route for travel unless one particularly wanted to go in those directions. A person could opportunistically drift down the river, but much travel in the region was along a north-south axis and was undertaken, at least in part, by overland expedition.

The "Client" Distribution

There were, however, routes westward to the Kobuk River, the Selawik and the coasts of northwestern Alaska. One possible route, starting in a northerly direction from Batza Téna, bypassed the Indian Mountains along their east side and the Sushgitit Hills on their west site, veered westward towards the Koyukuk River through a low pass just northeast of Kohokachalla Mountain, crossed the river, continued northwestward through the low pass north of Niitltoktalogi Mountain to the headwaters of Siruk Creek. From there were clear routes westward to the Kobuk River where Batza Téna obsidian appears abundantly in archaeological sites. The distribution of the various obsidian source groups in Alaska is being studied by John Cook. Here a very general statement will be offered. Batza Téna obsidian is found throughout Interior Alaska in the region extending from the Bering Sea coast to the Yukon. It is found as far east as Eagle whereas obsidian from Moosehide, located adjacent to Dawson, has the fingerprint of other sources (Jeff Hunston personal communication). Most obsidian from the northern Yukon has not been identified with specific sources. Trace element analysis done for the Archaeological Survey of Canada by V.C. Armstrong, Atomic Energy of Canada, Commercial Products Ltd. shows fingerprints vaguely similar to the main Koyukuk obsidian, but the match is imprecise and outside the generally tight pattern for the Koyukuk obsidian. There is a rapid decrease in abundance of obsidian within and north of the Brooks Range though occasional or minor occurrences are widespread and frequent. The same situation occurs along the Bering and Chukchee Sea coasts, with one notable exception: the high incidence of obsidian microblades in the Denbigh Flint complex site on Norton Sound (Giddings 1964).

There are possible temporal limits that set a floor on the earliest use of obsidian from the Koyukuk River outside that area. None is found in the c 9000-year-old Akmak component at Onion Portage (Anderson 1988) though it appears there slightly later in the Kobuk complex. None is found in any of the 11,100/11,400-year-old Nenana complex sites (Powers and Hoffecker 1989) though it is present in the 10,700-year-old component II at Dry Creek and to a minor extend at Healy Lake site XBD-020 (cf Davis 1977) during about the same period. An obsidian fluted point was found on the north side of the Brooks Range in the Putu complex, although obsidian otherwise is not part of the Putu lithics (Alexander 1987), and may indicate wide travel by the fluted point hunters.

The incidence of obsidian in sites at Batza Téna nears 100 percent. It may be instructive to note the frequency of obsidian away from that source. Not all the obsidian found elsewhere, though, comes from the Koyukuk River, so these figures provide only an approximate guide.

An extremely simple but powerful truism applies to the obsidian distribution that may allow us to recognize the camps of inbound people and outbound people. Sites containing obsidian to any notable extent must be outbound sites, the leavings of people travelling from Batza Téna after having obtained a supply of obsidian. Trade from the source complicates the situation, but here a simplified model is under consideration. Conversely, to a substantial degree flaked artifacts not of obsidian represent inbound movements. In this model, as distance from the source increases trade becomes dominant as a distribution mechanism, and transport by local bands who exploited the source becomes subordinate. The case here may have exceptions. For instance, we found two cores of charcoal-grey colored low-grade cherty material which probably was picked up on local gravel bars and was "tried" out of expediency or as an alternative to obsidian. There is a low-frequency basalt knapping industry at Batza Téna although no cores were found and the small amount of basalt debitage recovered cannot account for the moderate recovery of basalt artifacts there. Cortical basalt flakes appear to be from river-rounded cobbles. It would be useful to know how far away from the obsidian source this material came, and how far those equipped with basalt tools travelled to reach Batza Téna.

With this information in the background, we can list some frequencies of extraterritorial obsidian.

Hahanudan RkIk-3, flaked implements, (Clark 1977)	93.8%
Hahanudan RkIk-5, flaked implements, includes opaque obsidian not from Batza Téna	85.9%
Onion Portage, Itkillik, all implements (Anderson 1988)	45.7%
" ", flaked implements	c47.0%
Onion Portage, Norton-Ipiutak, all implements	18.0%
" ", flaked implements	c21.0%
Onion Portage, Interior Choris, all implements	9.5%
Onion Portage, Denbigh, all implements	23%
Onion Portage, Northern Archaic, all implements	42%
Anaktuvuk Pass, Kayuk, flakes & implements (Campbell 1962)	c3%
Anaktuvuk Pass, Tuktu, (Campbell 1962), 8 implements =	4.4%
" ", all lithics, Campbell's estimate	c1%
Minchumina, MMK-12, waste flakes (Holmes 1986)	45%
Dry Creek, Smith reports c 800 obsidian flakes from 1977 excavations; Powers, Guthrie and Hoffecker report total flake recovery from 2 seasons and all lithologies of 26,757 flakes and clusters generally with nil but with obsidian up to...	13%
Minchumina, composite, waste flakes (calculated by author)	22.6%
Minchumina Birches, all flaked material, site may date to about A.D. 1300 (West 1978), not all Koyukuk obsidian?	90+%
K-9 (Cathedral Mt.) Koyukuk R. South Fork (Holmes 1970, Fetter and Shinkwin 1978), an unusual nil situation	0%

TABLE 9.2. COLLATION OF FLAKED NON-OBSIDIAN ARTIFACTS

Site	End Scrapers Others		Bifaces (knives)		Projectile points		Flakes & cores	
	C&O	B	C&O	B	C&O	B	C&O	B
Basecamp Ridge								
RkIg-1	3		1					
RkIg-2							1	
RkIg-11			1				1	5
RkIg-12							2	
RkIg-14			1					
RkIg-20	1							
RkIg-22	2							
RkIg-23							1	
RkIg-24					1			
RkIg-26							1	
RkIg-41	1							
RkIg-46	1							
RkIg-49		1		1				22
Subtotals	8	1	2	2	1	0	7	27
Little Lake Ridge								
Main Ridge								
RkIg-51		2						
RkIg-5	1	1						17
RkIg-10	1	1					1	2
RkIg-39						2		+
RkIg-40			1					
RkIg-27	1					1		2
RkIg-28	1	3		3		8		149
RkIg-29	1	1						
RkIg-30	3	1		7		1	30	144
RkIg-31			2		1		12	
Subtotals	8	9	3	10	1	12	43	314+
East End of Main Ridge								
RkIg-32			1					
RkIg-38						1	1	
RlIg-41			1					+
Subtotals			2			1	1	+
L. Takbatzahullanten and High Ground Northwest of the Ridge								
RkIg-37		1	1					1
RkIg-8	1							
RlIg-34								1
Subtotals	1	1	1					1
Lake 324 and Vicinity								
RlIg-52	1	1		1			1	8
RlIg-52-324	2		5		4		tr	tr
RlIg-33						1	1	
RlIg-35	1				3		1	
RlIg-45		1						
RlIg-37							1	
Subtotals	4	2	5	1	7	1	4+	8+
Obsidian Source Highland								
RkIg-17							2	
RkIg-36			1					
Subtotals			1				2	
Middle Indian River Valley								
RlIg-46	5		3		2		3	3
RlIg-47		1						
RlIg-48			1				1	
RlIg-49		1						

Site	End Scrapers Others		Bifaces (knives)		Projectile points		Flakes & cores	
	C&O	B	C&O	B	C&O	B	C&O	B
RlIg-48			1				1	
RlIg-49		1						
Subtotals	5	2	4		2		4	3
Batzatiga and Vicinity								
RkIh-32	5	1			1			
RkIh-33	1							
RkIh-35	5				1		2	
RkIh-36	7	1		1	2	2	16	1
RkIh-37	1	1					2	
RkIh-38	1							
RkIh-28	1		1				3	1
Subtotal	21	3	1	1	4	2	23	2
Totals:	47	**18**	15	**18**	15	**16**	84+	**355+**
Group totals:	64		33		29		417+	

* Others are largely retouched flakes but include also a burin, a microblade core platform tablet and a quartz crystal graver spur.
** C&O means chert and other lithics not identified as basalt.

More than a Lithic Reduction Zone

We have noted that some Batza Téna localities also are composite or multipurpose camp sites. The strongest case for this is the Batza Téna Tuktu sites (Chapter 5). The various and numerous classes of artifacts present there amply fulfil Fladmark's (1985) requirement for implement diversity at sites of this category. The massive recovery of flaking detritus and biface reduction material further indicates that these sites were, concurrently or serially, lithic reduction sites. The Lake 324 complex is another example. Obsidian debitage within the close area of Lake 324-type artifacts was modest, but the complex locus was surrounded by massive obsidian flake clusters of undetermined cultural affiliation. At several other sites there are hints of diversity though elements of the assemblages not related to lithic reduction are low in number. RkIh-32, which yielded a notched pebble and the only ground adze, and RkIg-22 which had a Kayuk-style biface and a giant notched cobble chopping tool are examples.

There also are cases of narrowly focused sites that must be accounted for by more than lithic flaking, though that also is present. In particular I am thinking of such places as Locus E of RkIg-1 where there were 10 end scrapers (some of chert), a damaged notched point, an amorphous basalt biface, and traces of a hearth consisting of calcined bone; and of one of the loci of RkIg-10 where there were 6 end scrapers one of which was chert. Although end scrapers are abundant, another implement commonly used to alter materials or make implements is all but absent. These are burins. Because of the brittleness of obsidian, burins commonly are not produced from that material (and if they were, hundreds of broken flakes might have served as expedient burins), but it was possible to bring in harder stone if it was required. As burins are rare in many phases of the Northern Archaic tradition and during late prehistoric times, this observation suggests to me that certain periods or cultures are poorly represented in the nonlithic reduction sites or that activity at Batza Téna was narrowly focused on tasks like hunting, hide processing and lithic reduction that did not require use of burins.

Another special case entails the microblade industry which is represented at at least eight sites. One does not rough out or preform a microblade. It is possible that in some cases considerable flaking was done to make a microblade core, though there are cases in which natural preforms needed little further alteration. At Batza Téna they did not stop at this point but went on to produce microblades, in some cases to the point where the cores were exhausted. This activity fits the general model of producing preforms and blanks (in one sense microblades are blanks) and then going away with the usable product. But there is a certain degree of refinement to making microblades that I find difficult to lump with the production of relatively rough biface preforms. We can note that in three cases microblades or cores were found on multipurpose sites.

Special attention must be given to finished projectile points that occur in various contexts (Appendix II Table 4). These are found as isolated finds, as finds on sites that are mainly flaking stations, and on camp sites, often are made of basalt or other stone not obsidian (Table 10.2) though obsidian predominates, and frequently consist of basal fragments. Taken separately and jointly these finds point strongly to the use of Batza Téna as a hunting grounds. During the late 1960s and early 1970s game was especially abundant at Batza Téna. Moose were plentiful, bear so numerous that they were a hazard, and it is reported that formerly caribou lived on the source uplands. Points sometimes were lost at large; they also were broken and discarded at large; at other times people retipped weapons at their camps (or composite camps and lithic reduction sites). Several such sites have been described in this volume. Reger and Reger (1972) also recorded several point fragment finds on a ridge near the Utopia airstrip. It is especially telling that both finished and unfinished fluted point fragments occur on some fluted point sites that plainly are in part lithic reduction sites. We do not believe the finished points were broken on the very verge of their being finished. They were discarded by returning hunters who, concomitantly, were making new points and engaged in producing obsidian tools and roughouts. RkIh-28 (Chapter 3), a site with a high frequency of basalt artifacts is an interesting case though I am not certain how to interpret it. Were the massive obsidian flake clusters at this site left by the same people to whom the basalt tools belonged; e.g.,did a group arrive equipped mainly with basalt tools, produce new tools of obsidian, discard some broken basalt items, and then depart or move to another Batza Téna sites where they are difficult to recognize because they had expended most of their basalt implements?

Chert implements are sparser than those of basalt (Table 10.2) but they may be more useful for interpretation. For the most part, and if not entirely, they belonged to incoming or inbound people. With more complete information we may learn from their distribution where the entry points where, and from which directions or by which routes nonresident people reached Batza Téna. The relative high frequency of nonobsidian artifacts at Batzatiga indicates one such point.

CHAPTER 10:

SUMMARY AND DISCUSSION: PREHISTORY

The two sections of this chapter first summarize the historiography of Batza Téna. Then, there follows a more broadly-focused discussion of northwestern North American prehistory.

Summary

The basis for ordering prehistory was noted briefly in the Chronology section of Chapter 1. It may be appropriate to repeat the primary members of the sequence, each of which has been the basis for a chapter or section in this report.

1.   Palaeo-Indian occupation identified by fluted points.
2.   A phase of uncertain age characterized by leafshaped and oblanceolate points.
3.   Microblade and blade industries.
4.   A late-dating approximation of the Tuktu complex, of the Northern Archaic tradition, that is about 2000 years old.
5.   A late microblade component possibly dating to the same period as Batza-Téna Tuktu.
6.   First millennium A.D. Norton/Ipiutak-related assemblages from Hahanudan Lake.
7.   The Lake 324 complex is possible Athapaskan, although its industry emphasising tools made on bladelike flakes has not been traced to the Koyukon Athapaskans.
8.   The late-prehistoric Koyukuk Koyukon who are represented by sparse isolated artifacts.
9.   Protohistoric and early historic houses. They have yielded limited collections of persisting precontact type implements as well as an array of European items.

Fluted Point Palaeo-Indian

Thirty or more fluted points or fragments have been recovered from the Koyukuk drainage by various projects. Those from Batza Téna, which comprise the majority, come from one cluster of flaking stations and a few additional sites located within the radius of a few km. These points have been the subject of a number of descriptive articles and discussions (Clark, Clark and Clark, Holmes, Gal, and West references). The Koyukuk and other Alaskan and northern Yukon fluted points form a largely isolated distribution but probably are related to the fluted points of midcontinent North America. The precise lineage of the Alaskan points has not been determined, nor, in my estimation, are they acceptably dated. The fluted point problem, e.g., northern <u>versus</u> southern origin, has paramount bearing on questions of New World settlement.

Of the Batza Téna specimens, all except a basalt fragment are made of obsidian. The points usually are triple fluted with the medial flute having been detached last. Some are better described as basally thinned instead of fluted. Both finished and unfinished specimens were recovered. They range from 20 to 28 mm wide and tend to be 4 to 5 mm thick, which is small compared to most fluted points from the Great Plains and adjacent areas of the United States.

The fluted point sites at Batza Téna contain a very limited range of artifact associations, some of which may be incidental due to component mixture. One candidate for a discrete fluted point culture assemblage, on the basis of tight clustering of implements, came from RkIg-30, even although obsidian hydration measurements suggest that that collection represents two widely spaced occupations. Artifacts there were recovered from 40 shallow 6-by-6 foot sections. They include fragments of finished and unfinished fluted points and finished and unfinished ovoid and leafshaped bifaces. The latter are of various sizes and some are complete. There also are lanceolate or leafshaped points. Microblades, blades, and end scrapers are absent, uncertain specimens of the last excepted, and retouched flakes are uncommon. Some investigators have found microblades to occur with fluted points in the Koyukuk drainage (Gal 1976, Holmes 1971, 1973) but this association is lacking at Batza Téna.

Leafshaped and Oblanceolate Points

Points of generalized leafshaped, oblanceolate and lanceolate outline have a very wide temporal and spatial distribution in Alaska and elsewhere in the north, ranging from more than 11,000 years old to protohistoric age. These forms therefore do not constitute proof of any specific or considerable antiquity. We believe, though, that considerable age can be assigned to those from site RkIg-28, in part because this site is located within the cluster of flaking stations that yielded the majority of fluted points. Two RkIg-28 specimens are of a very broad oblanceolate form, found in ten to eleven thousand year-old components at Dry Creek (Powers, Guthrie and Hoffecker 1983), at Healy Lake (Cook 1975), and also in the south where it is known as the short Lake Mohave type. Relatively thick hydration measurements come from three specimens. The possibility remains that this assemblage is younger than suggested here or, conversely, that it actually is older than the fluted points.

The setting of site RkIg-28 is very much like adjacent fluted point site RkIg-30. Spectacular obsidian flake concentrations exposed on the surface were examined, but these produced few or no implements. The formalized artifacts come from less obvious clusters of obsidian and basalt detritus or are isolated surface finds. There are no blades, microblades or end scrapers in this collection though three thick planoconvex unifacially retouched basalt flakes probably served as scraping implements. RkIg-28 is the main site to yield a significant number of basalt implements. Assemblages of this nature are becoming recognized in Alaska as a logical complement to the fluted point phase (Dixon 1985) or as a separate Palaeo-Indian phase (Kunz personal communications 1993). They predate and postdate the microblade dominated Palaeoarctic tradition of early Holocene times (Clark 1983b, 1991; Kunz 1982; Powers and Hoffecker 1989).

Microblade and Blade Industries

Microblade and core assemblages were recovered from three sites while small numbers of microblades or cores also were found at other locations, including the Batza Téna Tuktu assemblage. One site produced both micro- and macroblades. These may be special-function sites for cultures otherwise represented in the sequence (if not fortuitously missing) by a broader spectrum of implements. Batza Téna Tuktu, which yielded a modest microblade industry together with numerous other implements is a case in point.

RkIh-28 is a low elevation lookout and flaking station. Artifacts in the small collection include macrocores, a microblade core, apparent rotated platform tablets, numerous microblades, a few blades, end scrapers on flakes and blades, and bifaces. The blade cores are basically amorphous obsidian pebbles. The single microblade core recovered is a rudimentary wedge-shaped specimen made on a decapitated pebble, but the microblades are unambiguous classic examples. The larger blades are not ideal prismatic specimens, a condition that may be accounted for by the fact that most probably are rejects or debitage. Although microblade technology in Alaska based on use of wedge-shaped cores has an antiquity going back nearly 11,000 years, there is no indication that any of the Batza Téna assemblages are more than half that age.

At RkIg-47 a small number of microblades and microblade cores with rounded to tabular faces were recovered from a series of four flake clusters. Only the platform on the cores has been prepared. In some respects they are like the tabular Tuktu type, but several core platform tablets more suggestive of rejuvenated cylindrical or conical cores also were recovered. Such platform tablets are not a characteristic of Tuktu cores. The only other artifacts recovered were a hammerstone and retouched flake. Obsidian hydration measurements that apply to a single core suggest an age possibly between 3500 and 6000 years, the age tentatively assigned also to RkIh-28.

Microblade components of more or less comparable or greater antiquity have been excavated along the Bonanza Creek or Fish Creek tributary of the South Fork River (Holmes 1971, 1973) and farther north in the Koyukuk drainage at the Girls' Hill site (Gal 1976). Some are associated with fluted points. Some Bonanza Creek and Girls' Hill cores have the Campus or Denali mode of platform preparation entailing lateral shaping from the sides and a burin-like rejuvenation process that detaches platform tablets through a blow directed to the top of the fluted face. This variety of wedge-shaped core occurs in both very early contexts, as at Dry Creek (Powers, Guthrie and Hoffecker 1983) and in contexts possibly only 2000 years old as at Lake Minchumina (Holmes 1983). The Denali technique of platform preparation was not seen on any of the Batza Téna wedgeshaped cores.

Late Microblade Component

The third microblade site, RlIg-37, appears to be very late. Microblades and fragments of wedgeshaped cores not of the Campus-Denali type were recovered at RlIg-37 in an area a few meters in diameter. They were accompanied by platform tablets and the base of a small sidenotched point. The cores had elliptical platforms with a bifacially prepared wedge element, though they lack the distinctive features of platform preparation and rejuvenation noted above. The average obsidian hydration layer thickness taken on microblades is 1.48 microns, probably indicating an age between 2000 and 3000 years (Clark 1984).

Batza Téna Tuktu

An approximation of the Tuktu complex (Campbell 1961), a facies of the Northern Archaic tradition (Anderson 1968), comes from two adjacent sites located at Batzatiga. At one large site, tested by widely spaced sections, artifacts are dispersed. At the other site, RkIh-36, an apparent camping area is indicated by the distribution of fire-altered cobbles and by more than 40 end scrapers. This living area is located within a larger flaking station which is not necessarily coeval with or a part of the Batza Téna Tuktu phase. Microblades are rare and only two microblade cores, neither of the tabular Tuktu variety, were recovered. Other artifacts include sidenotched and leafshaped points, bifaces of larger format, a retouched hide scraping stone, a notched pebble axe, notched and roughened pebble sinkers or weights and hammerstones, cores for ridged flakes, a copper awl, the occasional retouched flake, and a single burin on a chert blade.

Batza Téna Tuktu differs from Tuktu proper, as defined at Anaktuvuk Pass in the Brooks Range, through its relatively low frequency of sidenotched and leafshaped points, microblades and cores. The last, however, is a point of conformity with the related Northern Archaic tradition at Onion Portage (Anderson 1968). Tuktu or Northern Archaic correspondences also include a high incidence of end scrapers and larger bifaces, notched pebble sinkers, notched pebble axes or choppers, and retouched hide scraping stones (somewhat like chithos). Most of these elements also are found in the Northwest Microblade tradition of R. S. MacNeish (1964). On the basis of the most accepted Tuktu site radiocarbon date, and dates for the Palisades complex (early Northern Archaic) (Anderson 1988), it was anticipated that Batza Téna Tuktu would be approximately 5500 years old. However, a single radiocarbon date on calcined bone, evidently from a disturbed hearth, in a frost involution at RkIh-36 and a series of obsidian hydration measurements on various artifacts suggest that this phase is only about 2000 years old. Possibly related material from the Girls' Hill site of the upper Koyukuk drainage is characterized by abundant microblades, several types of microblade cores, and peripherally occurring sidenotched points as well as fluted points (Gal 1976, personal communications). Girls' Hill radiocarbon dates are approximately 2000 to 4500 years ago.

Norton-Ipiutak Occupation at Hahanudan Lake

Precisely how one would classify this phase depends upon the role and place assigned to the Ipiutak phase within a Norton tradition. The final report on this material is presented elsewhere (Clark 1977). The two housepit sites, one open site, and several cache pits excavated at Hahanudan Lake are located approximately 70 km (45 miles) southwest of Batza Téna. One site,

RkIk-3, consists of three house depressions and one ill-defined feature depression. Two more houses are located somewhat more than 1 km distant at RkIk-5. The older site, RkIk-3 is radiocarbondated to 450-500 A.D., the other a couple centuries later. They can be placed in a single Ipiutak-related phase.

The houses are rectangular to slightly irregular in plan, variously with and without entrance passages. When present, the entrance trench is short and at house floor level which is 2 to 3.5 feet (about 60 cm to slightly less than 1 m) below present ground surface. The pit floors range from a maximum size of 12 by 13 feet ($\underline{c}$ 4 m) down to a minimum of 8.5 by 9 feet (slightly less than 3 m). The simple hearths, without retaining structures, are centrally located or, in the case of one small elongate structure, near a side wall. Light poles of the superstructure and roof were found in the latter, burned structure, but heavier posts and beams were not recovered, nor was any trace of postholes recognized. Rotted birchbark found in one structure evidently covered the roof together with turf and soil.

Implements, produced largely from obsidian, include side scraper and flakeknife forms of retouched flakes. Bifaced scrapers of more or less discoidal or variable format also are common, but no conventional snubnosed end scrapers and stone slab and boulder spall scrapers were recovered. Other implements include lanceolate and leafshaped points, sideblades, small lateral inset sideblades, abrasive stones, ground adze bits, a large ground burin, a flint effigy or lancet tip, a hammerstone with red ochre stains, a chalcedony drill bit, a burinated (unintentional?) blade, and unmodified beaver incisors (intended for use in carving tools?). A small open site at Hahanudan Lake, RkIk-4, produced a few additional artifacts that can be placed in the Norton tradition. Among these are endblades similar in form to Arctic Small Tool tradition specimens but which lack Denbigh-style ripple flaking. No points of that form were recovered from the houses and the RkIk-4 endblades could represent a different earlier Norton phase.

Hahanudan presents the earliest evidence of Eskimo influence on the Koyukuk River, although the distribution of obsidian in Denbigh Flint complex sites found west of the Koyukuk River indicates that the Denbigh people of about 4000 years ago had contacts with the Koyukuk region. On the basis of the radiocarbon dates on the houses (Table 1.1), the form of adze bit, and the absence of pottery in the houses, identification is closest with the Ipiutak phase of Norton.

Kayuk Complex

Kayuk artifacts from Anaktuvuk Pass have attracted attention due to the distinctive parallel flaking found on the numerous points and bifaces recovered from a single site (Campbell 1962). Although some experts consider Kayuk to be part of the Anaktuvuk Ipiutak assemblage, there remains the probability that the two are unrelated. A few Kayuk-style artifacts have been recovered from the Koyukuk drainage and from farther south at Lake Minchumina (Holmes 1983). In both cases they lack, on the one hand, the Palaeo-Indian level of antiquity proposed by Campbell and MacNeish (1964) for the Kayuk assemblage or, on the other hand, Ipiutak associations. It is doubtful if any whole site assemblage from the Koyukuk drainage can be attributed to Kayuk, although a few implements with this style flaking are found in the Cathedral Mountain assemblage, from the South Fork of the Koyukuk, all of which Fetter and Shinkwin (1978) attribute to Kayuk.

Lake 324 Complex

The Lake 324 complex consists of an assemblage recovered from a small area within site RlIg-52. The greater site consists primarily of flaking stations possibly unrelated to this complex. Obsidian artifacts, comprising nearly 100 specimens, are produced in a distinctive mode that gives this material technological coherence. Large flakes, usually thin and elongate, have been extensively retouched into bifaces, or have been flaked along the edges to form end scrapers, knives and points. The end scrapers are of a relatively large size, for instance, 61 by 42 mm and 74 by 35 mm, and often are totally flaked on the dorsal surface. Most of the rough points, made on flat elongate flakes, were found in a single cluster where their owner apparently had left them. The reliance on elongate flake preforms is unique to this complex among Batza Téna collections. Late dating of the Lake 324 complex is based on an A.D. 1065 radiocarbon date of uncertain reliability (Table 1.1), and the presence of a longitudinally grooved stone pestle and four retouched stone slab and boulder flake scrapers. These occurred as a localized group and one cannot be certain that they belong together with the flaked obsidian implements. Microblades, burins and pottery are absent from the assemblage as also are Northern Archaic styles of points and any crossties with Hahanudan Lake and Batza Téna Tuktu. These limitations taken together also point to a relatively late age, but we cannot exclude the possibility of mixed components: one late prehistoric, the other possibly very early prehistoric.

Late Prehistoric Remains

Judging from its radiocarbon date, the Lake 324 complex fails to articulate with the ethnographic present of the 19th century by most of a millennium. No assemblages dating to the immediate precontact period have been recognized, but there are a few isolated artifacts or small groups of implements that fit the stylistic expectations of this period. Among these are a variant stemmed Kavik style point, large grinding slab and small scraping stone recovered from a single site, one occurrence of potsherds, and a grooved splitting adze seen in a private collection. One cache pit located at Hahanudan Lake is radiocarbondated to A.D. 1665±95 (without calibration which increases the age by nearly a century; Clark 1977: Table IV), but associations are limited to an obsidian flake and a potsherd.

Contact Period Houses

The final archaeological phase is documented by several protohistoric and early historic houses. Those excavated by the Canadian Museum of Civilization in the vicinity of Allakaket, the Okak, Kayak and Lake Creek sites, date approximately between 1870 and 1890 (A. Clark 1991,

Clark and Clark 1974). By the latter date log cabins were replacing semisubterranean houses on the lower Koyukuk River. Houses located there at Kateel and partially excavated by de Laguna (1947) are probably one to three decades earlier inasmuch as they yielded predominately aboriginal material even though at Kateel direct home territory contact was earlier, by 1842, than it was in the vicinity of Allakaket here home territory contact was in 1883-84. One house of this period also has been excavated on the Alatna River at the mouth of Siruk Creek (Morlan 1967).

Material from the houses may be classified according to three groups: indigenous aboriginal, indigenous manufactured from imported material, and imported European implements and goods. Indigenous aboriginal implements, some of which probably had gone out of style by the time of home territory contact, include plain ceramic pots, the grooved splitting adze, toothed split cannon bone fleshers, chitho hide scraping stones, snowshoe netting needle, red paint stone and its natural stone mixing basin, whetstones, large sandstone grinding slabs, antler wedge, antler comb, and slender barbed arrow points of various types. These items were recovered either from Kateel or the middle-river houses. The semisubterranean house, with numerous construction elements suitable for attribute analysis and comparison with other houses, is itself a prime artifact. Imported material, particularly powder canisters, was salvaged or recycled, for instance to make small metal pans. Knives and crooked knives were made from files and other pieces of metal. European goods particularly valuable as time markers are the various styles of beads and components of the firearms complex.

Crossroads and Eddies: Prehistory as Seen from a Tributary of the Yukon[1]

The Koyukuk River transects the most probable migration route from Asia into the New World. It does not matter whether people came by land bridge, ice floe or by boat, the configuration of the continents would have channelled all but littoral hunters and gatherers into the Koyukuk Region. And it does not matter whether or by what route people continued into the continent. Issues such as the "ice-free corridor" therefore are not pertinent. Conversely, and excepting maritime hunters, any people making a reverse trek, from North America to Siberia likely would have been Koyukuk people. A stone age people would have been sensitive to the properties of lithic materials and would have exploited a desirable, easily flaked stone like obsidian. Inasmuch as the Batza Téna source has more than one aspect, including the gravels of two streams, extending for several km, we believe that knappers did not take long to discover the Indian River sources. It is somewhat perplexing, then, that there is no obsidian in the earliest Alaskan sites, those of the Nenana complex (below). Possibly, this is a local problem, e.g., Nenana sourcing of raw material was local. Even during a later period, the Akmak people of the Kobuk River, which is closer to Batza Téna than the Nenana sites, did not utilize Koyukuk River obsidian although there likely was interregional contact and by this time, about 9000 years ago,

---

[1]The first archaeological research that included the Koyukuk River was published under the title "The Prehistory of Northern North America as seen from the Yukon" (de Laguna 1947).

obsidian was being taken eastward where it is found in several sites. Eventually, the explanation of such disjunctures in the distribution will permit a more precise delineation of prehistory. Fluted points from the Koyukuk region are made of obsidian, and this is further reason why it is important to know old their age.

As well as being a station along the crossroads between two continents, the Koyukuk region, together with neighboring terrain extending to the Arctic Ocean, literally is the corner of the North American continent.   Thus, at certain times this region appears not to have been a crossroads but instead, in keeping with continental geography, it was a corner or eddy.

Before Microblades: Were there Palaeo-Indians in the North?

Until recently, in Alaska and northwestern Canada, the earliest widely accepted evidence that occurred in sufficient frequency and regularity to be grouped into a culture tradition was the American Palaeo-Arctic (or simply Palaeo-Arctic) tradition. Convincing evidence for an earlier tradition now is available, especially as the Nenana complex. We will exclude the fluted point assemblages from consideration at this stage because of uncertainty surrounding their integrity and dating, and the possibility that fluted points in the north do not constitute a discrete culture or tradition but are an element of other traditions.   Options pertaining to the fluted points are discussed elsewhere in this section and in Chapter 2. The Palaeo-Arctic, which follows the Nenana complex and also in part follows the Northern Cordilleran tradition, is reasonably well established within a broader northern hemisphere context that accounts for its origins. Close Asian counterparts of the Palaeo-Arctic tradition can be found in Ushki I Layer VI excavated by Dikov (1978), and in artifacts assigned to the Dyuktai culture by Mochanov (1978a, b).

There is little, though, linking Palaeo-Arctic technology with Palaeo-Indian fluted point complexes in the midcontinent region (but see West 1981 for a differing opinion).   The most notable departure is the absence of microblade technology. Essentially different technological traditions are represented, and dating places the Palaeo-Arctic tradition slightly later than Clovis culture.   There are several reported Palaeo-Arctic dates between 9,000 and 11,000 years ago, including the single Dry Creek II date of 10,690±250 years (Powers and Hamilton 1978) that frequently is relied on to date this tradition in Alaska. The microblade industry at the Bluefish Caves possibly is older (Cinq-Mars 1979).

Since the fluted point tradition (Clovis culture) is not derived from the Palaeo-Arctic tradition, we must look for other evidence for its northern ancestors. To accommodate hypotheses of Clovis origins, these northern progenitors could be in the order of 20,000 years old and related only indirectly to the fluted point makers. Or they could be the direct antecedents of Clovis, in which case they should be about 12,000 years old. Until recently, the evidence (which recognized nothing older than the Palaeo-Arctic and discounted northern fluted points) strongly favored the view that there was no direct northern input into Clovis culture. The infusion of new information now prompts reexamination of previous proposals for early occupation of the north. MacNeish's

Cordilleran tradition (MacNeish 1959b, 1964), in particular, had been rejected because of its insubstantial, poorly defined basis and lack of radiocarbon dates. But in reexamining the problem "Is there a Northern Cordilleran Tradition?" (Clark 1983b), one of us wrote that a Northern Cordilleran tradition, or its local equivalent such as the Nenana complex (Powers and Hoffecker 1989), is necessary to accommodate an explanation of the origin of Clovis culture based on northern roots slightly predating the Palaeo-Arctic tradition.

An aspect of recognizing that there was prehistory before the Palaeo-Arctic tradition, is that there would have been surviving technological and perhaps ethnic diversity in the north during the period when Palaeo-Arctic microblade technology was becoming established in eastern Beringia. When the Palaeo-Arctic spread to present western Alaska, non-microblade antecedents would have continued to occupy easternmost Beringia. This evidently actually occurred near the end of the Pleistocene. Soon lands farther to the east, in northwestern Canada, were freed from glacial ice. These areas likely were occupied by persisting non-microblade-using or Northern Cordilleran people who had yet to be swamped by Palaeo-Arctic people or technology. Several diverse, old, non-microblade sites can be linked together primarily through this modelling of prehistory. Some in Alaska are dated between 11,000 and 11,500 years old; others are not dated or are later derivatives. They include, for example, Dry Creek I (Powers and Hamilton 1978), the lowest horizon of the Broken Mammoth site at Shaw Creek next to the Tanana River (C. Holmes personal communication), the oldest hearth at the Mesa site (Kunz 1992), and especially the Walker Road site in the Tanana Valley nearly completely excavated by Wm. Roger Powers. With the exception of the typologically distinct Mesa complex, this material from the "Golden Heart" of Alaska most commonly is termed the Nenana complex (Hoffecker, Powers and Goebel 1993; Powers and Hoffecker 1989, Simpson 1989).

Nevertheless, these earliest components of Palaeo-Indian age have failed to yield any fluted points, except Putu (Alexander 1987). The earliest Putu date, of c 11,000 years, might be valid but not applicable to fluted points from that locality (R. Reanier personal communication to D. Clark 1993). A short basally thinned or fluted point and fragment from the Broken Mammoth site are associated with the 9500-10,500 middle paleosol, not with the lowest component (D. Yesner, personal communication 1992). Without fluted points there is only a weak typological basis for closely identifying any northern assemblage with the Clovis Palaeo-Indian culture. Powers and his associates link the Nenana complex with Clovis and suggest that the two are only slightly diverged from a common ancestor (which should be found in the north), but the trait correspondences they note are general ones. Nenana complex points not only lack flutes but do not resemble Clovis artifacts in outline format, and Clovis seems to lack the thick heavy plane-shaped tools of Nenana.

Regardless of whether the search for Palaeo-Indian "origins" will be fulfilled in Alaska, especially in respect to Clovis, the identification of pre-microblade occupation in Beringia is pertinent to tracing relationships between the Asian and American continents. The interface between lithic technologies--without and with microblades--is one that we expect will be followed across Beringia, like a horizon, as more data become available.

The antecedents of the first Alaskans and the first people to occupy Batza Téna likely came to the New World without microblades, though thus far they have not been identified specifically on the Koyukuk River. The surficial occurrence of archaeological sites, subjected to a very long period of erosion and mass wastage, and the generalized nature of most Nenana complex artifacts impedes the recognition of any such remains. There is every reason, though, to believe that people of this period and cultural configuration were present in the Koyukuk drainage. For instance, if the Nenana complex represents an influx of people from Siberia, it probably would have appeared first in the Koyukuk area. And even if, instead of having genesis in recent migration, those people already had been long established in Alaska they should not have been confined to the Tanana drainage.

It remains to be demonstrated that any of these pre-11,000-year-ago inhabitants of the north, or their immediate antecedents, migrated southward to the midcontinent region. But in either case some of them remained local to the north. Both microblade-using Palaeo-Arctic folk and Northern Cordilleran peoples may be derived from these earlier inhabitants.

Microblade Industries: the Palaeo-Arctic Tradition

The arrival of microblade technology probably entails both cases of further migrations and the diffusion of new technology to inhabitants already established in Alaska. Elements of this tradition and their Asian crossties were long recognized for specific sites, Campus (Nelson 1937) for instance, and in synthetic constructs like the Northwest Microblade tradition (MacNeish 1964) and Denali complex (West 1967a) before the Palaeo-Arctic tradition was defined by Anderson (1970a). The most common link between assemblages is microblade production, usually based on prepared wedgeshaped cores. Formerly most assemblages were undated, and the few dates available were debated and, if not early, frequently were rejected because they failed to fit preconceptions. During the last 25 years, however, there have been four significant changes in the manner we understand this tradition.

First, excavations at Healy Lake (McKennan and Cook 1970 and unpublished reports), Onion Portage (Anderson 1970), the Tangle Lakes (West 1981 and references), Dry Creek (Powers 1978, Powers and Hamilton 1978), on the Alaska Peninsula (Dumond et al 1976; Dumond 1977), and the Bluefish Caves (Morlan and Cinq-Mars 1982) and elsewhere confirm an early age for some microblades in North America, back to about 10,700 years ago at Dry Creek. The appearance of microblade technology, thus, is within the later part of the time range of continental Palaeo-Indian cultures. This has resulted in some strained explanations for the co-occurrence of microblades and fluted points in the north (Clark this volume and references, Dumond 1980, West 1981).

Next, and this is our opinion, many archaeologists were willing to subordinate assemblage variability to dating and convenience. They grouped into a single tradition nearly all assemblages with microblades, excluding Palaeo-Eskimo complexes (cf. Dumond (1977, 1980). The term "Palaeo-arctic" is an extension of Anderson's (1970) designation for the Akmak and Kobuk complexes of the Onion Portage site. In our estimation, and evidently also Anderson's (1980:237 note), this lumping has gone farther than it should and reduces the precision of the Palaeo-Arctic construct and while enhancing its usefulness in a misleading manner.

The third point is that while early dating of the tradition has been confirmed, late dates for wedge-shaped microblade cores also have been verified. Many archaeologists, including the writers, see an amalgamation of late residual Palaeo-Arctic technological elements with features of the succeeding Northern Archaic tradition postdating 4000 BC.

Finally, when it was first defined the Palaeo-Arctic was considered to be a Beringian culture that initially spanned Bering Strait. Central Beringia now appears to have been all but flooded by the date of the earliest Palaeo-Arctic sites on the American side (Hopkins 1982). Unless Palaeo-Arctic people are in situ descendants of a pre-microblade people, they would have been familiar with the flooding coasts and might even have had a certain degree of maritime boating and hunting capability.

Not only do formalized wedge-shaped microblade cores also characterize later prehistory in northwestern North America, but a considerable variety of less well-prepared wedge-shaped cores and other varieties of microblade cores are present (see Chapter 4). This variety is found in certain assemblages of the Palaeo-Arctic tradition as well as in later sites. Platform rejuvenation through detachment of whole platform tablets is a characteristic of both the Palaeo-Arctic cores and less formalized cores, flat-faced tabular Tuktu cores possibly excepted. Some of these core forms are linked to later technological or style shifts in Siberia, to the Sumnagin culture in particular. Anderson (1980:236), Ackerman (1979, 1986) and Mochanov (Dolitsky 1985 and references) propose such Sumnagin links and recognize greater culture complexity in Alaska than the Palaeo-Arctic tradition alone implies. These proposals have yet to be fully incorporated into reconstructions of Alaskan and northwest Canadian prehistory, and any relationship to the Sumnagin culture remains to be demonstrated. We would, in fact, suggest that these relatively simple cores represent a case of parallel development and are not evidence for another migration or further diffusion across Bering Strait.

One point of discussion noted above bears expansion. Twenty years ago archaeologists were faced with a paucity of dated sites for the interior northwestern region and were reluctant to accept many of the radiocarbon dates which were available. They faced, as always, the spectre of mixed multiple components. Consequently there was a schism over the question of the age of microblade industries: 10,000 years or more proposed in some cases (West 1975), 4000 years or less in other cases, with the most youthful assemblages proposed as little as 1000 years old. New discoveries and further dating validate early components, as at Dry Creek. Nevertheless, an essentially identical microblade technology continued to about 4000 years ago, at Otter Falls in the southern Yukon for instance (Cook 1968) and in parts of Alaska to at least 500 B.C., and possibly to 500 A.D. (Holmes 1986). Details of core preparation and rejuvenation are remarkably similar between both the earliest and the latest assemblages. Paradoxically, while the 10,000 to 11,000 year maximum age of the Denali complex (usually regarded as part of the American Palaeo-Arctic tradition) has been validated, one specialist designates a Late Denali that may be as much as 8000 years younger and logically is unrelated (Dixon 1985; see also Bacon 1987). Moreover, the initial definition of Denali (West 1967a) may have been based more on younger sites of amalgamated Northern Archaic complexion than on the earlier sites.

Except initially, at the time microblades were first introduced into North America, it would be unwise to attribute microblade technology to any single culture, people or speech community. Nevertheless, more or less discrete broad-area microblade-using cultural traditions have been proposed, and this implies a certain degree of interaction and ethnic or linguistic unity within the tradition (cf. Borden 1969). Large unmixed assemblages from well-dated sites still are not numerous, and this leaves some chronological and spatial gaps in our knowledge, but it is possible to recognize a number of sequential and regional phases characterized by microblade industries. There also are many early and mid-Holocene sites that lack microblades.

The terms Denali or American-Palaeo-Arctic properly apply to the earliest phases with microblades. Assemblages are characterized by wedgeshaped microblade cores as discussed in Chapter 4, large and medium size bifaces (probably knives), and flakes burinated transversally, along one side, or multiply around the perimeter (the last and sometimes also the first are called Donnelly burins). Prismatic blades sometimes also are present, as in Akmak (Anderson 1970b). Stone projectile points are rare in many assemblages, although biface knives of point format often are present (at Dry Creek for instance). Assemblages of this nature are older than 8000 years in most cases, the majority actually dating more than 9000 years. They are best documented in Alaska though they apparently also are found in the Yukon Territory and, possibly, northern parts of British Columbia where they tend to be later though in many instances their dating has not been established.

We noted in Chapter 4 that there is no identified representative of the early Palaeo-Arctic tradition at Batza Téna. Classic Campus-type wedgeshaped cores of the variety commonly associated with the Palaeo-Arctic tradition have been found elsewhere in the Koyukuk drainage but it remains to be determined that any of these have great antiquity and do not represent assemblages of later "amalgamated" technologies. Association of fluted points and wedgeshaped microblade cores (Gal 1977; Holmes 1971, 1973) is suggestive, but it is not proven that these assemblages from superficial contexts are not mixed. This situation is interpreted as the result of insufficient exploration or the inability to control contexts and establish dating. Early-dated Palaeo-Arctic sites have been found in other regions northwest and southeast of Batza Téna and there is no apparent reason why people of the same technological tradition did not utilize the obsidian source. Obsidian is found in the Dry Creek II component but, surprisingly, none is present in the Palaeo-Arctic type site at Onion Portage.

The Significance of Fluted Points in Beringia

The most distinctive Palaeo-Indian artifacts are fluted points, of which the Clovis variety is best known. They appear in the archaeological record 11,400 years ago. To many archaeologists, Clovis culture forms the earliest occupation of the New World, though opinions accepting earlier occupations fluctuate (compare Marshall 1990 with Bryan et al 1980 and Irving 1985). We began the sequence, in Chapter 2, with fluted points, but because of uncertainty regarding their age they occupy a later position in this chapter. The age of these points actually is a secondary issue as the following discussion attempts to establish.

A modest number of fluted points have been recovered from Alaska and northwestern Canada (Clark 1984, 1990; Clark and Clark 1975). The gap that places northern fluted points in a group separate from the main distribution is being closed gradually in western Canada (Fladmark, Driver and Alexander 1988; Hanks 1991; Wilson 1989). This helps remove one caution, that the northern specimens may not be related to the Palaeo-Indian points (West 1981b). Although the northern points are not adequately dated, their temporal range at least partially overlaps that of the main Palaeo-Indian distribution.

An hypothesis which identifies fluted points with early migration to the New World gives special significance to these northern occurrences, for they would mark the trail of people from Asia, or from Beringia, into North America. (Actual fluted points are absent in Asia and were a later development made along this trail, in Alaska according to one hypothesis.) The rationale for Hibben's 1941 expedition to Alaska is a case in point (Hibben 1943). But the majority of prehistorians postulate development of fluted points farther south in the Americas from whence they spread northward at the end of the Pleistocene (Published discussion of this problem is extensive, cf Haynes 1964, 1971, 1982; Dixon 1985; Martin 1973). Present indications are that at least some of the northern fluted points date within the range 9500-10,500 years B.P., according with the so-called return migration hypothesis.

To amplify the two primary explanations for fluted points in the north, if fluted points developed in eastern Beringia, they should have been present there about 12,000 years ago in order to provide time slope to the south since they appeared in the United States 11,400 years ago. This would have been during the period of the inundation of central Beringia, possibly sundered by Anadyr-Bering Strait. Although there was migration farther into the American continent according to this hypothesis, there is no evidence of movement in the other direction, to Siberia.

If, on the other hand, the northern points are due to migration or diffusion from the midcontinent region, they very likely reached the north no more than 10,500 years ago. Palaeo-Indian migrants would have found the north already occupied by Palaeo-Arctic people, said to be an American branch of Dyuktai from Siberia, characterized by microblade technology (West 1981). The two appear to have interacted in Alaska inasmuch as microblades and fluted points sometimes co-occur at the same sites. Many of these cases, though, involve atypical points or suspected cases of component mixture (Clark 1984; Holmes 1971; Powers, Guthrie and Hoffecker 1983). Other fluted point-users, and also early non-fluted point Palaeo-Indians, may have kept their separate identity, leading to an ethnic mosaic in the north. There are, for instance, no microblades at the Mesa site or in the middle component at the Broken Mammoth site (Kunz 1992, Yesner personal communication 1992). Regardless of these considerations, fluted point technology was present near Bering Strait about 10,000 years ago (if not earlier), but it remained on the American side.

Had there been hemisphere-wide diffusion or cultural interchange extending across a northern zone of peoples with similar ecological adaptations, there is every reason to expect fluted points to have passed from America to Asia. That did not happen. Fluted points thus provide no evidence for contact between Asia and North America. The reasons for this merit examination.

One possible explanation, if the ethnic mosaic hypothesis is correct, is that people disinclined to use fluted points actually controlled the Seward Peninsula approaches to Bering Strait and the remnant landbridge. By virtue of its small size and limited access, Bering Strait was a bottleneck. Another factor, that might have been co-operative, is a flow of people or influence from Siberia into Alaska that held in check any diffusion in the opposite direction. Too, the fluted point people probably were a minority with less influence than the other inhabitants of the north.

Furthermore, if fluted points were fully part of the Palaeo-Arctic tradition, as Dumond (1980) and Morlan (1987) have suggested, and if there was communication between Asian Dyuktai and North American conjoiners of the Palaeo-Arctic tradition, then there is every reason to expect the fluted point trait to have passed from America to Asia. Obviously some of these conditions were not met. Perhaps ethnic differences were maintained and an ambivalence prevailed which resulted in fluted points not being fully accepted as part of the Palaeo-Arctic technological repertoire. Or Palaeo-Arctic people no longer had relations with Siberians. Preeminently, at this time the Koyukuk region was a cultural eddy.

Coeval with, Apart from the Microblade Users: The Cordilleran Cultures

Not many inland sites with microblade industries are dated to the next few millennia following the time of the earliest Palaeo-Arctic occupation. The specification "inland" excludes coastal assemblages of a somewhat different complexion found in British Columbia, southern and southeastern Alaska. This thinning of the record does not appear to be simply a matter of filling in the record, to be accomplished through continued field research. At this time, approximately 7000 to 8000 years ago prehistory in a substantial part of the northwestern region is characterized by lithic industries emphasising leafshaped and lanceolate spear points and lacking microblade technology (Clark 1983b). Isolated cases of large points notched for hafting also appear at this time, in the Acasta complex of the District of Mackenzie for instance (Noble 1971). In many instances archaeologists explain these points, and the cultures they represent, by an expansion northward of the terminal Palaeo-Indian Plano cultures of the northern plains. Whether or not Plano influence and people actually extended into Alaska, to the Mesa site (Kunz 1992) in the Range for instance (and at a date earlier than Plano in the south), is a matter for discussion. These lanceolate point, Plano-like assemblages presently are the earliest found in the western District of Mackenzie (Millar 1981), in northern Alberta (undated surface finds), the southern Yukon Territory as in the basal Canyon component (Workman 1974), and, excepting the Bluefish Caves, the northern Yukon Territory in the Rock River vicinity (Gotthardt 1985) and in the Engigstciak site Flint Creek phase (Cinq-Mars et al 1991, MacNeish 1959b). It is likely, however, that earlier remains exist in these areas. Such earlier remains should document the passage of fluted point Palaeo-Indians, and the expansion eastward, from Alaska, of pre-microblade people.

We have proposed from these data a western mountain and intermountain equivalent to the Plano tradition, e.g., a Northern Cordilleran tradition (Clark 1983b). This is not to be confused with the Old Cordilleran of southern British Columbia. MacNeish (1964) saw Plano and Cordilleran as distinct entities with the Cordilleran having earlier roots in the north preceding the advent of microblade industries there. We concur. With microblade industries validated for more than 10,000 years in Alaska, postulation of an older Cordilleran tradition in such terms is logically tied to hypotheses of Palaeo-Indian prehistory and even Palaeo-Indian origins as was discussed earlier (see also Powers and Hoffecker 1989). Accordingly, the microblade deficient industries of 7000 or 8000 years ago could represent either new inhabitants who had arrived from the south with a late continental western tradition (the Northern Cordilleran), or a people who had had a long antecedent history in the northwestern Arctic and Subarctic largely separate from that of the Palaeo-Arctic microblade users. By 8000 years ago they would have in some manner survived, at least locally, coexisting with the microblade tradition, rejecting microblade technology and perhaps later absorbing its former practitioners. At Batza Téna this tradition may be represented by the Site RkIg-28 assemblage which was described in Chapter 3.

Development of the Northern Archaic and Amalgamated Culture

Technologically and historically, the changes we have noted did not follow a straight-line course. Microblade industries again are well represented during the period 6000-7000 years ago. They may have remained absent in some areas of the far northwest--this is a question requiring further documentation. They also occur later, but are not universally distributed, and by this time there are significant stylistic changes in associated implements. Assemblages contain not only microblades but also various styles of lanceolate and leafshaped points and knives. Greater emphasis on bifacially prepared stone points is a departure from the early Palaeo-Arctic tradition. Microblades now appear in the Mackenzie drainage, and during this or during the next two millennia they reach the eastern limits of their distribution from Alberta to the Arctic Ocean.

Six thousand years ago, or a few centuries later in some areas, sidenotched points achieve a continent-wide distribution from Hudson Bay to Bering Strait. Antecedents are present in the archaic cultures of the south, and there are earlier local occurrences of notched lanceolate or leafshaped points that probably are not directly related, the Kamut and Acasta points for instance (Noble 1971, Gotthardt 1985). But for the vast subarctic region the advent of sidenotched spear points and knives begins what is essentially a new period in prehistory, viewable also as a temporally broad horizon. It is designated as the Northern Archaic tradition west of the Mackenzie drainage and is recognized as part of the Shield Archaic tradition eastward in the District of Keewatin and adjacent territory. A southern derivation is seen for notching, or for these points. The possibility of the notching attribute (and any change in weapons that prompted it) having been accompanied by other cultural elements also of southern derivation was brought up by some archaeologists several years ago, as the name for this tradition itself suggests. However, major population influx from south of the boreal forest has not been demonstrated.

The tradition name was first published for one of the components of the Onion Portage site in northwestern Alaska by Douglas Anderson (1968). Prominent in the assemblage from Onion Portage are large numbers of end scrapers with unprepared dorsal surfaces and many biface knives found together with relatively large sidenotched points and sidenotched cobble choppers and sinkers (see comparisons in Chapter 5). There are some slate pieces with ground surfaces, probably honing stones. Oblanceolate points are found in some phases of the tradition. Microblades and cores are absent. Certainly, then, this assemblage shows a break in technological traditions and there may have been other major undetermined changes, in language and ethnic identity. Selected sites, found at diverse locations in Alaska and the southwestern Yukon Territory (Taye Lake phase) show similar changes, suggesting marked change in prehistory between 5000 and 6000 years ago. In the southern Yukon the microblade tradition was terminated abruptly together with most forms of burins, and new styles of projectile points and knives appeared with equal abruptness (Workman 1978). However, in parts of the Subarctic the use of microblades terminated earlier, within the context of what I have called, in preceding paragraphs, the Northern Cordilleran tradition. Rather than seeing massive migration from the south replacing a substantial portion of the subarctic population, it appears to me to be more reasonable to see the origin of the Northern Archaic tradition in ongoing development, stimulated in part by southern archaic technology, that began initially within the Cordilleran tradition.

Many sites combine characteristics of the Northern Archaic Tradition with microblade technology. Some of the microblade sites described in Chapter 4 and the Batza Téna Tuktu phase described in Chapter 5 belong to this category. Various events could explain this situation: Northern Archaic elements simply could have been added to the technological repertoire of localized antecedent microblade using people; there could have been an amalgamation of peoples; microblades could have been reintroduced into the Northern Cordilleran/Archaic culture. Specifics vary from site to site, and many assemblages are too limited to determine which scenario prevails. Sites or taxa with these mixed characteristics have been published under the designation Tuktu complex (Campbell 1961) and Northwest Microblade tradition (MacNeish 1964) as well as later being included within the Northern Archaic. This characterization might also include some of the original constituents of the Denali complex (West 1967a), the Campus site for instance and ones recently classified as Late Denali (Dixon 1985). Knappers employed the formalized wedgeshaped cores as well as less formalized flat-faced Tuktu cores. Transverse burins and other forms of burinated flakes also continued. Nevertheless, the overall complexion of these later assemblages differs from the earlier Palaeo-Arctic tradition assemblages. Ground adze bits and chitho hide scrapers together with notched points and stem-notched knives are evidence of the passage of time and lead towards the "modernization" of prehistoric cultures (e.g., to the development of assemblages bearing the distinctive stamp of late-prehistoric times).

In our estimation, the northern Archaic tradition, including the microblade using aspect, is a congeries of local phases that differ from one another but which nevertheless possess many technological characteristics and in common. This entity might better be handled as a co-tradition. Initially, many archaeologists focused their conception of this co-tradition on its early interface with other archaeological traditions--a defacto horizon. Therefore, when characteristic elements, such as notched points, were found there was a tendency to expect them to be 5000-6000 years old. For several years this made it difficult to accept relatively recent dates of 2000 years or less for similar assemblages, some of which include microblades. At Onion Portage the Northern Archaic was defined on the basis of a sequent series of components with about 1500 years duration, ending about 4300 radiocarbon years ago (Anderson 1968, 1988). Assemblages with Northern Archaic characteristics now are known elsewhere which date as recently as 2000 or 1500 years ago. Moreover, some archaeologists also see threads of continuity from this middle time-range material through the remaining course of prehistory, and thence to the contemporary Athapaskan inhabitants of the Western Subarctic (Workman 1978). This interpretation may correctly identify a certain reality in technology and subsistence lifeways. But if cultural traditions are assumed to correlate with peoples in the sense of ethnic groups and speech communities, it puts us in the position of supporting an hypothesis of 6000 years of Athapaskan prehistory (or proto-Eyak/Athapaskan) throughout the western Subarctic. Linguists might find this interpretation excessive.

The Northern Archaic tradition in such a broadly drawn sense is too blunt a tool for research into the ethnogenesis of the northwestern peoples, nearly all of which are linguistic subdivisions of northern Athapaskan. Nor does it point out sufficiently the local variations, such as the Lake 324 complex discussed in Chapter 7, and in some cases contrastive differences, that have existed in the north over the last two millennia. Recently, attempts have been made to define local traditions and phases in some area, for instance in eastern Alaska and the adjacent Yukon by Shinkwin (1979) and Le Blanc (1984). The term "Athapaskan tradition," which sometimes appears in the literature, lacks sufficient definition to link these areas in a meaningful manner.

The Interlude that Set the Stage for History

The interlude is the Norton-Ipiutak penetration into the heart of Alaska. We have proposed that this was of considerable duration at Hahanudan Lake, while not far away at Batza Téna there is no evidence of this late Palaeo-Eskimo occupation (Clark 1977, Chap. 6 here). To the south, these people penetrated much deeper into the interior region, to at least as far as Lake

Minchumina (Holmes 1986). If we connect these two points and draw boundaries out to the nearest coastal regions it becomes apparent that 1000 years before historic contact there were few or no Kolchan, Ingalik and Holikachuk Athapaskans, at least in the territory where they now live, and half of the Koyukon lands also were occupied by an Eskimoan people. Holmes suggests that the Norton-Ipiutak occupation of Lake Minchumina simply intruded into the sequence there, displacing the Northern Archaic inhabitants for a time, but did not actually break the sequence (Holmes 1986:158). This interpretation requires further documentation. Concurrently, there was apparent Athapaskan occupation of the Kobuk, at Onion Portage in the Itkillik complex (Anderson 1988). Athapaskans already were caught up in the Koyukuk eddy system, but it was not until sometime after A.D. 800 that this whirl brought the historically known groups into western Alaska. Perhaps they replaced and displaced both late microblade people (Batza Téna Tuktu and at Lake Minchumina) who had persisted in a technological backwater and the interior Norton-Ipiutak people. Inter-area communication was established (or reestablished) rapidly, judging from the 90 percent incidence of obsidian at the Birches site (West 1978). One can query to what extent ancestral Eskimos were involved in the cultural and biological makeup of the several Athapaskan tribes of western Alaska, especially at an earlier time level than the one de Laguna used for interpreting late archaeological data from the lower Yukon River and ethnologists have used for assessing Eskimo-Indian crossties. The answers are still in the ground.

Figure 10.1. The Indian River; view looking upstream from a location north of "Lake 324" towards Benchmark "Cone." A primary obsidian outcrop is present in the middle background right. RlIg-46 (see Appendix I) is in the background left.

APPENDIX I: SITES RkIg-51 AND RlIg-46

Described here are two collections that we have been unable to place within the framework of the preceding chapters. One comprises an unaffiliated, undated collection or complex of rough triangular points. Several interesting artifacts were collected from the other site, RlIg-46, and are illustrated in the plates. Various components may be present in that surface collection.

A Unique Triangular Point Complex

Site RkIg-51 was surface collected in 1970 and small selected areas were excavated in 1971. One area on the north flank of the site was especially productive (Fig. Appendix 1.1). There, implements, including the noteworthy triangular bifaces, were found to a depth of 5 cm within a

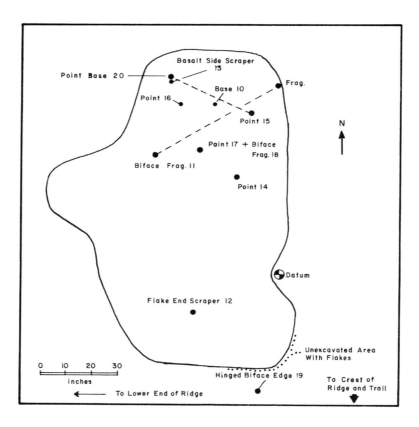

Figure Appendix 1.1. Sketch map of Site RkIg-51

broader distribution of flakes. The site is located on Little Lake Ridge, not far from its west end. A game trail that follows the crest of the ridge crosses the site. It is about 25 m in diameter.

Collection . In 1971, 1871 flakes weighing 1.4 kg were excavated. Catalog entries 1-8 are for 1970, 9 through 17 are for 1971.

Collected at large on the site:
Flake core fragment	51:4
Projectile tip fragment	51:9
Single-edged biface, roughout but not normal format 48x37	51:7
Point fragment, base, possibly lanceolate, thin	51:8
End scraper on large, arched, pointed flake, extensive ventral retouch (Pl. 20A)	51.1
Retouched flake (side scraper)	51:3
Utilized flakes (uncertain)	51:5, 51:6
Hinged biface edge fragment	51:2

Associated finds of the triangular biface complex excavated in 1971:
Point base or end, unfinished, trace of cortex remains	51:10
Bifacially edged flake, rough and damaged	51:11
Flake shaped and bevelled like an end scraper but retouch may be natural	51:12
Basalt side scraper	51:13
Unfinished point 29x23(c29 complete, Pl. 20C)	51:14
Point base fits No. 20, elongate triangular, unfinished	51:15
Point, short triangular 30x36 (Pl. 20D)	51:16
Point, elongate triangular, unfinished 30.5x53 (Pl. 20B)	51:17
Biface (fragment?), unfinished, subrectangular 33x40	51:18
Hinged biface edge fragment	51:19
Point tip fitted to No. 15, unfinished, 32.3x69 (Pl. 20E)	51:20
Retouched? basalt flake	51:21

The elongate triangular roughed-out points, of which there are four to six specimens, are highly unusual and almost are without parallel in other Batza Téna collection. However, inasmuch as most or all of these specimens are unfinished, it is difficult to make comparisons.

RIIg-46: A Mixed Component Surface Collection from The Indian River

The surface of this site was inspected in 1971. A number of distinctive implements collected and a few of the numerous flakes present were picked up. The site is located on a hill a few hundred metres away from the river south of a location where a meander of the Indian River abuts a high cliff on the south side (Fig. Appendix 1.2). Part of the top and backside of the hill is denuded and is littered with obsidian flakes, mostly in an area about 90 m long. Flakes also are present on the vegetated slope north of the denuded zone. This hillock is a lobe of a larger hill, lying to the south or southeast. These adjacent slopes were inspected and found to be archaeologically negative. Few implements were found, considering the large area and many thousands of flakes exposed.

Collection

Lanceolate chert point 70x25x4-5, base incipiently concave, basally thinned but not fluted, potlidded, very fine (Pl. 6I)	46:30
Point base, obsidian, tapers to a pointed base, spear size, edges ground (Pl. 20L)	46:37
Point, short, triangular on flake blank (Pl. 20M)	46:36
Biface roughout, oval 46 mm, 59 mm	46:4, 46:13
Biface roughout, slug shaped 63x33x24	46:12
Biface roughout fragment	46:2, 46:8, 46:11
Biface roughout, hinged edge frag.	46:3, 46:10, 46:16, 46:18, 46:22, 46:24
Biface, thick, triangular, unfinished, adze-shaped, 56x34x18max, possibly an end scraper (Pl. 20I)	46:35
Biface fragment, unfinished	46:6, 46:9, 46:15
Biface fragment, unfinished, very small format	46:21, 46:23
Biface fragment, chert	46:25, 46:27
Hinged biface edge fragment, chert	46:20
Ovoid-elongate uniface, edges partially bifaced (Pl. 20K)	46:40
Irregular uniface, narrow-nosed scraper 55 mm (Pl. 20J)	46:41
Endscraper	46:17, 46:34
Retouched flake, frag., 2 edges, chert	46:28, 46:29, 46:31(3 spec.)
Retouched flake, obsidian, 2 edges	46:29 #2
Retouched flake, pointed, gouge format (Pl. 20N)	46:38
Microblade core, exceptional, exhausted (Chap. 4)	Not cat.
Blade midsection	46:39

The triangular flake point is similar to specimens from the Lake 324 complex, but the microblade core and lanceolate chert point evidently belong with other phases. No particular cultural placement is proposed for the pointed-base point, bifaces, retouched flakes and end scraper.

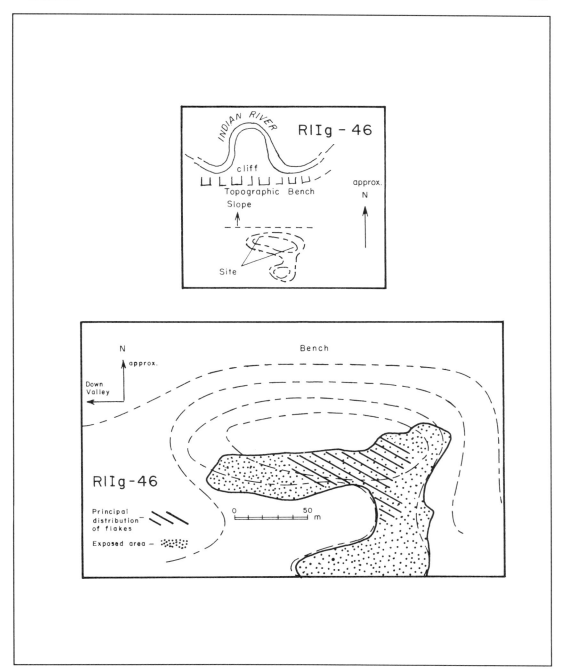

Figure Appendix 1.2. Sketch maps of Site RlIg-46.

APPENDIX II: COLLATIONS

Various information is drawn together in this appendix. Sites were listed in Chapter 1 Table 1.2 in their order of discovery and temporary field numbers. Here we provide a listing of sites according to location. Appendix II also collates data from all sites, including ones not described in this report. These data support the analysis and discussion in Chapter 9.

Sites Listed According to Subarea

Sites are listed below in the following area groups:
  North of the Indian River Flats
  Basecamp Ridge
  Little Lake Ridge
    The Main Ridge
    The East end of the Main Ridge South and Southwest of Lake 324
    High Ground to the Northwest and Sites Near Takbatzahullanten
  Lake 324 and vicinity
  The Source Upland
  Middle Indian River Valley, and
  Batzatiga.

The chapter in which the site is described also is indicated, and if no chapter reference is given, the site is one of those lacking substantial implement collections which described in Table 1.2 (or see Clark 1992).

The fact that Batza Téna falls into three Borden site designation code blocks, together with some areas having been examined and recorded during different reconnaissance traverses over three seasons obviates the possibility of any orderly progression of site numbers on a geographic basis. The order in which sites are listed below groups proximal sites and arranges sites in geographic order, as from west to east.

Site North of Indian River Flats
  RlIg-53

Basecamp Ridge
  RkIg-1 (Chap. 2)   RkIg-23
  RkIg-2   RkIg-24
  RkIg-3   RkIg-25
  RkIg-11   RkIg-26
  RkIg-12   RkIg-41

RkIg-13   RkIg-42
RkIg-14   RkIg-45
RkIg-18   RkIg-46
RkIg-19   RkIg-47, Chap. 4
RkIg-20   RkIg-49
RkIg-21   RkIg-50
RkIg-22 (Chap. 5

Little Lake Ridge
Main Ridge
Field No. 74   RkIg-39
RkIg-51   RkIg-40
RkIg-48   RkIg-27
RkIg-9   RkIg-28 Chap. 3
RkIg-6   RkIg-29--31 Chap. 2
RkIg-5   RkIg-44, -43 Chap. 2
RkIg-4
RkIg-10 Chap. 2

East End of Main Ridge South and Southwest of Lake 324
RlIg-40   RkIg-32
RlIg-39   RkIg-35
RkIg-33   RkIg-38
Field No. 59   RlIg-41

Lake Takbatzahullanten and High Ground Northwest of the Ridge
RkIg-37   RkIg-7
RkIg-8   RlIg-34

Lake 324 and Vicinity
RlIg-52   RlIg-38
RlIg-33   RlIg-43
RlIg-35   RlIg-44
RlIg-45   RlIg-36
                          RlIg-37 Chap. 4
                          RlIg-42

Obsidian Source Highland
RkIg-15   RkIg-36
RkIg-16   RkIg-53
RkIg-17

Middle Indian River Valley
RlIg-46 Chap. 2   RlIg-49
RlIg-47 Chap. 2   RlIg-50
RlIg-48   RlIg-51

Batzatiga and Vicinity
  RkIh-34, 35, -36, -37 Chap. 5
  RkIh-32, 28 Chap. 4
  RkIh-40   RkIh-27
  RkIh-33   RkIh-29
  RkIh-38   RkIh-30
  RkIh-39   RkIh-31

In addition to designated sites, there are numerous find spots represented by single collected
items, and in some cases by minor occurrences of lithic detritus that was not collected. Table II.1
below, lists these unassociated finds or so-called "found on the trail" artifacts, many of which are
featured in the plates. They are cataloged under the "non-site" designation RkIg-x or in some
cases in the "old system" catalog for Area XI-E. Only distinctive implements are listed in Table
II.1, which accounts for the fact that there are gaps in the numeric sequence.

TABLE APPENDIX II.1.   UNASSOCIATED FINDS

Number	Description	Location
RkIg-x:		
32	Point, base wide slightly convex	SW end Little Lake Ridge (Pl 21K)
37	Point, side notched	Basecamp Ridge 190 m below RkIg-41 (Pl. 21M)
38	Point, square stemmed	Basecamp Ridge S flank (Pl. 21L)
39	Lance or knife blade	Little L. Ridge W of site 28 (Pl.21B)
27	Flatfaced core	Basecamp Ridge (Pl. 24G)
28	Planoconvex object	Basecamp Ridge
41	Leafshaped biface, basalt	S of site 33 with few flakes (Pl.21S)
24	Biface, irregular damaged	Provenience lost
7	Biface, nonpointed fragment	Ridge behind 1969 basecamp
6	Biface, semipointed fragment	Little Lake Ridge trail
33	Biface, semipointed fragment	Outer end Little Lake Ridge
40	Biface, semipointed fragment	Between RkIh-33 & RkIh-34
10	End scraper	Basecamp Ridge
42	Retouched flake, steep bevel	Basecamp Ridge 3/4 way to end
25	Retouched flake, sharp unifacial	1969, Basecamp Ridge?
35	Retouched flake, sharp unifacial knife, not obsidian	Beach, SE corner of Lake Takbatzahullanten (Pl. 22N)
26	Retouched flake, bifacial, knife	1969, Basecamp Ridge
4	Utilized flake, steep thick edge	Basecamp Ridge
5	Utilized flake, steep thick edge	1969
13	Utilized flake like flakeknife	Provenience lost
36	Bladelike flake, basalt	(Pl. 22A)
XI-E:		
42	Biface	Behind Lake 324 camp (Pl. 21P)
25	Chopper-shaped core	Trail SW end of Batzatiga (Pl. 23D)
41	Platform core for small blades	Hillside behind RkIh-36 (Pl.23I)
23	Chert blade, small	West end of minor ridge just N of Little Lake Ridge (Pl. 22D)
19	Blade or bladelike flake	Very W end Little L. Ridge (Pl. 22C)

Incidence of Certain Flake Characteristics

The 1969 flake collections were studied for the following attributes:

1. Cortical flakes/non-cortical flakes. Most of the cortical flakes are only partially so or are what are called secondary cortical flakes.

2. The incidence of flakes not of obsidian, primarily chert and basalt (see also Table 9.2). It may be noted, however, that collection was biased towards this visibly different category and the percentage stated in Appendix Table II.2 could be halved to give a realistic proportion of its actual occurrence. The 0.22 percent represented by the combined recovery of chert and basalt flakes in 1969 is not representative. For the three seasons of field work the collection of chert and basalt flakes amounts to 84 and 355 respectively (Table 9.2) which would be in the approximately 0.5 percent of the total flakes.

TABLE APPENDIX II.2.   FLAKE DATA (1969)

Site RkIg..	Total	With cortex	Ra-tio	Without cortex	Chert & basalt	Colored obsidian	Speckled microlites	Weight kg
1	1307	620	0.96	644	0	45	1	3.3
2A	1792	811	0.85	950	1	24	0	8.0
3	692	325	0.90	361	0	77	15	2.2
5	354	109	0.49	223	0/16	23	0	0.8
6	287	161	0.42	382	0	5	0	0.8
7	111	–	–	–	0	1	2	0.2
8	288	164	1.40	117	0	4	0	1.5
9	650	368	1.35	273	0	6	3	1.3
10	2008	692	0.60	1146	1/2	34	12	7.4
11	1287	335	0.36	931	1/5	40	5	2.8
12	2556	1069	0.73	1459	2	45	7	5.1
13	1325	268	0.26	1041	0	128	15	1.8
14	679	236	0.55	432	1	27	4	1.9
15	841	259	0.46	561	0	8	0	2.9
16	59	14	0.33	42	1	2	0	0.3
17	718	298	0.73	406	2	12	0	2.2
18	73	11	0.18	62	1	4	0	0.3
19	493	248	1.02	242	0	0	0	1.1
20	229	93	0.72	130	0	20	0	0.9
21	553	294	1.18	249	0	12	26	1.6
22	1130	680	1.54	441	0	67	5	4.7
23	131	64	0.98	65	1	5	0	0.9
24	786	369	0.90	411	0	27	30	2.7
25	2032	963	0.93	1036	0	108	45	8.0
26	161	37	0.30	123	1	4	0	0.5
27	359	161	0.81	198	0/2	10	3	1.6
28	578	233	0.70	334	0/10	2	1	2.5
29	33	16	–	17	0	3	1	0.2
30	253	123	1.0	122	0/1	3	0	1.9
31	146	53	–	79	0/1	1	0	1.1
Total	21911	9074		12,477	12/37	747	175	70.5
Percent		41.4%		56.9%	0.22%	3.4%	0.80%	

Note: The total is for all flakes and includes also 426 flakes that had been held out for examination as possible implements. The total of flakes with and without cortex is based on an examination that did not include these items into account and therefore the first, total, column usually exceeds the amount of the next three columns. For this reason there is a low level inaccuracy in percentages based on the total column.

3. The incidence of coloured obsidian, primarily a combination of red-brown and black. Tested examples show that this is a colour of the common Type B or Group 2. As reported below the coloured category also includes a few blue-grey and milky-grey flakes that resemble chert and a very rare opaque enamel brown (which might not be Type B obsidian).

4. The incidence of obsidian with specks or microlites. Tested examples show that in all cases this variety is Type A or Group 3.

Although these time-consuming observations were extended only to the 1969 collections it is believed that they provide useful and generally applicable information on the ratio of cortical to noncortical flakes, an indication of the frequency of nonobsidian flakes, and an indication of the very low (0.8 %) frequency and distribution of Type A (Group 3) obsidian.

End Scrapers

End scrapers are one of the more numerous artifacts and have been recovered from many sites. Appendix II Table 3 brings together a listing of end scrapers and their description. The sequence in the table is the same as that followed in the first section of this appendix.

Classification and Description of Flake Cores

Flake cores are one of the more common artifacts recovered from Batza Téna, and their classification could bear further discussion. Any rock that was fractured to provide smaller pieces of material to be used directly as tools or for implement blanks could be considered as a core. Much shatter consists of fragments of cores. One of the fundamental relationships of lithic analysis is the core-flake diad. The existence of one generally supposes the other; where there are flakes it can be supposed that there also are or were cores unless the flakes were produced at one site and taken to another site for further processing or use. This is a potentially important relationship between cores and flakes in sites associated with and peripheral to lithic sources, and care was taken to note the presence of cores on the lithic sites collected or examined.

The cores recognized from Batza Téna are mainly (a) a platform core with variants, sometimes more or less of a conical shape, formed by removing flakes from one, two or more sides of a platformed pebble; (b) a more tabular or single flat faced core for flakes and bladelike flakes. This core also has a platform; (c) chopper-shaped cores or tools on which the edge and platform are concomitant; and (d) an amorphous group ranging from split pebbles to unclassifiable core fragments. Sometimes the cores have been rotated, which complicates their description. A rotated or multilateral variety is discussed in Chapter 5 (the present discussion and the Chapter 5 description were prepared on separate occasions a few years apart, thus complementary and supplementary remarks may appear here). There also are rare cores.

APPENDIX II TABLE 3. END SCRAPERS

Number	Material	L	W	Dorsum	Notes, Associations
Basecamp Ridge	(N=26, 6 not obsidian)				
RkIg-1:5	Obsidian	32	37	Cortex	Fluted point?
RkIg-1:51	Obsidian	42	27	Axial flake scars	Fluted point
RkIg-1:54	Obsidian	51	44	Single flake scar	Notched point
RkIg-1:56	Obsidian	33	31	Flake scars	" ", 60° convergent
RkIg-1:57	Chert	35	27+	Irregular flaked	Notched point
RkIg-1:58	Obsidian	27.5	23.5	Cortex	" ", 80° convergent
RkIg-1:59	Obsidian	24	27	Single flake scar	Notched point Spur (natural?)
RkIg-1:60	Obsidian	29	33	Flake scars	Convergent? bevelled @ 75°
RkIg-1:61	Obsidian	39	19-31	Flake scar/cortex	Notched point
RkIg-1:62	Basalt?	44.5	31	Axial flake scars	Notched point
RkIg-1:63	Chert	26	31	Flake scar	95° convergent
RkIg-1:65	Obsidian	32	33	Cortex	Hydration measured
RkIg-1 average		34.6	31.7		N = 12
RkIg-11:13	Obsidian	-	-	Flake scar	Fragment
RkIg-22:7	Obsidian	42	30	Cortex	Hydration measured
RkIg-22:27	Chert	47	37	Flake scars	
RkIg-25	Nonobsidian	41	29	Flake scars	1 side bevelled
RkIg-41:12	Obsidian	-	31.5	Cortex	With roughouts
RkIg-41:13	Obsidian	31	22	Flake scars	" "
RkIg-41:14	Bl. chert	47	28	Flake scars	End/side scraper
RkIg-42:2	Obsidian	34	37	Cortex	Almost isolated
RkIg-42:o	Obsidian	-	36	Cortex	" "
RkIg-45:1	Obsidian	47	31	Flake scar	Small bifaces
RkIg-47:94	Obsidian	27	24	Flake & retouch scars & cortex	Sharp bevel, sharp corner
RkIg-50:7	Obsidian	38	22	Cortex	Natural?
RkIg-x:10	Obsidian	42	29	Flake scar/cortex	Isolated find
RkIg-x:42	Obsidian	25	35	Cortex	Isolated find
Little Lake Ridge	(N=18, 5 not obsidian)				
RkIg-9	Obsidian	46	35	Cortex	Atypical
RkIg-5:2	Obsidian	33	30	Flake scar/cortex	
RkIg-5:3	Obsidian	27	27		Convergent
RkIg-5:9	Obsidian	46	32	Flake scars	
RkIg-5:10	Nonobsidian	33	25	Flake scars	
RkIg-10:11	Chert	30	18	Flake scars	
RkIg-10:12	Obsidian	32	23	Flake scar/cortex	Unfinished biface
RkIg-10:102	Obsidian	20.5	26	Cortex	Fluted point Hydration measured
RkIg-10:156	Obsidian	64	35	Flake scar/cortex	Fluted point Hydration measured
RkIg-10:184	Obsidian	53	36	Flake scar/cortex	Unfinished bifaces
Thick flake like 10:156, used as end scraper?					
RkIg-10:162	Obsidian	51	37	Flake scars, sides bevelled	
RkIg-10 average		41.7	29.2		N = 6
RkIg-28:49	Vol. rock	-	59?	Cortex & bevel	Scraper plane
RkIg-28:89	Obsidian	31	35	Flake scar	Edge worn
RkIg-29:5	Chert	30	23	Flake scars	
RkIg-30:100	Obsidian	53	40	Bevelled sides & cortex	Fluted point Unfinished bifaces
RkIg-30:321	Obsidian	50	36	Coarsely flaked from edges	Fluted point Unfin. bifaces
RkIg-30:409	Obsidian	26	29.5	Single flake scar	Fluted point
RkIg-8:3	Chert	30	26	Flake scars	Minor site

APPENDIX II TABLE 3--continued

Number	Material	L	W	Dorsum	Notes, Associations
RkIg-51:1	Obsidian	78	44	Cortex	Arched, ventrally flaked to shape

Lake 324 and Vicinity (N=14, 1 not obsidian)

Number	Material	L	W	Dorsum	Notes, Associations
RlIg-33:18	Obsidian	50	39	Cortex	
RlIg-33:17	Obsidian	30.7	29.8	Bevels & axial flake scar	
RlIg-52:186	Obsidian	67	76	Cortex	General area
RlIg-52:3	Obsidian	35	25	Flaked	General area, coarse vent. flaking, atypical
RlIg-52:4	Obsidian	57	38	Flake scars	Lake 324 complex
RlIg-52:8	Obsidian	74	35.5	Flake scar/cortex	" ", thick
RlIg-52:75	Obsidian	61	42	Prepared-flaked	" "
RlIg-52:76	Obsidian	58	41	Prepared-flaked	" "
RlIg-52:78	Obsidian	49	38	Cortex	" "
RlIg-52:79	Obsidian	62	33	Flake scars	" "
RlIg-52:80	Obsidian	62	32	Flake & cortex	" "
RlIg-52:81	Obsidian	58	30	Prepared-flaked	" ", thick
RlIg-52 average		60.1	36.2		" " N = 8
RlIg-52:41	Obsidian	25 atypical	55	Prepared	" "
RlIg-35:7	Dark chert	-	-		Fragment

Middle Indian River Valley (N=5, 1 not obsidian)

Number	Material	L	W	Dorsum	Notes, Associations
RlIg-46:17	Obsidian	-	26	Flake scars/bevel	Incomplete
RlIg-46:34	Obsidian	30	26	Flake scars	Rounded end
RlIg-47:1	Obsidian	43	30	Axial flake scars	Fluted & notched points
RlIg-49:3	Basalt	27	18	2 flake scars	Cores,
RlIg-49:6	Obsidian	29	29	Flake scars, lateral bevels	unfinished notched points

Batzatiga and Vicinity (N=70, 8 not obsidian)

Number	Material	L	W	Dorsum	Notes, Associations
RkIh-28:4	Obsidian	45	25.4	Axial flake scar, side bevels	Microblades
RkIh-28:14	Obsidian	57	36.3	Cortex, sides retouched	Sides also utilized?
RkIh-28:19	Obsidian	42+	41.4	Flake scar, bevels	" "
RkIh-28:24	Obsidian	35+	22	Cortex	Microblades
RkIh-28:30	Obsidian	32+	33.8	Axial flake scars	Made on blade
RkIh-28:31	Obsidian	27.5	24.3	Flake scars	Natural facet?
RkIh-32:2	Obsidian	32.5	30	Cortex	Various
RkIh-32:14	Obsidian	32	30	Cortex	Sharp corners
RkIh-32:18	Chert	23	27	Flake scars	Various
RkIh-32:49	Obsidian	27	26.5	Flake scar	Various
RkIh-32:51	Obsidian	51.5	40	Cortex	1 sharp corner
RkIh-32 average		33.0	30.7		N = 5
RkIh-33:2	Obsidian	57	44	Cortex	
RkIh-33:5	Obsidian	37	32	Cortex	Semi-convergent
RkIh-33:37	Obsidian	36	39	Cortex	
RkIh-36 average	42 obs. 5 other	37.9	31.5	See Table 5.6	N = 47 Batza Téna Tuktu
RkIh-35	6 obs. 1 chert				See Table 5.6
RkIh-37:19	Obsidian	42	26	Cortex	
RkIh-37:53	Chert	36	30	Flake/potlid	Convergent edges

apparently utilized for blades or bladelike flakes that do not quite reach the regularity in form shown by microblade cores. Some examples were discussed in Chapter 5. Finally, many implements or biface roughouts were made through a core-biface reduction procedure often starting from half of a split obsidian pebble.

Platform Cores

The platform cores are nearly amorphous, but not completely so. There are some regularities in their minimal preparation and subsequent mode of use. They consist of pebbles and cobbles, in all but two or three cases of obsidian, that have been split or "decapitated," e.g., from which a large primary decortication spall has been detached. If the pebble is elongate, it usually is one of the ends that is detached. The resulting flat surface serves as a platform for striking flakes from the sides of the pebble, from around one, two, or three sides. When the face is localized on one side of the core, and especially when the platform is angled, these cores tend to resemble blade cores. If the faces are distributed more or less around the perimeter of the core the specimen may become subconical and again resemble certain blade cores. However, usually the flakes removed are large and broad and it is common that only one or two flake scars are present on a face.

Often no more than a single course of cortical flakes, and sometimes only one or two flakes in addition to the platform spall have been removed. Many of the very numerous cores appear to have been abandoned because of imperfections and possibly they did not yield any usable flakes.

In reference to the primary axes of the raw pebble--length (front to back), width (side to side) and height--height usually is more or less vertical to the platform which may be horizontal, highly inclined in a single direction (e.g., front to back or monoclinic), or highly inclined in two directions (e.g., both front to back and side to side, or triclinic). The highly inclined (monoclinic) platform appears to be an intentional deviation from the horizontal platform. In many examples flakes have been detached from the acutely angled core surface adjacent to the bulbar end of the platform. Flakes may also be detached from the sides of the core. I am not certain though that the less common triclinic platforms were produced to that format intentionally. This platform has the feature of providing an acute platform-to-face angle along the side of the core as well as at the face that meets the bulbar end of the platform. Some monoclinic platforms are retouched at the lip as if the platform angle had been adjusted slightly, as is described for cores from RkIg-44 in Chapter 2.

Rotated cores that may or may not have originated as platform cores usually are smaller and consist of blocks of obsidian with five to seven sides, each side consisting of part of a surface formed by a single flake scar or sometimes two scars. The platforms usually consist of an adjacent side. Platform angles tend to be high, whereas in the platform cores the platform angles are extremely variable, ranging from 50 degrees, or less in a few cases, to 88 degrees.

Flatfaced Cores

Flatfaced cores represent an abstraction from the range of poorly formalized core variation present at Batza Téna, especially among the platform cores. At the least, the type may be useful for description. Most of these cores have a single generally flat face and they tend to be tabular in proportions. However the small sample is somewhat variable. They usually have a platform prepared through removal two or more flakes from the platform surface. Platform angles range from about 50 to 90 degrees (Fig. 4.1d).

V-Shaped Cores

In Chapter 5 a "chopper shaped" or "chopping tool-shaped" core was briefly described. A number of these simple pebble objects roughly bifaced along one edge are illustrated. They are a very common core at Batzatiga and are found elsewhere at Batza Téna. Here attention is drawn to a more formalized impressive V-shaped core (Pl. 24A, Append. II Fig. 1). This obsidian specimen was found on the surface at the site periphery at that site without associations. The edge has served as a platform for detaching large broad flakes from both faces of the core (strictly speaking, the faces near the edge were platforms). Superficially, this piece looks like a chopping tool. It measures 32 by 85 by 95 mm maximum thickness, width and height respectively. The core has been reduced from a cobble of approximately the same width but greater length and thickness. The interfacial angle is approximately 35 degrees except at the very edge where due to trimming or damage it is about 45 degrees.

In addition, there are many trimmed relatively flat pebbles and edge-trimmed split pebbles. Flaking is more or less distributed around the perimeter. These very likely represent (attempted) initial stages of biface tool production. There also is a very small discoidal core. The form is so uncommon at Batza Téna that we consider the discoidal format to be fortuitous and do not recognize this core or biface roughout as a type there.

Projectile Points

Appendix II Table 4 is intended to serve as a "finders' guide" to the projectile points recovered at Batza Téna. Some information not previously given also is provided in the table; for instance, the catalogue numbers of fragments. For the analysis in Chapter 9 several factors noted here will be called upon. In an abbreviated presentation such as this one it has been necessary to rely on conventions and judgemental procedures. Certain of them which the reader should be aware are as follows: Some points are in rough condition and might have been classified as unfinished were it not for surviving traces of stems heavily ground on the edges. I interpret stem grinding to be a criterion of finished production. An elongate specimen with part of the tip missing is classified as complete under the rationale that enough is left of the point for it to have been resharpened. Many specimens could have served well as small knife end blades as well as or instead as points.

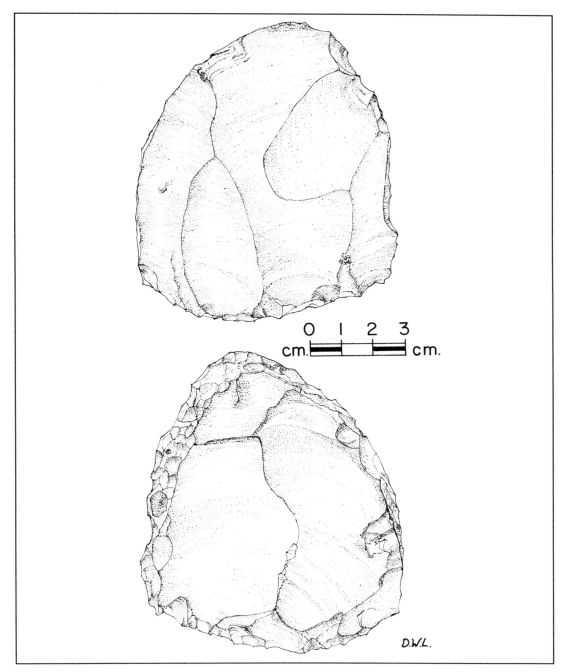

Figure Appendix II.1. Drawing of V-shaped flake core RkIg-1:83.

APPENDIX II TABLE 4.   PROJECTILE POINTS

Item	Style	Com-plete	Base	Tip/mid.	Fin-ished	Obsi-dian	Described	Illustr.
Basecamp Ridge								
RkIg-1:49	Fluted		x		x	x	Table 2.10	Pl. 1A, Fig. 2.1f
RkIg-1:53	Notched		x		x	x	Table 5.8	Pl. 19J
RkIg-11:47	Lanceolate		x		x	x	Clark 1993	Pl. 21J
RkIg-50:1	Lance?			x	o	x	" "	
RkIg-x:37	Notched	x			x	x	Table 5.8	Pl. 21M
RkIg-x:38	Stemmed	x			x	x	Clark 1993	Pl. 21L
Subtotal	6	2	2	1	5	6		
Little Lake Ridge								
Main ridge								
RkIg-x:32	Triangular		x		x	x	Clark 1993	Pl. 21K
RkIg-51:9	--			x	x	x	" "	
RkIg-51:8	Lanceolate?		x		x	x	" "	
RkIg-51:10	--			x	o	x	" "	
RkIg-51:17	Lanceolate?	x			o	x	" "	Pl. 20B
RkIg-51:14	" "	x-			o	x	" "	Pl. 20C
RkIg-51:15	" "	x			o	x	" "	Pl. 20E
RkIg-51:16	Triangular	x			x?	x	" "	Pl. 20D
RkIg-48:15	Lanceolate?	x			x?	x	" "	
RkIg-4:49	Lance?		x		o	x		
RkIg-10:36	Fluted		x		x	x	Table 2.10	Pl. 1B, Fig. 2.1i
RkIg-10:179	--		x		x	o	Chap. 2	
RkIg-10:155	--			x	x	x		
RkIg-39:3	Leafshaped	x			o	x	Clark 1993	
RkIg-39:4	Leafshaped		x		x	x	" "	
RkIg-39:5	Leafshaped		x		x	o	" "	
RkIg-39:6	Leafshaped		x		x	o	" "	
RkIg-27:18				x	x	o	" "	
RkIg-28:7	Oblanceolate	x			x	o	Chap. 3	
RkIg-28:9	Fluted?		x		x	x	Table 2.10	Pl. 7K, Fig. 2.1g
RkIg-28:43	Leafshaped			x	x	x	Chap. 3	Pl. 7E
RkIg-28:44	Leafshaped		x		x	x	" "	Pl. 7J
RkIg-28:63	--			x	x	x	" "	
RkIg-28:68	Lanceolate?		x		x	x	" "	Pl. 7G
RkIg-28:69	Lanceolate	x			x	x	" "	Pl. 7B
RkIg-28:71	Lanceolate	x			x	o	" "	Pl. 7L
RkIg-28:72	Leafshaped	x			x	o	" "	
RkIg-28:75	Leafshaped	x			x	o	" "	Pl. 7C
RkIg-28:76	Bipoint	x-			x	x	" "	Pl. 7F
RkIg-28:79	--			x	x	o	" "	
RkIg-28:85	--			x	x	o	" "	
RkIg-28:86	Leafshaped?			x	x	o	" "	Pl. 7D
RkIg-28:87	Leafshaped?		x		x	x	" "	Pl. 7H
RkIg-28:88	Lanceolate?		x		x	x	" "	Pl. 7J
RkIg-28:91-2	Leafshaped?			x	x	o	" "	Pl. 7N
RkIg-28:93	Leafshaped	x			x	o	" "	Pl. 7M
RkIg-28:81		x			x	x	" "	Pl. 7A
RkIg-29:16	Fluted		x		x	x	Chap. 2	Pl. 1C, Fig. 2.1c
RkIg-29:17	Bipoint	x			x	x		Pl. 6J
RkIg-30:42	Fluted		x		x	x	Chap. 2	Pl. 1D, Fig. 2.1a
RkIg-30:44	Leafshaped	x-			x	x	Chap. 2	Pl. 3C
RkIg-30:93	--			x	x?	x	" "	
RkIg-30:140	--			x	x	x	" "	

APPENDIX II TABLE 4--continued

Item	Style	Com- plete	Base	Tip/ mid.	Fin- ished	Obsi- dian	Described	Illustr.
RkIg-30:141	Ovoid	x			x	x	Chap. 2	Pl. 3A
RkIg-30:130	Oblanceolate	x			x	x	Chap. 2	Pl. 3B
RkIg-30:147	--			x	x	x	" "	" "
RkIg-30:160	Fluted		x		x	x	" "	Pl. 1J
RkIg-30:165	Fluted			x	o	x	" "	" "
RkIg-30:205 +213+206	Lanceolate	x			x	o	" "	Pl. 4Q
RkIg-30:208	--			x	x	x	" "	" "
RkIg-30:217	--			x	o?	x	" "	" "
RkIg-30:220	Fluted		x		o	x	" "	Pl. 1E
RkIg-30:247	Fluted			x	x	o	" "	Pl. 1G
RkIg-30:254	Fluted		x		x	x	" "	Pl. 1F
RkIg-30:321	Fluted		x		o	x	" "	Pl. 1H
RkIg-30:306	Fluted		x		x	x	" "	" "
RkIg-30:312	Lanceolate?		x		x	x	" "	Pl. 3D
RkIg-39:323	---		x		x	x	" "	Pl. 1I
RkIg-31:15	Fluted		x		o	x	" "	Pl. 2A, Fig. 2.1e
RkIg-31:110	--			x	x	x	Chap. 2	
RkIg-31:55	Notched	x			x	x	Table 5.8	Pl. 6D
RkIg-31:60	Fluted	x			x?	x	Chap. 2	Pl. 2B, Fig. 2.1h
RkIg-31:61	Notched	x			x	o	Table 5.8	Pl. 6E
RkIg-31:66	--			x	x	x		
RkIg-31:71	--			x	x	o		
RkIg-31:74	--			x	x	o		
RkIg-31:118	Fluted		x		x	x	Chap. 2	Pl. 2C
RkIg-31:120	Fluted		x		x	x	" "	Pl. 2D
RkIg-43:1	Fluted		x		x	x	" "	Pl. 2E, Fig. 2.16
RkIg-44:3	--			x	x	o		
RkIg-44:16	Leafshaped	x			o	x	Chap. 2	
RkIg-44:38	Lanceolate?		x		o	x	" "	Pl. 2F
RkIg-44:81	Fluted		x		x	x	" "	Pl. 2G, Fig. 2.1d
East end of main ridge								
RkIg-33:unc	Leafshaped	x-			x	x	Clark 1993	
RkIg-32:3	Lanceolate		x		x	x	Chap. 2	
Subtotal	76	24	29	23	69	62		
Lake 324 and Vicinity								
RlIg-13	Stemmed	x			x	x	" "	Pl. 19N
RlIg-33:8	Notched	x			x	x	Table 5.8	Pl. 19Q
RlIg-33:9	Notched	x			x	x	Table 5.8	Pl. 19O
RlIg-33:10	Notched	x			x	x	Table 5.8	Pl. 19S
RlIg-33:11	Notched	x			x	o	Table 5.8	Pl. 19R
RlIg-52:173	Leafshaped		x		x	x	Clark 1993	
RlIg-52:174	Oblanceolate	x			x	o	" "	
RlIg-52:11	--			x	?	o	Chap. 7	
RlIg-52:13	Leafshaped	x-			x	x	" "	Pl. 15B
RlIg-52:16	Leafshaped	x			x?	x	" "	Pl. 15A
RlIg-52:18	--			x	x	o	Chap. 7	
RlIg-52:17	--			?	?	x	" "	
RlIg-52:19	--			x	?	o	Chap. 7	
RlIg-52:20	Pentagonal	x			x	x	" "	Pl. 15C
RlIg-52:89	Leafshaped	x			x	x	" "	Pl. 15D
RlIg-52	Flakepoint	11+5				15/1	" "	Pl. 15

5 of these 16 items are incomplete but presumably they were broken on the site and the fragments remain there. Whether or not these are points and are finished are a matter of interpretation.

APPENDIX II TABLE 4--concluded

Item	Style	Complete	Base	Tip/mid.	Finished	Obsidian	Described	Illustr.
RlIg-35:5	Lance	x-			x	o	" "	Pl. 20H
RlIg-35:7	Leafshaped?		x		x	o	" "	Pl. 20G
RlIg-35:5	--		x		x	o	" "	
RlIg-37:168	Notched		x		x	x	Table 5.8	
RlIg-38:4	--		x		o	x	Clark 1993	
RlIg-38:5	Oblanceolate	x			x	x	Clark 1993	Pl. 21F
RlIg-44:3	Notched	x			x	x	Table 5.8	Pl. 21N
Subtotal	22+16	13+16	5	4	21+16 (4 are ?)	14+15		
Middle Indian River Valley								
RlIg-46:30	Lanceolate	x			x	o	Append. I	Pl. 16I
RlIg-46:36	Triangular	x			x	o	" "	Pl. 20M
RlIg-46:37	Pointed base		x		x	x	" "	Pl. 20L
RlIg-46:62	Fluted		x		x	x	" "	
RlIg-47:2	Notched		x		x	x	Table 5.8	
RlIg-47:4	Fluted			x	x	x	Chap. 2	
RlIg-47:	Fluted	x			x	x	" "	
RlIg-49:5	Lanceolate		x		x	x	Append. I	Pl. 21I
Subtotal	8	3	4	1	8	6		
Batzatiga and Vicinity								
RkIh-32:46	--			x	x	o	Chap. 4	Pl. 10G
RkIh-36:19	Notched	x-			x	x	Chap. 5	
RkIh-36:142	Notched	x			x	x	" "	Pl. 11D
RkIh-36:156	Stemmed	x			x	x	" "	Pl. 11B
RkIh-36:179	Notched	x			x	o	" "	Pl. 11F
RkIh-36:190	--			x	x	x	" "	
RkIh-36:204	Stemmed?		x		x	o	" "	
RkIh-36:215	Leafshaped	x			x	o	" "	Pl. 11A
RkIh-35:9	Stemmed	x-			x?	o	" "	Pl. 11C
RkIh-35:62	Notched	x			x	x	" "	Pl. 11E
RkIh-33:7	Lanceolate	x			x	x	Append. I	Pl. 6N
RkIh-35:60	--			x	?	o	--	
RkIh-35:62	Notched	x			x	x	Table 5.4	
RkIh-28:34	Large		x		x	x	Chap. 4	Pl. 8D
Subtotal	15	10	2	3	15	8		
Total A*	126	52	43	32	118**	90***		
Total B	142	68	43	32	134	105		

*   Total A does not include the 16 flake points from RlIg-52.
**   Of which about 10 are highly uncertain.
*** The balance of 36 points are made of basalt, chert and other stone not obsidian.

APPENDIX III:

CHARACTERISTICS OF KOYUKUK RIVER OBSIDIANS

With a Note on Basalt at Batza Téna

Trace Element Fingerprint and Other Characteristics

In order to provide an elemental characterization of Koyukuk River obsidian, and for comparison with other obsidian, the Canadian Conservation Institute analyzed 74 samples from archaeological sites and the natural source (Wheeler and Clark 1977). Source or geological obsidian included pebbles from the upland source area, transported pebbles from both Indian and Little Indian River and pebbles apparently derived from colluvium at Batzatiga. Archaeological obsidian was sampled from the Hahanudan Lake housepit sites as well as from Batza Téna. On the basis of that program three clearly distinguished chemical source groups were defined (Append. III Table 1, Append. III Fig. 1.). A possible fourth group is represented by a single specimen (Append. III Table 1:"x"). These groups can be distinguished on the basis of Mn histograms alone, although for broader comparisons three or more elements often are required to define a source group to the exclusion of others.

TABLE APPENDIX III.1. CHARACTERIZATION OF KOYUKUK RIVER OBSIDIAN BY ATOMIC ABSORPTION SPECTROPHOTOMETRY

Source group	Sodium %	Manganese ppm	Iron %	Potassium %	Zinc ppm	Na/Mn
1 (D)	3.95	432	1.36	3.89	60.3	92
2 geol. (B)	3.34	580	0.56	3.84	43.3	58
arch. (B)	3.33	595	0.55	3.85	41.8	56
3 (A)	3.46	722	0.42	3.60	42.7	48
* x (C)	3.28	412	0.65	3.76	--	80

From Wheeler and Clark 1977: Fig, 2-7 means.
* A single geological specimen from Batzatiga falls outside the pattern set by the three groups and tentatively is correlated with Griffin, Wright and Gordus' (1969) group C.

One source type (Group 1) was limited to Hahanudan archaeological specimens, although the most common Batza Téna variety also was found at the Hahanudan sites. This disjunct archaeological distribution leads us to believe that there are two geological sources in the Koyukuk drainage, the Indian River source or Batza Téna locality, and another source probably located closer to Huslia and Hahanudan Lake. Patton and Miller (1970: Fig. 1) note several volcanic deposits in the middle and lower Koyukuk valley where obsidian might be expected to occur. The proposed second source was sufficiently well known in prehistoric times to be represented among obsidian transported to the Kobuk drainage where it was reported by Griffin, Wright and Gordus (1969) at the University of Michigan as Group D. Nevertheless, Koyukuk people today appear to be familiar with only the Indian River source. The Group D (here Group 1) obsidian from Hahanudan has a notably higher percentage of iron than the others. Two distinct visual types are recognized in Group 1 specimens from Hahanudan Lake. One variety is translucent and has a very slight olive cast and a slightly resinous lustre. These characteristics provide a very subtle means for distinguishing between from Groups 1 and 2. The other form which Group 1 takes is opaque (except in microscopic thin sections). This gives it an enamel-like lustre. It occurs in black and other dark hues. When examined under low magnification they are seen to consist of a mottled mosaic of dark colours.

With the exception of the singular specimen of a possible fourth group, all geological specimens tested Group 2 (Group B from Kobuk River sites reported by Griffin et al 1969). The CCI analysis employed numeric identification of the obsidian groups to distinguish it from the Michigan analysis. Group 2 or B also is the most common archaeological type and has been widely recognized elsewhere in northern Alaska on the basis of other analyses (J. P. Cook personal communications). Group 2 occurs in a variety of colours and hues, ranging from nearly clear to dark grey and blue grey. Less common light or pearl grey resembling chert, rare black, mottled or streaked red and brown-red colours. Any obsidian from the Koyukuk area that is not visually apparent as a Group 1 or Group 3 material usually belongs to Group 2. Rare near-black Group 2 specimens resembling Group 1 are the exception. The high silica content of Group 2, reported at 77 percent SiO_2 by Michels (1981) and expressed by a high index of refraction between 1.484 and 1.487 (Patton and Miller 1970) makes it an especially desirable lithic material.

Unmodified pebbles with tiny white microlites, which invariably characterize the less common Group 3, occasionally are present in collections from Batza Téna. It probably is by chance that this variety was missed in the selection of geological specimens. The primary source of Group 3 evidently is essentially the same as Group 2. This group is the easiest one to distinguish in hand specimens, on the basis of the presence of white microlites and an essentially single colour of groundmass. Griffin, Wright and Gordus (1959) found Group 3 (their "A") in Kobuk River collections. The single Koyukuk specimen of a possible fourth group can be correlated with the Kobuk Group C.

The Archaeological Survey of Canada also collaborated with the Atomic Energy of Canada Limited, Commercial Products in the analysis of a small series of Alaskan obsidian specimens, together with a number of archaeological specimens from northwestern Canada. This INAA (instrumental neutron activation analysis) provided a somewhat different elemental composition and basis for comparison than the Canadian Conservation Institute analysis by atomic absorption spectrophotometry (AAS). The results of this analysis have not been published and pertinent portions of the data are given here in Table III.2. Only the Alaskan or Koyukuk source samples are given, except for one archaeological sample from the Little Arm site of the southwest Yukon,

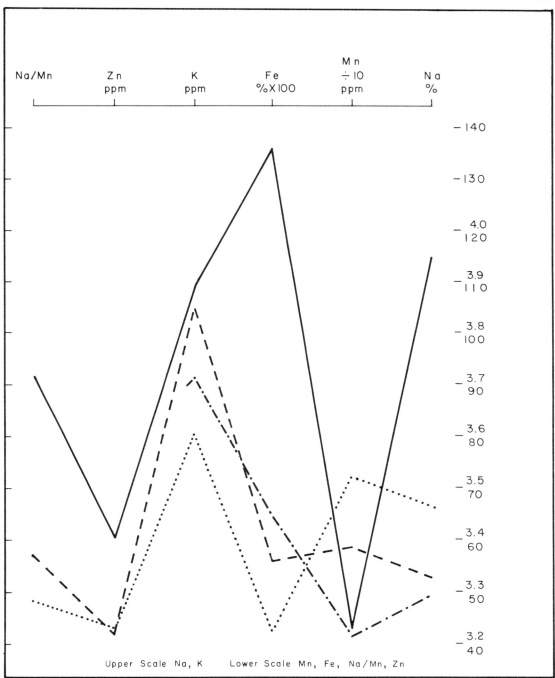

Appendix III Figure. 1. Diagram of Obsidian Analysis.

apparently derived from a northern British Columbia source, which is included to show how greatly obsidians sometimes differ in their trace element composition. Group 2 is relatively consistent and on the basis of this consistency numerous specimens from the northern Yukon Territory (not included in Table III.2), which are somewhat like Group 2 but variant, are considered to come from a different, unknown source. However, two small chips from more distant Colville Lake, located north of Great Bear Lake in the Northwest Territories, and a specimen from Eagle located near the Alaska/Yukon boundary clearly come from the Koyukuk River. Koyukuk obsidian specimens also have been analyzed by MOHLAB (Michels 1984) and in INAA programmes by John Cook and Cook and Larry Haskins (J. P. Cook personal communication; Haskins and Cook nd).

Surface texture

Obsidian pebbles and flakes exhibit various surface textures. Textures may intergrade or be mixed on the same specimen. Often one or two textures characterize the material at a particular site. Evidently, the textures represent different aspects of the primary and secondary sources. However, why these texture differences occur has not been determined, with the exception of one surface formed by rolling and abrasion during stream transport. The surface textures are as follow:

1. Frosted. This cortex occurs predominately on smooth angular pieces collected from the upland source. Under low magnification the frosting appears as a granular surface, or in some cases as a granular and very finely pitted surface. On archaeological specimens this cortex was found only co-occurring with other cortex types. Its presence indicates an absence of stream rolling, and, accordingly, in most cases as is discussed below, the fissured cortex is not to be attributed to rolling and impact among stream gravels inasmuch as the fissures and frosted cortexes co-occur on the same specimen. Patton and Miller (1970) identify the frosted and finely pitted cortex as a hydration surface.

2. Pitted. Closely spaced pits, often of coarse texture, cover much of the surface. This cortex occurs predominately on archaeological pieces and rarely is found on specimens collected from the upland source. Most pebbles collected from the shores of lakes at Batzatiga also are pitted with a frosted subtexture.

3. Fissured. The surface is covered with small curved fractures, fissures and rough areas. Some specimens show both fissured and pitted areas. This cortex occurs on some stream-rolled geological specimens but is found mainly on those from archaeological contexts. In the case of stream-rolled specimens the surface is somewhat smoothed and the fissured surface may be due to insufficient stream erosion to remove the original cortex. However, some fissuring appears to be due to battering along the stream bed. Fissures often are very coarse, but they also occur on a fine scale grading into relatively smooth surfaces.

4. Sugary. This cortex consists of minute impact fractures and is the result of stream rolling.

It is found, expectedly, near the edges and corners of angular pebbles collected from stream bars. Recognition of this cortex in archaeological specimens is uncertain, but only the 1969 and 1970 collections were examined for this attribute. It is probable that in some cases river bars were the actual collection locales for obsidian.

5. Silvery. A thin smooth, silvery to aluminous coating is found on some archaeological specimens. In a single specimen one surface may be frosted, another surface silvery. Specimens with this cortex often have angular shapes and smooth fused appearing edges.

6. Smooth. Smoothness in not the result of water rolling, judging from the fact that obsidian pebbles from the stream bars showed a different cortex. Pebbles and cobbles with this cortex generally lack angular edges, and the edges present lack any evidence of stream battering. This cortex is smoother and more transparent than the frosted cortex, though under low magnification the smooth cortex appears as a frosty rather than a polished surface. Specimens in this group also show circular fractures which penetrate the pebble at a low angle--characteristic indicators of high energy impact. The apex of these fracture cones is at the surface where sometimes a small amount of material has broken away. The smooth cortex also is found as a sub-texture on pitted and fissured specimens, in which case the pits and fissures usually are muted or shallow and smoothed.

Observations were made on the distribution of obsidian cortex types also were recorded for

APPENDIX III TABLE 2: NEUTRON ACTIVATION ANALYSIS

No.	Provenience	Group	Hf ppm	Rb ppm	Eu ppm	Th ppm	Ce ppm	La ppm	Sc %	Na %	Fe
1	Colville L.	2	4.8	206	0.1	47	48	33.9	2.1	3.13	0.52
2	" " NWT	2	4.7	199	N.D.	47	46	32.5	2.0	3.02	0.52
3	Koyukuk R.	2	4.9	195	0.1	48	47	31.9	2.0	3.02	0.53
4	" "	2	4.6	196	N.S.	39	49	32.0	2.2	2.87	0.50
5	" "	2	4.9	221	0.2	51	48	34.4	2.2	3.32	0.56
6	" "	2	4.7	179	0.2	41	51	35.7	2.3	3.11	0.53
7	" "	2	5.3	220	0.2	49	49	36.1	2.2	3.38	0.58
8	" "	2	5.2	214	0.2	52	52	34.7	2.2	3.24	0.55
8	" "	2	4.6	203	N.S.	39	50	32.7	2.2	2.73	0.53
9	" "	2	4.5	198	0.15	46	78	32.4	2.1	3.05	0.51
10	" "	1	7.7	144	0.69	19	64	42.7	5.4	3.53	1.23
11	" "	1	7.4	144	0.67	17	70	45.8	5.5	3.91	1.20
12	" "	2	4.7	205	0.3	45	60	38.5	2.4	3.28	0.59
13	" "	2	4.8	217	N.S.	40	51	33.6	2.3	3.01	0.53
14	" "	2	4.5	208	0.2	49	49	31.8	2.2	3.11	0.54
14	" "	2	4.5	208	N.S.	42	51	33.9	2.3	3.15	0.55
15	Eagle	2	4.8	220	0.1	49	52	34.4	2.2	3.24	0.56
16	Norutak L.	2	4.7	207	0.2	48	48	33.1	2.1	3.13	0.54
17	Norutak L.	2	4.9	208	0.1	51	54	35.0	2.2	3.27	0.53
28	SW Yukon	Mt. Edziza	27.7	217		32	152	97.0	0.1	3.77	1.94
94	Bering Str.	x						22.1	5.3	2.81	0.33

the 1969 collection. This showed that the type of cortex sometimes differed between sites. The reason for this probably lies in different local sourcing of the supply of raw materials. However we lacked specific information on he source of cortex types. The smooth cortex, for instance is very distinctive, and the presence of impact fracture cones makes this type all the more interesting. However we are not aware of its mode of occurrence--it is not the result of stream rolling. Being unable to put this data to practical use, we did not continue the observations and the detailed data will not be presented here.

Use and Identification of Basalt at Batza Téna

With Analysis by D. G. Fong

The second most common lithic material utilized at Batza Téna is basalt (Table 9.2). With less than 400 flakes and 52 implements or fragments recovered, though, it is less than one percent as abundant as obsidian flakes and less than ten percent as abundant as obsidian implements (very much less than ten percent if amorphously worked objects, biface roughouts and cores of obsidian are counted). Rock formations with basalt occur in the hills on the west side of the Koyukuk River, west of Batza Téna, and to the southwest at Bear Mountain, but the specific sources of the basalt and basaltic rock at Batza Téna have not determined. In several cases cortex flakes indicate that alluvial cobbles were utilized. This material is dark grey in colour, but weathers to very light grey shades on the surface with sufficient rapidity that no unbleached artifacts were recovered.

To establish the identification of this material four flakes were thinsectioned and examined by the Geological Survey of Canada in 1971. More than one variety of basalt is represented. Inasmuch as at the time this identification was made, some archaeologists were applying a completely different identification to similar material recovered from the eastern edge of the Koyukuk drainage during the Trans-Alaska Pipeline System project, details of the examination by D.G. Fong, Mineralogy Section, Geological Survey of Canada, Ottawa, may be of value. We reproduce here major portions of his report, including the two photomicrographs. The specimens analyzed are a flake catalogued as RkIg-30:34 and three unmarked chips from adjacent site RkIg-28 1970 locus 20 yards R, 30 yards +. The unused portions of these flakes have been reintegrated with the collection.

The four chips were examined in thin section and, where necessary, by X-ray diffraction.

Sample No. 30-34

This specimen is a basalt. In thin section it is seen to consist of fine to very-fine needles of plagioclase and pyroxene with some grains of opaque minerals in a matrix of transparent glass [Append. III Fig. 2]. A little of the plagioclase and pyroxene was observed also as microphenocrysts. Compositionally, the rock is estimated to consist of 56 percent plagioclase, as determined by X-ray diffraction, exhibits an average composition of An_{60} (labradorite). One medium-grained phenocryst of this labradorite was observed to contain abundant inclusions of glass.

Three Unmarked Chips [RkIg-28]

These are chips of a basaltic lava. They are described together as they show a great similarity in texture and mineralogical composition [they came from one context], though are quite unlike the previously described sample.

In thin section the chips consist essentially of microphenocrysts showing an alignment known as "fluidal or flow texture" [Append. III Fig. 3]. The plagioclase occupies approximately 33 percent of the examined sections and, as in the previous sample, shows an average composition near An_{60} (labradorite). Two pyroxenes, hypersthene and augite are present in minor amounts.

The matrix, which constitutes approximately 60 percent of the rock, is an extremely fine-grained intergrowth of fibrous plagioclase, fibrous pyroxene and opaque minerals. Glass is not common in the chips.

Appendix III Figure 2. Photomicrograph of specimen RkIg-30:34 (by D.G. Fong), showing very fine needles of plagioclase and pyroxene in a matrix of transparent glass.

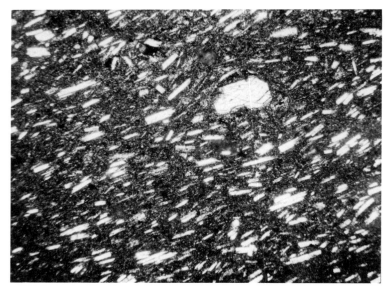

Appendix III Figure 3. Photomicrograph of specimen from RkIg-28 (by D.G. Fong) showing "fluidal texture" of aligned plagioclase microphenocrysts in a very fine grained matrix.

REFERENCES

Alaska Glacial Map Committee (see U.S. Geological Survey).

Ackerman, Robert
1979 [See Ackerman 1983 for published version.]

1983 Evaluation of the Late Pleistocene and Early Holocene Archaeology of Coastal Alaska, the Bering Sea, and Asia, in R.S. Vasil'yevskyed., Late Pleistocene and Early Holocene Cultural Contacts of Asia and America [translated title]. Novosibirsk: Nauka.

1986 A Mid-Holocene Lithic Tradition as Seen from Southwestern Alaska. Paper presented to the Alaska Anthropological Association, Fairbanks, Alaska, 1986. Typescript. 11 pp + references & figure.

Alexander, Herbert L.
1974 The Association of Aurignacoid Elements with Fluted Point Complexes in North America. In S. Raymond and P. Schledermann, eds., International Conference on the Prehistory and Paleoecology of Western North American Arctic and Subarctic. Calgary: University of Calgary Archaeological Association. 21-32.

1987 Putu, a Fluted Point Site in Alaska. Department of Archaeology, Simon Fraser University, Publication No. 17. Burnaby, B.C.

Allen, Henry T.
1887 Report of an Expedition to the Copper, Tanana, and Koyukuk Rivers in the Territory of Alaska, in the year 1885. Washington: Government Printing Office.

Anderson, Patricia M., Richard E. Reanier, and Linda B. Brubaker
1990 A 14,000-Year Pollen Record from Sithylemenkat Lake, North-Central Alaska. Quaternary Research 33:400-404.

Anderson, Douglas D.
1968 A Stone Age Campsite at the Gateway to America. Scientific American Vol 218(6):24-33.

1970a Athapaskans in the Kobuk Arctic Woodlands, Alaska? Canadian Archaeological Association Bulletin No. 2:3-12.

1970b Akmak: An Early Archaeological Assemblage from Onion Portage, Northwest Alaska. Acta Arctica 16. Copenhagen.

1972 An Archaeological Survey of the Noatak Drainage, Alaska. Arctic Anthropology 9(1):66-117.

1980 Continuity and Change in the Prehistoric Record from North Alaska. In Y. Kotani and W. B. Workman, eds., Alaska Native Culture and History. Senri Ethnological Studies No. 4., National Museum of Ethnology, Osaka. 233-251.

1988 Onion Portage: The Archaeology of a Stratified Site from the Kobuk River, Northwest Alaska. Anthropological Papers of the University of Alaska 22(1-2).

Andrews, Elizabeth F.
1977 Report on the Cultural Resources of the Doyon Region, Central Alaska. 2 vol. Occasional Paper No. 5, Anthropology and Historic Preservation Cooperative Park Studies Unit, University of Alaska, Fairbanks.

Anon.
1946 Diary of a Trip Down Yukon, Up Koyukuk, Up Alatna, Down Kobuk. Typescript. Copy in Government of Canada, Department of Indian Affairs and Northern Development Library.

Bacon, Glenn H.
1987 A Cultural Chronology for Central Interior Alaska: A Critical Appraisal. The Quarterly Review of Archaeology June 1987:3-5.

Borden, Charles E.
1969 Early Population Movements from Asia into Western North America. Syesis 2 (l&2):1-13.

Bowers, Michael
1982 The Lisburne Site: Analysis and Culture History of a Multicomponent Lithic workshop in the Iteriak Valley, Northern Alaska. Anthropological Papers of the University of Alaska 20(1-2):79-112.

Bryan, A.L.
1969 Early man in America and the Late Pleistocene Chronology of Western Canada and Alaska. Current Anthropology 10(4):339-375.

Bryan, Alan L., Arthur J. Jelinek and Irving Rouse
1980 Three Perspectives on the Archaeological Evidence for the Peopling of the Northern Hemisphere. Canadian Journal of Anthropology 1(2):239-245.

Burch, Ernest S., Jr.
1990 The Cultural and Natural Heritage of Northwest Alaska, Volume I Geology. Prepared for NANA Museum of the Arctic, Kotzebue, Alaska. E.S. Burch, Jr.

Campbell, John M.
1959 The Kayuk Complex of Arctic Alaska. American Antiquity 25:94-105.

1961 The Tuktu Complex of Anaktuvuk Pass. Anthropological Papers of the University of Alaska 9(2):61-80.

1962 Cultural Succession at Anaktuvuk Pass, Arctic Alaska. In J.M. Campbell, ed., Prehistoric Cultural Relations between the Arctic and Temperate Zones of North America. Arctic Institute of North America Technical Paper No. 11. 38-54.

1968 The Kavik Site of Anaktuvuk Pass, Central Brooks Range. Anthropological Papers of the University of Alaska 14(1):33-42.

Cinq-Mars, Jacques
1973 A propos de la signification archéologique d'un matériau découvert dans la région de la rivière Keele (T.N.O.). Canadian Archaeological Association Bulletin No. 5:1-25.

1973b An Archaeologically Important Raw Material from the Tertiary Hills, Western District of Mackenzie, Northwest Territories: Preliminary Statement. Appendix E in J. Cinq-Mars, ed., Preliminary Archaeological

Study, Mackenzie Corridor. Enviornmental-Social Committee, Northern Pipelines, Task Force on Northern Oil Development, Report No. 73-10. IAND Publication No. QS-1506-000-EE-A1.

1979 Bluefish Cave 1: A Late Pleistocene Eastern Beringian Cave Deposit in the Northern Yukon. Canadian Journal of Archaeology 3:1-32.

1982 Les grottes du Poisson-Bleu. GEOS 11(1):19-21.

Cinq-Mars, Jacques, C. Richard Harington, D. Erle Nelson and Richard S. MacNeish
1991 Engigstciak Revisited: a Note on Early Holocene AMS Dates from the "Buffalo Pit." In J. Cinq-Mars and Jean-Luc Pilon, ed., NOGAP Archaeology Project: An Integrated Archaeological Research and Management Approach. Canadian Archaeological Association Occasional Paper No. 1.

Clark, A. McFadyen
1975 Upper Koyukuk River Koyukon Athapaskan Social Culture: an Overview. In A. Clark, ed., Proceedings: Northern Athapaskan Conference, 1971, Vol. 1. National Museum of Man Mercury Series, Canadian Ethnology Service Paper No. 27. 146-180.

1977 Trade at the Crossroads. In J. Helmer, S. Van Dyke and F. Kense, eds., Prehistory of the North American Sub-Arctic: The Athapaskan Question. Calgary: Archaeological Association, Department of Archaeology, University of Calgary. 130-134.

1991 Who Lived in this House? An Ethnoarchaeological Study of Koyukuk River Semisubterranean House Construction, Contents and Disposition of Faunal Remains (provisional title). Manuscript in the possession of the author. Approx. 300 p.

n.d. "Koyukuk Settlement Pattern Paper" [working title, c 400 p draft].

Clark, A. McFadyen and Donald W. Clark
1974 Koyukon Athapaskan Houses as Seen through Oral Tradition and through Archaeology. Arctic Anthropology 11(Supplement):29-38.

Clark, D. W. and A. McF. Clark
1975 Fluted Points from the Batza Téna Obsidian Source of the Koyukuk River Region, Alaska. Anthropological Papers of the University of Alaska 17(2)31-38.

1980 Fluted Points at the Batza Téna Obsidian Source, Northwestern Interior Alaska. In D. Browman, ed., Early Native Americans. The Hague: Mouton. 141-159.

1983 Paleo-Indians and Fluted Points: Subarctic Alternatives. Plains Anthropologist 28(102 Pt. 1):283-292.

Clark, Donald W.
1972 Archaeology of the Batza Téna Obsidian Source, West-central Alaska. Anthropological Papers of the University of Alaska 15(2):1-21.

1974a Filaments of Prehistory on the Koyukuk River, Northwestern Interior Alaska. In S. Raymond and P. Schledermann, eds., International Conference on the Prehistory and Paleoecology of Western North American Arctic and Subarctic. Calgary: University of Calgary Archaeological Association. 33-46.

1974b Archaeological Collections from Norutak Lake on the Kobuk-Alatna River Portage, Northwestern Alaska. National Museum of Man Mercury Series, Archaeological Survey of Canada Paper No. 18. 65 p.

1975 Archaeological Reconnaissance in Northern Interior District of Mackenzie: 1969, 1970 and 1972. National Museum of Man Mercury Series, Archaeological Survey of Canada Paper 27. 397 p.

1977 Hahanudan Lake: An Ipiutak-Related Occupation of Western Interior Alaska. National Museum of Man Mercury Series, Archaeological Survey of Canada Paper No. 71. 168 p.

1978 Discussion on "Clovis Culture." American Quaternary Association Abstracts of the 5th biennial meeting. Edmonton: University of Alberta. 136-139.

1981 Prehistory of the Western Subarctic. In June Helm, ed., Wm. Stutervent, general ed., Handbook of North American Indians, Vol. 6, Subarctic. Washington: Smithsonian Institution. 107-129.

1983a Mackenzie--River to Nowhere? Musk-Ox 33:1-9.

1983b Is there a Northern Cordilleran Tradition? Canadian Journal of Archaeology 7(1):23-48.

1983c Archaeology of the Alaska Peninsula (review). Canadian Journal of Archaeology 7(1):93-103.

1984a Northern fluted Points: Paleo-Eskimo, Paleo-Arctic, or Paleo-Indian. Canadian Journal of Anthropology 4(1):65-81.

1984b Some Practical Applications of Obsidian Hydration Dating in the Subarctic. Arctic 37(2):91-109.

1986 Archaeological Reconnaissance at Great Bear Lake. Archaeological unit, Records Section, Library, Canadian Museum of Civilization. Typescript 660 p.

1987 Archaeological Reconnaissance at Great Bear Lake. Canadian Museum of Civilization Mercury Series, Archaeological Survey of Canada Paper 136. 312 p.

1991 The Northern (Alaska-Yukon) Fluted Points, in R. Bonnichsen and K. Turnmire, ed. Clovis: Origins and Adaptations, pp. 35-47. Corvallis: Center for the Study of the First Americans.

1992 A Microblade Production Station (KbTx-2) in the South Central Yukon. Canadian Journal of Archaeology 16:3-23.

1993 The Minor Sites at Batza Téna: Supplement to "Batza Téna: Obsidian Trail" by D.W. Clark (CMC Mercury Series), manuscript on file, Archaeological unit, Records Section, Library, Canadian Museum of Civilization.

Clark, D. W. and Richard E. Morlan
1982 Western Subarctic Prehistory: Twenty Years Later. Canadian Journal of Archaeology 6:79-93.

Cook, John P.
1968 Some Microblade Cores from the Western Boreal Forest. Arctic Anthropology 5(1):121-127.

1975 Archaeology of Interior Alaska. Western Canadian Journal of Anthropology 5(3-4):125-133.

REFERENCES

Cook, John P., ed.
1970 Report of Archeological Survey and Excavations along the Alyeska Pipeline Service Company Haulroad and Pipeline Alignment. Typescript. Fairbanks, University of Alaska, Department of Anthropology. 216 p.

1971 Final Report of the Archeological Survey and Excavations along the Alyeska Pipeline Service Company Pipeline Route. University of Alaska, Department of Anthropology, Fairbanks.

1977 Pipeline Archeology: Investigations along the Trans-Alaska Pipeline Fairbanks: University of Alaska, Institute of Arctic Biology. 982 p.

Cotter, John L.
1937 The Occurrence of Flints and Extinct Animals in Pluvial Deposits near Clovis, New Mexico, part 4. Report on Excavation at the Gravel Pit, 1936. Proceedings of the Academy of Natural Sciences at Philadelphia 89:1-16.

Davis, Emma Lou, and Richard Shutler, Jr., appendix by Donald R. Tuohy
1969 Recent Discoveries of Fluted Points in California and Nevada. Nevada State Museum Anthropological Papers No. 14. Carson City. 154-177.

Davis, Leslie B.
1977 Preliminary Hydration Rate Determination and Associated Hydration Age Alternatives: the Alyeska Archaeology Project. In J.P. Cook, ed., Pipeline Archeology. Fairbanks: University of Alaska, Institute of Arctic Biology. 10-65.

Dikov, N.N.
1978 Ancestors of Paleo-Indians and Proto-Eskimo-Aleuts in the Paleolithic of Kamchatka. In A.L. Bryan, ed., 1978. 68-69.

Dixon, E. James
1975 The Gallagher Flint Station, an Early man site on the North Slope Arctic Alaska, and its Role in Relation to the Bering Land Bridge. Arctic Anthropology 12(1):68-75.

1985 Cultural Chronology of Central Interior Alaska. Arctic Anthropology 22(1):46-66.

Dolitsky, Alexander B.
1985 Siberian Paleolithic Archaeology: Approaches and Analytic Methods. Current Anthropology 26(3):361-378.

Dumond, Don. E.
1977 The Eskimos and Aleuts. (Ancient Peoples and Places). Thames and Hudson.

1980 The archeology of Alaska and the peopling of America. Science 200:984-991.

Dumond, Don E., W. Henn and Robert Stuckenrath
1976 Archaeology and Prehistory on the Alaska Peninsula. Anthropological Papers of the University of Alaska 18(1):17-29.

Fetter, Sharon and Anne D. Shinkwin
1978 An Analysis of Archaeological Materials from the Cathedral Mountain Area, North Central Alaska. Anthropological Papers of the University of Alaska 19(1):27-43.

Figgins, J.D.
1927 The Antiquity of Man in America. Natural History 27:229-239.

Fladmark, Knut R.
1981 Paleo-Indian Artifacts from the Peace River District. BC Studies 48:124-135.

1985 Glass and Ice: The Archaeology of Mt. Edziza. Publication No. 14, Department of Archaeology, Simon Fraser University, Burnaby, B.C. 217 p.

Fladmark, K.R., J.C. Driver, D. Alexander
1988 The Paleoindian Component at Charlie Lake Cave (HbRf 39), British Columbia. American Antiquity 53(2):371-384.

Flenniken, J. Jeffrey
1987 The Paleolithic Dyuktai Pressure Blade Technique of Siberia. Arctic Anthropology 24(2):117-123.

Franklin, U.M., E. Badone, R. Gotthardt and B. Yorga
1981 An Examination of Prehistoric Copper Technology and Copper Sources in Western Arctic and Subarctic North America. Canadian Museum of Civilization Mercury Series, Archaeological Survey of Canada Paper 101. 158 p.

Gal, Robert
1976 Paleo-Indians of the Brooks Range: a Tradition of Uncontrolled Comparison. Paper presented at the Society for American Archaeology annual meeting, St. Louis, 1976. Typescript 16 p.

1982 Appendix I: An Annotated and Indexed Roster of Archaeological Radiocarbon Dates from Alaska North of 68#Latitude. Anthropological Papers of the University of Alaska 20:159-180.

1982b Evaluation of the Tunalik Site, Northwestern National Petroleum Reserve in Alaska. Anthropological Papers of the University of Alaska 20(1-2):61-78.

Giddings, James L., Jr.
1951 The Denbigh Flint Complex. American Antiquity 16(3);193-202.

1962 Onion Portage and Other Flint Sites of the Kobuk River. Arctic Anthropology 1(1):6-27.

1962 The Arctic Woodland Culture of the Kobuk River. Museum Monographs. Philadelphia: University Museum. 143 p + 46 pl.

1964 The Archeology of Cape Denbigh. Brown University Press. 331 p.

Gotthardt, Ruth
1985 The Archaeological Sequence in the Northern Cordillera: limits of a typological approach. Paper presented to 18th annual meeting of the Canadian Archaeological Association, Winnipeg, April 1985. Typescript, 11 p.

Griffin, James B., G. A. Wright and A. A. Gordus
1969 Preliminary Report on Obsidian Samples from Archaeological Sites in Northwestern Alaska. Arctic 22(2):152-156.

REFERENCES

Gryba, Eugene M.
  1983 Sibbald Creek: 11,000 Years of Human Use of the Alberta Foothills. Archaeological Survey of Alberta Occasional Paper No. 22.

  1985 Evidence of the Fluted Point Tradition in Alberta. In D. Burley, ed., Contributions to Plains Prehistory; Archaeological Survey of Alberta Occasional Paper 26. 22-38.

Hall, Edwin S., Jr.
  1969 CA comment to A.L. Bryan (1969) Early Man in America and the Pleistocene Chronology of Western Canada and Alaska. Current Anthropology 10(4).

Hamilton, Thomas D.
  1969 Glacial Geology of the Lower Alatna Valley, Brooks Range, Alaska. Geological Society of America Special Paper 123. 181-223.

  1982 A late Pleistocene Glacial Chronology for the Southern Brooks Range: Stratigraphic Record and Regional Inference. Geological Society of America Bulletin 93:700-716.

Hanks, Chris
  1991 A Pass to the South: Anatomy of a Traditional Route Across the T'logotsho Plateau--Mackenzie Mountains, NWT. Canadian Parks Service, Department of the Environment, Yellowknife. Typescript.

Haskin, L.A. and J. P. Cook
  1980 Characterization of Obsidian Source Groups and Distribution in Alaska. Research proposal submitted to U.S. National Science Foundation. 39 p.

Haury, Emil W.
  1953 Artifacts with Mammoth Remains, Naco, Arizona: Discovery of the Naco Mammoth and the Associated Projectile Points. American Antiquity 19(1):1-14.

Haynes, C. Vance, Jr.
  1964 Fluted Projectile Points: their Age and Dispersion. Science 145:1408-1413.

  1966 Elephant Hunting in North America. Scientific American 214(6):104-112.

  1969 The Earliest Americans. Science 166:709-715.

  1971 Time, Environment, and Early Man. Arctic Anthropology 8(2):3-14.

  1980 The Clovis Culture. Canadian Journal of Anthropology 1(1):115-121.

  1982 Were Clovis Progenitors in Beringia? In D. M. Hopkins et al., eds., Paleoecology of Beringia. New York: Academic Press. 383-398.

Hibben, Frank C.
  1943 Evidence of Early Man in Alaska. American Antiquity 8(3):254-259.

Hoffecker, John F., W. Roger Powers and Ted Goebel
  1993 The Colonization of Beringia and the Peopling of the New World. Science 259:46-53.

Holmes, Charles E.

1971 The Prehistory of the Upper Koyukuk River Region in Northcentral Alaska. In J. P. Cook, ed., Final Report of the Archeological Survey and Excavations along the Alaska Pipeline Service Company Pipeline Route. Department of Anthropology, University of Alaska, Fairbanks. 326-400.

1973 The Archaeology of Bonanza Creek Valley, North-central Alaska. Unpublished M.A. thesis. University of Alaska, Department of Anthropology, Fairbanks. 83 p.

1977 3000 Years of Prehistory at Minchumina: the Question of Cultural Boundaries. In Prehistory of the North American Sub-Arctic. Proceedings of the Ninth Annual Chacmool Conference. Calgary: University of Calgary Archaeological Association. 11-15 + 3 pl.

1982 Norton Influence in the Alaskan Hinterland. Arctic Anthropology 19(2):133-142.

1983 The Prehistory of the Lake Minchumina Region, Alaska: An Archeological Analysis. Ph.D. thesis. Washington State University,, Pullman. 333 p.

1986 Lake Minchumina Prehistory: An Archeological Analyis. AURORA Alaska Anthropological Association Monograph Series No. 2. 176 p.

Hopkins, David M.

1982 Aspects of the Paleogeography of Beringia during the Late Pleistocene. In D.Hopkins et al, ed., Paleoecology of Beringia. Academic Press. 3-28.

Hopkins, D.M., J.V. Mathews, C.E. Schweger and S.B. Young, eds.

1982 Paleoecology of Beringia. New York: Academic Press.

Humphrey, Robert L.

1966 The Prehistory of the Utukok River Region, Arctic Alaska: Early Fluted Point Tradition with Old World Relationships. Current Anthropology 7(5):586-588.

1969 CA Comment to A.L. Bryan (1969) Early man in America and the Late Pleistocene Chronology of Western Canada and Alaska. Current Anthropology 10(4).

Huntington, James, as told to Lawrence Elliott

1966 On the Edge of Nowhere. New York. Crown Publishers.

Irving, William N.

1962 1961 Field work in the Western Brooks Range, Alaska: Preliminary Report. Arctic Anthropology 1(1):76-83.

1963 Northwest North America and Central United States: A Review. Anthropological Papers of the University of Alaska 10(2):63-71.

1968 The Barren Grounds. In Science, History and Hudson Bay, C.S. Beals and A. Shenstone, eds., Vol. 1, 26-54. Ottawa: Dept. of Energy, Mines and Resources.

1971 Recent Early Man Research in the North. Arctic Anthropology 8(2):68-82.

1985 Context and Chronology of Early Man in the Americas. Annual Review of Anthropology Vol. 14:529-555.

REFERENCES

Irving, William N. and Jacques Cinq-Mars
1974 A Tentative Archaeological Sequence for Old Crow Flats, Yukon Territory. Arctic Anthropology XI(supplement):65-81.

Kunz, Michael L.
1982 The Mesa Site: an Early Holocene Hunting Stand in the Iteriak Valley, Northern Alaska. Anthropological Papers of the University of Alaska 20:113-122.

1984 Upper Kobuk River Drainage Archeology: Report of Phase 1 of A Culture Resources Survey and Inventory in Gates of the Arctic National Park and Preserve. Draft. Fairbanks: Gates of the Arctic National Park, National Park Service, Department of the Interior. 377 p.

1991 A Prehistoric Overview of Gates of the Arctic National Park and Preserve. Anchorage: US Department of the Interior, National Park Service. 307 pp.

1992 The Mesa Site. Alaska Anthropological Association Newsletter 17(2):4-5.

n.d. (1992) The Obsidian Hydration Dating Technique and Problems Associated with its Application in the Arctic. Paper presented to Alaska Anthropological Association annual meeting, Fairbanks, March 1992. 37 pp typescript.

de Laguna, Frederica
1947 The Prehistory of Northern North America as Seen from the Yukon. Society for American Archaeology Memoir No. 3.

Le Blanc, Raymond J.
1984 The Rat Indian Creek Site and the Late Prehistoric Period in the Interior Northern Yukon. National Museum of Man Mercury Series, Archaeological Survey of Canada Paper No. 120. Ottawa. 504 p.

1991 Prehistoric Clinker Use on the Cape Bathurst Peninsula, Northwest Territories, Canada: the Dynamics of Formation and Procurement. American Antiquity 56(2):268-277.

.......and John W. Ives
1986 The Bezya Site: A Wedge-shaped Core Assemblage from Northeastern Alberta. Canadian Journal of Archaeology 10:59-98.

Lind, Carl O.
1906 Extracts from the Diary of Rev. Carl O. Lind, M.D. In Sheldon Jackson, Fifteenth Annual Report on Introduction of Domestic Reindeer into Alaska, 1905. Washington: Government Printing Office. 84-160.

MacNeish, Richard S.
1959a A Speculative Framework of Northern North American Prehistory as to April 1959. Anthropologica ns 1:1-17 & chart.

1959b Men Out of Asia as Seen from the Northwest Yukon. Anthropological Papers of the University of Alaska 7(2):41-70.

1964 Investigations in Southwest Yukon: Archaeological Excavations Comparisons, and Speculations. Papers of the Robert S. Peabody Foundation for Archaeology Vol. 6 No. 2:199-488. Phillips Academy, Andover.

1976 Early Man in the New World. American Scientist 63(3):316-327.

Marshall, Eliot
1990 Clovis Counterrevolution. Science 249(17 Aug.):738-741.

Marshall, Robert
1933 Arctic Village. New York: The Literary Guild.

Martin, Paul S.
1973 The Discovery of America. Science 179:969-974.

McKennan, Robert A. and John P. Cook
1970 Prehistory of Healy Lake, Alaska. Proceedings VIIIth Congress of Anthropological and Ethnological Sciences, 1968, Tokyo, Vol. 3:182-184.

Michels, Joseph W.
1984 Hydration Rate Constants for Batza Tena Obsidian, Alaska [Revised]. MOHLAB Technical Report No. 1.

Millar, James F.V.
1981 Interaction between the Mackenzie and Yukon Basins during the Early Holocene. In P. Francis, F.J. Kense and P.G. Duke, eds., Networks of the Past: Regional Interaction in Archaeology. Calgary: Archaeological Association of the University of Calgary. 259-294.

Mochanov, Iuri A.
1978a Stratigraphy and Absolute Chronology of the Paleolithic of Northeast Asia. In A.L. Bryan, ed., 1978. 54-66.

1978b The Paleolithic of Northeast Asia and the Problem of the First Peopling of America. In A.L. Bryan, ed., 1978. 67

Morlan, Richard E.
1967 Siruk House 1, Alatna River Alaska: the Mammalian Fauna. University of Wisconsin, Department of Anthropology. Typescript (copy in the possession of the authors). 34 p.

1970 Wedge-shaped Core Technology in Northern North America. Arctic Anthropology 7(2):17-37.

1973 The Later Prehistory of the Middle Porcupine Drainage, Northern Yukon Territory. Canadian Museum of Civilization Mercury Series, Archaeological Survey of Canada Paper No. 11. 583 p.

1987 The Pleistocene Archaeology of Beringia. In M.H. Nitecki and D.V. Nitecki, ed., The Evolution of Human Hunting. Plenum. 267-307.

Morlan, Richard E. and J. Cinq-Mars
1982 Ancient Beringians: Human Occupations in the Late Pleistocene of Alaska and the Yukon Territory. In D.M. Hopkins, J.V. Mathews Jr., C.E. Schweger and S.B. Young, eds., Paleoecology of Beringia. New York: Academic Press. 353-381.

Morrison, David A.
1987 The Middle Prehistoric Period and the Archaic Concept in the Middle Mackenzie Valley. Canadian Journal of Archaeology 11:49-74.

Nelson, N. C.
1937 Notes on Cultural Relations between Asia and America. American Antiquity 2(4):387-392.

Noble, William C.
1971 Archaeological Surveys and Sequences in Central District of Mackenzie, N.W.T. Arctic Anthropology 8(1):102-135.

Orth, Donald J.
1967 Dictionary of Alaska Place Names. Geological Survey Professional Paper 5671. Washington.

Patton, William W. and Thomas P. Miller
1970 A Possible Bedrock Source for Obsidian found in Archaeological Sites in Northwestern Alaska. Science 169:760-761.

Patton, W.W., R.M. Chapman and Warren Yeend
1979 Geological Map of the Melozitna Quadrangle, Alaska. Open File Map 77-147. U.S. Geological Survey.

Péwé, Troy L.
1975 Quaternary Geology of Alaska. Geological Survey Professional Paper 835. Government Printing Office. 145 p.

Pilon, Jean-Luc
1990 Vihtr'iitshik: A Stone Quarry Reported by Alexander Mackenzie on the Lower Mackenzie River in 1789. Arctic 43(3):251-261.

Powers, W. Roger
1978 Perspectives on Early Man. Abstracts of the Fifth Biennial Meeting, American Quaternary Association, Edmonton, September 2-4, 1978. 114-122.

Powers, William R. and Thomas Hamilton
1978 Dry Creek: a Late Pleistocene Human Occupation in Central Alaska. In A.L. Bryan, ed., Early Man in America. Edmonton: Archaeological Researches International. 72-77.

Powers, William R., R. Dale Guthrie and John F. Hoffecker
1983 Dry Creek: Archaeology and Paleoecology of a Late Pleistocene Alaskan Hunting Camp. Park Service Contract CX-9000-7-0047. University of Alaska, Fairbanks. Typescript. 461 p.

Powers, W. Roger and John F. Hoffecker
1989 Late Pleistocene Settlement in the Nenana Valley, Central Alaska. American Antiquity 54(2):263-287.

Rainey, Froelich G.
1939 Archaeology in Central Alaska. Anthropological Papers of the American Museum of Natural History 36:351-405.

1940 Archaeological Investigations in Central Alaska. American Antiquity 5(4):299-308.

Reger, Douglas R. and R. D. Reger
1972 An Archaeological Survey in the Utopia area, Alaska. Anthropological Papers of the University of Alaska 15(2):23-38.

Schoenberg, Kenneth M.
  1985 The Archaeology of Kurupa Lake. National Park Service Research/Resources Management Report AR-10. Anchorage: National Park Service, Alaska Region.

Schrader, F.C.
  1900 Preliminary Report on a Reconnaissance along the Chandalar and Koyukuk Rivers, Alaska, in 1899. Washington: U.S. Geological Survey, 21st Annual Report, 1899-1900.

Shinkwin, Anne D.
  1979 Dakah De'nin's Village and the Dixthada site: a Contribution to Northern Athapaskan Prehistory. National Museum of Man Mercury Series, Archaeological Survey of Canada Paper No. 91. Ottawa. 197 p.

  1964 Early Man in the Brooks Range: the Tuktu-Naiyuk Sequence. Unpublished MA thesis. The George Washington University.

Simpson, Sherry
  1989 Archaeologists in Alaska dig for Traces of the First Americans. Heartland Magazine 6(36):H4-H9. (supplement to the Fairbanks Daily News-Miner. Fairbanks, Alaska.

Solecki, Ralph S.
  1951 Notes on Two Archaeological Discoveries in Northern Alaska, 1950. American Antiquity 17(1):55-57.

Smith, Jason W.
  1971 The Ice Mountain Microblade and Core Industry, Cassiar District, Northern British Columbia, Canada. Arctic and Alpine Research 3(3):199-214.

Stevenson, Marc
  1982 Preliminary Prehistoric Sites Survey in Kluane National Park, 1978 and 1979. Research Bulletin No. 177, Parks Canada.

Stuck, Hudson
  1917 Voyages on the Yukon and its Tributaries. New York: C. Scribner's Sons.

Thompson, M.
  1948 Notes on the Archaeology of the Utukok River, Northwestern Alaska. American Antiquity 14(1):62-65.

United States Geological Survey, Alaska Glacial Map Committee
  1965 Map Showing Extent of Glaciations in Alaska. Miscellaneous Geological Investigations Map I-415. Government Printing Office.

Weber, Florence R. and Troy L, Péwé
  1978 Surficial and Engineering Geology of the Central Part of the Yukon-Koyukuk Lowland, Alaska. Miscellaneous Geologic Investigations Map I-590. U.S. Geological Survey.

West, C. Eugene
  1978 Archeology of the Birches Site, Lake Minchumina, Alaska. Unpublished Master's thesis, University of Alaska, Fairbanks.

West, Fred Hadleigh

1967a The Donnelly Ridge site and the Definition of an Early Core and Blade Complex in Central Alaska. American Antiquity 32(3):360-382.

1967b A system of Archaeological Sites Designation for Alaska. American Antiquity 32(1):107-108.

1975 Dating the Denali Complex. Arctic Anthropology 12(1):76-81.

1981 The Archaeology of Beringia. New York: Columbia University Press.

1982 Making Points with Points. The Quarterly Review of Archaeology 3(3):6-7.

Wheeler, M. E. and D. W. Clark

1977 Elemental Characterization of Obsidian from the Koyukuk River, Alaska, by Atomic Absorption Spectrophotometry. Archaeometry 19(1):15-31.

Wilson, Ian

1987 The Pink Mountain Palaeo-Indian site. Archaeological Survey of Alberta Occasional Paper No. 31. Edmonton. 217-219.

1989 The Pink Mountain Site (HhRr-1): An Early Prehistoric Campsite in Northeastern B.C. Canadian Journal of Archaeology 13:51-67.

Workman, William B.

1974 First Dated Traces of Early Holocene man in the Southwest Yukon Territory, Canada. Arctic Anthropology XV Supplement:94-103.

1978 Prehistory of the Aishihik-Kluane Area, Southwest Yukon Territory. National Museum of Man Mercury Series, Archaeological Survey of Canada Paper No. 74. 592 p.

Wormington, H. M.

1957 Ancient Man in North America. Denver: Denver Museum of Natural History, Popular Series No. 4. 322 p.

PLATE 1

FLUTED POINTS

No.	Description	Catalog No.	Reference*
A.	The first Batza Téna find	RkIg-1:49	Fig. 2.1, 68
B.	The first convincing fluted point from Batza Téna	RkIg-10:36	Fig. 2.1, 49
C.	Finished	RkIg-29:16	Fig. 2.1
D.		RkIg-30:42	Fig. 2.1, 58
E.	Unfinished	RkIg-30:220	58
F.		RkIg-30:254	58
G.	Basalt, base missing, traces of ends of flutes present	RkIg-30:247	58
H.	Unfinished	RkIg-30:321	58
I.	Unfluted counterpart of fluted point	RkIg-30:323	58
J.	Fluted basal corner	RkIg-30:160	58

* All the points are described in Table 2.10

Scale: A is 34 mm long, J is 26 mm.

NOTE: OBSIDIAN FLUTED POINTS (PLATES 1 & 2) HAVE BEEN COATED WITH INDIA INK. OTHER OBSIDIAN ARTIFACTS ARE COATED WITH RED OPAQUE.

a

b

c

d

e

f

g

h

i

j

k

PLATE 1. FLUTED POINTS

PLATE 2

FLUTED POINTS

No.	Description	Catalog No.	Reference*
A.	One side fluted, other face convex	RkIg-31:15	Fig. 2.1, 68, 80
B.	Complete point	RkIg-31:60	Fig. 2.1, 68
C.	Unfinished	RkIg-31:119	68
D.		RkIg-31:120	
E.		RkIg-43:1	Fig. 2.1, 71
F.	Unfinished, not fluted, basal bevel present	RkIg-44:38	Fig. 2.1, 74
G.		RkIg-44:81	75
H.		RlIg-46:62	75
I.		RlIg-47:4	76
J.	Fluted on one side only	RlIG-47:13	76
K.	Pl. 1A & 1B points, here coated with red opaque and reduced slightly.		

* All the points are described in Table 2.10 and Appendix II Table 4.

Scale: Complete point B is 53 mm long.

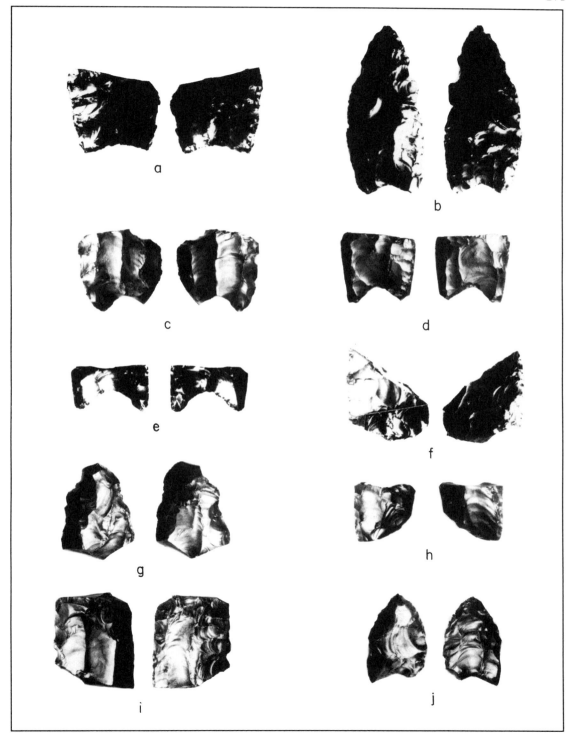

PLATE 2. FLUTED POINTS

PLATE 3

IMPLEMENTS FROM RkIg-30, A FLUTED POINT SITE

No.	Description	Catalog No.	Reference
A.	Point (stem edges ground)	RkIg-30:141	58
B.	Point (stem edges ground)	RkIg-30:130-31	58
C.	Point (stem edges ground, incomplete)	RkIg-30:44	57
D.	Point stem (edges ground)	RkIg-30:312	58
E.	Small biface (on a flake blank)	RkIg-30:30	Tab. 2.6
F.	Small biface (nearly finished)	RkIg-30:154	Tab. 2.6
G.	Small biface (incomplete)	RkIg-30:134	Tab. 2.6
H.	Biface (form altered by damage?)	RkIg-30:117	Tab. 2.6
I.	Small biface (nearly finished)	RkIg-30:43	Tab. 2.6
J.	Biface (unfinished)	RkIg-30:163+ 467	Tab. 2.6
K.	Biface (unfinished)	RkIg-30:16	55
L.	Biface (unfinished)	RkIg-30:80+81	Tab. 2.6
M.	Biface (roughout)	RkIg-30:175	---*
N.	Biface (roughout)	RkIg-30:29	---
O.	Biface (roughout)	RkIg-30:143	---
P.	Biface (point roughout?)	RkIg-30:178	---
Q.	Large biface (unfinished)	RkIg-30:149-50	55
R.	Large biface (unfinished)	RkIg-30:83+88	55
S.	Thick flake with curved bevel	RkIg-30:16	56
T.	Thick flake with curved bevel	RkIg-30:366	56

Scale: F is 46 mm long, Q is 94 mm.

* Artifacts lacking specific text references may be described summarily.

PLATE 3. IMPLEMENTS FROM RkIg-30, A FLUTED POINT SITE

PLATE 4

IMPLEMENTS FROM RkIg-30, A FLUTED POINT SITE

No.	Description	Catalog No.	Reference
A.	End scraper (bevelled edge down)	RkIg-30:100	57*
B.	Thick end scraper	RkIg-30:321	57
C.	End scraper	RkIg-30:409	56
D.	Thick bevelled flake (bevel left)	RkIg-30:249	57
E.	Thin flake uniface	RkIg-30:23	56
F.	Utilized flake (along concave edge)	RkIg-30:10	56
G.	Utilized flake (edges finely bevelled)	RkIg-30:65	56
H.	Utilized flake (along right edge)	RkIg-30:41	56
I.	Bevelled flake (both edges, incomplete)	RkIg-30:349	56
J.	Bladelike flake (lacks proximal end, utilized or edge naturally damaged)	RkIg-30:449	56
K.	Core	RkIg-30:49	---
L.	Spur (quartz crystal)	RkIg-30:244	57
M.	Flake (utilized or naturally damaged)	RkIg-30:191	---
N.	Shaped basalt flake (top is edged unifacially, right edge is bifaced)	RkIg-30:33	Tab. 2.7
O.	Basalt biface (unfinished)	RkIg-30:35	Tab. 2.7
P.	Asymmetrical basalt biface (complete)	RkIg-30:139	Tab. 2.6, 56
Q.	Basalt biface or point (irregularities are due to damage)	RkIg-30:206+ 213+245	Tab. 2.7
R.	Discoidal basalt uniface	RkIg-30:156	Tab. 2.7

Scale: A is 453 mm long, P is 81 mm.

* End scrapers from all sites are listed and described in Appendix II Table 3.

PLATE 4. IMPLEMENTS FROM RkIg-30, A FLUTED POINT SITE

PLATE 5

IMPLEMENTS FROM RkIg-44

No.	Description	Catalog No.	Reference
A.	Biface roughout (failed at end of flute-like thinning flake)	RkIg-44:47+49	Tab. 2.9
B.	Biface roughout (fragment showing same thinning technique as A)	RkIg-44:2	Tab. 2.9
C.	Bevelled flake (showing same face thinning technique as A and B	RkIg-31:57	Tab. 2.8
D.	Biface roughout	RkIg-44:11	Tab. 2.9
E.	Biface roughout (showing same face thinning technique as A-C)	RkIg-44:3+48y	Tab. 2.9
F.	Biface roughout	RkIg-44:12	Tab. 2.9
G.	Biface roughout	RkIg-44:6+53	Tab. 2.9
H.	Core	RkIg-44:42	75
I.	Core	RkIg-44:15	74
J.	Microblade core	RkIg-44:13	75
K.	Split cobble tool	RkIg-44:80	Tab. 2.9
L.	Blade core	RkIg-44:40	74

Scale: A is 72 mm long, K is 124 mm.

PLATE 5. IMPLEMENTS FROM RkIg-44

PLATE 6

IMPLEMENTS FROM FLUTED POINT SITES RkIg-31, RkIg-10 AND OTHER SITES

No.	Description	Catalog No.	Reference
A.	Preform (compare with RkIg-44, Pl. 5)	RkIg-31:65	Tab. 2.8
B.	Biface fragment (attrition or grinding present on all edges--natural?)	RkIg-31:64	Tab. 2.8
C.	Bevelled flake (sidescraper)	RkIg-31:14	Tab. 2.8
D.	Notched point	RkIg-31:62	Tab. 2.8, Tab. 5.8
E.	Notched point (chert)	RkIg-31:55	Tab. 2.8, Tab. 5.8
F.	Multilateral core, face and platform	RkIg-31:52	Tab. 2.8
--	Multilateral core, reverse side	---	
G.	Bevelled flake "spokeshave"	RkIg-31	Tab. 2.8
H.	Flake shaped along 2 edges	RkIg-31:53	Tab. 2.8
I.	Lanceolate point (chert, not associated with fluted point from the same site)	RlIg-46:30	76, 232
J.	Bipoint (not from fluted point locus)	RkIg-29:17	Tab. 2.4
K.	End scraper	RkIg-10:156	50
L.	End scraper	RkIg-10:162	Tab. 2.2
M.	Biface	RkIg-10:157	50
N.	Projectile point	RkIh-33:7	---

Scale: A is 64 mm long, I is 70 mm.

PLATE 6. IMPLEMENTS FROM FLUTED POINT SITES RkIg-31 AND OTHER SITES

PLATE 7

IMPLEMENTS FROM RkIg-28

No.	Description	Catalog No.	Reference
A.	Point	RkIg-28:81	Tab. 3.2
B.	Point	RkIg-28:69	Tab. 3.2
C.	Point	RkIg-28:75	Tab. 3.2
D.	Point (incomplete)	RkIg-28:86	Tab. 3.2
E.	Point (incomplete)	RkIg-28:43	Tab. 3.2
F.	Biface	RkIg-28:76	Tab. 3.2
G.	Point base	RkIg-28:68	Tab. 3.2
H.	Point base	RkIg-28:87	Tab. 3.2
I.	Point base	RkIg-28:88	Tab. 3.2
J.	Point base	RkIg-28:44	Tab. 3.2
K.	Point base	RkIg-28:9	Tab. 3.2
L.	Biface	RkIg-28:71	Tab. 3.2
M.	Biface (fitting fragment reduced through weathering)	RkIg-28:40+93	Tab. 3.2
N.	Biface (incomplete)	RkIg-28:91+92	Tab. 3.2
O.	Bevelled flake	RkIg-28:73	Tab. 3.1, 87
P.	Biface	RkIg-28:72	Tab. 3.2
Q.	Uniface (biface equivalent)	RkIg-28:74	Tab. 3.1
R.	Biface tip	RkIg-28:47	Tab. 3.1
S.	Thick, bevelled planoconvex implement (incomplete)	RkIg-28:44	Tab. 3.1, 86

C-D, K-Q are of basalt

Scale: A is 53 mm long, O is 92 mm.

PLATE 7. IMPLEMENTS FROM RkIg-28

PLATE 8

IMPLEMENTS, BLADES AND CORES FROM RkIh-28

No.	Description	Catalog No.	Reference
A.	Microblade core	RkIh-28:23	Tab. 4.1, 98, 115
B.	Small blade	RkIh-28:32	Tab. 4.1
C.	Five microblades	RkIh-28:27	Tab. 4.2
D.	Base of biface point	RkIh-28:34	Tab. 4.1
E.	Unfinished biface	RkIh-28:5	Tab. 4.1
F.	Unfinished biface	RkIh-28:60	Tab. 4.1
G.	Unfinished biface, hinged fragment	RkIh-28:12	Tab. 4.1
H.	Blade/edge of core	RkIh-28:16	Tab. 4.1
I.	Blade	RkIh-28:11	Tab. 4.1
J.	Blade	RkIh-28:32	Tab. 4.1
K.	Unifacially bevelled flake (incomplete)	RkIh-28:21	Tab. 4.1, 98
L.	End scraper (made on a blade segment)	RkIh-28:30	Tab. 4.1
M.	Small blade core	RkIh-28:15	Tab. 4.1, 98
N.	Core	RkIh-28:35	Tab. 4.1, 95
O.	Microblade core platform tablet (not obsidian)	RkIh-28:18	Tab. 4.1, 98
P.	End scraper	RkIh-28:19	Tab. 4.1, 9.4

Scale: A is 38 mm long, H is 69 mm.

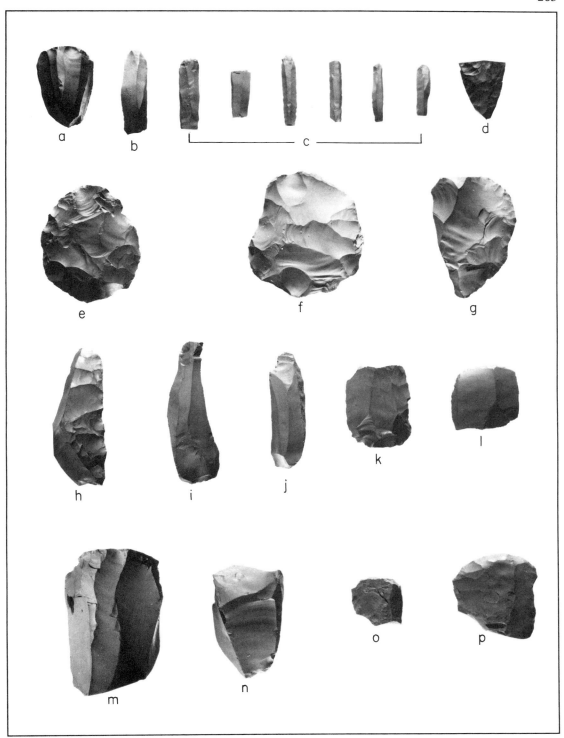

PLATE 8. IMPLEMENTS, BLADES AND CORES FROM RkIh-28

PLATE 9

MICROBLADE CORES AND RELATED PRODUCTS, VARIOUS SITES

No.	Description	Catalog No.	Reference
A.	Microblade core (face-platform views)	RkIg-47:110	Tab. 4.7, 116
B.	Microblade core (face view)	RkIg-47:93	Tab. 4.7, 116
C.	Microblade core (face-side-platform)	RkIg-47:10	Tab. 4.7, 116
D.	Microblade core (face-one side)	RlIg-46---	113
E.	Microblade core (face-side-platform)	RkIn-1:1	113, 115
F.	Microblade core tablet (platform-side)	SaEw-1:1	114
G.	Face rejuvenation flakes (rejoined)	RkIg-47:11+12	Tab. 4.5, 115
H.	Microblade core tablet/top of core	RlIg-37:223	100
I.	Hammerstone	RkIg-47:90	Tab. 4.5
J.	Microblade core platform tablet	RkIg-47 Area A	Tab. 4.8, 106
K.	Microblade core platform tablet	RkIg-47:4	Tab. 4.8, 106

Scale: A is 27 mm high, I is 62 mm wide.

PLATE 9. MICROBLADE CORES AND RELATED PRODUCTS, VARIOUS SITES

PLATE 10

CORES AND IMPLEMENTS FROM RkIh-32

No.	Description	Catalog No.	Reference
A.	Flat-faced flake core	RkIh-32:20	Tab. 4.9, 111
B.	Flake core	RkIh-32:17	Tab. 4.9, 4.10, 110
C.	Core	RkIh-32:21	Tab. 4.9, 4.10, 110
D.	Core for small linear flakes	RkIh-32:24	Tab. 4.9, 4.10, 110
E.	Microblade or small blade core (face and side views)	RkIh-32:48	Tab. 4.10, 110, 116
F.	Microblade core	RkIh-32:25	Tab. 4.9, 4.10, 115
G.	Biface (point?, chert, incomplete)	RkIh-32:46	Tab. 4.9
H.	Blade (chert, incomplete, retouched on one edge)	RkIh-32:8	Tab. 4.9
I.	End scraper	RkIh-32:2	Tab. App. II.3
J.	End scraper	RkIh-32:14	Tab. App. II.3
K.	End scraper (chert)	RkIh-32:18	Tab. App. II.3
L.	Adze	RkIh-32:55	Tab. App. II.3
M.	Notched pebble	RkIh-32:52	Tab. 4.9
N.	Retouched flake fragment (along L edge)	RkIh-32:50	Tab. 4.9

Scale: A is 65 mm high, L is 103 mm long.

PLATE 10. CORES AND IMPLEMENTS FROM RkIh-32

PLATE 11

PROJECTILE POINTS AND SMALL IMPLEMENTS
BATZA TENA TUKTU SITES RkIh-35 AND RkIh-36

No.	Description	Catalog No.	Reference
A.	Leafshaped point (basalt)	RkIh-36:215	Tab. 5.5
B.	Stemmed point	RkIh-36:156	Tab. 5.5
C.	Stemmed or notched point (stem-base area incomplete, not obsidian)	RkIh-35:9	Tab. 5.5, 154
D.	Notched point	RkIh-36:142	Tab. 5.5
E.	Stem-indented point	RkIh-35:62	Tab. 5.5, 154
F.	Notched point (chert)	RkIh-36:179	Tab. 5.5
G.	Notched biface (chert, incomplete)	RkIh-36:175	Tab. 5.5
H.	Finished biface (incomplete)	RkIh-36:112	143
I.	Small biface	RkIh-36:225	143
J.	Copper awl	RkIh-36:186	148
K.	Burin on a retouched blade (chert)	RkIh-36:81	146
L.	Triangular ridge flake (from microblade core, retouched on two facets)	RkIh-36:106	141
M.	(Description same as L)	RkIh-36:169	141
N.	Microblade (large, medial-distal segment)	RkIh-35:16	Tab. 5.3, 141
O.	Microblade core (side-face-platform)	RkIh-36:123	116, 140
P.	Microblade core fragment	RkIh-36:454	140
Q.	Perforated pebble (natural)	RkIh-36:235	---
R.	Bifacially edged flake	RkIh-35:6	154
S.	Unifacially retouched triangular ridge flake from face of a blade core, views of the two dorsal facets	RkIh-36:552	---

Scale: A is 52 mm long, E is 58 mm.

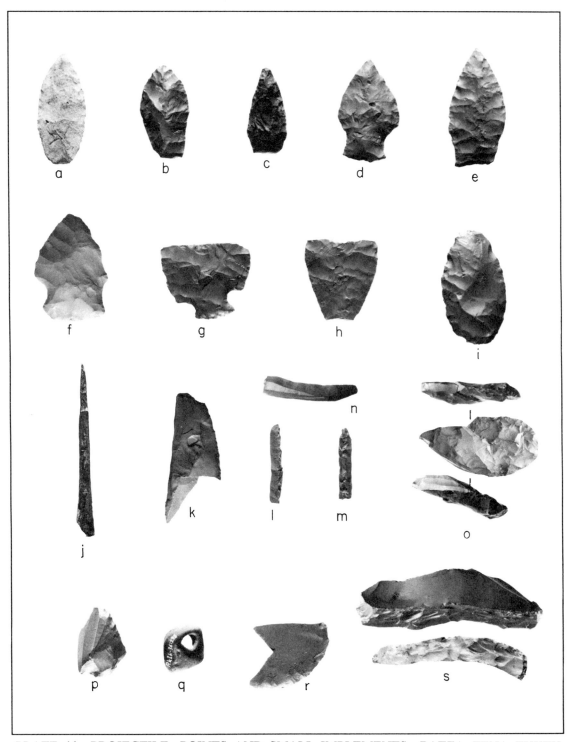

PLATE 11. PROJECTILE POINTS AND SMALL IMPLEMENTS: BATZA TENA TUKTU

PLATE 12

BIFACES FROM BATZA TENA TUKTU SITES RkIh-35 AND RkIh-36

No.	Description	Catalog No.	Reference
A.	Biface roughout	RkIh-35:81	152
B.	Discoidal biface (unfinished)	RkIh-36:160	143
C.	Subrectangular biface roughout	RkIh-35:65	152
D.	Pointed biface (nearly finished)	RkIh-35:43	154
E.	Roughout/unfinished	RkIh-36:73	Tab. 5.4, 142
F.	Biface (nearly finished)	RkIh-35:63	154
G.	Biface (nearly finished)	RkIh-35:14	154
H.	Biface (incomplete, nearly finished)	RkIh-35:7	154
I.	Adze-shaped biface (unfinished)	RkIh-35:31+32 +26	152
J.	Subrectangular early stage roughout	RkIh-36:77	Tab. 5.4
K.	Roughout	RkIh-36:216+ 241	Tab. 5.4
L.	Biface (unfinished at the ends)	RkIh-36:149+ 180	143
M.	Biface roughout (fragment)	RkIh-35:71	154
N.	Biface roughout (fragment)	RkIh-36:5	---

Scale: A is 56 mm long, L is 134 mm.

PLATE 12. BIFACES FROM BATZA TENA TUKTU SITES RkIh-35 AND RkIh-36

PLATE 13

BLADELIKE FLAKES AND END SCRAPERS
FROM BATZA TENA TUKTU SITE RkIh-36

No.	Description	Catalog No.	Reference
A.	Blade or bladelike flake	RkIh-36:220	135
B.	Blade of bladelike flake	RkIh-36:246	138
C.	Blade or bladelike flake	RkIh-36:76	138-139
D.	Bladelike flake	RkIh-36:173	138
E.	Bladelike flake	RkIh-36:257	138
F.	Blade (with cortex and retouched notch on one facet)	RkIh-36:560	138
G.	Small blade (not obsidian)	RkIh-36:85	138
H.	Battered obsidian pebble (problematical object, miniature chopper-shaped core)	RkIh-36:171	---
I.	End scraper (chert, flat dorsum)	RkIh-36:68	Tab. 5.6
J.	End scraper (not obsidian, flat dorsum)	RkIh-36:92	Tab. 5.6
K.	End scraper (chert, flat dorsum)	RkIh-36:88	Tab. 5.6
L.	End scraper (chert, flat dorsum)	RkIh-35:149	Tab. 5.6
M.	End scraper (cortical back, trimmed to petaloid format)	RkIh-36:141	Tab. 5.6, 143
N.	End scraper (flat back, trimmed to petaloid format)	RkIh-36:182	Tab. 5.6, 143
O.	End scraper (cortical back)	RkIh-36:497	Tab. 5.6, 143
P.	End scraper (cortical back)	RkIh-36:447	Tab. 5.6, 143
Q.	Elongate scraper (dorsally trimmed sides and butt end)	RkIh-36:89	Tab. 5.6, 143
R.	End scraper, limace uniface format	RkIh-36:159	Tab. 5.6, 143
S.	End scraper (left side retouched)	RkIh-36:238	Tab. 5.6, 143
T.	End scraper (left side coarsely flaked)	RkIh-36:133	Tab. 5.6

Scale: A is 59 mm long, Q is 67 mm.

PLATE 13. BLADELIKE FLAKES AND END SCRAPERS: BATZA TENA TUKTU SITE

PLATE 14

LARGE OBJECTS FROM BATZA TENA TUKTU SITES RkIh-35 AND RkIh-36

No.	Description	Catalog No.	Reference
A.	Notched flat cobble	RkIh-35:58	156
B.	Notched chopper	RkIh-36:125	147
C.	Retouched flake (on left edge)	RkIh-35:19	156
D.	Flat pebble battered on edges	RkIh-36:130	Tab. 5.7
E.	Hammerstone (lightly used)	RkIh-36:102	Tab. 5.7
F.	Flat shingle uniface (incomplete large bevelled flake)	RkIh-35:8	156
G.	Retouched flake (dorsally around right and lower edges, bifacial at top)	RkIh-36:150	147
H.	Small maul or large hammerstone	RkIh-35:38	Tab. 5.7
I.	Hammerstone (heavily utilized)	RkIh-35:92	Tab. 5.7
J.	Hammerstone (heavily utilized)	RkIh-36:185	Tab. 5.7

Scale: A is 138 mm long, H is 145 mm.

PLATE 14. LARGE OBJECTS FROM BATZA TENA TUKTU SITES RkIh-35, RkIh-36

PLATE 15

POINTS FROM THE LAKE 324 COMPLEX

No.	Description	Catalog No.	Reference*
A.	Leafshaped point (unfinished?)	RlIg-52:16	Tab. 7.1, 179
B.	Stemmed point (base missing)	RlIg-52:13	Tab. 7.1, 179
C.	Pentagonal point	RlIg-52:20	Tab. 7.1, 179
D.	Point (finished but edge damaged)	RlIg-52:89	Tab. 7.1
E.	Flake point (not obsidian)	RlIg-52:42	Tab. 7.1
F.	Flake point (base missing)	RlIg-52:12	Tab. 7.1
G.	Semi-biface tool on a flake (gouge?)	RlIg-52:38	Tab. 7.1
H.	Flake uniface	RlIg-52:107	Tab. 7.1, 182
I.	Flake point (incomplete)	RlIg-52:12	Tab. 7.1, 7.2, 181
J.	Flake point	RlIg-52:23+24	Tab. 7.1, 7.2, 181
K.	Flake point	RlIg-52:34	Tab. 7.1, 7.2, 181
L.	Flake point	RlIg-52:33	Tab. 7.1, 7.2, 181
M.	Flake point	RlIg-52:66+67	Tab. 7.1, 7.2, 181
N.	Flake point	RlIg-52:9	Tab. 7.1, 7.2, 181
O.	Flake point	RlIg-52:31	Tab. 7.1, 7.2, 181
P.	Flake point	RlIg-52:14	Tab. 7.1, 7.2, 181
Q.	Large blade made in flake point mode	RlIg-52:64	Tab. 7.2
R.	Large blade made in flake point mode (from a side-blow flake)	RlIg-52:39+40	Tab. 7.2

Flake points are shown in their dorsal aspect. The ventral edges are retouched more or less in the same manner as the dorsal edges.

Scale: A is 66 mm long, Q is 89 mm.

PLATE 15. POINTS FROM THE LAKE 324 COMPLEX

PLATE 16

SCRAPERS AND BIFACES FROM THE LAKE 324 COMPLEX

No.	Description	Catalog No.	Reference
A.	End scraper	RlIg-52:6	Tab. App.II.3, 183
B.	End scraper (flaked dorsum)	RlIg-52:75	Tab. 7.1, 183
C.	End scraper (flaked dorsum)	RlIg-52:76	Tab. 7.1, 183
D.	End scraper	RlIg-52:78	Tab. App.II.3, 183
E.	End scraper (on a thick uniface)	RlIg-52:81	Tab. 7.1, 183
F.	End scraper (thin format)	RlIg-52:4	Tab. 7.1, 183
G.	End scraper (thin format)	RlIg-52:80	Tab. 7.1, 183
H.	End scraper (thin format)	RlIg-52:79	Tab. 7.1, 183
I.	Retouched flake (bevelled side-blow flake, technically an end scraper)	RlIg-52:41	Tab. 7.1, 183
J.	Retouched flake (2 thick bevels)	RlIg-52:43	Tab. 7.1, 183
K.	Retouched cortical flake (2 thick bevels, right and left)	RlIg-52:57	Tab. 7.1, 183
L.	Bevelled cortical flake (fragment, 2 thick bevels, right and left)	RlIg-52:29	Tab. 7.1, 183
M.	Thick uniface (fragment, dark chert)	RlIg-52:181	Tab. 7.1, 182
N.	Thin-edged uniface	RlIg-52:108	Tab. 7.1, 182
O.	Thin-edged uniface (on side-blow flake, N-O also show slight bifacial retouch)	RlIg-52:46	Tab. 7.1, 182
P.	Thin-edged retouched flake (R-L edges)	RlIg-52:47	Tab. 7.1, 183
Q.	Thin-edged retouched flake (Left edge)	RlIg-52:55	Tab. 7.1, 183

Scale: A is 72 mm long, Q 80 mm.

PLATE 16. SCRAPERS AND BIFACES FROM THE LAKE 324 COMPLEX

PLATE 17

BIFACES AND HEAVY IMPLEMENTS FROM THE LAKE 324 COMPLEX

No.	Description	Catalog No.	Reference
A.	Biface (unfinished at one end)	RlIg-52:88	Tab. 7.1, 181
B.	Biface	RlIg-52:	Tab. 7.1
C.	Biface (unfinished)	RlIg-52:52+62	Tab. 7.1, 180
D.	Biface	RlIg-52:10	Tab. 7.1, 181
E.	Boulder flake (with ventral edge retouch, not found at Lake 324 locus)	RlIg-52:151	Tab. 7.1, 186
F.	Biface (unfinished at one end)	RlIg-52:63	Tab. 7.1, 180
G.	Grooved pestle	RlIg-52:87	Tab. 7.1, 184
H.	Split cobble (hide scraper)	RlIg-52:83	Tab. 7.1, 179, 184
I.	"Chitho" tabular hide scraper	RlIg-52:81+82	Tab. 7.1, 179, 184

Scale: A is 92 mm long, G 194 mm.

PLATE 17. BIFACES AND HEAVY IMPLEMENTS FROM THE LAKE 324 COMPLEX

PLATE 18

LARGE OBJECTS

No.	Description	Catalog No.	Reference
A.	Grinding slab (incomplete)	RlIg-33:29	187, 190
B.	Notched chopper or axe	RkIg-22:13	158

Scale: A is 130 mm wide left to right.

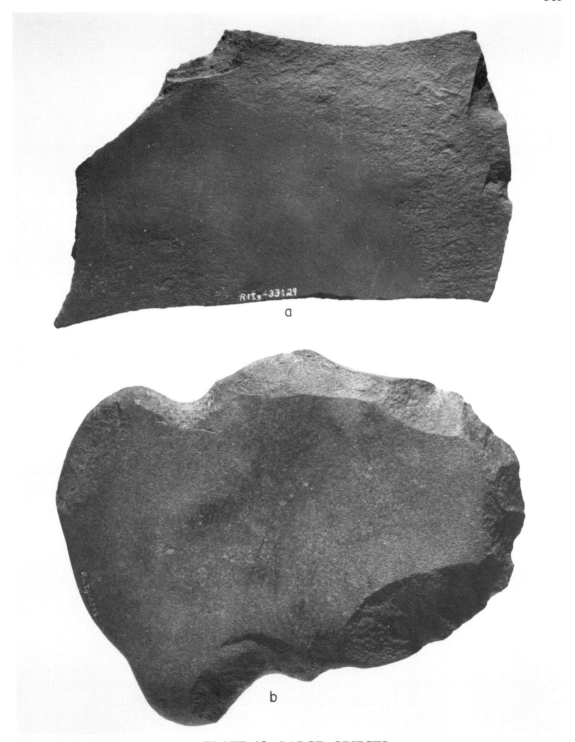

a

b

PLATE 18. LARGE OBJECTS

PLATE 19

IMPLEMENTS FROM RkIg-1 LOCUS E AND RlIg-33

No.	Description	Catalog No.	Reference
A.	End scraper	RkIg-1:54	Tab. App.II.3, 46
B.	End scraper (2 or 3 bevels)	RkIg-1:56	45-46
C.	End scraper (chert)	RkIg-1:57	45
D.	End scraper (2 bevels)	RkIg-1:58	45
E.	End scraper	RkIg-1:59	45
F.	End scraper (2 bevels)	RkIg-1:60	45
G.	End scraper	RkIg-1:61	45
H.	End scraper (not obsidian)	RkIg-1:62	45
I.	End scraper (not obsidian, 2 bevels)	RkIg-1:63	45
J.	Side-indented point (incomplete)	RkIg-1:53	Tab. 5.8, 45
K.	End scraper (sides shaped)	RlIg-33:17	188
L.	Bevelled implement (made from a biface roughout fragment?)	RlIg-33:16	188
M.	Pointed flake tool (in mode of RlIg-52 flake points)	RlIg-33:14	188, 190
N.	Stemmed point	RlIg-33:13	187-188
O.	Notched point	RlIg-33:10	Tab. 5.8, 188
P.	Retouched shingle (hideworking stone?)	RlIg-33:19	188, 190
Q.	Notched point	RlIg-33:8	Tab. 5.8, 188
R.	Notched point	RlIg-33:11	Tab. 5.8, 188
S.	Notched point	RlIg-33:9	Tab. 5.8, 188

Scale: P is 96 mm long, S 41 mm.

PLATE 19. IMPLEMENTS FROM RkIg-1 LOCUS E AND RlIg-33

PLATE 20

IMPLEMENTS FROM RkIg-51, RlIg-35 AND RlIg-46

No.	Description	Catalog No.	Reference
A.	End scraper (dorsal and ventral views)	RkIg-51:1	Tab. App.II.3, 231
B.	Point (unfinished)	RkIg-51:17	Tab. App.II.4, 231
C.	Point (unfinished, incomplete)	RkIg-51:14	231
D.	Point	RkIg-51:16	231
E.	Point (unfinished)	RkIg-51:15+20	231
F.	Biface (unfinished at ends)	RlIg-35:8	172
G.	Point base (chert)	RlIg-35:7	172
H.	Point (chert, missing tip, both faces)	RlIg-35:5	172
I.	Adze-shaped biface	RlIg-46:35	232
J.	Uniface	RlIg-46:41	232
K.	Thin uniface (with slight ventral ret.)	RlIg-46:40	232
L.	Point stem (ground edge)	RlIg-46:37	232
M.	Point made on a flake (not obsidian)	RlIg-46:36	232
N.	Bevelled flake (gouge?)	RlIg-46:38	232
O.	Kayuk-style biface	RkIg-22:29	Fig. 5.14c, 158
P.	Kayuk-style biface	RkIh-37:17	---
Q.	Small end scraper (compare size with A)	RlIg-49:3	150

Scale: A is 78 mm long, H is 86 mm.

PLATE 20. IMPLEMENTS FROM RkIg-51, RlIg-35 AND RlIg-46

PLATE 21

BIFACES AND POINTS FROM MINOR ASSEMBLAGES, AND ISOLATED FINDS

No.	Description	Catalog No.	Reference
A.	Asymmetrical biface (basalt, base not finished)	RkIg-38:1	---
B.	Asymmetrical biface (edges ground)	RkIg-x:39	---
C.	Point (basalt, poorly formed but an edge is ground)	RlIg-41:3	---
D.	Biface (unfinished)	RlIg-36:3	---
E.	Biface blade (basalt, edges of tongue-shaped stem are ground)	RlIg-52:174	186
F.	Blade or point (stem edges ground)	RlIg-38:5	Tab. App.II.4
G.	Point (damaged, edge of stem ground)	RkIg-33:--	---
H.	Biface blade (incomplete)	RkIg-49:4	---
I.	Point base (edges ground)	RlIg-49:5	Tab. App.II.4
J.	Point base (edges ground)	RkIg-11:47	Tab. App.II.4
K.	Triangular point	RkIg-x:32	Tab. App.II.4
L.	Stemmed point	RkIg-x:38	Tab. App.II.4
M.	Notched point	RkIg-x:37	Tab. App.II.4
N.	Notched point	RlIg-44:3	Tab. 5.8
O.	Bevelled flake tool (chert, incomplete, format of Ipiutak flake knife)	SaEw-1:2	---
P.	Biface	XI-E:42	Tab. App.II.4
Q.	Thick bifaced roughout, or scraping tool (faintly suggestive of Kayuk-style scraper)	RlIg-51:3	---
R.	Uniface blade (in format of a biface)	RkIg-2:9	---
S.	Biface (basalt, unfinished)	RkIg-x:41	Tab. App.II.4
T.	Thin biface	RkIg-48:16	---

Scale: A is 68 mm long, R is 94 mm.

PLATE 21. BIFACES AND POINTS FROM MINOR ASSEMBLAGES, ISOLATED FINDS

PLATE 22

VARIOUS OBJECTS FROM MINOR ASSEMBLAGES AND ISOLATED FINDS

No.	Description	Catalog No.	Reference
A.	Bladelike decortication flake (basalt)	RkIg-x:36	Tab. App.II.1
B.	Bevelled flake or blade (basalt, both edges retouched, lacks distal end)	RlIg-45:3	--
C.	Blade or bladelike flake	XI-E:19	Tab. App.II.1
D.	Small chert blade (lacks proximal end)	XI-E:23	Tab. App.II.1
E.	Bladelet (retouch may be natural)	RkIg-17:10	--
F.	Limace on a flake (with ventral retouch)	RkIh-38:10	157
G.	Plano convex object (poorly finished)	RkIg-18:1	Fig. 5.14e
H.	Bevelled flake (basalt, all edges retouch)	RkIg-44:1	Tab. 2.9
I.	Bevelled flake (along concave edge)	RkIg-22:14	158
J.	Utilized flake (spokeshave)	RkIg-22:1	158
K.	Cortical flake with low-angle bevel	RkIg-46:12	Fig. 5.15b
L.	Basalt flake, low-angle bevel to right	RkIh-37:52	150
M.	Basalt flake, low-angle bevel to right	RlIg-47:3	76
N.	Basalt flake bevelled along top and right edges, pseudo burin on L edge)	RkIg-x:35	Tab. App.II.1
O.	Biface roughout (early stage, shaping technique similar to fluting)	RkIg-12:18	---
P.	Biface (unfinished, thinning technique similar to fluting)	RkIg-35:3	---

Scale: A is 86 mm long, O is 172 mm.

311

PLATE 22. OBJECTS FROM MINOR ASSEMBLAGES, AND ISOLATED FINDS

PLATE 23

CORES

No.	Description	Catalog No.	Reference
A.	Early-stage biface roughout or discoidal core (only cortical flakes have been removed)	RkIh-36:8	141
B.	Rough discoid (spent discoidal core?)	RkIg-21:1	---
C.	Chopper-shaped core	RkIh-40:2	---
D.	Chopper-shaped core	XI-E:25	Tab. App.II.1
E.	Chopper-shaped core	RkIh-36:74	135
F.	Chopper-shaped core	RkIh-36:294	135
G.	Platformed core (decapitated pebble bladelets removed mainly for decortication, oblique view)	RkIh-34:14	156, Fig. 4.1c
H.	Platformed core (like G, oblique view)	RkIh-35:55	152
I.	Platformed core (like G, oblique view)	XI-E:41	Tab. App.II.1, 114
J.	Core with bladelet facets (side, face)	RkIh-36:57	138, 150
K.	Platform core	RkIh-32:l5	111
L.	Platform core	RkIh-37:16	---
M.	Platform core	RkIh-37:--	150
N.	Platform core (unsuccessful, flakes hinged off short)	RkIh-33:29	---
O.	Flatfaced core or reduced platform core	RkIh-35:25	152

Scale: A is 64 mm high, O is 72 mm.

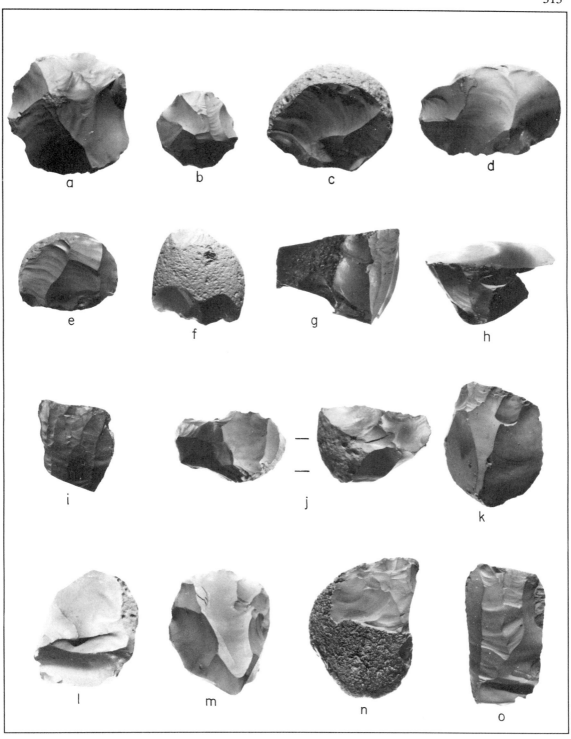

PLATE 23. CORES

PLATE 24

CORES

No.	Description	Catalog No.	Reference
A.	Rotated core	RkIh-33:3	---
B.	Multilateral core	RkIh-32:54	---
C.	Multilateral core	RkIh-36:52	135
D.	Multilateral core	RkIh-36:51	135
E.	Spent core (reduced multilateral)	RkIh-37:8	---
F.	Flatfaced variant of platformed core	RkIh-38:8	157
G.	Flatfaced core (coarsely shaped top)	RkIg-x:27	Tab. App.II.1
H.	Wedgeshaped core	RkIg-1:83	45-46
I.	Large biface (chert)	RlIg-48:2	---
J.	Flatfaced core	RkIh-37:20	138, 150

Scale: H is 96 mm high, I is 136 mm in long dimension.

PLATE 24. CORES

Some Recent Titles in the Mercury Series:

Orders must be prepaid with cheque or postal order payable to the Canadian Museum of Civilization, or charged to Visa or Mastercard (provide name of card and cardholder, card number, expiry date, and signature).

Add handling charges (10% in Canada; 20% outside Canada) and 7% GST (in Canada).

Write to:

Mail Order Services, Publishing Division
Canadian Museum of Civilization
P.O. Box 3100, Station B
Hull, Québec J8X 4H2